The Good Society

An Introduction to Comparative Politics

Second Edition

ALAN **DRAPER**

St. Lawrence University

ANSIL **RAMSAY**

St. Lawrence University

Longman
Boston   Columbus   Indianapolis   New York   San Francisco   Upper Saddle River
Amsterdam   Cape Town   Dubai   London   Madrid   Milan Munich   Paris   Montreal   Toronto
Delhi   Mexico   City   São Paulo   Sydney   Hong Kong   Seoul   Singapore   Taipei   Tokyo

Senior Acquisition Editor: Vikram Mukhija
Project Editor: Toni Magyar
Editorial Assistant: Beverly Fong
Senior Marketing Manager: Lindsey Prudhomme
Production Manager: Frances Russello
Cover Design Manager: Jayne Conte
Cover Designer: Bruce Kenselaar
Full-Service Project Management: Niraj Bhatt/Aptara®, Inc.
Cover Illustration/Photo: © Artkey/Corbis
Printer and Binder: Courier Companies, Inc.

Photo Credits: Chapter 1: © Ken Straiton/Corbis; Chapter 2: © ATEF HASSAN/Reuters/Corbis;
Chapter 3: AP Photo/Jeff Widener; Chapter 4: © Hanan Isachar /Godong/Corbis; Chapter 5:
© Atlantide Phototravel/Corbis; Chapter 6: © PHILIMON BULAWAYO/Reuters/Corbis;
Chapter 7: © Andrew Lichtenstein/Corbis; Chapter 8: AFP/Getty Images; Chapter 9: © CHRIS
WATTIE/Reuters/Corbis; Chapter 10: © Paulo Fridman/Sygma/Corbis; Chapter 11: © CHINA
DAILY/Reuters/Corbis.

Library of Congress Cataloging-in-Publication Data
Draper, Alan.
    The good society : an introduction to comparative politics / Alan Draper, Ansil Ramsay.—2nd ed.
    p. cm.
    ISBN-13: 978-0-205-08278-0
    ISBN-10: 0-205-08278-5
    1. Comparative government—Textbooks.   I. Ramsay, Ansil.   II. Title.
    JF51.D73 2012
    320.3—dc22

                                                                  2010054546

1 2 3 4 5 6 7 8 9 10—CRS—14   13   12   11

Longman
is an imprint of

www.pearsonhighered.com   ISBN-10:   0-205-08278-5
                                 ISBN-13: 978-0-205-08278-0

BRIEF CONTENTS

DETAILED CONTENTS

iv

CHAPTER 3
State and Society 54

CHAPTER 6
Authoritarianism   138

CHAPTER 9
Developed Countries and the Good Society   222

CHAPTER 10
Less Developed Countries and the Good Society   265

CHAPTER 11
Communism, Postcommunism, and the Good Society   310

PREFACE

Juarez in Mexico and El Paso, Texas in the United States are separated by the narrow band of the Rio Grande River. The two cities are so close to each other that the Mayor of El Paso can actually see downtown Juarez from his office window. But the quality of life for residents of the two cities could not be more different. In 2008, El Paso was ranked as the third safest city over 500,000 in the United States, with only 16 homicides, while over 1,550 people were murdered in Juarez that same year. The infant mortality rate—the number of newborns who die before their first birthday—in El Paso was 6.6 per 100,000 births. In comparison, the infant mortality rate was five times higher across the river in Juarez, and while 63 percent of El Paso residents completed high school, only 10 percent did so in Juarez.

Just as the Rio Grande divides Mexico from the United States, the Moie River forms the border between Thailand and Myanmar. And like the Rio Grande, the Moie River is so narrow in some places that people can actually swim across it. But if they were to do so, they would find conditions of life to be very different from one shore to the other. In Thailand, most people have enough to eat, receive good health care, and can afford modern amenities. There are shopping malls, and traffic jams, and citizens have intermittently enjoyed political freedom. In Myanmar, however, many people suffer from malnutrition, health care is primitive, and poverty is widespread. The shelves in stores are bare, people use bicycles as their main form of transportation, and a brutal military government deprives people of basic human rights.[1]

This tale of two rivers is at the heart of our book *The Good Society*, whose central theme is: Why are some countries more successful than others at creating conditions that promote their citizens' well-being? Why do people in Thailand or the United States live so much better than those who live just across the border in Myanmar and Mexico, respectively? How can a river loom as wide as an ocean in terms of the quality of life for those who live on opposite shores? These questions give unity to a wide range of topics in comparative politics by asking how political institutions in different countries affect citizens' quality of life. Students are interested in comparative politics—and appropriately so—because of what it might teach them about how different political institutions affect people's lives. It is our experience that few students who enroll in "Introduction to Comparative Politics" are intrinsically curious about the details of other countries' political institutions or about the conceptual repertoire of comparative politics. But they are curious why some countries do a better job than others of providing for their citizens. Students want to know how political systems work because they are interested in how they

---

[1]Thomas Fuller, "Across the River: 2 Divergent Paths in Southeast Asia," *New York Times* (October 25, 2007), p. A8.

can work better. The wonderful, exciting quality of comparative politics is that it is in a privileged position to pose and answer such large and meaningful questions. Comparison permits students to make normative judgments about the merits of different political systems. These are the kinds of issues that first attracted us as students to comparative politics. We believe today's students will find the fresh, normative approach to comparative politics in *The Good Society* equally compelling.

The second edition of *The Good Society* gives us an opportunity to introduce students to new scholarship and to show them new ways of how comparative politics can answer important questions. For example, new approaches to the good society have gained currency since the last edition appeared, such as using happiness to assess government performance, and we have broadened the reach of the book by addressing new issues and regions of the world. But the second edition is not only an opportunity to include new scholarly material. It also permits us to show students how powerful the comparative method can be to address questions that matter. As a result, we now devote more time to introducing students to the logic and practice of comparative politics. We expanded the section on the comparative method in the opening chapter and build upon this in succeeding chapters where we set up hypotheses and test them. We also include examples of how leading political scientists use comparative methods to address issues raised in these chapters. These examples model how to define terms, form hypotheses, and test them so that students can see how practitioners do comparative analysis. Finally, we have added Critical Thinking Questions at the end of each chapter to encourage students to reflect upon what they have read and to encourage discussion among them.

We believe the fresh, normative approach to comparative politics that the *Good Society* offers is a bold departure from existing comparative politics textbooks. Most textbooks in the field use the case study approach, in which students study a series of individual countries in depth. We find such textbooks to be richly descriptive but oddly uninformative. The case studies provide evocative detail but are not related to one another, nor is their collective meaning and significance clear. Textbooks using a thematic approach are also unsatisfying. They familiarize readers with core concepts in comparative politics but often fail to explain how those concepts could be applied or would be useful to explain the politics of any particular country. In short—and to be blunt—existing comparative politics textbooks generally offer either too little comparison or too little politics. They leave students asking "so what?" and wondering in what ways the fine detail and conceptual clarity these textbooks offer matters.

We have not dispensed with case study and thematic approaches to comparative politics. We believe each is valuable and we make use of them here by situating them within a larger argument about the *purpose* of government. We use case studies to typify different political models and we illustrate how concepts can be applied to the study of individual countries. We offer case studies of individual countries in order to assess their performance against the standards of the good society. We review the conceptual nuts and bolts of the field because such terms as state, markets, and democracy represent ways people have organized their lives. But they are means to an end, not the end itself, which is to maximize people's ability to live well. The *Good Society* introduces students to the variety of countries and the conceptual apparatus of comparative politics in ways that we hope they will find relevant and meaningful.

NEW TO THIS EDITION

This is the second edition of the *Good Society*. While we continue to introduce concepts, describe political institutions, and assess government performance in different countries against the standards of the good society, there is also much that is new here. Some chapters are completely new and others have been revised significantly. Changes to *The Good Society* have moved along two tracks. The first track is expanded coverage of various topics along with integrating the good society theme more thoroughly into the book. Expanded coverage includes the following:

- **More coverage of core concepts in comparative politics:** Some conceptual material was expanded, such as that covering parliamentary and presidential governments, globalization, democracy, and authoritarianism, while other concepts are included for the first time, such as electoral systems, nationalism, political culture, ethnicity, race, and religion.
- **More coverage of methodological issues in comparative politics:** The second edition contains more material on how to form hypotheses, operationalize variables, test hypotheses, and connect normative and empirical analyses.
- **Expanded discussion of the concept of "the good society" in Chapter 1 and fuller integration of the concept into each chapter:** Each of the thematic chapters (2–8) begins with an anecdote linked to the theme of "the good society" and ends with an examination of how the central concepts discussed in the chapter affect citizens' lives. The remaining chapters (9–11) that contain case studies end with a comparison of the countries discussed in the chapter and how they measure up to the criteria of the good society.
- **Expanded coverage of the state:** There are new sections devoted to the origins of the state as well as separate treatment of the bureaucracy and military as arms of the state.
- **New chapter on state and society:** This chapter considers linkages that connect citizens to the state, such as political parties, interest groups, and social movements, how these may create weak or strong states, and what the consequences of each may be for ordinary citizens.
- **New chapter on political culture:** An entire chapter is now devoted to political culture and the politics of identity. This chapter examines how political identities are acquired and some of the different forms they can take, such as nationalism, religious, and ethnic bases of identification.
- **More coverage of democracy and authoritarianism:** In contrast to the first edition, both democracy and authoritarianism are now given their own, separate chapter-length treatments. One chapter includes new material

covering transitions to democracy while the other contains new material regarding the persistence of authoritarianism.

■ **More coverage of the Middle East:** Iran is now included among the case studies we offer of developing states, which is current enough to include the presidential election of 2009 and its aftermath. In addition, there is more coverage of the Middle East throughout the text, especially in the chapters on political culture (Chapter 4); authoritarianism (Chapter 6); and development and underdevelopment (Chapter 8).

■ **Stronger integration of conceptual and case study material:** We profile countries that represent distinctive models of politics. The subheadings we use in the country case studies that appear in chapters 9 through 11 mirror the conceptual material provided in the preceding chapters. Each case study in these chapters is divided into sections covering the state (from Chapter 2), state and society (from Chapter 3), political culture (from Chapter 4), and political economy (from Chapter 5) so that students can see how those concepts are applied to specific countries in practice.

The second type of change we made to *The Good Society* is to provide more pedagogical assistance to users of the book. Several pedagogical features were retained from the first edition. These include using boldface type to identify key terms; "In Brief" text boxes to highlight key concepts in the chapter; figures and tables; and maps with accompanying economic and demographic data. Other significant pedagogical features that were added to this second edition include the following:

■ **New emphasis on the practice of comparative politics:** The thematic chapters (2–8) now contain "Comparative Political Analysis" text boxes that focus on controversial issues designed to engage students. The text boxes begin with an issue related to the topic of the chapter and present an example of good comparative analysis that examines it.

■ **Application of concepts to countries:** We profile certain countries in "The Good Society In Depth" boxes to show how concepts that appear in the thematic chapters can be applied. These boxes illustrate how the issues discussed in the thematic chapters actually play out in the politics and history of particular countries.

■ **Critical Thinking Questions at the conclusion of each chapter:** Along with Comparative Political Analysis text boxes, Critical Thinking Questions are designed to promote discussion among students and encourage them to use the material in the chapter to think beyond it. These questions ask them to apply the concepts and address the normative and empirical issues from the chapter they just finished.

■ **Key terms are highlighted and placed in a Glossary:** This feature draws students' attention to important terms and makes it easier to find and review them.

■ **Annotated suggested readings:** Selected readings at the end of each chapter guide students to some of the best and most recent scholarship on the topic.

FEATURES

CHAPTER 1. GOOD SOCIETIES.   The opening chapter introduces students to the field of Comparative Politics and the comparative method. It then proceeds to ask: What does the good society look like? The answer to this question becomes the measure, the standard, by which we will compare and evaluate how well different countries perform. We consider alternative visions of the good society before presenting our own view that is based on "the capability approach," developed by Amartya Sen and Martha Nussbaum. According to the capability approach, the good society is one in which certain minimal conditions are met that permit people to flourish or thrive. These include physical well-being, safety from violence, the ability to make informed choices about one's life, and the freedom to participate in meaningful political activity. After reviewing this approach, we respond to different criticisms, including those condemning it as a form of imperialism that uses culturally biased ideas derived from the West to judge and evaluate other countries.

CHAPTER 2. THE STATE.   Chapter 2 introduces students to the concept of the state. States are sovereign, meaning they are the ultimate authorities within a territory, creating and enforcing rules within it. As a result, groups struggle to gain control over the state and try to influence its procedures and decisions. The chapter then proceeds to describe the origins of the modern state and examines its components or parts, such as legislatures, judiciaries, executives, bureaucracies, militaries, and more local or regional authorities.

CHAPTER 3. STATE AND SOCIETY.   Chapter 3 examines the ways in which states and societies are linked together through political parties, interest groups, social movements, and patron–client relations. The chapter also explores ways in which states try to use these linkages to gain more influence over society, at the same time groups in society try to exploit these linkages to increase their influence over the state. The chapter ends with a discussion of weak and strong states and their consequences for the good society.

CHAPTER 4. POLITICAL CULTURE.   This chapter describes different approaches to the study of political culture. It then proceeds to show how political identities are formed, and how groups with common national, ethnic, and religious identities engage in collective action to achieve their goals. Finally, the chapter asks whether the level of generalized trust within countries affects the degree to which they approach the good society.

CHAPTER 5. POLITICAL ECONOMY.   Chapter 5 looks at different economic systems, especially the relationship between states and markets. It begins by arguing that markets are not antagonistic to states but presume them. Markets require states to set the rules so that production and exchange can take place. We then discuss the market's virtues and vices, and the different means through which states intervene in the operation of market economies. The chapter then proceeds to discuss globalization. Finally, we examine whether economies that are more market-oriented do a better job promoting the capability of citizens than those economies in which the state intervenes more substantially.

CHAPTER 6. AUTHORITARIANISM.   Chapter 6 defines authoritarianism as well as describing its different forms, such as monarchy, military rule, single-party rule, electoral authoritarianism, and personal rule. It also examines the surprising persistence of authoritarianism in many countries, despite the trend toward democracy in recent decades. This section examines why authoritarian rule has been so enduring in the Middle East, in general, and in Arab societies, in particular. The chapter ends with a discussion of how well different types of authoritarian rule do in meeting the criteria of the good society.

CHAPTER 7. DEMOCRACY.   Chapter 7 parallels the previous chapter by defining democracy and describes its two dominant forms, parliamentary and presidential systems. It also considers the successive waves of democratization and how electoral rules shape party competition. The chapter ends by assessing whether democracies perform better than authoritarian states in meeting the standards of the good society.

CHAPTER 8. DEVELOPMENT AND UNDERDEVELOPMENT.   This chapter begins with a discussion of the concepts of development and underdevelopment and distinguishes between economic development and human development. The chapter next examines five different explanations for why development gaps have emerged among countries: imperialism, geography, culture, institutions, and leadership. It concludes with an examination of the relationship between economic development and the good society.

CHAPTER 9. DEVELOPED COUNTRIES AND THE GOOD SOCIETY.   Chapter 9 begins our analysis of the developed countries, which include the rich democracies of North America and Western Europe, as well as those of Japan, New Zealand, and Australia. It examines three "families of nation," or distinct models of politics and policy found within them: social democracies, Christian democracies and extreme-market democracies. We then offer case studies for each of the three types: Sweden represents the social democratic model; Germany exemplifies the Christian democratic model; and the United States typifies the extreme-market model. Finally, the chapter compares these countries' performance to see which of them—and the political models they represent—most nearly approximates the good society.

CHAPTER 10. LESS DEVELOPED COUNTRIES AND THE GOOD SOCIETY.   This chapter begins with a description of the main features of less developed countries, while noting that they are a more numerous and diverse lot than their developed counterparts. Many of them are not democracies—and the quality of democracy varies considerably among those that are—and they differ considerably in terms of economic performance. Taking the "family of nations" approach of the previous chapter, we focus on just three of the more common types of regimes found among developing countries: weak democracies, electoral democracies, and electoral authoritarian regimes. Nigeria is offered as a model of weak democracies; Brazil is presented as an example of electoral democracies, and Iran is submitted as a case study of electoral authoritarianism. The chapter concludes with a comparison of how well these countries—and the models they represent—perform in promoting their citizens' well-being and meeting the criteria of the good society.

CHAPTER 11. COMMUNISM, POST-COMMUNISM, AND THE GOOD SOCIETY.   Chapter 11 begins with a discussion of the institutional features of communist regimes prior to their demise. It asks why many communist regimes collapsed and why a few of them survived. The chapter then focuses on Russia, which emerged from the collapse of the communist Soviet Union, and then shifts its focus to China where the communist party still rules despite its collapse elsewhere. It then concludes by comparing the two countries' success in promoting their citizens' well-being and approximating the good society.

SUPPLEMENTS

Longman is pleased to offer several resources to qualified adopters of *The Good Society* and their students that will make teaching and learning from this book even more effective and enjoyable. Several of the supplements for this book are available at the Instructor Resource Center (IRC), an online hub that allows instructors to quickly download book-specific supplements. Please visit the IRC welcome page at **www.pearsonhighered.com/irc** to register for access.

MYPOLISCIKIT FOR *THE GOOD SOCIETY*.   This premium online learning companion features multimedia and interactive activities to help students connect concepts and current events. The book-specific assessment, video case studies, mapping exercises, comparative exercises, *Financial Times* newsfeeds, current events quizzes, politics blog, MySearchLab, and much more encourage comprehension and critical thinking. With Grade Tracker, instructors can easily follow students' work on the site and their progress on each activity. Use ISBN 0-205-09668-9 to order MyPoliSciKit with this book. To learn more, please visit www.mypoliscikit.com or contact your Pearson representative.

PASSPORT FOR COMPARATIVE POLITICS.   With Passport, choose the resources you want from MyPoliSciKit and put links to them into your course management system. If there is assessment associated with those resources, it also can be uploaded, allowing the results to feed directly into your course management system's gradebook. With over 150 MyPoliSciKit assets like video case studies, mapping exercises, comparative exercises, simulations, podcasts, *Financial Times* newsfeeds, current events quizzes, politics blog, and much more, Passport is available for any Pearson introductory or upper-level political science book. Use ISBN 0-205-11147-5 to order Passport with this book. To learn more, please contact your Pearson representative.

INSTRUCTOR'S MANUAL/TEST BANK. Written by the authors, this resource includes chapter overviews, learning objectives, lecture outlines, key terms, and numerous multiple-choice, short answer, and essay questions for each chapter. Available exclusively at the IRC.

PEARSON MYTEST. This powerful assessment generation program includes all of the items in the instructor's manual/test bank. Questions and tests can be easily created, customized, saved online, and then printed, allowing flexibility to manage assessments anytime and anywhere. To learn more, please visit www.mypearsontest.com or contact your Pearson representative.

THE ECONOMIST EVERY WEEK. *The Economist* analyzes the important happenings around the globe. From business to politics, to the arts and science, its coverage connects seemingly unrelated events in unexpected ways. Use ISBN 0-205-09530-5 to order a 15-week subscription with this book for a small additional charge. To learn more, please contact your Pearson representative.

FINANCIAL TIMES. Featuring international news and analysis from journalists in more than 50 countries, *Financial Times* provides insights and perspectives on political and economic a developments around the world. Use ISBN 0-205-09531-3 to order a 15-week subscription with this book for a small additional charge. To learn more, please contact your Pearson representative.

LONGMAN ATLAS OF WORLD ISSUES (0-205-78020-2). From population and political systems to energy use and women's rights, the *Longman Atlas of World Issues* features full-color thematic maps that examine the forces shaping the world. Featuring maps from the latest edition of *The Penguin State of the World Atlas*, this excerpt includes critical thinking exercises to promote a deeper understanding of how geography affects many global issues. Available at no additional charge when packaged with this book.

GOODE'S WORLD ATLAS (0-321-65200-2). First published by Rand McNally in 1923, *Goode's World Atlas* has set the standard for college reference atlases. It features hundreds of physical, political, and thematic maps as well as graphs, tables, and a pronouncing index. Available at a discount when packaged with this book.

ACKNOWLEDGMENTS

We took out a mortgage on the first edition, leaving us with extensive debt to a number of people who contributed to *The Good Society*. The renovation was so substantial for the second edition that we needed a home equity loan to repay all those who played a role in the book's revision. Among our creditors are Vikram Mukhija at Pearson Longman who worked closely with us on the architectural blueprint for this edition. He also put us in the skilled and patient hands of our editor Toni Magyar who guided us through the revision process. She was a perspicacious and energetic editor who really had faith and confidence in our approach to the field of comparative politics. Beverly Fong at Longman took over from Toni as the manuscript moved into production, while Niraj Bhatt oversaw the magical process of turning a manuscript into a book. We would also like to thank Barbara Geddes and Jan Teorell who responded to our questions as we ventured into their fields of expertise, as well as the reviewers Longman commissioned who offered suggestions in response to our revision proposal. J.D. Bowen, St. Louis University; Robert Dayley, The College of Idaho; Maria Fornella-Oehninger, Old Dominion University; Peggy Kahn, The University of Michigan—Flint; Steven L. Taylor, Troy University; and Jiangnan Zhu, University of Nevada—Reno.

Our colleagues in the Government Department at St. Lawrence University (SLU) provided a collegial atmosphere in which to work, and Paul Doty, a librarian at SLU, was like a forensic investigator, hunting down the odd requests for sources and information we forwarded to him. But we owe the greatest debt to our former colleague Sandy Hinchman who, again, patiently edited almost every chapter of the book. She turned our prose from analog to HD. She added pixels to the page by sharpening our prose and clarifying its meaning.

Finally, we dedicate this book to those who mean the most to us—our parents and our families—Robert and Clarice Draper; Pat Ellis; Sam and Rachel Draper; Bryan and Trevor Ellis; Estelle K. Ramsay; Eva Turknett-Ramsay; Douglas and David Ramsay; Brian and Alan Mobley; and Jeni Flint.

ALAN DRAPER
ANSIL RAMSAY

ACKNOWLEDGMENTS

Good Societies

INTRODUCTION

All of us want to enjoy richer, fuller lives. We may disagree as to exactly what richer and fuller means—it may involve becoming the next Nobel Prize winner in medicine or an Olympic gold medalist in track and field—but we all want to realize our dreams, whatever they may be. Our ability to make our dreams come true depends in part on raw talent. As much as we would like to find a cure for a deadly disease or be an athletic star, most of us are not smart or athletic enough no matter how hard we try or how much we practice. But our potential is constrained not only by the limits of our innate talents but by the kind of society we live in. As President Lyndon Baines Johnson explained in a famous address he gave in the 1960s, ability is not simply "the product of birth," but is "stretched or stunted by the family that you live with, and the neighborhood you live in—by the school you go to and the poverty or richness of your surroundings. It is the product of a hundred unseen forces playing upon the little infant, the child, and finally the man."[1] According to Johnson, our ability to realize our potential is conditioned by the circumstances in which we live. For example, it would be difficult at best to be a great scientist or outstanding athlete if we had to work six days a week making bricks, as some children do in Pakistan; if we had to subsist on one dollar a day, as millions do in India; or if we could not read or write, as is true for three-quarters of the adult population in the African country of Niger. People in such dire circumstances—deprived of childhood, devoid of income, and denied an education—would find it exceedingly difficult to fulfill their potential, regardless of their natural gifts. On the other hand, some people are more fortunate and live in countries that help them realize their potential. These countries require children to attend school, ensure that people have sufficient income to purchase necessities, and make sure their citizens are literate. The famed investor Warren Buffet attributes his economic success to the fact that "When I was a kid, I got all kinds of good things. I had the advantage of a home where people talked about interesting things, and I had intelligent parents and I went to decent schools. . . . I was born at the right time and place."[2] Of course, not everyone who went to good schools and grew up in a good home with loving parents is as economically successful as Warren Buffet. But Buffet is wise and humble enough to know that his success would not have been possible without them. In short, the quality of our lives is improved or impoverished depending upon the type of society we live in.

This book argues that some countries are better than others at creating conditions that permit citizens to realize their potential. This issue is our entrance into the field of comparative politics. **Comparative politics** identifies similarities and differences between countries, explains why they occur, and probes their consequences. For example, some countries are organized in ways that permit their citizens to flourish and thrive, while in others people's lives are blighted and stunted. Take the case of Botswana and neighboring Zimbabwe in Africa. In 2008, infant mortality rates were twice as high in Zimbabwe as in Botswana, life expectancy was fifteen years shorter, and Zambabwe's GDP per capita was just $100 compared with almost $14,000 in Botswana.[3] Why is the quality of life so much better in Botswana than Zimbabwe? Or take the example of Thailand in Asia and Ghana in Africa. Thirty years ago, the two countries had nearly identical per capita incomes. In the ensuing years, Thailand's economy grew at an annual rate of 4.5 percent, while Ghana's grew by only 0.4 percent. Currently, life expectancy is considerably shorter in Ghana; infant mortality rates are twice as high; and the literacy rate in Ghana is only two-thirds what it is in Thailand. Why did Thailand progress further and faster than Ghana when both countries were once at the same developmental level?

By comparing Botswana to Zimbabwe, and Thailand to Ghana we can try to identify what it is that might explain such divergent outcomes in the quality of their citizens' lives. Comparative politics enables us not only to compare different countries but to appreciate what is special or distinctive about our own. It provides a standard or point of reference that permits us to recognize unique features of our country by comparing it to something else. As Rudyard Kipling, the British writer, once remarked, "What should they know of England, who only England know."[4]

Comparative politics is a subfield of political science and is distinct from international relations, another subfield of the discipline with which it is sometimes confused. The former studies politics *within* countries, while the latter studies politics *among* them. But the border separating these subfields is quite porous, as what happens among countries can and often does affect what happens within them, and vice versa. For example, international trade agreements that promote commerce among countries—which are within the domain of international relations—have led states to abandon policies that protected their industries from foreign competition. This, in turn, altered their policy-making processes in ways that shifted authority from the legislative to the executive branch, and required them to develop new capacities to enforce these agreements and manage their consequences—all of which is the stuff of comparative politics.[5] Comparative politics is not walled off from the other branches of political science but bleeds into them, just as it accepts transfusions from them as well.

THE LOGIC AND PRACTICE OF COMPARATIVE POLITICAL ANALYSIS

Just like the man who was pleased and surprised to learn he always had been speaking prose, readers might similarly be surprised to learn they have been doing comparative analysis all their lives. We compare all the time. Students compare the merits of different colleges when they decide where to enroll, and men and women compare the merits of potential partners when they decide whom to date. Instead of comparing colleges or potential dates, comparative politics analyzes how and why the politics of countries differ, and what consequences those differences may have. However, **comparative political analysis** differs from comparative analysis in everyday life in its use of systematic procedures. Comparative political analysis requires practitioners to form hypotheses about how different variables or concepts are related to one another. **Hypotheses** simply present relationships that we expect to find among these variables. They often take the form of "if, then" statements, such as if a country's wealth increases, then its citizens will be healthier. The two variables in this hypothesis are a country's wealth and health. Differences in health among countries are the **dependent variable,** or, what we are trying to explain, whereas differences in wealth among countries are the **independent variable,** or, what we believe explains them.

But how do we know which countries are wealthier or healthier? Wealth and health are only concepts. They are abstract and do not provide specific criteria with which to make comparisons among countries. For example, we might safely assume that Germany is wealthier than Bangladesh, but is it wealthier than Austria its neighbor to the south? We might reasonably believe that Canadians are healthier than Haitians, but are they healthier than Americans? In order to make comparisons like these, we need to find measurable, real-world approximations for wealth and health to see whether Germans are wealthier than Austrians and Canadians are healthier than Americans. We need to **operationalize** our variables. This means finding specific, concrete alternatives to use in place of such abstract terms as wealth and health. For example, we can operationally define health, our dependent variable, in terms of life expectancy and compare it across countries. We can do the same for our independent variable, wealth, by using per capita gross domestic product (GDP) in place of it. Per capita **GDP** refers to the total amount of goods and services sold within a country divided by the number of people in it. Both life expectancy and per capita GDP are measurable; they actually exist in the real world, and capture the concepts of health and wealth they are meant to represent. Once we operationally define our variables, we can now determine whether and to what degree wealth influences health.

We might find that as per capita GDP increases so does life expectancy, as our hypothesis anticipated. But this only reveals a **correlation** or pattern between our variables; it does not prove that our independent variable wealth actually caused life expectancy to increase. It could be that the positive result confirming our hypothesis was due to other factors that we did not take into account. For example, before the polio vaccine was discovered, public health experts noted that polio outbreaks increased with the consumption of ice cream, leading to speculation that ice cream contributed to the crippling disease. It turned out that polio outbreaks were more common in the summer when people ate more ice cream, and that the summer treat was only associated with the disease but did not cause it.[6] Ice cream was innocent of the vicious charge leveled against it once researchers included **controls** in their tests. Controls hold other factors constant in order to see whether we still obtain the same results, or if they were spurious due to other intervening factors. An excellent example of comparative research using controls was one recently conducted by Dan Zuberi. Zuberi was interested in whether Canadian workers lived better than their American counterparts. He conducted research in cities that were otherwise quite similar on either side of the border, Vancouver and Seattle, on workers who did the same job for the same employer and belonged to the same union in each city.[7] By doing so, Zuberi could have confidence that any difference in Canadian and American workers' life chances was not due to differences in occupation, employer, union status, or urban environment, but, as he concluded, could be attributed to the political power Canadian workers enjoyed in comparison to their American counterparts. When we control for variables, we are more confident that any correlations we find are not accidental but are the result of **causation**. We are more confident that it is safe to eat ice cream without the fear that it increases our chances of contracting polio.

▶ COMPARATIVE POLITICAL ANALYSIS

Does Gender Equality Help Girls Do Better in School?

Problem

Being able to read, write, and do math well are important skills. Students proficient in all three of these skills are in a better position to succeed at school, at work, and in life. Comparisons of girls and boys in different countries who took the same math test found that girls on average had lower scores than boys. Is this because girls are simply not as good at math as boys, or is it because they have been socialized to believe the subject is too difficult for them, just as they have been taught that they lack what it takes to manage a business or be a political leader? Countries differ considerably in beliefs about what girls can and should do. In countries with very high gender equality, old sexist myths about what girls can do have been dismantled, leading researchers to wonder whether gender equality can affect girls' performance in math.

Methods and Hypothesis

One recent study uses comparative analysis of 40 countries to answer whether sexist expectations influence girls' performance. The authors note that while boys have a higher average test score on international math tests than girls, in some countries there are large gaps between their test scores, while in other countries there are almost none. The authors hypothesize that the more gender equality in a country (independent variable), the smaller the gender gap in test scores (dependent variable).

Operationalizing Concepts

To test this explanation the authors needed to define what they meant by "being better at math" and "gender equality." They needed to operationalize their variables.

1. For "math test scores" they used the results of a math test administered to 15-year-olds in 40 countries in 2003.
2. To measure "gender equality" they used the World Economic Forum's Gender Gap Index (GGI). The index measures economic, cultural, and political opportunities for women compared to those for men.

Results

The results confirmed the researchers' hypothesis. In countries where there is a large gender gap, such as Turkey, there is a large gap in math scores between boys and girls. In countries where there is gender equality, such as Sweden, the gap disappears.

Continued

For Further Discussion

1. Why should greater gender equality lead to more equal math scores between boys and girls?

2. Should countries with differences in gender equality move toward greater gender equality even if this conflicts with prevailing cultural norms?

Sources: "Vital Statistics," *The Economist*, May 29, 2008; Luigi Guiso, Ferdinando Monte, Paola Sapienza, and Luigi Zingales, "Culture, Gender, and Math," *Science*, Volume 320, May 30, 2008.

Comparative political analysis uses three methods to test hypotheses. One approach is to do a case study that examines a topic in depth within a single country. Case studies use specific actors and events to draw inferences about how larger forces and structures behave. For instance, the political scientist Kellee Tsai's case study of China tested the hypothesis that capitalists (independent variable) promote democracy (dependent variable). Entrepreneurs allegedly would come to resent the restrictions imposed by the Communist Party and want political power equal to the wealth they enjoy. But contrary to these expectations, Tsai found that as the number of entrepreneurs in China has increased, they have not demanded or been in the vanguard of democratic reform because they have been able to advance their interests through other means. Chinese entrepreneurs have succeeded so well in promoting their interests through the one-party dictatorship of the Chinese Communist Party that they have little need, or appetite, for democratic reform.[8]

The case study approach offers detail and depth but it does so at the expense of breadth. Like a camera that zooms in for a close-up, the high definition that the case study of a single country provides comes at the expense of how much is included in the picture. Using the case study method, researchers may be confident about their results for the country they studied, but cannot generalize beyond it with any assurance.

Another approach, the comparative cases method, attempts to make broad generalizations by examining a few countries in depth instead of just one, as case studies do. For example, Ann Swidler analyzed why Uganda had more success at AIDS prevention than Botswana. She found that both countries were successful at providing people with information about how AIDS is contracted, but Uganda did better when it came to engaging them in AIDS prevention programs.[9] But Uganda and Botswana have many other differences between them that may account for why AIDS prevention was more successful in the former than the latter. It is hard to control for all the variables that may influence results when researchers use the comparative cases method.

Finally, researchers can compare many countries instead of just a few or just one. Such studies often make use of quantitative data. An example of this approach is provided in the scattergram below, testing the hypothesis whether wealth affects health that we mentioned previously. The independent variable, wealth—operationally defined as per capita GDP—is located along the horizontal "x" axis on the bottom of the scattergram, and the dependent variable, health—

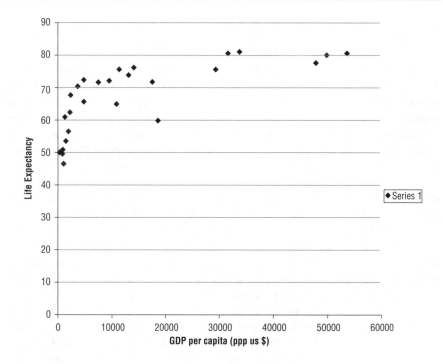

FIGURE 1.1
Wealthier Is Healthier

GDP per capita (PPP US$)
Data Source: Human Development Report 2009,
http://hdrstats.undp.org/en/indicators/91.html
Life expectancy index
Data Source: Human Development Report 2009,
http://hdrstats.undp.org/en/indicators/92.html

operationalized as life expectancy—is located along the vertical "y" axis. As can be seen in Figure 1.1 above, the relationship between wealth and health generally follows the pattern we expected to find: As per capita GDP increases, so does life expectancy. The advantage of comparing many countries in this way is that it gives researchers confidence that their results apply broadly because of the number of countries included. But while this approach may reveal statistical relationships among variables, it does not provide as much insight as the other approaches as to why those relationships exist. Depth is sacrificed for breadth. In addition, it is more difficult to find reliable and comparable data as the number of countries included in the data set increases. Countries may differ in how they define activities and in their accuracy and efficiency in recording them.

In summary, proceeding systematically with comparative political analysis requires a lot more effort than proceeding intuitively, as we do when we make everyday comparisons. But it is worth the effort because forming hypotheses, operationally defining variables, and choosing a method to test them leads to more accurate results than relying upon intuition and common sense.

Proceeding systematically gives us a procedure to validate whose intuition is correct when people disagree. What is more, judgments relying upon common sense are sometimes flat-out wrong because they do not incorporate controls. Relying upon common sense to wean people from ice cream would not have done much to prevent polio. Also, sometimes, what we think we see plainly with our own eyes deceives us. The absence of conflict in a society marked by inequality and discrimination may falsely lead us to believe that those who are its victims accept their fate as fair and legitimate, as opposed to passively tolerating conditions they consider unjust because they are powerless to change them. Finally, doing systematic comparative political analysis can be very satisfying because it poses puzzles to solve. But these are not just ordinary puzzles. They pertain to the quality of people's lives. It is important to solve them, to find the right answer, because people's welfare depends upon it.

We have argued that the value of comparison is that it offers us insight into how countries' political conditions differ and the consequences those differences have for them. It permits us to check our intuitions about a country's politics by examining whether they apply in other circumstances. But comparison is also useful because it permits us to evaluate and form judgments that help us make sense of the world around us. Those judgments may be **empirical** and objective, such as when we say that Sweden spends more on its welfare state (35.7 percent of GDP) than the United States (15.8 percent of GDP) or that Germany has higher turnout in parliamentary elections (77 percent of eligible voters) than Switzerland (48 percent of eligible voters). Or, our judgments may be **normative** and moral, such as when we say that something is better or worse than something else; such as when we say that Sweden is kinder and gentler than the United States because it makes a greater welfare effort, or that democracy is more robust in Germany than in Switzerland because it has higher voter turnout. Comparison permits us to make objective and normative judgments that help us make sense of the world.

This book tries to combine both forms of comparison, the empirical and the normative, in order to probe more deeply into the political life around us. We are interested in how countries govern themselves not only because such knowledge gives us insight into our own circumstances, but also because it helps us make moral judgments about them. The question at the heart of our text is: What constitutes a good society and why are some countries better than others at creating one?[10]

This chapter asks what it means to be better governed. We develop some general criteria by which to examine and evaluate government performance in creating a good society. Our argument begins by suggesting that there are some kinds of behavior that are widely condemned throughout the world, whose presence would not meet most people's criteria of a good society. We then discuss why wealth and happiness are inadequate to serve as bases to compare and evaluate government performance. Next, we offer standards to compare the performance of countries and evaluate the degree to which they create the conditions in which people can flourish. Finally, the chapter anticipates and responds to the criticism that it is a form of cultural domination for us to impose our standards of a good society on others.

VISIONS OF THE GOOD SOCIETY: GROSS NATIONAL PRODUCT AND GROSS NATIONAL HAPPINESS

Few people anywhere in the world would argue that a society based on slavery, where some individuals have no rights and can be bought and sold like cattle, is a good society, especially if one happened to be a slave. Few would agree that a society in which one group of people slaughters fellow citizens from another ethnic or religious group exemplifies good governance, especially if one happened to be part of the persecuted minority. And few would say that a society in which thousands of children die each year of easily preventable diseases is desirable, especially if one of those children happened to be yours.

These are not hypothetical examples. If slavery is defined as "the total control of one person by another for the purpose of economic exploitation," there were an estimated 27 million persons in slavery in the world at the end of the twentieth century.[11] These included girls as young as fifteen who were held in brothels in Thailand and children as young as six who made bricks all day in Pakistan. Likewise, ethnic killings are widespread in the world. In 1994, members of the Hutu ethnic group in the central African country of Rwanda killed approximately 800,000 of their fellow citizens, including both Tutsi and moderate Hutus.[12] Finally, millions of infants suffering from preventable diseases die each year.[13] In the African country of Angola, almost two out of ten babies die before their first birthday.

It would be relatively easy to get widespread agreement that these are undesirable and morally unacceptable outcomes in any country or culture. Our sense of moral outrage might be particularly acute if they were to happen to us. But is it possible to move beyond these specific examples to develop general criteria that can be used to decide what constitutes a good society? In the following paragraphs, we discuss the merit of using wealth and happiness to judge societies.

It is generally and appropriately assumed that the higher a country's level of economic development, the better off its citizens will be. In wealthier countries, few people are held as slaves, large-scale ethnic violence is rare, and few people die from preventable diseases. Economic development is often measured by a country's per capita gross domestic product, which we defined earlier, in which purchasing power is held constant.[14]

By this criterion, the small European principalities of Liechtenstein and Luxembourg were some of the most successful countries in the world, with per capita GDPs of $85,362 and $78,489, respectively. The least successful was the Democratic Republic of the Congo in Africa, with a per capita GDP of only $288.[15] Countries with high levels of per capita income to purchase an array of goods and services can afford to have children go to school instead of to work, can satisfy the competing claims of different ethnic groups instead of having them slaughter each other, and can provide health care services to people instead of having them die needlessly.

Yet, political leaders and social scientists are increasingly dissatisfied with this measure of a good society and good governance. In fact, in February 2008, the president of France, Nicholas Sarkozy, was so disgruntled that he

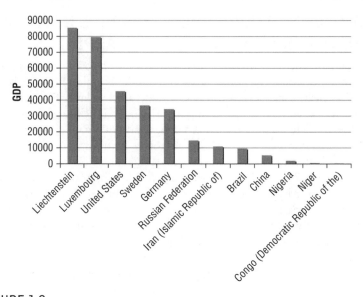

FIGURE 1.2
Countries Ranked by GDP, 2005

Data Source:
GDP per capita (PPP US$)
Source: Human Development Report 2009,
http://hdrstats.undp.org/en/indicators/91.html

commissioned a group of the world's leading economists, including two Nobel Prize winners, to propose a better alternative.[16] One problem with using wealth or per capita income as the measure of a good society, Sarkozy's commission noted, was that it treats money spent on desirable goods and services as equivalent to money spent on goods and services that most of us would consider detestable. For example, major oil spills from ocean-going tankers contribute to economic growth because of the expense to clean them up. But few of us would regard a coastline ravaged with oil slicks as something that improves people's lives. High crime rates lead people to purchase more locks for their doors and security systems for their homes. But few people would regard such purchases as indicators of a good society. Most of us would see them as indicators of fear and insecurity. Or, to take one final example, GDP treats money spent on prisons as equivalent to money spent on education, but few of us believe that money spent on prisons is as productive for society as that devoted to education. In short, economic growth includes not only "goods" but also "bads."

Moreover, a focus on growth alone may ignore its hidden costs and thus misrepresent the benefits society derives from it. For example, China has achieved remarkable rates of economic growth recently, but this has been achieved at the expense of increasing inequality, environmental degradation and ruinous corruption. High-quality economic growth needs to be distinguished from low-quality growth where the costs to society of achieving it are great. The kind of growth that occurs is as important to social well-being as the rate of growth.

A second problem with using GDP as a standard is that it omits behavior many of us consider desirable. People who care for their children or aging parents out of selfless devotion do not contribute to the GDP because such work is unpaid. One would better contribute to economic growth by hiring and paying others who have no emotional investment in or attachment to those they care for.[17] GDP only measures what people do for cold, hard cash; what people do out of the goodness of their hearts is irrelevant from this perspective. As Robert F. Kennedy put it: "GDP measures everything, in short, except that which makes life worthwhile."[18]

Finally, using GDP per capita as a measure of good governance may hide considerable differences in how it is distributed. According to this standard, it makes no difference whether the national income is captured by a few rich people to buy yachts while their fellow citizens cannot afford to eat, or if it is distributed broadly so that all citizens have enough income to purchase necessities. Whether higher per capita incomes increase well-being depends upon how wealth is distributed. Charles Dickens, in his novel *Hard Times*, captured this notion that higher national incomes only contribute to well-being when their benefits are distributed widely. The teacher in Dickens's novel tries to convince students that wealth equaled well-being by telling them to imagine that their classroom is a nation endowed with "fifty millions of money." He then asks whether this didn't make them collectively prosperous, to which one of the students replies: "I couldn't know whether it was a prosperous nation or not . . . unless I knew who got the money and whether any of it was mine."[19]

We do not mean to suggest that economic development and the accumulation of wealth is unimportant. It is the only way to raise large numbers of people out of absolute poverty in very poor countries. According to economist Paul Collier, "Growth is not a cure all, but lack of growth is a kill-all."[20] Countries that fail to grow economically lack the financial resources to improve citizens' health care, increase their educational opportunities, and insure their safety. Poor countries are also more prone to debilitating corruption and destructive civil wars that threaten people's well-being.

As much as economic growth is desirable, it is only a means to an end; it is not an end in itself. Consequently, some social scientists have proposed happiness as the goal of a good society that wealth can help us achieve. They argue that a country's Gross National Product is only important as much as it contributes to a country's Gross National Happiness (GNH), which is the true measure of the good society. More is better only if it makes us happier.

One country that took happiness seriously as the measure of the good society was the Kingdom of Bhutan, located high in the Himalayan mountains, between China and India. Under a new constitution that Bhutan adopted in 2008, government programs are judged according to the happiness they produce, not the economic benefits they bring.[21] The government then proceeded to classify happiness in terms of four pillars (economy, culture, environment, and good governance), with nine domains under them, which could, in turn, be measured by seventy-two indicators. The domain of psychological well-being, for example,

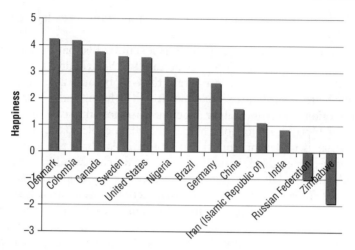

FIGURE 1.3

Countries Ranked by Happiness

Data Source:
Countries Ranked by Happiness
Source: "Despite Frustrations Americans Are Pretty Darned Happy." National Science Foundation Press
Release, June 30, 2008. nsf.gov.www.nsf.gov/news/newsmedia/pr111725/pr111725.pdf

came under the pillar of culture and was indicated by the frequencies of prayer and meditation, fewer feelings of selfishness and jealousy, and more feelings of calm and compassion.[22]

Bhutan developed complex mathematical formulas for measuring happiness. But it is hard to apply these formulas comparatively to other countries. Fortunately, beginning in 1981, the World Values Survey began to investigate how happy people were in different countries, making such comparisons possible. Figure 1.3 above is based on combined World Values Survey data from 1995 to 2005.

According to this survey, Denmark comes closest to being a good society with the highest average score on reported happiness and life satisfaction, with Zimbabwe bringing up the rear. But there are good reasons to be skeptical of happiness as an indicator of the good society.

First, the happiness standard suffers from many of the same flaws that afflict the wealth standard. Just as GDP measures ignore the purpose for which goods and services are produced, so do happiness measures overlook the different ways in which people find satisfaction. Genghis Khan is alleged to have said, "The greatest happiness is to vanquish your enemies, to chase them before you, to rob them of their wealth, to see those dear to them bathed in tears, to clasp to your bosom their wives and daughters."[23] Most people would agree that happiness derived in this fashion perverts its meaning. But people who get pleasure from humiliating others may report the same level of life satisfaction as those who derive pleasure from helping their victims. Just as GDP measures ignore differences between low- and high-quality economic growth that we mentioned previously, so do happiness surveys ignore differences between how people find pleasure and what makes them happy.

Second, while happiness may be a good thing, it is not the only thing. Indeed, people may desire other worthy goals that require sacrifice and hardship in order to attain them. As Elizabeth Kolbert argues, making sure the environment is sustainable may be more important than trashing it, even if we derive more pleasure from the latter than the former.[24]

Third, different cultures don't attach the same value to happiness. In some countries, people are expected to be optimistic and exuberant in the face of adversity, while in others the prevailing norm is to be dour and grim. Survey comparisons of happiness across countries may thus be measuring differences in the cultural approval given to happiness as opposed to actual differences in happiness.[25] Moreover, happiness may have different meanings to people in different circumstances. People "come to want only what they can have" and be content with this. Consequently, poor people tend to apply lower standards to evaluate their happiness than wealthier citizens.[26] Amartya Sen writes that "hopelessly deprived people adjust their desires and expectations to what little they see as feasible . . . [and] train themselves to take pleasure in small mercies."[27] While reports of happiness by poor people may be genuine, they are also expressions of acceptance to conditions they would probably change if they had the power to do so.

Happiness is a function of expectations. Where life is hard, people adapt to adversity and find happiness with less. Similarly, when more is available, people expect it and ratchet up their standards for happiness. This may explain why citizens in some developing countries report higher levels of contentment than Americans, even though Americans live better according to most social indicators. It may also explain why crime victims report lower levels of happiness where crime is less prevalent than in those areas where it is more common and why, according to Carol Gable, "freedom and democracy makes people happier, but the effect is greater when they're used to such liberties than

---

IN BRIEF

Criticisms of GNP and GNH as Measures of the Good Society

GNP
- Treats all spending as the same (of equal value) regardless of the purpose for which it is used.
- Is not sensitive to issues of distribution and equality.
- Devalues activity that is not bought and sold.

GNH
- Is indifferent to the ways people might find happiness.
- Discounts that people's sense of satisfaction may depend more upon their reference group or expectations than upon their actual circumstances.
- Ignores cultural differences in the approval or sanction given to happiness.

when they are not."[28] It appears that happiness depends heavily on one's reference group.

Neither Gross Domestic Product nor Gross Domestic Happiness is satisfactory as a standard to evaluate government performance and compare quality of life across countries. The question remains: What standard is appropriate by which to measure the good society? We have adopted the capability approach, which has been developed by Amartya Sen and Martha Nussbaum to answer this question. According to the capability approach a good society "enhances the **capabilities** of people to pursue the goals important to their own lives, whether through individual or collective action."[29] We suggest that empowering people, giving them the capacity to pursue values of importance to them, rather than wealth or happiness, is the most satisfactory way of assessing individuals' quality of life and the degree to which countries measure up to the good society.

CAPABILITIES AND THE QUALITY OF LIFE

If the concept of enhancing persons' capabilities is to be useful in comparative analysis, we need to make it more precise and measurable. The first step is to make it less abstract by suggesting there are four dimensions that are essential to making people free to live the life they choose, which apply in all countries.[30] Instead of one dial, such as GDP or GDH, to measure the quality of life in different countries, we propose a dashboard containing different gauges. Just as one dial won't tell you how well a car is running, so do you need to check various gauges on the dashboard—electricity, gas, temperature, and pressure—to assess how well a car is performing.[31] In a good society, people are able to

- meet their physical needs;
- make informed decisions;
- live in safety; and
- exercise democratic rights.

Physical Well-Being

Physical well-being includes nourishment, health care, and housing sufficient to support a long life. People cannot lead rich, full lives if they are malnourished, chronically sick, or exposed to the elements because they lack shelter. One way of assessing physical needs is to compare poverty rates across countries. But doing so is problematic. Many countries do not draw a poverty line, an income threshold below which people are considered poor, as the United States does. And a poverty line of $22,000 (2008–2009) for a family of four in the United States would look like riches to the millions of poor people in the rest of the world whose total income amounts to a dollar a day, even if we were to adjust for living costs. Alternatively, poverty can be defined as including those whose income is 50 percent below the median income in a country. But this measure really compares inequality among countries, not poverty, since the median income differs from one country to the next. People who are below 50 percent where the median income is high would live much better than those who were below that threshold where the median income was low.

In order to avoid these problems, we will steer clear of poverty rates entirely. We propose to examine physical well-being across countries by comparing infant mortality rates (see Table 1.1 in the Appendix), the number of children who die during their first year of life. Infant mortality rates provide a revealing window into social conditions because new babies are particularly susceptible to poor diets, deadly diseases, and extreme weather. Some countries do an excellent job of keeping infants alive and healthy, while others do not. In developed countries, such as Sweden and Japan, fewer than three newborn babies die per 1,000 births. In contrast, in the West African country of Sierra Leone there were 154 deaths for every 1,000 babies born in 2006 and in Afghanistan nearly 20 percent of babies died before they reached their fifth birthday.[32]

THE GOOD SOCIETY IN DEPTH

Costa Rica—Doing More With Less[59]

People can only develop capabilities if they survive to adulthood, and they are more likely to do so in some countries more than in others. The general pattern is that wealthier countries are healthier, as we saw in Figure 1.1, and that the wealthiest countries have the lowest infant mortality rates. Costa Rica is an exception. This small democratic country of four and a half million people in Central America has one of the best infant mortality records in the world for a country at its income level. More impressively it nearly matches infant mortality rates in the United States, even though its per capita income is only one-fourth as large. In 2003, for every 1,000 infants born alive in Costa Rica, eight died in their first year of life as compared to seven deaths per 1,000 live births in the United States.

Dramatically reducing infant mortality rates does not require expensive, sophisticated medical technology. It does, however, require safe drinking water, adequate nutrition, and basic health care for pregnant mothers and newborns. Costa Rica has done an excellent job of providing these necessities to poor mothers and infants who need them most. The government began to provide safe drinking water in the 1940s. By 1995, safe drinking water was available to over 90 percent of the population. The result was a dramatic drop in infant mortality caused by parasites and diarrhea. In the 1950s, Costa Rica began nutrition programs for poor families to help reduce severe malnutrition, expanding them in succeeding decades. It has also provided basic medical care to mothers by placing teams of doctors, nurses, and trained health care workers in all parts of the country, especially rural areas that traditionally lacked access to health care workers. These health care providers advised pregnant women on nutrition, assisted them in child birth, inoculated infants, and treated them for parasites.

Continued

Costa Rica's success in reducing infant mortality is due, first, to the traditions and vibrancy of its democracy. The country is one of the oldest, most established democracies in the Americas, boasting competitive political parties and high voter turnout by peasants and workers. Second, for most of the latter part of the last century the government was controlled by a political party whose leaders were determined to help the rural poor. Finally, groups opposed to its policies were politically weak. Doctors, hospitals, and insurance companies were publicly controlled and funded, which weakened their ability to oppose the government's policies.

For Further Discussion

1. Why is per capita income an inadequate indicator of a population's health?

2. Nearly half of the public spending that paid for health care services for poor mothers and infants came from payroll, income, and property taxes on other Costa Ricans. Is this appropriate?

Informed Decision Making

Knowledge is Power. In the modern world, the ability to make choices that improve one's quality of life depends on access to information and the skills to understand its meaning. In India, a new right to information law permits poor people to hold the bureaucracy accountable and find out what happened to the money that was budgeted for them. Whereas previously an unresponsive bureaucracy had to be bribed, activists now say that "simply filing an inquiry about a missing ration card, a wayward pension application, or a birth certificate is nowadays enough to force the once stodgy bureaucracy to deliver."[33] But access to information is insufficient without the skills to make sense of it. People need to be literate and numerate so they can negotiate their lives more effectively. People who are illiterate are said to be "blind"; they cannot decipher street signs, understand medical prescriptions, and are handicapped in trying to provide for their families.[34] Without literacy and mathematical skills, individuals are excluded from many occupational choices. Their awareness of the ways in which their lives could be improved is limited, and they are vulnerable to others who can take advantage of these limitations. One study found that Americans who lacked basic knowledge about finances and could not do simple calculations were more likely to lose their homes to foreclosure in the recent recession than those who were more financially literate. "The less people know," James Surowieki writes, "the more they run into trouble."[35] Citizens' ability to protect their interests and make thoughtful choices about their lives can be dramatically improved by access to education. For example, in her book, *A Quiet Revolution*, Martha Chen tells the story of how learning to read and calculate changed the lives of poor, illiterate women in a village in Bangladesh. The change began when volunteers working for the Bangladesh Rural Advancement Committee came to the village to help the women learn to read. Initially, most of the women said they didn't need to learn to read and saw no reason to spend their time doing so. However, eventually they realized that literacy and math skills could help them earn money to provide health care, clothes, and food for their children. The new skills, coupled with new women's organizations, also gave them self-confidence, even to the point of defying local religious leaders who threatened to break their legs if they began doing work that had been traditionally reserved for men. Becoming literate not only helped these women earn more income, but also substantially enhanced their ability to improve their lives in ways that were important to them. None of them would ever be satisfied going back to their previous status.[36]

In order to assess informed decision making, we compare literacy rates across countries (see Table 1.2 in the Appendix). Literacy rates differ among countries and within them. Access to education is often much lower for women than it is for men. In Pakistan, for example, the literacy rate for women in 2003 was only 57 percent that of men.[37] In other countries, race can affect one's chances of receiving an education. In South Africa, the literacy rate for whites is 99 percent, while it is only 75 percent for blacks.[38] Where these gender and racial inequalities occur, they limit severely the ability of individuals to improve their life prospects.

Safety

People cannot lead a good life if they are in constant fear of being beaten, shot, raped, or tortured. Even if they are not direct victims of assault, living in a place where the probability of assault is very high means they must alter their preferred routines and diminish their lives in order to avoid such threats. The link between insecurity and poor government performance goes in both directions: Insecurity makes it more difficult for governments to create the conditions in which citizens can thrive. Conflict discourages trade and investment and diverts resources from schools and hospitals at the same time poor government performance contributes to instability.

Just as there are substantial differences in the degree to which countries meet their citizens' physical needs, there are also profound differences in the extent to which they meet their citizens' need for safety and security. In order to measure physical safety, we compare homicide rates across countries (see Table 1.3 in the Appendix). Homicide rates avoid different definitions of criminal offenses that might exist in different countries and minimize the different rates at which crimes are reported and recorded by police. Being dead is the same everywhere, and people are more likely to report a murder and the police are more likely to record it than other crimes.

According to this measure, countries differ greatly in their ability to provide a safe environment for their citizens. Residents of Canadian, European, and Japanese cities are less likely than urban-dwelling Americans to be victims of homicide. The differences between Canada and the United States are particularly dramatic because these countries are similar in so many other respects. Both are former British colonies that have become wealthy economically and have strong democracies. Yet Ottawa, Canada's capital city, had only 0.9

homicides for every 100,000 citizens in 2000, while Washington, D.C., had 41.7. A broader, national comparison reveals the Canadian homicide rate (1.5 per 100,000 in 2004) was much lower than the U.S. (5.9 per 100,000) rate.

Where appropriate, we supplement the use of homicide rates to capture our standard of safety by looking also at the incidence of war. People's safety is not only threatened by murderers but by soldiers and the collateral damage that accompanies warfare. Millions of people have died in violent political conflicts between states, and especially in civil wars within them, in places ranging from Bosnia in Europe to the Democratic Republic of the Congo in central Africa. In the Congo, which is about the size of the U.S. east of the Mississippi River, a civil was began in 1998 and officially ended in 2003, although fighting still persists in parts of the country. The International Rescue Committee estimated that more than five million people died as a result of the war, nearly half of them children under five years old. Only a fraction of these deaths was combat-related; most of the loss of life occurred because the war ruined the Congo's economy and health care services, leading to widespread starvation and disease.[39]

Democracy

The ability "to participate effectively in political choices that govern one's life; . . . the right of political participation; protections of free speech and association" underpin the other three conditions for a good society.[40] Without influence over the laws that govern them, people cannot press for improvements in their physical well-being, safety, and education. Nor can they defend gains they have already made, as former slaves discovered in the American South in the aftermath of the Civil War. By the end of Reconstruction, many southern blacks lost access to their farms, lived in fear of being lynched, and sent their children to segregated and inferior schools once they had lost the right to vote.

There have been striking improvements in **civil rights** that the state guarantees to all its citizens, such as the right to public accommodations, **civil liberties**, such as freedom of speech or assembly, that permit people to participate in their society without fear of repression or discrimination by the government, as well as improvements in **political rights,** such as the right to vote or hold office that permit people to participate in the political process. In 1900, "a scant 10% of the world's people lived in independent nations."[41] Most countries in the world were colonies or dependencies of European powers, and even within Europe itself, not a single country had universal adult suffrage. By 2000, in contrast, almost all of the world's people lived in independent countries, and the majority of countries had universal suffrage and multiparty elections.

However, these positive trends hide considerable differences. The former Soviet Union's constitution guaranteed citizens considerable freedom, but their ability to actually exercise that freedom was severely limited. These limits gave rise to the joke in the Soviet Union that Americans did not really understand freedom of speech: "What's important is not freedom of speech, but rather freedom *after* speech." Just because a constitution enumerates rights does not mean that they are enforced or that people are free to enjoy them. In many countries, people are unable to exercise their civil and political rights because they are subject to the vindictive power of employers, landlords, urban bosses, or even their relatives. In these circumstances, people are reluctant to exercise their legal rights because it might cost them their jobs, access to land, or even their lives.[42]

Unlike our other standards, there is no shortage of indexes measuring democracy. Efforts by governments and international agencies to promote democracy led to more efforts to monitor and assess it. For example, the U.S. government's Millennium Challenge Account program uses various data sets on democracy to allocate aid among foreign countries. The problem with democracy indexes is not their frequency but their quality. Some indexes define democracy in such a way that it includes too much while others include too little. According to Gerardo L. Munck, the best of the lot is the Polity IV index (see Table 1.4 in the Appendix) developed by Monty G. Marshall and Keith Jaggers, which rates countries from negative 10 (highly authoritarian) to positive 10 (highly democratic).[43]

Some Caveats

The four categories we have described represent the minimum that people need to fulfill their potential and enhance their quality of life. Several points must be stressed here before we respond to criticisms of these criteria to define the good society. First, it may be that all "good things do not necessarily go together" and trade-offs among physical well-being, safety, education, and democracy may be necessary.[44] Progress on one dimension of capabilities may require concessions on others. Second, the goal of a good society is to make it possible for each individual in a country to enjoy a high quality of life, and not just for the average quality of life to be high. Third, our approach does not specify a particular set of economic, political, or social institutions that are necessary for a good society. Some argue that good societies can be created only by relying on free markets, private property rights, and a minimal role for states. Others argue that a good society requires institutions that do just the opposite. Finally, our approach does not assert that it is the state's responsibility to ensure that all individuals thrive. It is, however, the role of the state to create conditions in which persons can *choose* a flourishing life. One way of thinking about this difference, Nussbaum suggests, is to distinguish between dieting and starving. People may choose to go on a diet, even if the diet severely restricts their intake of food. By contrast, starvation is not a choice. It is the role of states to provide the circumstances in which people are able to choose to diet if they so desire, but also to ensure that adequate supplies of food are available so they do not starve.[45] Conversely, a state can help create conditions in which individuals can lead long healthy lives, but citizens who choose to smoke cigarettes, drink excessive amounts of alcohol, and subsist on fast food are unlikely to do so.

> **IN BRIEF**
>
> **Operationalizing Capabilities**
> - Meeting physical needs: infant mortality rates
> - Informed decision making: literacy rates
> - Safety: homicide rates
> - Democracy: the Polity IV index

RESPONDING TO CRITICISMS OF THE CAPABILITY APPROACH

The capability approach has won widespread support in recent years from eminent scholars and important international organizations. Recently, Peter A. Hall of Harvard and former president of the Comparative Politics section of the American Political Science Association encouraged his colleagues to move beyond their concern with how societies distribute income and to think more broadly "about the distribution of life chances and about the ways in which institutional and cultural frameworks . . . contribute to individual and collective well-being."[46] He and a number of colleagues have collaborated on a project that investigates the sources of successful societies.[47] A number of organizations, such as the United Nations, have also adopted the capability approach. The 2002 Human Development Report issued by the U.N. stated: "Fundamental to enlarging human choices is building capability: the range of things that people can do or be."[48] There is even a scholarly journal, *The Journal of Human Development and Capabilities,* devoted to work using the capability perspective. Despite support from prominent scholars and influential organizations, the capability approach still has its critics.[49] A skeptic might dismiss this approach as too idealistic, asserting with some justification that no country can meet these conditions for every single citizen. Not even the wealthiest countries in the world have met these standards, no less the poor countries in Africa, Asia, and Latin America.

While it may be idealistic to assume that every citizen in every country enjoy a high quality of life, it is not idealistic to believe that many countries can do a much better job than they currently do. Some countries already are more successful than others in providing health care to their citizens. Some are safer than others, with much lower rates of homicide and political violence. Some offer better guarantees of civil and political rights. Performance on these standards varies widely among countries that are quite similar to one another in other respects, indicating that there is probably room for improvement.

Other readers will argue that our approach is contrary to "human nature." Some critics may be sympathetic to the goals of the capability approach but believe that people are too competitive, greedy, and selfish to create the kind of good society we envision. But people are capable of a wide range of behavior, from the most greedy and selfish to the most altruistic and cooperative. It is not any more natural to be greedy and selfish than to be caring and cooperative. As Amartya Sen reminds us, we do not have to be a Gandhi, a Mandela, or a Mother Teresa "to recognize that we can have aims or priorities that differ from the single-minded pursuit of our own well-being only."[50] In addition, insisting that there is a universal human nature makes it hard to explain why there are dramatic differences in citizens' capability from one country to another. Those who insist that flaws in human nature prevent substantial improvements in people's lives cannot explain why Americans kill each other more frequently than do Canadians; why Denmark has remarkably little government corruption while it is routine in Nigeria, or why South Korea has achieved extraordinary economic growth since 1960, while North Korea has plunged into poverty and famine. People behave differently in different institutional settings. When institutions work well, they enable people to act cooperatively to achieve their goals. But when institutions "are weak or unjust, the result is mistrust and uncertainty."[51]

Another group of critics advances a different line of argument. For them, humans are clearly selfish, but this is seen as a desirable trait rather than a flaw. Perhaps the best known statement of this viewpoint occurred in the 1987 movie *Wall Street,* in which an aggressive corporate raider asserted, "The point is, ladies and gentlemen, greed is good."[52] This point of view is not limited to movies. A nationally syndicated columnist argues, "You can call it greed, selfishness, or enlightened self-interest; but the bottom line is that it's these human motivations that get wonderful things done."[53]

Yet, there are problems with this assertion. The first is that even persons who argue that greed can be beneficial do not claim that it achieves wonderful results under all circumstances. Unrestrained greed and selfishness would leave the advocates of greed themselves vulnerable to being cheated, robbed, or even killed. Whether the pursuit of self-interest leads to good results for individuals depends a great deal on the institutional setting in which that pursuit takes place. In the Nigerian context, institutions create incentives for people to pursue their self-interest in ways that lead to high levels of corruption, poor health, illiteracy, and limited political rights for most citizens. In the Danish setting, people pursue their self-interest in ways that yield the opposite outcomes. One of the major goals of this book will be to examine why some societies do a much better job than others of creating conditions in which an individual's self-interest can be aligned with the self-interest of others to create a good society.

Finally, **cultural relativists** believe that it is inappropriate to try to establish criteria for a good society that apply to all of the world's countries. They claim that each society should be evaluated only by using criteria from that society.[54] If some countries choose not to practice democratic politics, that is up to them. If some countries do not want female children to be educated, that is their prerogative. These are not necessarily practices that we would approve of but other countries and cultures have the right to decide upon their own rules, just as we do. Cultural relativism is attractive because it appeals to our desire to be tolerant and open-minded toward people who have different beliefs from our own.[55]

But cultural relativism is not as innocent and impartial as it appears. Cultural relativists simply legitimize the power of those who have triumphed over others in the conflict over prevailing social values. Cultures are seldom, if ever, monolithic in which everyone agrees, but are often filled with different, and sometimes conflicting, interpretations. For example, the extremist Muslim Taliban government in Afghanistan banned education for girls from 1996 until 2001. But this policy was not supported by female teachers or by all women in Afghanistan. Even the male leaders of some fundamentalist Islamic political parties in Afghanistan supported education for girls. Where many different interpretations of a culture's values exist, cultural relativism sides with those who are able to enforce their values on others. To say that Afghani culture should not be condemned for barring girls from being educated accepts the Taliban prohibition on educating girls as representative of the national culture over those who opposed it.

Cultural relativism is difficult to apply with consistency. It is particularly difficult in countries headed by authoritarian governments to find out about internal value differences because citizens are not free to voice differing opinions. Cultural relativism "provides no independent footing" for choosing among competing values within a country.[56] The approach we use, by contrast, offers a reasoned way to establish standards by which to compare and evaluate societies, one that has been used and accepted by the United Nations Human Development Program. It provides general criteria for evaluation and comparison but does not specify a particular institutional arrangement. Moreover, it gives individuals considerable freedom of choice by creating conditions that permit them to pursue the kind of lives they value. If people want to live frugally they should be free to do so, but they should not have to live that way due to unwanted poverty. If people who are sick choose not to take advantage of health care resources that is their business; but it is quite another matter if sick people cannot take advantage of heath care resources because they are unavailable or unaffordable.[57] This is not to say that our approach is uncontroversial. In many countries, authoritarian leaders who object to giving citizens civil and political rights would certainly oppose our emphasis on them. These rights, however, are not just Western values that are being imposed on other cultures, but are valued by many people around the world.[58]

CONCLUSION

Comparative politics examines why countries are organized in different ways and what consequences those differences may have. It examines differences within countries as opposed to relations between them, which is the domain of international relations, another subfield within political science. Comparative politics is a valuable field of study not only because it makes us familiar with other countries but because it gives us perspective about our own. Comparative politics provides a reference point or standard by which we can make judgments about our government's performance.

Comparative political analysis proceeds systematically, which entails forming hypotheses, operationally defining variables, and selecting a method to test those hypotheses. We then proceeded to assess different standards of the good society by which to compare countries. One standard defined the good society according to wealth, while another did so according to happiness. Both were inadequate because they were insensitive to distributional issues. A society may be wealthy but the people within it are not because its wealth is unevenly distributed, while the poor may use lower standards than the rich to define happiness because that is all they think they can obtain or deserve.

We then proceeded to defend the capability approach, which defines the good society as one in which certain minimal conditions exist that permit people to flourish. These conditions include physical well-being, safety from violence, the ability to make thoughtful choices about one's life, and the possession of civil and political rights.

Finally, the chapter responded to critics of the capabilities approach who condemn it for idealism or cultural imperialism. But it is not idealistic to suggest that some countries can do better at promoting their citizens' capabilities because other countries with similar levels of resources are outperforming them. Nor is the capabilities approach guilty of imposing values on another culture. Rather, it provides consistent standards to apply in making normative judgments among competing values within and between societies.

EXERCISES

Apply what you learned in this chapter on MyPoliSciKit (www.mypoliscikit.com).

 ASSESSMENT
Review this chapter using learning objectives, chapter summaries, practice tests, and more.

 VIDEO CASE STUDIES
Analyze recent world affairs by watching streaming video from major news providers.

FLASHCARDS
Learn the key terms in this chapter; you can test yourself by term or definition.

 COMPARATIVE EXERCISES
Compare political ideas, behaviors, institutions, and policies worldwide.

CRITICAL THINKING QUESTIONS

1. What principles does your vision of the Good Society reflect? What prerequisites do you think the Good Society should include?

2. We use concepts, such as democracy or freedom, all the time. Or we often say that workers in some country are more class conscious than workers in another, or that ethnic tensions are greater here than there. But operationally defining these concepts so they can be used in comparative political analysis is tricky and takes a great deal of imagination. How would you operationally define these concepts

(democracy, freedom, class consciousness, ethnic tension) so they can be compared across countries?

3. What are the advantages and disadvantages of the different comparative methods we reviewed: the case study approach that examines one country intensively; a paired country approach that tries to find countries that are similar to each other so that other variables can be held constant; or comparisons that involve many countries so analysts can test their hypothesis against many cases? Which method do you think is best and why?

4. Even if we accept that wealth (GDP per capita) is not sufficient for the Good Society, do you think it is, at least, necessary?

5. What criteria do you believe should be used to evaluate how states perform?

KEY TERMS

Comparative Politics 2	Control Variables 4	Civil Rights 18
Comparative Political	Correlation 4	Civil Liberties 18
Analysis 3	Causation 4	Political Rights 18
Hypothesis 3	GDP 4	Cultural Relativism 21
Dependent Variable 3	Empirical Analysis 8	
Independent Variable 3	Normative Analysis 8	
Operationalize	The Capabilities	
Variables 4	Approach 14	

SUGGESTED READINGS

Alexander Kaufman, (ed) , *Capabilities Equality: Basic Issues and Problems* (New York: Routledge 2006). Chapters by authors sympathetic to the capabilities approach but also includes criticisms of it.

Todd Landman, *Issues and Methods of Comparative Politics: An Introduction* (New York: Routledge, 2000). Makes the case for why we compare countries and how to make comparisons using a single country, a few countries, and many countries.

Darrin McMahon, *Happiness: A History* (New York: Grove Press, 2006). A lively, well-written account of changing views of happiness and of the pursuit of happiness as an inalienable right.

Andrew J. Nathan, "The Place of Values in Cross-Cultural Studies," in Andrew J. Nathan, *China's Transition* (New York: Columbia University Press, 1997), pp. 198–216. One of the world's leading China scholars makes a case for evaluative universalism.

Martha Nussbaum, *Women and Human Development: The Capabilities Approach* (New York, NY: Cambridge University Press, 2000). Asserts there are universal norms of human capability that apply to all societies. These norms should provide the basis for constitutional guarantees of women's rights to choose the kinds of lives they have reason to value.

Amartya Sen, *Development as Freedom* (New York, NY: Alfred A. Knopf, 1999). An introduction to the capabilities approach. It suggests the success of a society should be evaluated primarily by the freedoms its members enjoy.

Amartya Sen. *The Idea of Justice* (Cambridge: Belknap Press, 2009). The book examines egalitarian, libertarian, and happiness-based theories of justice. It does not attempt to describe a perfectly just society as an alternative to these theories, but rather a framework for thinking about justice based on the kinds of lives people are actually able to lead.

NOTES

1. President Johnson is quoted in Ira Katznelson, *When Affirmative Action Was White: An Untold History of Racial Inequality in Twentieth Century America* (New York: Norton, 2005), p. 175.
2. Alice Schroeder, *The Snowball: Warren Buffet and the Business of Life* (New York: Bantam, 2008), p. 43.
3. These figures are from the *CIA Factbook* for 2009.
4. Kipling is quoted in Niall Ferguson, *Empire: The Rise and Demise of the British World Order and the Lessons for Global Power* (New York: Basic Books, 2003), p. 203.
5. Richard H. Steinberg, "The Transformation of European Trading States," in *The State After Statism: New State Activities in the Age of Liberalization*, ed. Jonah Levy, (Cambridge: Harvard University Press, 2006), pp. 340–365.
6. Steve Lohr, "For Today's Graduate, Just One Word, Statistics," *The New York Times*, August 5, 2009.
7. Dan Zuberi, *Differences that Matter: Social Policy and the Working Poor in the United States and Canada* (Ithaca: Cornell University Press, 2006).
8. Kellee S. Tsai, *Capitalism without Democracy: The Private Sector in Contemporary China* (Ithaca: Cornell University Press, 2007).
9. Ann Swidler, "Responding to AIDS in Sub-Saharan Africa: Culture, Institutions, and Health," in Peter A. Hall and Michele Lamont, eds., *Successful Societies: How Institutions and Culture Affect Health* (New York: Cambridge University Press, 2009), pp. 151–168
10. This goal is adapted from Harvard economist Dani Rodrik's statement of his research focus as "what constitutes good economic policy and why some governments are better than others in adopting it." Accessed December 9, 2010: http://ksghome.harvard.edu/~drodrik.academic.ksg.
11. Kevin Bales, *Disposable People: New Slavery in the Global Economy* (Berkeley: University of California Press, 1999), pp. 6–8.
12. Philip Gourevitch, *We Wish to Inform You that Tomorrow We Will Be Killed With Our Families: Stories from Rwanda* (New York: Farrar, Strauss, and Giroux, 1998), p. 29.
13. Kenneth Hill and Rahim Pande, "Trends in Child Mortality in the Developing World: 1965–95," (New York: United Nations, 1995).
14. A country's gross domestic product is the value of all final goods and services produced within a country. The total gross domestic product must be divided by the total number of persons in a country to get the GDP per person (or per capita). It is important to compare countries on the basis of per capita GDP because otherwise a very large country such as China would appear to be wealthier than a small country such as Denmark. China's GDP is bigger, but its population is also much bigger than Denmark's.
15. "Getting and Using Data." Human Development Reports. United Nations Development Programme. Accessed April 10, 2010: www.hdr.undp.org. These amounts show the actual purchasing power of what citizens can buy when their currency is converted to dollars.
16. The group was called the Commission on the Measurement of Economic Performance and Social Progress.

17. Nancy Folbre, *The Invisible Heart: Economics and Family Values* (New York: The Free Press, 2001), p. 62.

18. Kennedy is quoted in Louis Uchitelle, "G.D.P. = Happiness," *The New York Times*, (August 31, 2008), Week in Review, p. 3.

19. Dickens is quoted in Martha Nussbaum and Amartya Sen, eds., *The Quality of Life* (New York: Oxford University Press, 1992), p. 1.

20. Paul Collier, *The Bottom Billion: Why the Poorest Countries are Failing and What Can be Done About It* (New York: Oxford University Press, 2007), p. 190.

21. Eduardo Porter, "All They Are Saying Is Give Happiness a Chance," *The New York Times*, November 12, 2007; and Daniel Kahneman, Alan B. Krueger, David Schkade, Norbert Schwarz, and Arthur Stone, "Toward National Well-Being Accounts," American Economic Association, Papers and Proceedings, May 2004.

22. Seth Mydans, "Recalculating Happiness in a Himalayan Kingdom," *The New York Times*, May 7, 2009, p. A8.

23. William C. Martel, "Formulating Victory and the Implications for Policy," *Orbis* 52:4 (2008).

24. Elizabeth Kolbert, "Everybody Have Fun," *The New Yorker* (March 22, 2010), pp. 72–74.

25. Alberto Alesino, Rafael Di Tella, and Robert MacCulloch, "Inequality and Happiness: Are Europeans and Americans Different?" *Journal of Public Economics* 88 (2004), pp. 2009–2042.

26. Martha Nussbaum, "Poverty and Human Functioning: Capabilities as Fundamental Human Entitlements," in David B. Grusky and Ravi Kanbur, eds., *Poverty and Inequality* (Berkeley: University of California Press, 2006), pp. 48–49.

27. Sen, *The Idea of Justice*, (Cambridge: Harvard University Press, 2009), p. 283.

28. Carol Graham, "The Economics of Happiness," *Washington Post* (January 3, 2010), p. B1

29. Peter Hall and Michele Lamont, "What Makes a Society Succeed?" *Reach Magazine* (Spring 2007), p. 9.

30. Both Nussbaum and Sen have written extensively on this subject. For Nussbaum's most recent version of the capabilities approach, see Martha Nussbaum, *Women and Human Development: The Capabilities Approach* (New York: Cambridge University Press, 2000). Sen's fullest account can be found in his *Development as Freedom*. The list of four ways of functioning here draws from the work of both authors.

31. Jon Gertner, "The Rise and Fall of the G.D.P.," *The New York Times* Magazine Section (May 10, 2010).

32. World Bank, *World Development Report 2000/2001* (New York: Oxford University Press, 2000), p. 287.

33. Lydia Polgreen, "Right-to Know Law Gives India's Poor a Lever," *The New York Times* (June 28, 2010), p. 1.

34. Carlotta Gall, "Long in Dark, Afghan Women Say to Read Is Finally to See," *The New York Times*, September 24, 2002.

35. James Surowieki, "Greater Fools," *The New Yorker* (July 5, 2010), p. 23.

36. Martha Alter Chen, *A Quiet Revolution: Women in Transition in Rural Bangladesh* (Rochester, VT: Schenkman Books, 1983).

37. United Nations Development Programme, *Human Development Report 2005* (New York: Oxford University Press, 2005), p. 309.

38. Accessed on June 3, 2010 at: http://www.justice.gov.za/policy/african%20charter/afr-charter01.html

39. "The Deadliest War," *The Atlantic Monthly* (July/August 2003), p. 38. See also Adam Hochschild, "Chaos in Congo Suits Many Parties Just Fine," *New York*

Times (April 20, 2003); and Philip Gourevitch, "The Congo Test," *The New Yorker* (June 2, 2003), pp. 33–35.

40. Nussbaum, *Women and Human Development*, p. 80.
41. United Nations Development Programme, *Human Development Report 2000* (New York: Oxford University Press, 2000) p. 29.
42. Patrick Heller, "Degrees of Democracy: Some Comparative Lessons from India," *World Politics* 52:4 (July 2000), pp. 484–519.
43. Gerardo L. Munck, *Measuring Democracy: A Bridge Between Scholarship and Politics* (Baltimore, MD.: Johns Hopkins Press, 2009), p. 37.
44. Adam Przeworski, Michael E. Alvarez, Fernando Limongi, and with contributions by Mary Margaret McCabe, *Democracy and Development: Political Institutions and Well-Being in the World, 1950–1990* (New York: Cambridge University Press, 2000), p. 1.
45. Nussbaum, *Women and Development*, p. 88.
46. Peter A. Hall, "A Capabilities Approach to Successful Societies," *Perspectives on Europe* (Spring 2010), Vol. 40, No. 1, p. 11.
47. Peter A. Hall and Michelle Lamont, *Successful Societies: How Institutions and Culture Affect Health* (New York: Cambridge University Press, 2009).
48. United Nations Development Programme, *Human Development Report 2002* (New York: Oxford University Press, 2002), p. 13.
49. These criticisms have come from our students who have read drafts of this chapter. For examples of scholarly critiques, see G.A. Cohen, "Amartya Sen's Unequal World," *New Left Review* 203 (1994), pp. 117–129; Peter Evans, "Collective Capability, Culture, and Amartya Sen's Development as Freedom," *Studies in Comparative International Development* 37:2 (Summer, 2002), pp. 54–60; and Nivadita Menon, "Universalism without Foundations," *Economy and Society* 31:1 (February 2002), pp. 152–169.
50. Amartya Sen, *The Idea of Justice*, pp. 18–19.
51. World Bank, *World Development Report 2003: Sustainable Development in a Dynamic World* (New York: Oxford University Press, 2003), p. 37.
52. Cited in Paul Krugman, "Greed is Bad," *The New York Times* (June 4, 2002), p. A19.
53. Walter E. Williams, "The Virtue of Greed," *Capitalism Magazine* (January 5, 2001), accessed on November 15, 2010 at: http://www.capitalismmagazine.com/culture/69-The-Virtue-G.
54. Andrew J. Nathan, "The Place of Values in Cross-Cultural Studies," in Andrew J. Nathan, *China's Transition* (New York: Columbia University Press, 1997), p. 200. See also Martha C. Nussbaum, *Sex and Social Justice* (New York: Oxford University Press, 1999), p. 121.
55. Ibid., 122.
56. Nathan, *China's Transition*, p. 207.
57. Amartya Sen, *The Idea of Justice*, p. 238.
58. Andrew Nathan, *China's Transition*.
59. The following material is from James W. McGuire, "Politics, Policy, and Mortality Decline in Costa Rica," Paper prepared for delivery at the 2007 Convention of the American Political Science Association, Chicago, IL, August 30–September 2, 2007.

The State

INTRODUCTION

States viewed forests initially as sources of revenue, for the timber that could be extracted and sold from them. In order to increase their yields, states turned to scientific forestry, which involved replacing the diverse, chaotic old-growth forest with one that was easier to manipulate, measure, and assess. The underbrush needed to be cleared, the number of species needed to be reduced, and the trees needed to be planted at the same time and in straight rows for easy harvesting. The forest had been replaced by tree farming. Scientific forestry promised to deliver maximum production of a uniform commodity that could be managed, extracted, and sold easily.[1]

In the short run, the simplification of the forest to a single commodity was a success. Timber yields increased. But after the second rotation of saplings had been planted, the quality of the timber began to decline. Scientific forestry destroyed the complex ecology that the forest had once provided to nourish and protect the trees. The absence of biomass on the forest floor due to the clearing of underbrush led to thinner and less nutritious soil. Trees that were all of the same species attracted pests that specialized in that species, and James C. Scott writes, "same age, same-species forests . . . were more susceptible to massive storm-felling."[2] Efforts to bring order and control to the forest in pursuit of higher yields were incompatible with the complex ecosystems on which healthy trees depended.

But scientific forestry matured. The regimentation of nature as a way to manage forests and increase their yield was abandoned. New ways of cultivating forests were developed that did not destroy the biodiversity that trees required. Scientific forestry, which initially imposed an order on nature that harmed it, now permitted the state to extract more revenue from it in ways that also maintained this vital resource. The kind of planning and order that states impose became the basis for realizing higher timber yields that would not have been possible without it.

This parable of the forest tells us a lot about states. They have certain interests—in this instance, raising revenue—and they try to bring order to chaos in pursuit of them. Like the forest, society is diverse and complex, with a complicated ecology, and the state's efforts to impose order on such a complex social organism can make things worse. In these cases, as Scott quips, "the state can't see the forest for the trees."[3] At other times, the state's effort to plan, coordinate, and administer permits societies to achieve wonders that could not have been attained otherwise. The state can both frustrate society's ambitions and help it realize them.

This chapter argues that the good society depends on a society's institutional arrangements, and the most powerful institution of all is the state. The good society, as we established earlier, is based on a set of defensible universal values. First, people should be able to meet their physical needs: People should be able to obtain the food, shelter, and health care they need to work, play, and procreate. It is hard to achieve your life's goals if you are hungry from lack of food, cold from lack of shelter, or sick from lack of medical care. Second, people should be safe from harm: They should be secure enough that others, including agents of the government, will not arbitrarily harm them physically or take their personal property. Third, people should have the ability to make educated choices about how they live: To do so, they must have the opportunity to obtain the knowledge they need to make informed decisions. Finally, people should have civil and political rights in order to protect the conditions in which they might freely develop their capabilities. People should be allowed to participate in open public debate about the policies and leaders most likely to produce conditions in which they can thrive.

States can promote conditions that develop people's capabilities or impede them. They can manage forests in ways that destroy their ecology or contribute to it. Since states loom so large in thwarting or enhancing people's lives, this chapter examines the origins of the state and its different parts or components. These include its legislative, executive and judicial branches, its bureaucratic and military arms, and its subnational or federal levels. Since states matter so much, it is important to look inside them.

INSTITUTIONS AND POWER

The degree to which countries meet the standards of the good society depends upon their institutional arrangements. **Institutions** create and embody written and unwritten rules that constrain individuals' behavior into patterned actions. These rules make a social life together possible by giving it order and predictability. Without these rules our lives together would be chaotic and fraught with anxiety. Just as individual words in a paragraph would sound like gibberish if we did not use them within the context of established rules, so do institutions give meaning and structure to our relations with each other. Institutions provide the grammar of our lives.

To appreciate the importance of institutions, just imagine how dangerous the simple act of driving a car would be if there were no traffic laws. We could not be sure that incoming traffic would stop at red lights, that cars on our side of the road would go in the same direction, or that drivers would operate at safe speeds. The result would be chaos and danger. This is precisely what happened in Baghdad, Iraq, "when the rules vanished in the chaos of the American invasion, when there was no electricity for stoplights, and no police officers to enforce the law." According to *New York Times* reporter John Tierney, "Every intersection became a perpetual game of chicken among cars, trucks, buses and carts drawn by horses and donkeys. Every lane became potentially two-way, even on expressways, where there quickly became no distinction between entrance and exit ramps."[4] In order to make traffic flow smoothly, in order to create the order and predictability that makes daily life tolerable, institutions must constrain people's conduct. They must exert power. Some people make and enforce the traffic rules that drivers follow so there can be a safe and predictable flow of traffic. Investing institutions with power over our behavior is the price we pay in order to enjoy the benefits of a social life together, of keeping traffic moving safely and smoothly. Institutions, one might say, are "the ground of both our freedoms and unfreedoms."[5] They make it possible for drivers to get from place to place safely, but only by exerting power, imposing and enforcing rules on them.

There are all kinds of institutions that impose rules, such as families and schools. Parents tell their children when they should be home and teachers tell students how they should behave in class. They exert **power**, which is the ability to get people to do things they would not have chosen to do on their own, or to prevail in getting what you want in the presence of opposing claims and competing interests.[6] To paraphrase Dr. Martin Luther King, power is the ability to get people to say "Yes" when they really want to say "No."

Power is one of the most contested and elusive terms in political science. It is hard to pin down or measure precisely. Sometimes the exercise of power is overt, such as when force or coercion is used. At other times, power is concealed, such as when people are manipulated without realizing it. Sometimes power is used to get people to do something, to elicit change, while at other times it is used to ensure that people do nothing, to preserve the status quo. Power is distinct from authority in which those who comply think it is legitimate or morally appropriate that they do so. **Authority** is a form of power that has been accepted as right and proper by those who submit to it.

Power takes three forms: cultural, economic, and political. Cultural power exists when some people are able to convince others to adopt their values, ideas, and premises as their own. People comply with what others want because they think it is the right thing to do. For example, students sit quietly through a painfully boring lecture because they are socialized to think that is the proper way to behave in school. This form of power can be insidious because people may not even be aware they are subject to it. The values and ideas they thought were their own are actually those they have been socialized to adopt and accept. They obey because they have been led to believe the rules to which they submit are fair and legitimate.

The second form of power is material or economic power. People who control critical scarce resources, such as land or capital, are able to obtain compliance from those who do not. For example, to return to our example above, students may sit quietly through boring lectures because they don't want to risk offending professors who grade them. Professors dispense rewards that students are willing to feign interest to obtain. Economic power occurs when rewards are offered or denied in order to obtain compliance.

Finally, there is political power. Political power is grounded in coercion and control over the means of violence. Returning to the classroom example, students sit quietly because professors can tell disruptive students to leave the class or have the campus police evict them. Not all forms of political power involve the use of violence. But they do involve the threat of violence; that is, if people do not obey commands those who wield political power have ways of making them do so.[7]

The power institutions exert is based on control over the content of social beliefs, control of essential material resources, and control of the means of violence. Institutions wield cultural, economic, and political power to create rules that channel people's behavior into regular patterns. Rules grounded in power make civilization possible. Of course, the quality of that civilization depends upon what the rules are and how they are enforced.

THE STATE

But not all forms of power are created equal. Political power trumps all others. Only in so far as the threat of violence works can cultural and economic power be exercised in a peaceable and orderly manner. For example, all economic systems presuppose political power to enforce rules of exchange and trade. Political power, thus, takes functional priority over other forms.[8] In addition, political power is necessary to protect cultural and economic power from outside threats. Political power is paramount because it keeps rivals who are not subject to ideological indoctrination or material incentives in check. Political power not only comes first but it is foremost.

The institution that embodies political power is **the state**. The state refers to a set of organizations imbued with sovereignty over a given area through its control of the means of violence. There are four distinct parts to this definition. First is the notion of the state as an organization, a distinct administrative entity. People who are vested with political power are granted it by virtue of their place within this organization. Power belongs to the office, not the person. This is as true of presidents who are elected as it is of kings who ascend to the throne by accident of birth.

Second is the concept of sovereignty, which refers to absolute power. The state has ultimate power over the population. The only limits to its power are those it creates and accepts itself. It sets the rules by which others must play.

Third is the idea of territoriality. The state's power extends over a specific area with clear boundaries. It exercises sovereign rule over this territory, whose integrity it protects against encroachment by other states.[9]

Finally, there is the issue of coercion and violence. The state enjoys a monopoly over the means of violence within its territory. That is, the only legitimate or legal use of violence is by those whom the state mandates or authorizes to use it. Control over the means of coercion permits the state to make its rules effective against internal challengers and foreign rivals. This does not mean that the state exercises power primarily through coercion and violence, but that these are available as a last resort in enforcing its laws.

These different dimensions of the state—an organization that is sovereign within a bounded territory through its control of the means of coercion— are captured in the pithy phrase: one government, one land, one law, one gun.

The powers of states can be truly awesome. States can dictate what people wear, what language they speak, and what job they do. Consequently, groups struggle for control of the state and its power to make rules that others will follow. Groups that are successful in gaining control of the state are said to form **the government**. The term "government" refers to the group of leaders in charge of directing the state. States and governments are often treated as equivalent expressions but they need to be distinguished from each other. The state, as we argued, refers to a set of organizations imbued with sovereignty over a given area, while the government refers to the people who run those organizations. The state is the car; the government is the driver.

While states are often powerful, they are not all-powerful. Indeed, some states are not powerful at all. "One law" and "one gun" are aspirations that states often find difficult to achieve. Their rule may be challenged by other institutions that have their own rules they want to enforce and their own resources with which to do so. Foreign governments may threaten their territorial rule, and groups inside their borders—clans, tribes, employers, landlords, and religious leaders—may threaten their sovereignty. Under such circumstances states may find it difficult to govern, to assert their authority, and to implement their decisions. In general, then, the ability of states to govern—to process demands, develop policies, and implement them—cannot be taken for granted. In some countries, states are strong and effective; in others, they are weak and vulnerable.

▶ THE GOOD SOCIETY IN DEPTH

Somalia—The Weightlessness of Statelessness

If you are a libertarian or an anarchist who believes that states are a threat to freedom, then you should consider moving to Somalia where there has been no permanent national government since 1991. The criteria we use to define a state— one government, one land, one law, and one gun—are absent there. Instead of the state enjoying a monopoly of violence, the country is ablaze with competing armies. Instead of the state ruling over a bounded territory, the country's borders are porous, with refugees and foreign troops crossing into its territory. Instead of the state being governed by one set of rules, many laws compete for supremacy. Some parts of Somalia are ruled by Islamic *Sharia* law, while more rural areas subscribe to the *Xeer*, a form of common law indigenous to Somalia. And instead of the state being sovereign, the government's authority does not extend beyond a couple of city blocks in Mogadishu, the nation's capital. Elsewhere whoever has the most guns rules. The Somali state has not simply failed, it has disappeared.

Prior to 1991, Somalia was ruled by a dictator, Major General Mohamed Siad Barre, who took power in a military coup d'etat in 1969. Barre ruled capriciously. His government was guilty of numerous human rights violations, economic policies that led to shortages, and social policies that promoted identification with Greater Somalia as opposed to one's clan. But clans that were marginalized by Barre resisted and deposed the government. Soon the clans fell to fighting among themselves for political power, claiming the state itself as a victim of their struggles.

Without a state, "Somalia," according to *New York Times* reporter Jeffrey Gettleman, has returned to a Hobbesian "state of nature where life is nasty, brutish, and short."[42] The level of daily violence is catastrophic. Death comes frequently and randomly. Social conditions are deplorable. Infant mortality rates are among

Continued

the highest in the world. A quarter of all children do not live beyond five years of age. Economically, the private sector has grown and even prospered. Business now operates in a thoroughly deregulated environment, which has unleashed entrepreneurial energy among Somalis to provide services, such as telecommunications and transport, in place of the government doing so. But the provision of services has been narrow in scope, and dependent on remittances from Somalis living abroad because the lack of government discourages foreign investment. Not only is capital sent by expatriate Somalis the basis of private business ventures, but in some urban areas remittances from abroad account for 40 percent of household income. Without a state to promote development, the economy of Somalia is dependent on the charity of Somalis who have left.

For Further Discussion

1. Which is preferable: bad government, as Somalia experienced under Barre, or no government, as Somalis experience today after Barre?

2. Why hasn't Somalia without a state become the paradise that libertarians anticipate? Why hasn't statelessness enhanced the capabilities of Somalis, increased their life chances?

THE ORIGINS OF THE STATE

"As recently as 1500," Jared Diamond writes, "less than 20 percent of the world's land area was marked off by boundaries into states run by bureaucrats and governed by laws."[10] Today, in contrast, the entire world is organized into states. Choose any speck of land on a map, with the exception of Antarctica, and some state claims control over it. There are different views as to why and how states emerged. Modernization theorists argue that states arose as a result of the increasing division of labor in society. As societies became more complex, they became more functionally specialized, requiring states to oversee the integration of their diverse parts. Modernization theorists see a parallel between the way states develop and how species evolve: as societies become more mature and differentiated, they require states to coordinate their more specialized parts. States emerge to solve coordination problems posed by society's increasing complexity.[11]

Modernization theory is helpful in drawing our attention to the coordination role that states play. But modernization theory perceives states as benign and stabilizing society, knitting its disparate parts together, when, in fact, states can be malign and highly destabilizing. States can be corrupt and prey on society and they can upset social routines instead of harmonizing them. In addition, modernization theory perceives the emergence of states occurring in a peaceful, rational fashion when, in fact, the process of state building was filled with bloody turmoil. It was a process in which fragmented, local patterns of authority resisted state builders who wanted to centralize authority and promote coordination at their expense.[12]

Marxists take a different approach. Whereas modernization theorists saw states emerge as part of the requirements of society as a whole, Marxists perceive states emerging as a result of one of the interests within it. [13] According to Marxists, the dominant class uses the state and its monopoly over the means of violence in society to impose its rule over subordinate classes. In *The Communist Manifesto*, Marx and Engels describe the modern state as "the executive committee of the bourgeoisie," by which they meant that the state reflects the general interests of the ruling, capitalist class. The state is not some neutral mechanism coordinating a complex society, as it is for modernization theorists. For Marxists the state is much darker, representing the repressive apparatus that the dominant class wields against other classes to cement its rule and exploit them.

The Marxist theory of the state has the advantage of drawing us closer to the defining aspect of states based on violence and coercion than modernization theory. But the Marxist theory of the state too narrowly confines state-building to the requirements of class conflict. It ignores other actors with other motives from the story.

Finally, according to realists, "Wars made the state, and the state made war."[14] States defined by violence were forged in violence. According to these theorists, state building proceeded under pressure from external and internal rivals. Externally, states competed with each other to further their interests. No international law or organization regulated their behavior or sanctioned them. Consequently, states posed threats to each other. In order to protect themselves in such a lawless, threatening environment, states need to create armies. But provisioning and maintaining an army was expensive, placing a heavy burden of requisitions, taxes, and conscription on the populace. It also required the state to develop new bureaucracies and administrative innovations in order to increase the efficiency of its tax collection and armed forces, which often led citizens to oppose what they considered extortion by the state to subsidize its expenses. Popular resistance occurred in the form of tax rebellions, conscription movements, and food riots. This defiance further promoted the development of state capacities, as states had to contend with internal rivals as well as challengers lurking beyond their borders.

States, in this view, developed in response to the extractive necessities of war, whose possibility is always lurking in an unruly, unstructured international system of competing states. "Without war," the German historian and politician Heinrich von Treitschke wrote in the 1890s, "there would be no state."[15] "Sovereignty," Mustafa Kemal, the founder of modern Turkey told his followers, "is acquired by force, power, and by violence."[16] States emerged dripping with the blood of their local subjects as they developed new coercive and administrative means to extract revenue from them to prepare for war. Expansion of the armed forces, increases in taxation, and popular rebellion all go together in this narrative of state building.[17]

This perspective hews closely to the genetic origin of states in coercion and violence. It also includes some elements of both modernization and

Marxian arguments. It incorporates the coordinating role that modernization theorists discuss by alluding to the state's attempt to bring order to society so it can increase its tax take from it.[18] It also includes the notion of interests that Marxists present but offers a different interpretation of them. According to this perspective, states pursue their own interests in a threatening international environment, as opposed to the interests of the ruling class. While including key elements of alternative explanations, the idea that states developed from the requirements of war has the added advantage of drawing attention to the role that the international system played in state building. The other explanations perceive states as emerging wholly to solve domestic problems of order or domination. In contrast, this perspective explains the emergence of states by looking at relations between states as well as those within them.

POLITICAL INSTITUTIONS

Groups not only struggle for control of the state, giving them the power to set its policies, but they also struggle over what the state should look like. One need only recall the fierce debates in the United States between delegates from small and large states, and from slave and free states at the 1787 Constitutional Convention, as they debated how to construct the new American state. Small states, such as Delaware and Rhode Island, demanded the creation of a Senate in which each state would receive two votes as protection against the power that large states, such as New York and Massachusetts, wielded in the House of Representatives by virtue of their larger populations. Or consider the more recent conflict in Europe between small and large states, and between those wanting to integrate faster and those wanting to go slower as they each tried to shape the form of the European Union. New permutations, new ways of organizing the state, result from these struggles.

The distribution of power among the different levels and branches of the state is contested because groups have a stake in the outcome. A group may win or lose depending on which part of the state is making the decision. Whether policy is made by the executive, legislative, or judicial branch, or at the national or local level, influences the result. For example, Antonia Maioni attributes the failure of doctors to prevent the passage of national health insurance in Canada and their success in blocking similar legislation in the United States to different policy-making processes in the two countries. American doctors could exert influence upon an independent and powerful Congress to block national health insurance in the United States, while the subordination of the legislature to the executive in Canada precluded doctors in that country from following a similar strategy.[19]

Groups with interests at stake seek to empower those parts of the state in which they have the most advantage. Levels and branches of the state rise and fall in power along with the groups whose interests they represent. In the

United States, for example, the increasing power of the presidency in relation to Congress is often attributed to the rise of large corporations that shared the same national and international perspective of the president, while the influence of small business that shared Congress' more local and parochial perspective declined. The fact that different group interests are tied to different parts of the state accounts for conflict between them. Groups take an active interest in "turf" wars or jurisdictional conflicts within the state when it better positions them to advance their interests.

The way in which power is distributed within a state is presented in its constitution. **Constitutions** are blueprints that display the state's architecture. They are "power maps" describing the internal distribution of power within the state and between the state and its citizens. Constitutions depict how power is dispersed within the state and its limits; where the power of the state stops and the rights of citizens begin. But the map may be inaccurate. The actual distribution of power often diverges from what is given in the constitution. Power depends on political factors as well as legal, formal, constitutional arrangements. For example, presidents elected by a landslide or with a legislative majority from their party will find it easier to govern than presidents who were narrowly elected or who must contend with an opposing majority in the legislature. In France, for example, the power of presidents has depended far more on whether the prime minister is also from their party than on what is legally stipulated regarding presidential powers in the Constitution. Power is fluid, dependent on circumstances, not static, as constitutions make it appear.

The power map of constitutions sometimes is not only inaccurate but also incomplete. The constitution only maps what is included within the formal state. Absent are other organizations outside the state that influence political actors, such as political parties, the media, and interest groups. While constitutions provide helpful maps to the distribution of power among the different levels and branches of government, they may be missing interesting highlights and important destinations. Below we review the different parts or components of the state that are featured in many constitutional maps. These include its legislative, executive and judicial branches, subnational levels, and the state's bureaucratic and military arms.

Federal and Unitary Systems

Constitutions may divide power vertically between national and local levels, and horizontally between the legislative, executive, and judicial branches. For example, some constitutions create **unitary systems** in which power is concentrated at the national level. Local levels of the state have little autonomous power to raise revenue, spend money, or make their own policies. They operate more as administrative arms of the central government than as independent authorities. In unitary systems, all sovereignty resides at the top, in the national government. Subnational units are created at the discretion of national governments and can be reorganized or abolished by them because they lack constitutional protection. China, France, and Japan are often cited as examples of unitary systems where regional and local governments lack significant policy-making powers and act largely as agents of the national government.

In **federal systems,** on the other hand, constitutions divide sovereignty between national and subnational levels of the state. "The essence of federalism," Brian Galligan writes, "is two spheres of government neither of which is sovereign but each of which has defined and limited powers."[20] Federal systems have a long tradition among developed countries, such as the United States and Switzerland, and are evident in developing countries, such as India and Brazil, as well. Authority in these countries is not concentrated at the national level but divided between national and lower, more local units of the state, with each level sometimes responsible for policy in a certain domain. For example, state governments in the United States play a leading role in education policy, the *Länder* in Germany play a prominent role in education and cultural policy, while the provinces in Canada have jurisdiction over the management and sale of public lands. In some countries, the specific tasks that the national and subnational levels of the state perform are neatly separated from each other as in a layer cake. In others, it more resembles a marble cake in which functions are interwoven and shared among the different levels.[21] Lower levels of the state in federal systems also have more fiscal independence than their counterparts in unitary systems. Local and regional governments can raise their own revenue, giving them more resources with which to strike out on their own, independent of the central government. Finally, in federal systems, subnational political units also enjoy control over their own administrative agencies. A separate administrative apparatus controlled by local and regional governments exists to implement their policies.

Unitary state forms are more common than federal systems. In most countries the national government does not share power with other levels. Where federal systems do exist, they are found predominantly among large countries, such as the United States and India, where the central government is challenged to extend its power over a large population spread across a large land mass.[22] They may also be found in smaller states with intense ethnic, religious, and linguistic cleavages that are territorially based. Federal systems offer such groups a stake in the larger, national government by giving them influence in a smaller, regional government, incorporating them into the wider polity by giving them a political space they can call their own. This, for example, is the case in Switzerland, where powerful regional governments called *cantons* reflect divisions among French, German, and Italian speakers, as well as between Protestants and Catholics. It has also been the case in Canada, where powers guaranteed to the provinces have mollified to some extent the worries of French speakers in Quebec who are concerned about losing their cultural identity in a predominantly English-speaking country.

▶ IN BRIEF

Federal and Unitary Systems

In federal political systems:

- The central state shares sovereignty with lower political units.
- Regional governments can raise their own revenue and make their own policy.
- Lower state units have their own officials, agencies, and administrative integrity.

In unitary political systems:

- Political power is concentrated at the national level.
- Subnational levels of the state are primarily administrative arms of the central government.
- Lower levels of the state do not have the power to levy taxes or make policy.

The Legislature

Political power is distributed not only vertically between national and subnational levels but also horizontally among the different branches of the state: the legislature, executive, and judiciary. **Legislatures** appear under different names in different countries. In the United States, the legislature is referred to as Congress; in Britain as Parliament; and in France as the National Assembly. Regardless of their different title, they all do the same thing: they are assemblies that approve of policies on behalf of a larger political community that they represent.[23] This holds true in authoritarian states as well as in democratic polities. In authoritarian political systems, legislatures are tolerated because they provide the government with the fig leaf of public consent. They infrequently and only marginally influence policy. Their main function is simply to transmit local concerns to those actually in charge. For example, in China, the National People's Congress only passes those bills proposed by the government and not a single bill from an individual deputy has ever been enacted. Delegates to the National People's Congress lack the time and staff to evaluate bills and are under pressure to conform rather than challenge the ruling Communist Party.

In contrast to authoritarian political systems, legislatures in democracies are more than rubber stamps. They actually influence policy either by amending or rejecting executive proposals, or by substituting their own measures for them. In addition, legislatures in democracies play an important role in overseeing the executive branch. They scrutinize the activities of the executive to make sure that laws are implemented fairly and effectively.

Most legislatures are **unicameral,** meaning that they have only one chamber. The **bicameral** structure of the United States Congress, with a House of Representatives and a Senate, is atypical. Where bicameralism occurs, each chamber is based on a different principle of representation. For example, in the United States the House of Representatives is based on population while the Senate represents states. Larger countries tend towards bicameralism because the different principles of representation in each chamber can better reflect the diversity of interests within them. Bicameralism is also more common in countries with federal systems, where lower, regional political structures are represented by one of the chambers. This is true not only in the United States and Australia, where states are represented in the Senate, but also in Germany where the *Länder* are represented in the upper house, or *Bundesrat*. This gives territorially based interests confidence that their interests will be reflected within the national government. The advantage of a unicameral legislature is that it is more efficient. There is no second chamber to delay, veto, or amend bills that the first chamber has already passed. The advantage of bicameralism is that it can offer a broader basis of representation than one chamber. This is especially valuable in large, diverse, and regionally divided countries.

Another comparative dimension to legislatures concerns their internal organization, especially their committee system. Even more than size— legislatures with fewer members tending to be more powerful than larger assemblies—a strong committee system is a good indicator of a legislature's power to influence policy, demonstrating whether it is a show horse or a workhorse. Legislative committees armed with clear jurisdictions and adequate resources permit their members to specialize. Legislators can develop expertise on narrow issues, which permits them to negotiate with the executive on an equal basis and knowledgably oversee its actions. Again, the United States Congress is unusual in this regard because its committee system is exceptionally strong. Compared with other legislatures, congressional committees have ample staff and budgets to collect information and draft legislation on their own. The strength of its committee system is a tip-off that the United States Congress is one of the most powerful legislatures in the world.

In practice, most legislatures today, at least in democracies, are reactive, not proactive; they reject and modify bills but do not often propose their own. They respond to the agenda proposed by the chief executive, rather than setting their own priorities. Their subordination to the executive branch is attributed to the increasing significance of foreign policy, growth in the scope of government activity and the size of the bureaucracy to carry it out, the rising power of the media to portray politics in terms of personality, and the emergence of organized political parties that can deliver disciplined majorities for the government. But it would be facile to regard legislatures as mere window dressing in democracies, despite their loss of power to the executive branch. At a minimum, legislatures in democracies retain "the capacity to influence, as opposed to determine; the ability to advise, rather than command; the facility to criticize but not to obstruct; [and] the competence to scrutinize rather than initiate."[24] At a maximum, they have the power to veto legislation, make policy by considering their own proposals instead of those submitted to it by the executive, and even bring down the government itself.

While legislatures have lost ground overall, they tend to be more powerful when they have a strong committee system, permitting legislators to build up expertise, and when parties are weak, depriving governments of disciplined legislative majorities to vote for their proposals. Finally, legislatures display more influence in some issue areas than in others. They generally exert little influence over foreign affairs or economic policy. These arenas tend to be dominated by the executive branch whose perspective tends to be more national than the parochial view legislators take, reflecting the local constituencies from which they come. While seemingly content to play background vocals on foreign and economic policy, legislatures are more apt to project their voice when it comes to social welfare policy, such as housing, health care, education, and pensions, which directly touch their constituents.[25]

The Executive

The **executive branch** is supposed to elaborate, coordinate, and implement the legislature's decisions. In fact, it does much more. The executive branch is often the energy center of the government, providing it with leadership. It sets the agenda of government, creating priorities and proposing bills. In most democracies, not only do a greater proportion of all bills that legislatures consider come from the executive, but those that originate there have a better chance of being approved.[26] We discuss below three distinct parts of the executive branch: (1) the **core executive**, which includes the ruling government; (2) the bureaucracy, which is directly below the core executive and includes the different departments and agencies of the executive branch; and (3) the military, which includes the armed forces.

At the center of the executive branch is the core executive. The core executive includes all the significant policy-making and coordinating actors in the executive branch, such as the president or prime minister, members of their cabinet, their personal advisors, and senior civil servants. The core executive pulls together and coordinates the diverse political and bureaucratic interests in a sprawling executive branch into a coherent and coordinated program to present to the legislature and the public. The core executive is at the apex of the executive branch, resolving disputes within it and setting priorities for it. It sets the wheels of the state in motion as the core executive tries to shape society according to its own designs.

At the top of the core executive are its political leaders, the **head of state** and the **head of the government**. The former represents the country, while the latter directs the executive branch. Sometimes these two positions are unified in the same office and person, as they are in the United States where the president is both the head of state—the leader of the nation—and the head of the government—in charge of the federal bureaucracy. In many other countries, such as Great Britain, the two positions are separated. In Britain, the reigning monarch is the head of state, and the ruling prime minister is the head of the government. In such countries, the head of state usually plays only a ceremonial role, as the monarchy does in Britain. But there are countries, such as France, where power is shared between the head of state (the president) and the head of the government (the prime minister), and some rare cases, such as

Jordan, where power resides in the head of state, who is the king, and not the head of the government, who is the prime minister.

As the executive branch has grown in size to keep pace with increasing state responsibilities, the central coordinating role that political leaders play has become more significant. Among developed countries, according to one study, "There is general agreement that over the last thirty to forty years there has been a steady movement toward the reinforcement of the political core executive . . . and, that within the core executive, there has been an increasing centralization of power around the person of the chief executive—President, Prime Minister, or both."[27] Their position at the top of government gives presidents and prime ministers a commanding view of the entire ground that other political actors lack. In addition, political leaders can shape and manipulate public opinion through the media attention they attract. Presidents and prime ministers also now have more staff at their disposal to coordinate policy, provide expertise, manage their image, and help them develop political strategy. When Herbert Hoover was president of the United States (1928–1932), he was assisted by three confidential secretaries, a stenographer, and some clerks. Today, the Executive Office of the President—which didn't even exist as a formal office in Hoover's time—includes over 3,000 people who serve the president in all sorts of capacities. Finally, political leaders embody the national interest, which permits them to take charge of foreign policy. This policy domain is now of more concern because globalization has tied the fate of countries more closely together. As the world gets smaller, presidents and prime ministers get bigger. The result of these changes has been to personalize power and raise the profile of political leaders in relation to other political actors inside and outside the core executive.

The core executive includes not only political leaders such as the head of state and the head of the government, but also those ministers who serve under them. These ministers direct state ministries or departments and are often members of the president's or prime minister's **cabinet**. Jean Blondel estimated there are about 3,000 ministers throughout the world, with an average of 20 in each country.[28] In some countries, ministers serve on average for as long as five years, while in others there is quick turnover and a minister's average tenure is as short as a year. Some are specialists who are familiar with the problems and issues of the department they lead, while others are amateurs who come to office with little specialized knowledge of the issues for which their department is responsible. Finally, some ministers may rotate among different posts within the government, while others fill only one post in the course of their ministerial career.

Presidents and prime ministers are not simply first among equals in relation to their cabinet; they are first without equal. That is, presidents and prime ministers set the direction of the government, not the collective Cabinet. The cabinet is more a collection of isolated ministers concerned with their particular departments than a group of political executives concerned with strategic planning for the government as a whole.[29] While ministers might not enjoy much standing through their participation in the cabinet, they often do so through the substantial discretion they enjoy when it comes to managing their departments. Ministers often manage their departments without much direction by presidents and prime ministers. Presidents and prime ministers cannot look everywhere at once and must practice "management by exception," given the pressures on their time and attention.

The Bureaucracy

The core executive directs the **bureaucracy**, or the different agencies and bureaus within the executive branch. The bureaucracy is supposed to be an extension of the government in power and its political leadership. The core executive makes policy while the bureaucrats or career civil servants below execute it in an impartial and professional way. But, in fact, core executives often have a hard time imposing their will on bureaucrats. Political control of the bureaucracy is an aspiration, not a guarantee. The core executive has no choice but to delegate power to those below them to carry out policies. But delegating power to lower-level officials permits them to shape policy in how it is administered. Policies get altered subtly, as if in a game of telephone with multiple players, as it gets passed down the chain of command.[30] President Harry Truman remarked ruefully as he was about to be replaced in office by former General Dwight D. Eisenhower, "He'll sit here and he'll say, 'Do this! Do that! *And nothing will happen.* Poor Ike—it won't be a bit like the Army. He'll find it very frustrating."[31] Policies can be thwarted by bureaucrats who have their own interests separate from political executives and their own sources of power with which to pursue them.[32] For example, bureaucrats can use their experience and knowledge to frustrate the will of political executives. They can share information with them or withhold it. They can also leak information that threatens their interests to the government's opponents. A notorious example of this occurred when FBI Assistant Director Mark Felt, known for decades only as "Deep Throat," leaked information about White House efforts to cover up the Watergate break-in because he believed President Nixon was trying to besmirch the reputation of his agency. Moreover, while bureaucrats are supposed to be neutral and impartial, they have their own interests they want to protect. They want to maximize their agency's budget and jurisdiction, which means higher pay and more career opportunities for them, and defend their professionalism from policies that threaten it.

Political leaders try to counter the bureaucracy's influence by strengthening their own personal staffs. Consequently, as we saw when we discussed the core executive, the number of people who work in the president's or prime minister's office has grown. They also try to increase the number of political appointees who work within the bureaucracy. The greater the number of political appointees, the more responsive the bureaucracy is to the administration in power. At one extreme are many African states where the bureaucracy is bloated with political appointees. Instead of being staffed by a permanent civil service selected on the basis of merit, rulers give state jobs to loyalists who then use their official posts to extract bribes and exploit the public they are supposed to serve. For example, in the Democratic Republic of the Congo (DRC), formerly called Zaire, the political faction allied with President Sese Seko Mobutu (1965–1997) controlled "lucrative positions in the state, diplomatic corps, party, army and secret police" from which they plundered their country.[33]

At the other end of the continuum are countries like Great Britain. Its bureaucracy is staffed by a highly professional civil service that reaches up to the highest levels. A change in administration does not create turnover in a department's staff, except at the very top for the ministers who run them and their assistants. Unlike Zaire's Mobutu, the British prime minister does not have the opportunity to salt the bureaucracy with supporters and thus ensure its cooperation. The United States lies somewhere in between these two polar cases, combining elements of both patronage and civil service systems in its staffing practices. The lower levels of the federal government are filled by protected civil servants selected on the basis of merit, while the upper tiers are filled through political appointment. While civil service regulations prevent the bulk of federal jobs from being given to political supporters, as in Zaire, positions at the higher rungs are filled by the president and are not occupied by civil servants, as in Britain.

IN BRIEF

Bureaucracy

According to Max Weber, an eminent German sociologist, the essential features of bureaucracies include:

- a division of labor in which people are given specific tasks to perform,
- a hierarchy in which there is a clear chain of command, and
- a set of rules and regulations that govern the conduct of people in positions and limit their discretion.

The Military

Seven Days in May, published in 1962, describes a military plot to take over the U.S. government. In the book, the Joint Chiefs of Staff are thwarted in their conspiracy to remove the president of the United States. *Seven Days in May* is fiction, a novel that became a Hollywood motion picture. It is a gripping political thriller because its plot is so plausible. But it is also far-fetched because civilian control of the military is such an intrinsic part of the American political tradition. It requires a novelist's imagination to conceive of a military coup occurring in the United States. But what novelists must invent with regard to the United States is all too real elsewhere. Military takeovers are common in other countries. They are fact, not fiction.

The military is just one specialized department within the bureaucracy. We devote special attention to it because the military embodies the essence of the state. It is organizationally coherent, enjoying a centralized command structure; it has a corporate sense of purpose, binding it together; and it controls the armed forces, making it possible to impose its will on others. Consequently, the military needs to be treated differently than other parts of the state. For example, the core executive does not have as much to fear being removed by angry clerks as it does by aggrieved colonels.

The relationship between the government and the military takes many forms. At one end of the spectrum is civilian control of the military's budget, command structure, and the promotion and assignment of its commanders. Civilian control also implies that the military does not intervene in political affairs. Politics is for civilians, not for soldiers. But even civilian control of the military has its limits. In return for the military respecting the authority of the government, the government respects the autonomy and professionalism of the military and defers to its expertise within its appointed sphere. Of course, the boundary separating political from military issues is unclear and civilians and the military often trespass on each other's domain. The military often injects itself into policy debates about national security and budget appropriations, while civilians often project their values on to the military and seek to use it for political advantage. Thus, even in countries where civilian control of the military is the norm, that control is not absolute but has to be negotiated. Samuel P. Huntington writes, "Objective civilian control [involves] the recognition and acceptance [by civilian leaders] of an area of professional competence and the autonomy of the military [and] the minimization of . . . political intervention in the military."[34] Civilians are careful to respect the professional norms of the military in order to receive respect from it in return.

Civilian control of the military is more likely to exist in those countries where both state and military institutions are strong. That is, the state has legitimacy and is capable of governing society, while the military has a strong ethos of professionalism and autonomy.[35] This is the case in much of the developed world. But in many developing countries, states are weak and unable to maintain order. Nor is the military highly professionalized. The army abuses its power to rob civilians, and officers give loyalty to their own ethnic group instead of to the government. When professionalism is low, military intervention in politics is more common.[36] In these circumstances, the armed forces will exercise veto power over government decisions, without taking power itself. The military, in effect, holds a sword over government to ensure that its policies remain within acceptable bounds. For example, fear of the military prevents elected Muslim governments in Turkey from diverging too far from the army's secular preferences. In such cases, the military is reluctant to take power itself and often finds it unnecessary since its goal is simply to prevent change. It can afford to let civilians rule since the military's objective to preserve the status quo is so minimal.[37]

But sometimes the military has more ambitious goals than simply maintaining the status quo. It wants faster economic growth that could provide the wealth and technology that the army needs to improve its fighting capacity. The military believes it must remove civilian governments that are too inept, corrupt, or unwilling to achieve these goals. Civil–military relations then shift from the military having veto power over the government to the military actually taking it over. Not only is the civilian government replaced by military officers in these circumstances, but political rights are typically rescinded. Authoritarian rule quickly ensues in which political parties are banned, the news is censored, and protests are outlawed. The military tries to create the same sense of discipline in society that exists in the army as it pursues its program of economic modernization.

The Judiciary

The third branch of the state is the **judiciary**. It is a political institution that is, theoretically, above politics and outside of the policy-making process. The courts are supposed to be neutral and impartial, above the tug of sordid interests that sully legislators and executives. Their role is to interpret the laws, not make them. But interpreting the law—settling disputes about its meaning and how it should be applied—requires courts to exercise power, to issue decisions that produce winners and losers. As Charles Evan Hughes, former Chief Justice of the U.S. Supreme Court, once remarked, "We are under a Constitution and the Constitution is what judges say it is."[38] And because courts do exercise power, they are the object of intense conflict. Court jurisdictions, the manner in which judges are selected, and the content of judicial decisions are all political questions of the first order.

In authoritarian political systems, the powers of the judiciary are quite limited. While laws and constitutions may exist, the judiciary is often too weak to uphold them. Dictators and tyrants do not want to be constrained by tedious and bothersome laws. The rule of law in authoritarian states is compromised because the judiciary lacks independence and is subordinate to the executive. Judges often owe their jobs to the ruler and can be removed easily if they decide a case "incorrectly." While the rule of law may be weak under authoritarian regimes, they still subscribe to rule by the law. That is authoritarian governments find it convenient to rule through the law. Consequently, they make great efforts to stage show trials of dissidents, to ground their authority in emergency decrees that suspend the law temporarily, or make use of alternative forums outside the regular court system, such as military tribunals, to try cases and issue decisions. Authoritarian regimes are not lawless. They have court systems and judges. But the courts are distinguished by their independence in democracies and their lack of it in authoritarian regimes.

By contrast, the judiciary enjoys more autonomy and political power in democracies. In some cases, the courts may even exercise the power of **judicial review**, which empowers courts to nullify and invalidate laws that they believe violate the constitution. Judicial review can be conducted through special constitutional courts set up for that purpose, as in France and Germany, or within the regular court system, as in Ireland and the United States. But regardless of where judicial review takes place, its practice is controversial. It has the same impact on policy as an executive veto and belies the claim that courts do not influence policy. For example, the U. S. Supreme Court in the 1954 case *Brown v. Topeka Board of Education,* famously ruled that state laws requiring segregated schools were invalid because they violated the Fourteenth Amendment's "equal protection clause" of the Constitution.

Critics of judicial review believe that it is undemocratic for unelected judges to overturn laws passed by elected governments and thereby subvert the will of the people. Defenders respond that judicial review is necessary to prevent the majority from using the state to trample on the rights of the minority. They insist that constitutional limits need to be placed upon what the majority can do.

Judicial review permits judges to influence policy by nullifying laws. But judges typically will not exercise this power unless their positions are secure. The independence of the judiciary depends on how its members are selected, how long they have tenure, and how difficult it is to remove them once they are on the bench. The U.S., for example, safeguards the independence of federal judges by awarding them lifetime tenure. With their jobs secure, federal judges do not have to worry about shaping their decisions to suit either the president who nominated them or subsequent officeholders. And once seated, they can only be removed from office by being impeached by Congress, which is such a difficult process that it rarely occurs. Other countries seek to insulate the judiciary from political influences at the appointment stage. In Italy and Portugal, for example, the appointment and promotion of judges is taken out of the hands of voters, legislatures, and chief executives alike and given predominantly to judges themselves. Judges are insulated from political pressure by having control over their own career paths. An alternative strategy for ensuring the judiciary's independence is to appoint judges to nonrenewable terms, as is the practice in France. And in still other countries, such as Canada and South Africa, appointments follow recommendations by special judicial selection commissions.

Political scientists have noticed a trend toward the "**judicialization of politics**" in which political disputes are settled in courtrooms rather than legislatures. According to John Ferejohn, "Since World War II, there has been a profound shift in power away from legislatures and toward courts and other legal institutions."[39] Citizens are making increasing use of courts to "contest government decisions or to assert and defend their rights."[40] Alexis de Tocqueville's complaint that Americans frequently turn political issues into legal contests is becoming a common practice throughout the world.

The judicialization of politics is also evident in the eagerness with which courts intervene in political thickets that they previously avoided, such as struggles for power. In the 1990s, Italian judges brought down the Christian Democratic Party, which had been in the government from 1947 to 1994, on charges of corruption, and the United States Supreme Court issued rulings that decided the outcome of the 2000 presidential election. But the most stunning example of all might have been the role the judiciary played in the 2004 presidential election in the Ukraine. The Ukrainian Supreme Court nullified the results of that election and mandated new elections that produced a different winner. Remarkably, despite having so much at stake, Ukrainian politicians respected the power of the court to rule that electoral laws had been violated in a country not otherwise known to be so law abiding. The Ukrainian example shows how powerful courts have become, even in countries where one would least expect it. Finally, judges are not only intervening more frequently in struggles for political power, but they are also more aggressively using the power of judicial review to look over the shoulders of politicians and evaluate their decisions. The prospect that the courts might intervene forces public officials to anticipate the court's possible objections when they make laws and decisions. Policy makers increasingly legislate in the shadow of the courts.[41]

COMPARATIVE POLITICAL ANALYSIS

Does the Design of Political Institutions Make a Difference in People's Lives?

Problem

Do people live better under one set of political institutions than another? According to the political scientist Arend Lijphart, political institutions in democracies go together in consistent patterns that conform to either majoritarian or consensus principles. Majoritarian democracies have unitary systems in which authority is concentrated in the national government; unicameral legislatures in which authority is based in a single house or chamber; weak courts that lack the power of judicial review; and strong core executives that dominate the legislature. Consensus democracies, on the other hand, operate on the principle that policies should be supported by broader agreement than a majority, which often involves sharing, dispersing, and limiting power in a variety of ways. Political institutions commonly found together in consensus democracies include: federal systems, bicameral legislatures, courts with the power of judicial review, and weak core executives. Having distinguished between majoritarian and consensus democracies, Lijphart then asks the "so what" question: what difference do these ways of organizing democracy make for people's lives? Do people live better under democracies with majoritarian institutions than they do in democracies with institutions that follow the principle of consensus?

Methods and Hypothesis

Lijphart ranked selected democracies according to the degree that their political institutions conformed to his models of majoritarian and consensus democracies and then statistically compared their economic, political, and social performance. He hypothesized that consensus democracies would produce better results because their policies have broader support and are not as prone to abrupt policy shifts as typically occur in majoritarian democracies.

Operationalizing Concepts

To test his hypothesis Lijphart had to clarify what he meant by economic, political, and social performance and develop indicators for each.

1. Some of his proxies to test the relative economic performance of majoritarian and consensus democracies included: average annual growth in GDP, average annual rates of inflation, and unemployment levels.
2. His measures of political performance were turnout rates in elections, the number of women holding national political offices, and survey data concerning how satisfied citizens were with the workings of democracy in their country.
3. Lijphart's measures of social performance were welfare state expenditures, foreign aid contributions, pollution levels, and prison incarceration rates.

Results

Lijphart found that consensus democracies performed better socially, devoting more money to the welfare state, spending more on foreign aid, recording less pollution, and imprisoning fewer citizens. They also performed better politically, with more citizens participating in elections, more women elected to office, and more citizens expressing satisfaction with their political system. However, the form of democracy had little apparent impact on economic performance. Consensus democracies did not have more economic growth or lower unemployment than majoritarian democracies, although the former did have a significantly better record in regard to checking inflation.

For Further Discussion

1. Do you think Lijphart's indicators of economic, political, and social performance were appropriate? What other tests of performance do you think would have been more suitable?
2. Why did consensus democracies perform better than their majoritarian counterparts on political and social indicators but not on economic ones?

Sources: Arend Lijphart, *Patterns of Democracy: Government Forms and Performance in Thirty-Six Countries* (New Haven: Yale University Press, 1999).

CONCLUSION

The state is the supreme sovereign authority within a country. The government, which controls the political institutions of the state, sets priorities and marshalls society's resources in support of them.

The modern state emerged in response to the insecurity of the international system. It required states to build up their administrative capacities to prepare for the ever present danger of war. States come in a variety of shapes and forms as laid out in their constitutions. Some are unitary, with authority centralized at the national level, while others have a federal structure in which subnational levels of the state are able to raise their own revenue and make their own policies.

States also differ in how they arrange their essential building blocks, the legislative, executive, and judicial branches. In some states the legislative branch is strong, with strong committee systems that permit members to build up expertise and propose their own bills, while in others the legislature is weak and only rubber stamps what the core executive submits to it. In some states, the core executive is able to command the bureaucracy, including the military. In others, the bureaucracy and military are able to thwart the will of the core executive. Finally, in some states, the judiciary is independent and has the authority to overturn laws approved by the legislative and executive branches. In others, the judiciary is subordinate to the executive, although even here the government makes an effort to subscribe to rule by law, if not the rule of law.

The form states take—the manner in which power is divided within them—is not neutral or innocent in its effects. Some groups win and others lose depending on these arrangements. As a result, the balance of power among the state's different levels and branches is constantly being challenged. The distribution of state power is not frozen in law but changes subtly—and sometimes not so subtly—in response to political pressure. Political actors try to shape how power is distributed because their success in influencing policy depends upon the state's structure.

myposcikit EXERCISES

Apply what you learned in this chapter on MyPoliSciKit (www.mypoliscikit.com).

ASSESSMENT
Review this chapter using learning objectives, chapter summaries, practice tests, and more.

VIDEO CASE STUDIES
Analyze recent world affairs by watching streaming video from major news providers.

FLASHCARDS
Learn the key terms in this chapter; you can test yourself by term or definition.

COMPARATIVE EXERCISES
Compare political ideas, behaviors, institutions, and policies worldwide.

CRITICAL THINKING QUESTIONS

1. We argued at the beginning of the chapter that power takes three forms: economic, political and ideological. Are these three forms of power equal? What claims for preeminence can be made about each of them?
2. Do states promote individuals' capabilities or restrict them?
3. If your country was just emerging and was writing a constitution, how would you organize your political institutions? What judicial, legislative, federal, and executive arrangements would you create and why?
4. Over time, the legislative branch has lost ground to the executive in almost all countries. Why has this happened and is this state of affairs constructive or harmful?

5. Since the military has all the guns, why don't they take over governments more frequently? Why does the military accept civilian control in some countries while it is reluctant to consent to it in others?

KEY TERMS

Institutions 30
Power 31
Authority 31
The state 32
The government 32
Modernization
  theory 34
Marxism 35

Constitutions 37
Unitary systems 37
Federal systems 38
Legislature 39
Unicameral 39
Bicameral 39
Executive branch 41
Core executive 41

Head of State 41
Head of Government 41
Cabinet 42
Bureaucracy 43
Judiciary 46
Judicial Review 46
Judicialization of
  Politics 47

SUGGESTED READINGS

Ludger Helms, *Presidents, Prime Ministers and Chancellors: Executive Leadership in Western Democracies* (New York: Palgrave, 2005). A good, comprehensive review of different political executive offices and styles.

Arend Lijphart, *Patterns of Democracy: Government Forms and Performance in Thirty-Six Countries* (New Haven: Yale University Press, 1999). How certain executive, legislative, and judicial institutions have an affinity for each other in democracies.

Steven Lukes, *Power: A Radical View* (New York: Palgrave, 2005). Argues that there are three different faces, or levels, of power: the first is associated with government decision-making, the second with agenda control and determining what issues are defined as political, and the third is ideological, which is concerned with socialization to certain values and beliefs.

Gianfranco Poggi, *The State: Its Nature, Development, and Prospects* (Stanford, CA.: Stanford University Press, 1990). A short and rich analysis of the origins and future of the state.

James C. Scott, *Seeing Like a State: How Certain Schemes to Improve the Human Condition Have Failed* (New Haven: Yale University Press, 1998). How and why states seek to manage society.

NOTES

1. James C. Scott, *Seeing Like a State: How Certain Schemes to Improve the Human Condition Have Failed* (New Haven: Yale University Press, 1988).
2. Scott, *Seeing Like a State*, p. 20.
3. This material on scientific forestry is drawn from Scott, *Seeing Like a State*.
4. John Tierney, "A Baghdad Traffic Circle is a Microcosm for Chaos," *The New York Times*, September 12, 2003, p. 1.
5. Scott, *Seeing Like a State*, p. 7.
6. Robert A. Dahl, "The Concept of Power," *Behavioral Scientist* (July 1957), pp. 201–215.
7. Gianfranco Poggi, *The State: Its Nature, Development, and Prospects* (Stanford, CA.: Stanford University Press, 1990), pp. 3–19.

8. Poggi, *The State*, p. 9.

9. Poggi, *The State*, p. 22.

10. Jared Diamond, *Guns, Germs and Steel: The Fate of Human Societies* (New York: W.W. Norton, 1999), p. 266.

11. Poggi, *The State*, pp. 86–93.

12. Sheri Berman, "From the Sun King to Karzoi," *Foreign Affairs* (March–April, 2010), Vol. 89, No. 2, pp. 2–9.

13. Poggi, *The State*, p. 94.

14. Charles Tilly, "The History of European State-Making," in *The Formation of National States in Western Europe*, ed. CharlesTilly (Princeton, NJ: Princeton University Press, 1975), p. 42.

15. Von Treitschke is quoted in James J. Sheehan, *Where Have all the Soldiers Gone?: The Transformation of Modern Europe* (New York: Houghton Mifflin, 2008), p. 3.

16. Kemal is quoted in Sheehan, *Where Have All the Soldiers Gone?*, p. 96.

17. Tilly, "The History of European State-Making," p. 135.

18. Scott, *Seeing Like a State*.

19. Antonia Maioni, *Parting at the Crossroads: The Emergence of Health Insurance in the United States and Canada* (Princeton, NJ: Princeton University Press, 1998).

20. Brian Galligan, "Comparative Federalism," in *The Oxford Handbook of Political Institutions*, ed. R. A. W. Rhodes, Sarah A. Binder and Bert A. Rockman (New York: Oxford University Press, 2006), p. 268.

21. Morton Grodzins, *The American System: A New View of Government in the United States* , ed. Daniel J. Elazar (Chicago: Rand McNally, 1966).

22. China is a major exception to this rule.

23. Nicholas D. J. Baldwin, "Concluding Observations: Legislative Weakness, Scrutinizing Strength?," *Journal of Legislative Studies* Vol 10, No 2/3 (Summer/ Autumn 2004), p. 295.

24. Ibid., p. 302.

25. Paul Heywood, "Executive Capacity and Legislative Limits," in *Developments in West European Politics 2*, ed. Paul Heywood, Erik Jones, and Martin Rhodes (New York: Palgrave, 2002), pp. 151–167.

26. Ludger Helms, *Presidents, Prime Ministers and Chancellors: Executive Leadership in Western Democracies* (New York: Palgrave, 2005), p. 5.

27. B. Guy Peters, R. A. W. Rhodes and Vincent Wright, "Staffing the Summit—The Administration of the Core Executive: Convergent Trends and National Specificities," in *Administering the Summit,* ed. B. Guy Peters, R. A. W. Rhodes, and Vincent Wright (New York: St. Martin's Press, 2000), p. 7.

28. Jean Blondel, *Government Ministers in the Contemporary World* (New York: Sage, 1985), p. 4.

29. Thomas T. Mackie and Brian W. Hopwood, "Decision-Arenas in Executive Decision-Making: Cabinet Committees in Comparative Perspective," *British Journal of Political Science*, Vol 14., No. 3 (July 1984), p. 304.

30. Jeffrey L. Pressman and Aaron J. Wildavsky, *Implementation: How Great Expectations in Washington Are Dashed in Oakland: Or, Why It's Amazing That Federal Programs Work at All, This Being a Saga of the Economic Development Administration as Told by Two Sympathetic Observers Who Seek to Build Morals on a Foundation of Ruined Hopes* (Berkeley: University of California Press, 1973).

31. Truman is quoted in Richard E. Neustadt, *Presidential Power: The Politics of Leadership* (New York: Wiley, 1960), p. 9 (emphasis in original).

32. Max Weber, "Bureaucracy," in *From Max Weber: Essays in Sociology* , ed. H. H. Gerth and C. Wright Mills (New York: Oxford University Press, 1958).

33. Georg Sorensen, *Democratization and Democracy: Processes and Prospects in a Changing World* (Boulder, CO: Westview Press, 1993), p. 79.
34. Huntington is quoted in Douglas L. Bland, "A Unified Theory of Civil-Military Relations," *Armed Forces & Society* Vol. 26, no. 7 (1999), p. 11.
35. Robin Luckham, "A Comparative Typology of Civil-Military Relations," *Government and Opposition*, Vol. 6, No. 1 (1971), pp. 5–35.
36. Samuel P. Huntington, *The Soldier and the State* (Cambridge: Harvard University Press, 1957).
37. Eric A. Nordlinger, *Soldiers in Politics: Military Coups and Governments* (Englewood Cliffs, NJ.: Prentice Hall, 1977), pp. 1–30; see also Alfred Stepan, *The Military in Politics: Changing Patterns in Brazil* (Princeton, NJ: Princeton University Press, 1971).
38. Hughes is quoted in Bernard Schwartz, *A Basic History of the U.S. Supreme Court* (Princeton, NJ: D. Van Nostrand Co., 1968), p. 9.
39. John Ferejohn, "Judicializing Politics, Politicizing Law," *Law and Contemporary Problems* (2002), Vol. 65: No. 3, p. 41.
40. Paul Heywood, Erik Jones, and Martin Rhodes, "Introduction: West European States Confront the Challenge of a New Millennium," in *Developments in West European Politics*, 2nd edition, ed. Paul Heywood, Erik Jones, and Martin Rhodes (New York: Palgrave, 2002), p. 10.
41. C. Neal Tate and Torbjorn Vallinder, eds. *The Global Expansion of Judicial Power* (New York: NYU Press, 1995).
42. Jeffrey Gettleman, "The Most Dangerous Place in the World," *Foreign Policy* (March/April, 2009), p. 63.

State and Society

INTRODUCTION

The crowd of farmers gathered behind the village church. To make sure everyone could come, the elders had called the meeting for a Sunday evening when people were not working, and to hide it from the hacienda foremen they had passed the word privately among themselves instead of ringing the church bell.

Almost all the men from the village were there as they waited for Jose Merino, president of the village council, to speak. He told his neighbors that the task of representing the village's interests had become too much for him and the other members of the village council. They were too old and infirm to defend the villagers' land titles and water rights, and with new laws and taxes being passed, the burden was only going to get worse. That was why he and the other four men of the village council had decided to resign. Merino then asked for nominations to replace him as council president.

Emiliano Zapata, a young farmer, was nominated and, to no one's surprise, was elected. He had been active in the village's defense, signing petitions, challenging local authorities, and making connections with opposition party leaders. As leader of his village, Zapata defended the land claims of small farmers against large landowners. This soon led to armed conflict with the government that defended the hacienda owners. Zapata's reputation rose quickly and he became the leader of the Liberation Army of the South, which joined forces with other peasant armies to depose the government in the 1910 Mexican Revolution.[1]

Fast forward about 100 years and half a world away to Beijing, China, where—like Mexican peasants before them—Chinese students were meeting, sharing grievances, choosing leaders, and trying to avoid the authorities. Students believed the Chinese Communist Party had betrayed its ideals that were represented by the recently deceased Hu Yaobang, a party official who had supported political reforms but had been ousted by hardliners. By marching on Tiananmen Square, the seat of the government, to mourn the death of Hu Yaobang, the students would be validating his criticisms that the Party had deviated from its principles. As more students arrived at the Square, they drafted a list of demands for more democracy and less corruption to present to the government. When the government refused to accept the student's petition, they occupied the Square and called for a boycott of classes. The protest escalated in terms of its demands, becoming more radical, and in its scale, attracting more support from workers and students outside Beijing. Finally, the government called in the People's Liberation Army that fired indiscriminately at its own citizens, murdering them in a bid to restore control.

These incidents reveal what can happen when the linkages between the state and society fail. Unaddressed demands for land reform in Mexico or democracy in China can become tinder that ignites to challenge the state. A few peasants in a remote village or a few students paying homage to a deceased leader can become the basis for mass protest and revolution.

The previous chapter dissected the state to expose and examine its internal organs: the legislature, the core executive, the bureaucracy, the military, and the judiciary. This chapter examines the links connecting state and society. Sometimes the state and society stand in implacable opposition to one another. Perhaps no image captures this better than the one at the beginning of this chapter in which a lone, unarmed man stands defiantly in front of a row of tanks as they approach Tiananmen Square. The awesome, impersonal power of the state represented by the tanks is confronted by society in the form of a single, determined individual. At other times, the state reflects society instead of being in opposition to it. Citizens' demands are transmitted to the state, which satisfies them. Demands for land reform or democracy from below are translated into policy from above.

The state and society are connected to each other through **political participation**. Political participation flows through political parties, interest groups, social movements, and patron–client relations that convey demands from below to the state. In some countries, these linkages can handle the volume of demands that flows through them. In other countries, such as Mexico in 1910 and China in 1989, the wires are overloaded and political participation overwhelms the ability of the state to process demands and make its authority stick. The state's sovereignty and legitimacy are challenged. Samuel P. Huntington argued that the "most important distinction between countries concerns not their form"—the kind of issues we touched on in the previous chapter—"but their degree of government."[2] The distinction between order and anarchy, Huntington offers, may be more fundamental than that between democracy and dictatorship.[3]

Some countries have "strong, adaptable, coherent political institutions," in which the probability is high that policies will be implemented as the government intended.[4] In these countries, you can be fairly sure that products are safe because regulators have inspected them, water will come out of the tap when you turn it on, police will arrive when you dial 911, and that children will receive an education when you send them to school. In other countries, the opposite is the case. These countries suffer from a **crisis of governability**. The government rules but does not govern. The authority of the state dissolves outside the capital as warlords and local strongmen effectively govern outlying areas. Regulations are not enforced, basic public services are not delivered, and corrupt state officials use public money for their own enrichment. Some states can manage their environments, they can effectively govern society. In others, the society overwhelms the state. The state is defeated by it.

POLITICAL PARTICIPATION

Political participation occurs in both democratic and authoritarian political systems. The former encourages citizens to influence policy, while the latter promotes participation if only to register approval for what the government does. It can also take many different forms. Where citizens fear for their lives, they engage in political activity furtively and anonymously by using satire to make fun of the powers that be, try to undermine rulers' legitimacy through rumor and innuendo, and carry out hidden acts of sabotage.[5] Political participation can also take the opposite form in which citizens engage in open, violent revolt against their rulers. Citizens can yell from a soap box or cast votes in a ballot box. Citizens use strategies they believe are appropriate given the resources they have and the opportunities that are available. Take the case, for example, of the environmental movement. Green Parties that compete for votes are common and relatively successful in Europe. Indeed, the Greens have been successful enough in elections in Europe to even participate in some governments. But Green parties have been unsuccessful in the United States, despite conditions being as propitious in terms of public support for environmentalism as in Europe.

At the same time Green parties are weaker in the United States, American environmental interest groups are more plentiful and powerful than they are in Europe. There are more than 10,000 environmentally oriented organizations registered as tax-exempt organizations in the United States, and they employ more staff and have bigger budgets than their European counterparts. The difference has to do with the opportunity structure for political participation in the two regions. In the United States, the decentralized, open structure of Congress is congenial to interest group activity. Interest groups can target their influence on congressional committees that have jurisdiction over their issues. At the same time, elections are not nearly as inviting. Third parties, such as the Greens, have a hard time competing in the United States due to winner-takes-all electoral rules, obstacles to getting on the ballot, and a lack of media coverage given to minor parties. **The opportunity structure** is quite different in many European countries, leading environmentalists to mobilize electorally as opposed to doing so through interest groups. Many European countries have proportional representation electoral systems in which small parties, such as the Greens, are awarded seats in the legislature based on the percentage of the vote they receive. This permits small parties to come away with some legislative influence so their voters do not feel they are wasting their vote as they would in the United States, where losing parties get nothing. In addition, parliamentary systems of government that exist throughout Europe deprive their legislatures of having the kind of influence on policy that Congress enjoys. Consequently, environmentalist interest groups in Europe tend to be smaller and weaker than those in the United States. Groups engage in different forms of political participation, depending on the opportunities for influence that different political structures create.

Of course, groups engage in different forms of political participation simultaneously, not one mode of participation at the expense or exclusion of another. While environmentalists in Europe and the United States may not engage in interest group and electoral activity in equal proportion, they are both part of the movement's repertoire as they supplement and support each other. It is also the case that one form of participation may pave the way to another. Recent elections in Serbia (2000), the Ukraine (2004), and Iran (2009) became the trigger for mass protests in which the initial mobilization for an opposition candidate later became the basis for mobilization against the state itself. One form of political participation, voting, morphed into another, street demonstrations. Groups can engage in different forms of political participation simultaneously, one form of political participation can change seamlessly into another, or groups can engage in different types of political participation sequentially. This, for example, was the case with the black civil rights movement in the United States. It shifted its strategy from protest to politics, from marches and demonstrations to voter mobilization and registration as the rewards of the former declined and opportunities for the latter increased. One can also see the same sequence occurring in terms of the history of the environmental movement. In Germany, the Green Party was the culmination of a process in which antinuclear peace activists shifted their focus from demonstrations to elections.

Like water trying to escape through the weakest part of a dam, political actors are always looking for the weakest point in the wall of power. They may engage in different forms of political participation simultaneously or move sequentially from one to another, depending on the resources political actors have and their opportunities to deploy them.

The early research on political participation found that voting was the most popular form of activism and that only a minority engaged in more demanding forms of participation beyond this, such as party work, and even fewer engaged in protests. People with more resources—more education, money, self-confidence, civic skills, and social contacts—were more likely to participate. Political activity was skewed to those who were most advantaged.[6] But these results drawn from individual level surveys that showed the impact of social inequality on participation ignored the impact of institutions, the rules of the game, on levels of political activism. A later generation of political scientists found that electoral rules, such as proportional representation systems, compulsory voting, and whether elections occurred during workdays, also affect turnout and why voting is skewed to the affluent and educated in some countries more than on others.[7] They also found that traditional forms of political participation in democracies, such as turnout in elections, was declining, but new forms of civic and political action, such as petitioning, demonstrating, or participating in consumer boycotts (or becoming vegan in protest to the cruel slaughter of animals for meat), were taking their place.[8] New forms of political expression are expanding political participation beyond more conventional forms.

Some political scientists found virtue in the limits of political participation, that so few engaged in it beyond the simple and infrequent act of voting. It was sufficient for democracy that citizens could choose among candidates in free and fair elections. It was not necessary that they participate in political activity beyond that. Others believed that activism had virtues in itself, promoting social tolerance, interpersonal trust, political knowledge, and more responsive government. But few considered the inextricable link between political participation and people's capabilities, that improving people's capabilities only occurs through political activity. As Peter Evans notes, "my ability to choose the life I have reason to value often hangs on the possibility of my acting together with others who have reason to value similar things."[9] People cannot create the institutional structures they need on their own, by themselves, to promote their capabilities. They can only realize these goals through politics, which requires them to act collectively with others if they are to succeed. This is especially true for the underprivileged who have few personal resources to develop their capabilities by themselves. They need to ally with others in political activity in order to create institutions that improve their lives. Individual capabilities depend on collective action, which occurs through parties, interest groups, social movements, and patron–client relations to achieve them. We review these forms of collective action below.

POLITICAL PARTIES

The Founders of the American Republic viewed **political parties** with contempt and believed they were a threat to liberty. Yet, even as the Founders condemned parties in theory, they helped create them in practice. Thomas Jefferson, who founded the Republican Party (the forerunner of today's Democratic Party), and Alexander Hamilton who led the Federalist Party, both viewed political parties as "sores on the body politic." Two hundred years later, in 1986, Uganda tried to do what the Founders could not. The National Resistance Movement took power and tried to establish a "no-party democracy." While political parties were permitted, party activity on behalf of candidates running for office was banned. But the equivalent of party activity emerged in response to the very effort to limit it, as those who opposed the ban on party activity ran against those who supported it.[10]

Political parties emerge even where they are ridiculed because people have diverse interests and values and find parties useful in expressing them to the state. Citizens turn to political parties to educate and mobilize voters, advocate policies that link voters to candidates, and connect elected officials from the same party to each other. But what distinguishes political parties most from other forms of political participation is that they recruit and nominate candidates for public office. Whereas interest groups seek to influence the state from the outside, political parties seek to influence it from the inside by offering candidates to form the government.

Political parties have often been condemned as baleful influences that threaten the unity and integrity of the political order. They "are *parts against the whole*," the political theorist Nancy L. Rosenblum writes, "not *parts of the whole*."[11] Other critics have attacked parties for being corrupt and corrupting, for pandering to special interests, or serving the selfish, predatory needs of office-seekers. But those who condemn parties for being divisive have a naïve view of politics. The unified political community that parties allegedly disrupt does not exist anywhere because people have diverse interests and values. Those diverse interests could not be denied within the new American state in 1787 any more than they could be ignored two hundred years later within Uganda's "no-party democracy." And while parties may have vices, they also contribute to the political community by structuring conflict and organizing government. They play a creative role, Nancy L. Rosenbloom suggests, that often goes unacknowledged in the way parties "stage the battle" by formulating issues and giving them political relevance. They take the raw material of interests and grievances that exist in society and create the practical art of governing, by offering voters a choice of policies and candidates, from it.[12]

Political parties emerged with democracy and the extension of voting rights in the nineteenth century. In some instances, they arose as extensions of factional disputes in the legislature. Legislators appealed to the people, organizing supporters among the broader public, to settle policy conflicts among themselves. Party in government gave birth to party in the electorate. This was the case in the United States where opposing congressional factions, what became the Federalists and the Republicans, took their dispute outside the halls of Congress and appealed to the public for support. In other instances, the opposite occurred. Groups outside the legislature formed political parties so as to have more influence within it. An example of this occurred in Britain where the trade unions, frustrated with their lack of political representation in Parliament, gave birth to the Labour Party in order to increase their political influence. This was also the case in many developing countries where political parties formed to express the interests of particular castes, religious groups, and tribes.[13] For example, the Zulu tribe in South Africa found representation through the Inkatha Freedom Party, and the Bahujan Samaj Party emerged as the expression of lower-caste voters in northern India.

Parties play significant roles in democracies, competing to win elections and form governments. A crude sense of what the public wants gets transmitted up to government through party competition in elections. But political parties are also common in authoritarian systems in the absence of elections. Here they are used not to transmit demands from below up to government, but to reverse the flow of information and convey government policies down to the people. Two political scientists suggested that parties in authoritarian regimes are used both as "an instrument of political recruitment as well as a device for management of the public."[14] The party facilitates mass mobilization in support of the government in order to assert its legitimacy, and to recruit and socialize people to staff it.

Beyond one-party authoritarian regimes, parties exist within party *systems* that entail enduring, stable forms of party competition. **Party systems** are distinguished by the number of parties they include. For example, people often refer to the American two-party *system* because electoral competition often takes the regular, patterned form of Democrats competing against Republicans. But the American two-party system is actually quite rare. Multiparty systems are much more common, where the effective number of parties that compete for votes and win legislative seats is greater than two. In Israel, for example, there were twelve parties that won enough votes in the 2009 elections to be represented in the Knesset, its legislature. Party systems are also distinguished by their ideological breadth. Some party systems are highly polarized because of the presence of extreme right and left wing parties that are absent from other party systems.[15] And finally, party systems differ in their degree of institutionalization, the degree to which they function as a system at all. This, for example, is a dilemma faced in many new democracies in Eastern Europe and Africa, where parties form and disappear quickly, party competition is highly unstable, and party organizations are weak, with few members or resilient local chapters.[16] Some party systems are characterized by strong parties that enjoy high memberships, loyal voters from one election to the next, and party discipline among their elected officials, while other party systems give rise to weak parties where there is volatility among voters from one election to the next, party membership is low, and there is little unity or party-line voting among legislators.

IN BRIEF

Strong and Weak Political Parties

Characteristics	Weak Parties	Strong Parties
Membership	low	high
Party identification among voters	low	high
Electoral volatility	high	low
Party unity in the legislature	low	high

Party systems reflect deep-rooted social divisions that are embedded in the history of a country. These cleavages give rise to group identities that find expression in political parties. Consequently, party competition assumes the characteristics of a system, with durable, recurrent patterns. According to two sociologists, Seymour Martin Lipset and Stein Rokkan, the party systems that emerged in Western democracies were the geological remains of violent economic and political conflicts from their pasts, specifically, the rise of industrial capitalism and the nation-state. The emergence of industrial capitalism gave birth to class and urban–rural conflicts, while the development of the nation-state gave rise to church–state and national–local conflicts. Just as ice, water, fire, and ice combined in unique ways to shape different regions of the earth, so did these four cleavages combine in distinctive ways to shape party competition in West European countries. The impact of these social divisions is still evident today in the form of socialist (class conflict), Christian democratic (church–state conflict), agrarian (rural–urban conflict), and regional parties (national–local conflict) in many European countries.

Party systems are also shaped by electoral laws. Different methods of counting votes, awarding seats in the legislature and choosing presidents, affect the shape of party systems. For example, the rules under which elections are held in the United States, where whoever-gets-the-most-votes wins, create a bias toward a two-party system. Under these rules, there are no rewards for losing. Consequently, voters do not want to waste their vote on parties that cannot win and strategically vote for the lesser of two evils among the two major parties that can. Under different electoral rules, such as proportional representation, where legislative seats are awarded to parties based upon the percentage of the vote they receive, multiparty systems flourish. Parties receiving less than a plurality still receive some representation in the legislature. Voters can now vote their conscience without the fear that they are throwing their vote away, as would be the case under winner-takes-all rules. Electoral rules shape the nature of party competition by influencing the number of parties that compete and the ideological space between them.

But not all parties and party systems are created equal. Some contribute more to developing citizens' capabilities than others. The quality of the link between state and society through political parties depends on the presence of well-organized, disciplined parties that articulate clear programs and appeal to a broad coalition of voters. Such parties are able to maximize the greatest asset of the underprivileged: their power of numbers. In their absence, when party systems are poorly institutionalized and parties appear and disappear rapidly—which is the case in many new democracies—it is hard for citizens to know what parties stand for and, thus, what they are voting for. Parties built around personalities tend to appear and these party leaders are less likely to be constrained when they govern and to favor elites who have privileged access to them when they do. Programmatic commitments and organizational discipline that could limit wheeling and dealing by politicians and hold them accountable are absent.[17]

Parties built on **patronage** are as suspect as those that are weakly institutionalized and develop around personalities. Parties that are built around rewards in return for political loyalty divide the underprivileged into multiple, competing parties. The less fortunate form political ties with elites who offer them rewards instead of allying with each other. Where such parties exist, people with low capabilities have a difficult time making improvements in their lives because their power of numbers has been diluted. Developing their capabilities depends upon political participation that flows through institutionalized and programmatic political parties that can harness their power of numbers, and can appeal and unite a wide variety of voters around a common program.[18] **Programmatic parties** that link citizens to the state contribute to people's capabilities by providing more public services that ordinary people depend on and by engaging in less corruption that common people cannot afford.[19]

◥ THE GOOD SOCIETY IN DEPTH

Iraq—From Bullets to Ballots (and perhaps back again)

Following the American invasion, political participation in Iraq took the form of suicide bombings, civil strife, and ethnic cleansing. Kurds, Shiites, and Sunnis used bullets not ballots to influence the government and settle differences with each other. Political participation escaped the institutional channels designed to contain and express it.

In March 2010, legislative elections were held in which Kurds, Shiites, and Sunnis ran candidates and appealed for votes. Despite election-day violence that claimed 38 lives, 62 percent of eligible Iraqis walked past cratered buildings and walls pockmarked with bullet holes in order to cast their ballot. Sunnis ignored provocations and turned out to vote instead of boycotting the election as they had done previously. Secular and religious parties competed for the vote of the dominant Shiite majority, and Kurds participated even though the election might cost them influence they enjoyed under the old government.

But Iraq's fragile institutions imperiled the election's success. A slow tallying of votes brought charges of vote tampering, tainting any government that emerges with suspicions that the election was stolen. When the election returns finally began to come in, they reflected the fragmentation of Iraq too well, yielding indecisive results. Sunni, Shiite, Kurdish, secular, and religious parties dithered in negotiating with each other to form a government, undermining confidence that elections could settle differences.

It is unclear whether Iraq's fledgling institutions will be up to the task of earning the trust of Iraqis as they exchange bullets for ballots. The social conflicts in Iraq may be too powerful for electoral forms of political participation to contain. If the institutional capacity is not sufficient to channel demands arising from electoral participation into effective government, then Iraqis may return to settling their differences with bullets instead of ballots again.

For Further Discussion

1. In what ways do the Iraqi elections support and undercut one of President George W. Bush's reasons to invade Iraq, that it would bring democracy to the country?

2. While the capability approach argues people are better off with civil and political rights, is it possible that democracy may be too much of a good thing in some places? Can democracy reflect social conflicts too well, leading participants to resort to violence in order to settle issues they could not resolve through elections?

INTEREST GROUPS

Political participation can also take the form of interest group activity in which people with common interests organize for the purpose of influencing policy makers. **Interest groups** engage in many of the same activities as political parties: raising money, mobilizing voters, and campaigning for candidates in order to influence policy. But unlike political parties, interest groups do not nominate candidates to run for office.

It may appear natural and easy for people with common interests to organize in pursuit of their shared goals. But interest group formation is not so simple and straightforward. Someone has to invest time, provide leadership, and commit resources to make it happen. Such skills and resources may not exist and are certainly not evenly distributed among groups. For this reason, organizations of poor people, who lack time, money, and leadership skills, are very rare, while those of higher status groups who have these resources are more common. In addition, interest group formation faces the **free rider problem**. It is rational for people to try and gain the benefits that interest groups create without paying the costs of joining or participating in them. For example, it is rational to not contribute to the Sierra Club and enjoy the benefits of clean air and water it helps promote while letting others pay dues and attend its meetings. But if everyone acted rationally in this way, free riding on the activity of others, no interest groups would form. The Sierra Club would not exist.

But the Sierra Club and interest groups like it do exist because they offer a variety of incentives that entice people to join them. Some groups offer material incentives, some tangible rewards for becoming a member, such as discounts on insurance or purchases. Other groups avoid the free rider problem by offering people an opportunity to feel fellowship in a common enterprise. They derive emotional satisfaction from joining with others in an organization that seeks to realize their shared values.[20]

To some extent, the challenges of interest group formation and mobilization have been reduced by technological innovations such as the internet. According to the political scientist Mark S. Bonchek, "electronic forms of communication reduce communication, coordination and information costs, facilitating group formation, group efficiency, membership recruitment and retention."[21] Organizers can recruit members, appeal for contributions, inform supporters, and coordinate their activity through a Web site, which is very inexpensive to create and maintain. The expense of a bureaucracy to carry out basic functions of recruitment and coordination can now be avoided because these tasks can be done cheaper and more quickly through computer-mediated communication. The internet permits interest groups to travel light because it reduces start-up costs.

The internet has not only facilitated interest group formation but also given impetus to professional advocacy organizations, such as the Children's Defense Fund in the United States. These interest groups, in contrast to older ones, dispense with dues paying members and local chapters and rely on foundations, direct mail, or internet fund-raising appeals for money. They have a head, but no body. Previously, members engaged in politics by participating in the life of the organization, developing civic values and leadership skills in the process. But these professional advocacy organizations do not need to involve their supporters in the life of the organization. They are creatures of their staff who simply appeal to the like-minded to support financially their efforts.[22]

Some countries have a plethora of interest groups. In the United States, special interests proliferate. In other countries, interest groups are not as plentiful, even when one controls for population. The interest group universe is larger in some countries than in others because their state structures are more conducive to pressure group influence. For example, the divided, decentralized political institutions of the United States create many access points where groups can influence policy: at the state level, in the Senate, the House of Representatives, and in the courts. The open, diffused, fractured structure of policy making in the United States invites groups with a stake in policy to lobby and exert influence. The more power is dispersed within the state, the more opportunities for special interests to apply pressure on it. In countries such as Sweden, where the state is unitary and policy making is centralized, there are not as many access points for interest groups to affect policy and, consequently, the incentive to form them is not as great.

Just as different types of party systems exist, so, too, are there different interest group systems. Groups in different countries that represent similar interests operate very differently depending on the type of interest group system in which they are embedded. For example, even though the AFL-CIO in the United States and the LO in Sweden represent the interests of labor unions in their respective countries, they are organized and act differently because they are embedded in different interest group systems with distinctive characteristics.

Some countries have what is called a **pluralist interest group system**. Such systems are characterized by large numbers of interest groups that compete with each other for members and influence. Pluralist interest group systems have the following characteristics. First, groups have to compete for members in order to survive and expand. They all want to increase their market share and recruit members who can provide them with the money, staff, resources, and significance they need to be influential. This is especially important because pluralist interest groups enjoy no special relationship with the government. They do not participate in policy making but have to exert influence from the outside through lobbying policy makers. Second, pluralist interest groups tend to capture a smaller share of their potential market because some people choose not to join. They are less encompassing. Finally, pluralist interest groups tend to be decentralized. They lack the authority to sanction their members and tell them what to do. For example, the AFL-CIO cannot require its affiliated unions, such as the United Auto Workers or the Machinists union, to support the same bills and candidates it has endorsed. The AFL-CIO lacks sanctions short of expulsion to prevent affiliated unions from freelancing and ignoring its decisions.

At the other end of the spectrum are corporatist systems of interest group representation in which there are fewer but larger interest groups. **Corporatist interest groups** are more encompassing. They recruit a higher percentage of those who are eligible to join because membership is often compulsory, not optional. They also enjoy a monopoly over their market, reducing competition for members. Finally, they are more hierarchically organized with the authority to sanction their member's behavior and they are often invited to participate in policy making by the state as insiders, not outsiders, as occurs with their pluralist counterparts. They are invited to negotiate directly with the government in return for complying with any agreement that is reached. In Table 3.1, countries that received high scores, such as Austria and Norway, have corporatist interest group systems, while countries with low scores, such as Canada and the United States, have pluralist interest group systems.

Corporatist and pluralist interest groups behave differently with consequences for people's capabilities. The pluralist interest group market is crowded with competing groups, which undermines their willingness to cooperate with each other. Internally, a lack of centralized control impedes efforts to operate efficiently. Both sap their collective strength. Corporatist interest groups, on the other hand, don't have to outbid other groups to attract members. They are not beset by organizational fragmentation nor do they suffer from as much organizational inefficiency due to a lack of centralized

TABLE 3.1

Interest Group Systems

Corporatism	Scores	Corporatism	Scores
Austria	5.000	Ireland	2.000
Norway	4.864	New Zealand	1.955
Sweden	4.674	Australia	1.680
Netherlands	4.000	France	1.674
Denmark	3.545	United Kingdom	1.652
Germany (West)	3.543	Portugal	1.500
Switzerland	3.375	Italy	1.477
Finland	3.295	Spain	1.250
Japan	2.912	Canada	1.150
Belgium	2.841	United States	1.150

Source: See Alan Siaroff, "Corporatism in 24 Industrial Democracies: Meaning and Measurement," *European Journal of Political Research* Vol. 36 (1999), p. 198.

authority. Hierarchy within corporatist interest groups is able to resolve problems of internal coordination that plague their pluralist counterparts. Finally, their encompassing memberships require them to synthesize the diverse interests of their members and articulate only the most general interest among them. This broadens the appeal of these groups. All of these qualities permit corporatist interest groups to unify and appeal to broader interests as well as use their limited resources more efficiently. For citizens who want to develop their capabilities and have to depend on their power of numbers to be politically effective, these are no small advantages. Fewer and bigger really is better.

IN BRIEF

Pluralist and Corporatist Interest Group

Characteristics	Pluralist	Corporatist
Number of interest groups	many	few
Internal organization	decentralized	hierarchical
Coverage	low density	encompassing
Relationship to government	lobbying	participates in policy-making.

SOCIAL MOVEMENTS

The mothers first came across each other by accident as they visited police stations, military prisons, and government offices. They were searching for their sons, daughters, and husbands who had been kidnapped as suspected subversives by the Argentine military after it seized power in 1975. In their desperation, mothers converged on the Plaza de Mayo in front of the presidential palace in Buenos Aires, the nation's capital, to demand answers. Every Thursday afternoon they would march around the plaza wearing white headscarves embroidered with the names of their "disappeared" family members. Week after week in hope and fear, month after month in sunshine and rain, and year after year in sickness and in health, they would appear demanding to know what happened to their abducted children and loved ones. Their witness helped shatter the fear and silence surrounding the military's rule and paved the way to the restoration of democracy in Argentina.[23]

The Mothers of the Plaza de Mayo, as they became known, is an example of a **social movement**. Social movements engage in more unconventional and confrontational forms of political participation to influence policy makers than interest groups or political parties. This may include peaceful assemblies in front of the presidential palace as the Mothers of the Plaza de Mayo did, protest marches that were the stock-in-trade of the American civil rights movement, or blocking the entrance to abortion clinics that pro-life activists use. Social movements are not as formally organized or hierarchical, tend to be more ideological and contentious, and move participation up to a more active and demanding level than other forms of political participation. Consequently, social movements tend to attract people with intense feelings about an issue who are more committed and willing to assume the increased risks that social movement activism entails. While social movements are often identified with liberal and progressive goals, conservatives have also formed social movements to influence policy makers. The ideological commitment to participate in social movements is not the monopoly of any one tendency but can be found across the political spectrum.

Social movements, according to Charles Tilly, first emerged in the 1700s when people began to engage in sustained campaigns that used disruptive performances to make claims on authorities. Social movement activists pressured officials and appealed to the wider public by conveying the worthiness of their claims in petitions and signs. They demonstrated the unity and breadth of their support in public assemblies and rallies, and substantiated commitment to their ideals by their personal attendance and sacrifice. Social movements engage in these tactics in order to advance two types of claims. First, some social movements want to promote group acceptance; that is, those who are considered outsiders want the same rights and privileges as insiders. The civil rights and feminist movements are examples of this type of claim in which blacks wanted what whites had and women demanded the same rights as men. Social movements also make claims on authorities to promote group goals, to enact changes in policy. This is not a simple case of outsiders wanting in, but of insiders forming a social movement because the normal channels are blocked and unresponsive to their demands. The environmental and antiabortion movements are examples of these types of claims.[24]

The emergence of social movements was facilitated by the spread of democracy. Democracy contributed to this distinctive and innovative form of political participation by removing prohibitions against mass rallies and other repressive measures; providing convenient and accessible targets in the form of legislatures and representatives upon whom social movements could focus demands; magnifying the political importance and respect given to sheer numbers; and increasing the significance of claims to represent "the people."[25] Where democracy flourished, so did social movements. Where democracy was sparse, it was difficult for social movements to gain traction (the Mothers of Plaza de Mayo being an exception).

Many early social movements were formed by occupational groups around economic demands. Peasant, farmer, and labor movements proliferated. But as industrialism gave way to postindustrialism, new forms of domination became prominent alongside familiar forms of economic power. The landlord's domination of peasants, the merchant's power over farmers, and the employer's control over workers were now joined by male domination of women, straights of gays, whites of blacks, settlers of indigenous people, and man of nature. Cultural domination, not simply economic domination, became a new source of social conflict, as groups affirmed their way of life, behavior, and needs against traditional standards that devalued them. These social movements were as interested in legitimizing alternative lifestyles as they were in promoting their policy goals. Politics was personal in a way that was not true for participants in older, more traditional social movements. **New social movements** were also distinguished from their predecessors by their flatter and more decentralized structures. They were much more skeptical of bureaucracy, which they believed would compromise their ideals. When the 1997 Nobel Peace Prize was awarded to the International Campaign to Ban Landmines (ICBL) and its founding coordinator Jody Williams, the ICBL had to wait nearly a year to receive its share of the money because it had no bank account or address to which the Nobel Committee could send it. New social movements believe that by prefiguring their goals in the means they used to achieve them and avoiding bureaucracy they could avert being domesticated and co-opted like the economically based social movements that preceded them.

As the breadth of issues covered by social movements increased, so did they expand in scope from the national to the international level. The increase in the power and number of international organizations created their own world of social movements to shadow them. This is best exemplified by the formation of the World Social Forum, which brings together global activists every year to discuss issues and network among themselves, which is modeled on the annual meetings of the World Economic Forum, which brings together political and economic elites to discuss issues and network among themselves. Globalization from above in the form of multinational corporations and international organizations is increasingly replicated by globalization from below in the form of social movements that cross borders. For example, when protesters greeted World Trade Organization representatives in what became known as the "Battle of Seattle," in 1999, coordinated protests also occurred in Britain, Canada, Ireland, Portugal, France, Switzerland, Germany, Turkey, Pakistan, and India. Social movement organizations are networked together across borders to coordinate activity, such as those surrounding the Battle of Seattle. Such linkages are made easier by the internet, which facilitates planning and dialogue among groups in different countries.

PATRON–CLIENT RELATIONS

The debt binding clients to patrons in the Philippines is greater than any exchange of money can expunge. In return for protection, which may take the form of work, access to land, school tuition for children, or money for a medical emergency, sugarcane cutters give plantation owners their loyalty, gratitude, and respect. As one owner explained, "[plantation owners] control the community, because everybody is dependent on you, and you can have a say in everything they do."[26] When owners need political support they simply call in their debt.

Patron–client relations, in which a patron offers or withholds some material benefit in return for political support, are another way in which citizens are linked to the state. Clients exchange their vote or participation in a rally in return for some tangible reward, such as money, jobs, or better land to rent. As a party official in a rural part of Spain explained: "The citizen who is worried about resolving problems with the doctor or the school, or the problem of an unjust accusation before the courts, or of delinquency in paying taxes to the state, etc. . . . has recourse to an intermediary . . . who can intercede on his behalf, but in exchange for pledging his very conscience and his vote."[27] Patron–client relationships occur among those in deeply unequal relationships in which the haves are in a position to bargain for political support from the have-nots.

The bargain struck between patrons and clients is reinforced by **norms of reciprocity**, that people should help those who do favors for them. When patrons intercede on behalf of their clients or offer small loans to them, clients become obligated to their patrons. These feelings of obligation are powerful and cannot easily be dismissed or avoided because of the regular face-to-face contact that patrons have with clients on a daily basis. Moreover, exchanges create a sense of ongoing dependence by clients on patrons to ensure they continue to provide gifts in the future. When a client was asked whether she was required to attend political rallies in return for free medicine she received from a party broker, she replied, "I know I have to go to her rally in order to fulfill my obligation to her, to show my gratitude. . . . [I]f I do not go to the rally, then, when I need something, she won't give it to me."[28] Of course, clients can always cheat and not go to the rally. But patron–client relations are embedded in local social networks that provide feedback as to whether clients deliver on their end of the bargain. According to Susan C. Stokes, this turns the normal meaning of democratic accountability in which parties are held accountable by voters into its opposite in which voters are held responsible for their actions by parties.[29]

Clientelism generates poverty, and poverty, in turn, generates clientelism. Clientelism flourishes when people are desperate for handouts. Their vote and political support may not seem like much to exchange when people need food, a job, or medicine. The poor value the benefits that patrons can deliver today more than the promises of redistribution others might promise tomorrow. Living so close to subsistence and vulnerable to abuse from powerful officials, clients appreciate the safety net that patrons offer and consider themselves luckier than those without one. But clientelism also contributes to poverty. Political parties that depend on patron–client networks for support provide targeted relief to individuals at the expense of providing public goods that might have bigger payoffs for all. Clientelist parties tend to forego developmental projects that contribute to economic growth and enhance the quality of life for everyone in order to provide private goods to their supporters.

WEAK AND STRONG STATES

Linkages such as political parties, interest groups, social movements and patron–client relations, which connect citizens to the state, are important because they convey demands to the government. These wires carry the electrical current from the base of society to policy makers. But these linkages do not simply carry the current, they manage and transform it. The way in which they are structured—clientelistic or programmatic parties, pluralist or corporatist interest groups—affects which demands get through and which are discouraged, advantaging some groups at the expense of others.

Some countries are able to handle the electrical current that political parties and other linkage organizations convey, while others are overwhelmed by it. Their wires and circuits become overloaded, causing the machinery of state to fail. Such countries are called **weak states**. Weak states lack autonomy from groups in society. They can be captured by narrow interests, just as the Mexican state was captured by landlords before Zapata led the revolution to defeat it. They also lack the capacity to govern. They cannot translate their power into policy. This incapacity is not a small, innocent matter of inefficiency, such as when the postal service loses a package or pension checks are late, but can have lethal results. Drinking water that is supposed to be safe carries dysentery, and garbage that is supposed to be collected breeds deadly diseases. Millions of people in Africa die from AIDS not simply because antiretroviral drugs are expensive, but because governments lack a public health infrastructure that could administer the complex protocols of AIDS prevention effectively.[30]

Not only are weak states unable to implement policies, but many cannot even do the bare minimum of what defines a state, which is to maintain law and order. They exert little authority beyond the immediate vicinity of the capital city, leaving local strongmen or warlords to rule over the rest of the country. Afghanistan and Pakistan are examples of this, where the Taliban effectively rules over sections of these countries and their law and order replaces that of the government. In some countries, such as Somalia, the state has collapsed entirely. There is no state to enforce laws, leaving people at the mercy of local warlords.

Finally, weak states are characterized by corruption, the use of public office for private gain. Prime ministers pocket foreign aid that was intended for their citizens, police officers threaten people with arrest if they are not bribed, and teachers sell grades to students in return for cash. One tale of corruption concerns Chinese and African civil servants who knew each other from graduate school. The African visits his counterpart in China and marveled at his large house and the luxury cars in his driveway. He asked, "How did you manage this on a bureaucrat's salary?" The Chinese official responded, "Do you remember that highway you took to get here?" Then, tapping his chest, he said, "ten percent," meaning he pocketed ten percent of the cost of highway construction. Five years later when the Chinese official visited his friend in Africa, he marveled at his palatial home and the expensive cars in his driveway. He asked, "How did you manage this on a bureaucrat's salary?" The African official responded, "Do you remember that highway you took to get here." The Chinese official was puzzled and replied, "What highway?" His friend responded, laughing and tapping his chest with satisfaction, "One hundred percent."

Strong states, on the other hand, display both capacity and autonomy. When we speak of capacity we are referring to the ability of states to implement policies effectively throughout their territory. They can process the electrical current coming in from political parties, interest groups, and other institutions that link society to the state and transform it into policy, which is then executed efficiently. They are able to defend their borders, maintain order within them, collect taxes, and execute policies with a minimum of slippage.

Strong states are not only characterized by capacity but they also display autonomy. Strong states are not captured by social interests but can make policy independent of them. Autonomy insulates the state from conflicts among social groups and permits the state to act in the public interest. Strong states that exhibit both capacity and autonomy are not necessarily authoritarian states. In fact, many strong states are democracies, such as Sweden and Germany, while many authoritarian states, such as Belarus and Laos, are weak. The government in these countries has a difficult time insulating itself from powerful social groups and implementing its policies.

◥ COMPARATIVE POLITICAL ANALYSIS

Why Do Some Political Institutions Work Better Than Others?

Problem

People's lives are better when political institutions deliver what they are supposed to: safe streets, clean water, and educated citizens. Yet some states perform better than others. In his book, *Making Democracy Work*, Robert Putnam asked why that might be so. He compared the effectiveness and responsiveness of fifteen new regional governments that Italy created in the 1970s to join five existing ones, each

Continued

of which essentially had the same legal, constitutional powers and responsibilities for public health and economic development. "On paper," writes Putnam, "these twenty institutions are virtually identical."[32] Putnam likened the problem to a botany experiment in which genetically identical seeds—the new regional governments—were placed in different soil so as to compare how they developed; if their diverse settings made a difference in how the seeds grew.

Methods and Hypothesis

Putnam used qualitative and quantitative methods to assess the performance of regional governments. He conducted interviews with officials and community leaders, surveyed voters and, like an anthropologist, immersed himself in the various regions of Italy, "soaking and poking" around to gather information. But he also tested his intuitions and supplemented his evidence with quantitative data he collected from among the various regions in Italy. He hypothesized that the new regional institutions in Italy would be shaped by and reflect the social context in which they operated.

Operationalizing Concepts

Putnam developed indicators to assess institutional performance as a problem-solver and service provider: Good performance depended on:

1. how well institutions managed their own affairs, which was evaluated according to whether they met budget deadlines and the amount of government turnover;
2. how appropriate and extensive their legislative solutions were, which was measured by whether regional governments established day care centers that the national government subsidized, and how much of their agricultural funds they actually dispersed;
3. how responsive bureaucracies were, which Putnam tested by mailing letters to each regional government requesting information about a problem and evaluating the quality of their reply and if he received any at all.

Results

Putnam found those regional institutions that performed best were located in areas where there was a great deal of civic trust that was cultivated by a rich array of local voluntary organizations, such as sports clubs and unions. He found that good citizens and good government reinforced each other.

For Further Discussion

1. What circumstances contribute to a vibrant civic life that creates civic trust, which Putnam believes is so essential to good government? Why were some regions blessed with such fertile conditions while others were cursed with distrust and disengagement that was the source of poor government performance?
2. Can states create civic trust? Can states turn vicious circles of mutual suspicion among citizens into virtuous circles of mutual confidence?

Source: Robert D. Putnam with Robert Leonardi and Raffaella Y. Nanetti, *Making Democracy Work: Civic Traditions in Modern Italy* (Princeton, NJ: Princeton University Press, 1993).

WEAK STATES, STRONG STATES, AND THE GOOD SOCIETY

Are stronger states better, in the sense of promoting people's capabilities? Or does the quality of life for citizens improve when states are weak? In order to distinguish strong from weak states, we turn to the Failed States Index developed by The Fund for Peace in conjunction with the journal *Foreign Policy*. The Failed States Index that appears as Table 3.1 in the Appendix used twelve indicators, including social factors such as the amount of internal violence, economic parameters such as stability, and political indicators such as the quality of its public services to assess state strength and weakness. States that performed the best on these indicators—what we would call the strongest—were labeled "sustainable." As Table 3.1 in the Appendix indicates, Canada and Australia were members of this select group. The index proceeds down to the next group, which included much of Western Europe and the United States, where state performance was good, or "moderate" as the Index referred to it. The next group of states, such as Mexico and India, earned a "warning" because there was cause for concern about the quality of these states. The Index issued an "alert" to the last and worst performing group of states, which included Somalia and Yemen, because it doubted their continuing viability, or because these states had collapsed entirely.

Physical Well-Being

A good society, we argued, is one that meets the physical needs of its citizens. People should be fed, sheltered, and healthy, and that the best way to measure this was to look at infant mortality rates. It is apparent from Figure 3.1 that state quality has a significant effect on infant mortality rates.[31] As we move along the horizontal "x" axis of Figure 3.1, from the weakest to the strongest states, the average infant mortality rate improves. The average infant mortality rate for states on alert was 68.96 per 1,000 babies; for states that earned a warning it was 35.27; for states that were labeled moderate it was 7.55; and for sustainable states, the average infant mortality rate was just 4.23. According to these results, higher quality states—those considered in the top two categories—performed much better than those in the bottom two categories. But as stark as the differences may be between the top and bottom two categories, the differences within the top and bottom categories are also noteworthy, that is, between states rated "moderate" and "sustainable," and between states given a "warning" and those rated on "alert." Countries with states that were regarded as sustainable had average infant mortality rates that were almost twice as good as those whose states were considered moderate, and the same was true for the two lowest categories: countries with states that drew warnings had average infant mortality rates that were almost twice as good as those that were placed on alert. The quality of the state appears to matter when it comes to meeting people's physical needs. Strong states, which have the capacity to translate demands into effective policies and are not captured by social interests but enjoy some autonomy

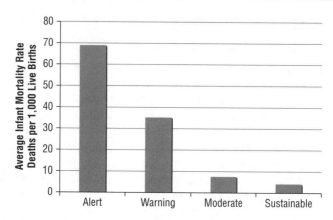

FIGURE 3.1
State Quality and Infant Mortality Rates

Failed State Index 2009

Data Source: The Fund for Peace, http://www.fundforpeace.org/web/index.php?option=com_content&task=view&id=391&Itemid=549

Country Comparison: Infant Mortality Rate Data Source: CIA World Factbook, https://www.cia.gov/library/publications/the-world-factbook/rankorder/2091rank.html

from them, are better able to meet the physical needs of their citizens than weak states.

Informed Decision Making

Good societies also equip their citizens with skills to make informed decisions regarding their lives. Citizens can read and write. When we look at literacy rates in Figure 3.2, we find again that the quality of the state matters. Most countries that scored well on the Failed States Index had high literacy rates, while those countries that were in danger of failing had lower ones. Both sustainable (99 percent) and moderate states (96 percent) on the Failed States Index had very high average literacy rates. But as the quality of the state declines below those rated as moderate, literacy rates drop precipitously. Countries that were issued a warning because their states were regarded as problematic had an average literacy rate of 83 percent, while countries that were placed on alert, the lowest rated group of states in terms of quality, had an average literacy rate of only 61 percent. Strong states better equip citizens with the skills to make informed decisions about their lives.

Safety

A good society is also one in which people are safe from violence. A disproportionate number of those countries listed as on alert for state weakness, such as Somalia, the Sudan, Iraq, Afghanistan, and Sri Lanka among others, have been wracked with civil conflict. Many of these countries have been in the headlines

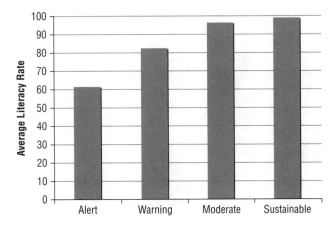

FIGURE 3.2
State Quality and Literacy Rates

Failed State Index 2009
Data Source: The Fund for Peace, http://www.fundforpeace.org/web/index.php?option=com_content&task=view&id=391&Itemid=549
Adult Literacy Rate (% aged 15 and above)
Data Source: Human Development Report 2009, http://hdrstats.undp.org/en/indicators/89.htm

for the number of casualties they have suffered as a result of the wars they have endured. Those countries rated as sustainable have experienced nothing comparable. Their citizens have been safe from political violence. Similarly, as Figure 3.3 reveals, states listed as on alert tended to average higher homicide rates, (14.32 per 100,000 citizens), than those states that earned a warning (12.53); states that were rated as moderate had still lower average homicide rates (3.58); and those countries considered sustainable had the lowest homicide rates of all, just 1.38 murders per 100,000 citizens. Again, the great divide appears to be between the top two categories on the Failed States Index and the bottom two categories. Clearly, countries with strong states are safer than those with weak states.

Democracy

Finally, as Figure 3.4 reveals, the quality of the state also seems to be correlated with the form of government, the extent to which countries have democratic or authoritarian political systems. Every state that was judged sustainable, the best score on the Failed States Index, also received a perfect 10 on the Polity IV Index, indicating they were the most democratic. As one moves down the Failed States Index, Polity IV scores fall, indicating less democracy and more authoritarianism. States judged moderate on the Failed States Index received an average Polity IV score of 6.68; states that received a warning on the state performance index received an average Polity IV score of 3.09;

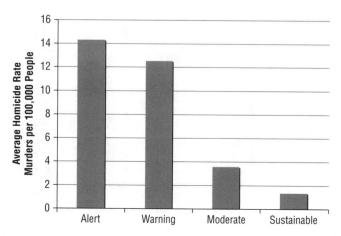

FIGURE 3.3

State Quality and Homicide Rates

Failed State Index 2009

Data Source: The Fund for Peace, http://www.fundforpeace.org/web/index.php?option=com_content&task=view&id=391&Itemid=549

Murder Rates around the World Data Source: Guardian.co.uk, http://www.guardian.co.uk/news/datablog/2009/oct/13/homicide-rates-country-murder-data

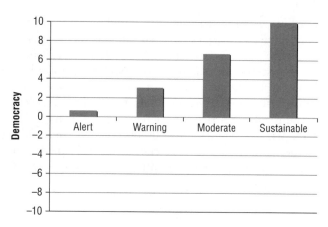

FIGURE 3.4

State Quality and Democracy

Data Source: The Fund for Peace,
http://www.fundforpeace.org/web/index.php?option=com_content&task=view&id=391&Itemid=549
Polity IV Country Reports, 2007
Data Source: Polity IV, http://www.systemicpeace.org/polity/polity06.htm

and states that were placed on alert were the most authoritarian, with an average score of .93. Contrary to those who applauded the Italian fascist dictator Benito Mussolini for making the trains run on time, it appears that democracies have a better record in this respect than authoritarian states.

The alleged benefit of authoritarianism, that it is more efficient than democracy, is a myth.

CONCLUSION

States not only differ in their institutional design but in their effectiveness, their ability to actually govern. Some states are able to process demands and implement policies, while others have trouble making their rules stick. Strong states develop linkages to society that can manage the volume of demands that flow through them; in contrast, weak states are overwhelmed by political participation from below. Such linkages that connect society to the state include political parties, interest groups, social movements, and patron–client relations. Citizens engage in these different forms of political participation depending on the resources they have and their opportunities to deploy them. We then found that strong states are more conducive to developing citizens' capabilities than weak states. Infant mortality rates are lower, literacy rates are higher, people are safer, and political systems are more democratic in strong than weak states.

EXERCISES

Apply what you learned in this chapter on MyPoliSciKit (www.mypoliscikit.com).

 ASSESSMENT
Review this chapter using learning objectives, chapter summaries, practice tests, and more.

VIDEO CASE STUDIES
Analyze recent world affairs by watching streaming video from major news providers.

 FLASHCARDS
Learn the key terms in this chapter; you can test yourself by term or definition.

 COMPARATIVE EXERCISES
Compare political ideas, behaviors, institutions, and policies worldwide.

CRITICAL THINKING QUESTIONS

1. Is more political participation by citizens always better? Can there be too much of a good thing when it comes to political participation?
2. Can democracy exist without political parties?
3. What are some of the differences distinguishing political parties, interest groups, social movements, and patron–client relations as forms of political participation? Under what circumstances do people use one as opposed to another form of participation?
4. How would you operationally define strong and weak states?
5. What can be done to improve state quality, to transform failed states into sustainable states?

KEY TERMS

Crisis of
  Governability 56
Political
  Participation 56
Opportunity
  structures 57
Political Parties 59
Party Systems 60
Programmatic
  parties 62

Patronage 62
Interest groups 63
Free rider
  problem 63
Pluralist interest group
  systems 65
Corporatist interest
  groups 65
Social Movements 67

New Social
  Movements 68
Patron–Client
  Relations 69
Norms of
  Reciprocity 69
Clientelism 69
Weak States 70
Strong States 71

SUGGESTED READINGS

Samuel P. Huntington, *Political Order in Changing Societies* (New Haven, CT: Yale University Press, 1968). A classic work in comparative politics that argues the greatest challenge for developing states is developing the institutional capacity to manage increasing rates of participation.

Joel S. Migdal, *Strong States and Weak States* (Princeton, NJ: Princeton University Press, 1988). An examination of why so many states in developing countries have a hard time actually governing, making their laws effective.

Mancur Olson, *The Logic of Collective Action: Public Goods and the Theory of Groups* (Cambridge, MA: Harvard University Press, 1971). The obstacles interest groups face in forming and the strategies they use to overcome them.

Nancy L. Rosenblum, *On the Side of Angels: An Appreciation of Parties and Partisanship* (Princeton, NJ: Princeton University Press, 2008). A spirited defense of political parties and their contributions to democracy.

Charles Tilly and Lesley J. Wood, *Social Movements, 1768–2008* (Boulder, CO.: Paradigm Publishers, 2009). A primer on social movements by Charles Tilly, one of its leading scholars.

NOTES

1. John Womack, Jr., *Zapata and the Mexican Revolution* (New York: Vintage, 1968)
2. Samuel P. Huntington, *Political Order in Changing Societies* (New Haven, CT: Yale University Press, 1968), p. 1.
3. Samuel P. Huntington, *The Third Wave: Democratization in the Late Twentieth Century* (Norman, OK: University of Oklahoma Press, 1991), p. 28.
4. Huntington, *Political Order*, p. 1.
5. James C. Scott, *Weapons of the Weak: Everyday Forms of Peasant Resistance* (New Haven, CT: Yale University Press, 1985).
6. SidneyVerba, Kay Schlozman, and Henry E. Brady, *Voice and Equality: Civic Voluntarism in American Politics* (Cambridge: Harvard University Press, 1995).
7. Mark N. Franklin, *Voter Turnout and the Dynamics of Electoral Competition in Established Democracies since 1945* (New York: Cambridge University Press, 2004).

8. Bruce Cain, Russell Dalton and Susan Scarrow, eds., *Democracy Transformed: Expanding Political Opportunities in Advanced Industrial Democracies* (New York: Oxford University Press, 2003).

9. Peter Evans, "Collective Capabilities, Culture, and Amartya Sen's *Development as Freedom,*" *Studies in Comparative International Development* (Summer 2002), Vol. 37, No. 2, p. 56.

10. Giovanni Carbone, *No Party Democracy: Ugandan Politics in Comparative Perspective* (Boulder, CO.: Lynne Reimer, 2008).

11. Nancy L. Rosenblum, *On the Side of Angels: An Appreciation of Parties and Partisanship* (Princeton, NJ: Princeton University Press, 2008), p. 12 (emphasis in original).

12. Rosenblum, *On the Side of Angels,* p. 272.

13. Maurice Duverger, *Political Parties* (New York: Wiley, 1955).

14. Myron Weiner and Joseph Lapalombara, "The Impact of Parties on Political Development," in *Political Parties and Political Development,* ed. Joseph Lapalombera and Myron Weiner (Princeton, NJ: Princeton University Press, 1996), p. 403.

15. Giovanni Sartori, *Parties and Party Systems: A Framework for Analysis:* (New York: Cambridge University Press, 1976).

16. Scott P. Mainwaring, *Rethinking Party Systems in the Third Wave of Democratization: The Case of Brazil* (Stanford: Stanford University Press, 1999).

17. Mainwaring, *Rethinking Party Systems in the Third Wave of Democratization.*

18. Kurt Weyland, *Democracy without Equity: Failures of Reform in Brazil* (Pittsburgh, PA.: University of Pittsburgh Press, 1996).

19. Philip Keefer, "Programmatic Parties: Where Do They Come From and Do They Matter?" presented at the 2009 American Political Science Association Convention, Philadelphia, Pa.

20. Mancur Olson, *The Logic of Collective Action: Public Goods and the Theory of Groups* (Cambridge, MA: Harvard University Press, 1971).

21. Mark S. Bonchek, "Grassroots in Cyberspace: Using Computer Networks to Facilitate Political Participation," Paper presented at the Midwest Political Science Association, Chicago, IL, (April 1995), p. 1.

22. Theda Skocpol, *Diminished Democracy: From Membership to Management in American Civic Life* (Norman, OK.: University of Oklahoma Press, 2003).

23. Rita Ardetti, *Searching for Life: The Grandmothers of the Plaza de Mayo and the Disappeared Children of Argentina* (Berkeley, CA: University of California Press, 1999).

24. William A. Gamson, *The Strategy of Social Protest* (Homewood, IL: Dorsey Press, 1975).

25. Charles Tilly and Lesley J. Wood, *Social Movements, 1768–2008* (Boulder, CO.: Paradigm Publishers, 2009).

26. Alan Berlow, *Dead Season: A Story of Murder and Revenge* (New York: Vintage, 1996), p. 81.

27. Quoted in Richard Gunther and Larry Diamond, "Types and Functions of Parties," in *Political Parties and Democracy,* ed. Larry Diamond and Richard Gunther (Baltimore, MD: Johns Hopkins Press, 2001), pp. 14–15.

28. Quoted in Susan C. Stokes, "Political Clientelism," in *The Oxford Handbook of Comparative Politics,* ed. Carles Boix and Susan C. Stokes, (New York: Oxford University Press, 2007), pp. 609–610.

29. Stokes, "Political Clientelism," p. 613.

30. Patrick Heller, *The Labor of Development* (Ithaca, NY: Cornell University Press, 1999), p. 28. The examples are from Francis Fukuyama, *State Building* (Ithaca: Cornell University Press, 2004), p. x.

31. See Gary King and Langche Zeng, "Improving Forecasts of State Failure," *World Politics* (July 2001), pp. 623–658, for further support of the close fit between state quality and infant mortality rates.

32. Robert D. Putnam with Robert Leonardi and Raffaella Y. Nanetti, *Making Democracy Work: Civic Traditions in Modern Italy* (Princeton, NJ: Princeton University Press, 1993).

Political Culture

INTRODUCTION

In November 2009, several armored police cars appeared at the headquarters of the Iraqi Soccer Association in Baghdad. No one at the Association had called for the police or expected their arrival. Uniformed men jumped out, quickly seized control of the building, and set up machine gun positions. The Soccer Association had just become a hostage in the continuing struggle between Sunni and Shia Muslims to control Iraq.[1]

During Saddam Hussein's dictatorship from 1979 to 2003 Sunni Muslims, who are the minority Muslim sect in Iraq, controlled the state. After the United States toppled Saddam, Shia Muslims won parliamentary elections held in 2005 and formed a government. But public institutions, including the Soccer Association, remained under Sunni control. The Sunni directors of the Association were quite successful in improving the quality of soccer in Iraq. The Iraqi team won the Asian Soccer Cup in 2007, and the Association hosted an international meet in 2009. These accomplishments were not enough to guarantee the directors' jobs. The Shia- dominated Iraqi Olympic Committee accused them of mismanagement and asked them to step down. When they refused, the Olympic Committee sent in the police.

The soccer struggle provides a window into the ways in which religious identity and political culture create obstacles to the creation of a democratic Iraq. Saddam's government killed many Shia political leaders during the years it was in power. When he was removed from power, Shia saw an opportunity to retaliate. Battles between Shia and Sunni militias killed thousands of citizens between 2003 and 2007. Although the number of killings has declined considerably since 2007, the struggle between Sunni and Shia to control the state continues. Intimidation, threats of violence, and assassinations are used by both sides in a deadly game of winner takes all.

Deep distrust among politicians makes compromise and cooperation difficult. Some Iraqis refer to their political culture as a "culture of *kundara*," the Iraqi word for shoe. One Iraqi explained the meaning of kundara: "When anyone is against you, when anyone has differences with me, I will put a *kundara* in his mouth, I will shove a *kundara* down his throat, I will hit him with a *kundara*."[2]

There are some indications that Iraqi political culture has begun to change. The March 2010 parliamentary election was one of the freest in Iraq's history. Sunni citizens participated in the election instead of boycotting it as they did in 2005. The political party that won the most parliamentary seats appealed to both Sunni and Shia voters. But there is still considerable uncertainty as to whether Iraqi political culture can support democratic institutions.

Iraq's difficulties raise the question what kind of political culture is needed to support democracy? Can countries divided by ethnicity and religion avoid conflicts that threaten to turn into civil wars? Can politicians promote cooperation among diverse ethnic and religious groups that improves capabilities for everyone, and not just those from their own ethnic or religious background? These are the questions this chapter addresses.

In Chapter 2 we examined important state institutions: the legislature, the core executive, the bureaucracy, the military, and the judiciary. In Chapter 3 we examined the institutions that connect the state and society: political parties, interest groups, social movements and patron–client relations. In this chapter we turn to the differing beliefs, norms, and values that help explain why people behave as they do. These beliefs, norms, and values can differ dramatically from one society to another, as well as within societies. This chapter is about these differences; how they help us understand why political institutions work differently in different societies, and the consequences they have for people's capabilities.[3]

The chapter is divided into four sections. The first defines culture and political culture and cautions about traps to avoid in studying them. The second looks at the kind of political culture needed to sustain stable and effective democracy, and the aspects of political culture that either facilitate or frustrate civic cooperation. The third explores how ethnic, national, and religious identities can divide countries, to the detriment of political stability and intergroup cooperation. The final section of the chapter assesses how political culture and identity affect citizens' capabilities.

CULTURE AND POLITICAL CULTURE

Culture can be defined as a society's widely shared values, beliefs, norms, and orientations toward the world. It provides individuals with a sense of who they are, "what is the good life, what is possible, what is just, who counts, and who doesn't."[4] Culture gives us a road map that instructs us how to interact with others. These maps can differ significantly from society to society, as students who participate in their school's study abroad programs quickly discover. One of the greatest rewards of living in another country is learning to use its cultural road map. For example, students studying in Thailand are told never to point the sole of their shoe toward another person, as this is considered a supreme insult in Thai culture. At first students have to remind themselves continually not to do this, but eventually the behavior becomes automatic. It becomes analogous to driving along a familiar street at home. For most students and political scientists learning about another society's culture is a reward in itself. But political scientists have an additional goal. They want to understand how culture and political culture affect political behavior and institutions.

Political culture is a narrower concept than culture. It is a society's shared values, beliefs, and norms, and orientations toward politics. A society's political culture shapes how people think about their country's political system as a whole, its decision-making process, and their own role in that process. It determines whether citizens feel proud or ashamed, hopeful or cynical, loyal or rebellious, and powerful or impotent.

Before turning to examine the specific ways political scientists use culture and political culture, it is useful to keep in mind that cultural analysis is full of traps that should be avoided. First, we should rely on evidence about what people actually believe rather falling back on stereotypes. One common stereotype is that Muslims in the Middle East are hostile to democracy. Careful surveys of people's attitudes in five Muslim countries in 1995–1996 and 2000–2002 found that they are not.[5] Second, we must bear in mind that people are not cultural robots. Culture does not completely determine how they think and behave. Individuals can step outside accepted cultural norms and imagine different ways of thinking. Third, we should be careful about making sweeping statements such as "Muslims believe," or "Chinese believe." There are well over a billion Muslims and a billion Chinese in the world. They disagree among themselves about what it means to be Muslim or to be Chinese. Finally, culture and political culture are never the sole factor explaining differences in politics and capabilities among countries. Factors such as the countries' level of economic development, distribution of power in society, the kind of institutions that prevail, and the quality of leadership also matter.

THREE APPROACHES TO THE STUDY OF CULTURE AND POLITICAL CULTURE

In this section, we examine three ways of using culture and political culture to explain political similarities and differences among countries: the social character, congruence, and social capital approaches.

The Social Character Approach

The **social character approach** begins with the assumption that culture "is crucial in understanding how societies and political systems function and how and why they differ from one another."[6] Deeply held cultural beliefs shape the way people see the world and how they behave. These ideas and values often originate in religious traditions, but become embedded in institutions and therefore persist long into the future.[7]

The social character approach proposes to explain political differences between countries. The political scientist Seymour Martin Lipset uses it to explain why the United States adopted a presidential form of democracy and an aversion to state intervention in the economy and society, while Canada adopted a parliamentary form of democracy combined with greater acceptance of state intervention. According to Lipset, the differences stem from "the two countries' values and the ways they affect behavior, beliefs, and institutional arrangements."[8] The American Revolution, in his view, was the historical turning point that set them on their differing paths. American political elites held revolutionary beliefs and were willing to fight to free themselves from British control, while Canadian elites chose to remain part of the British Empire. These differences were sharpened as British loyalists in the United States emigrated to Canada in order to live under a government whose beliefs matched their own.

For the American revolutionaries "the objectives of the good society" were "life, liberty, and the pursuit of happiness." They believed these objectives would be threatened by a strong state. Their views were reinforced by a religious tradition characterized by the separation of church and state and the existence of voluntary association among believers. In contrast, Canadian leaders defined the good society in terms of "peace, order, and good govern-ment."[9] They believed a strong state was needed to guarantee peace and order. Their political values were reinforced by a hierarchical religious tradition with close links between church and state.

The values of Americans and Canadians found institutional expression in different forms of government. The American Constitution reflected the Founders' skepticism regarding the state. They devised a complex system of checks and balances intended to make it difficult to legislate and to use the state to solve social problems. In contrast, Canadians, being more sympathetic to the state, chose a parliamentary form of government that permitted leaders to appropriate the state's powers more easily. Prime ministers and their cabi-nets had relatively unchecked power and did not have to worry so much about legislative support or judicial approval.[10]

A big strength of the social character approach is its ability to provide a rich sense of countries' cultural nuances and how people think about politics. It draws upon a wide range of evidence—historical and religious documents, histories, public opinion surveys, novels, and popular culture—to understand how values and beliefs fit together to form coherent patterns of meaning that bind people together. However, the approach has its limitations. First, it requires researchers to have considerable knowledge of the culture of the countries they are comparing. A second limitation is that it can be used effec-tively only when countries are very similar to each other. Ideally, they should differ only on the dependent variable one wants to explain and the independ-ent variable that allegedly causes the differences in the dependent variable. Canada and the United States come close to meeting this requirement. Both are large, affluent, democratic countries that were former British colonies. They differ in regard to political institutions, Lipset's dependent variable, and in political culture, his independent variable. Lipset makes the case that the difference in political culture accounts for the difference in the forms of democracy they chose. The problem is few countries match up so well. As a result, the social character approach does not lend itself to comparison of large numbers of countries. If we want to make such generalizations, we have to proceed differently.

The Congruence Approach

One of the possible candidates is the **congruence approach**. Its basic claim is that a lack of congruence, or match, between a country's political culture and its institutions is likely to create political instability. That is, for the sake of sta-bility democratic political institutions require a democratic political culture, while authoritarian political institutions require an authoritarian political cul-ture.[11] According to this approach the Nazis were able to take power in Germany in 1933 mainly because of the mismatch between the Weimar Republic's democratic institutions and widespread authoritarian attitudes within the German public. As one author put it, "democracy failed in Weimar Germany because it was 'a democracy without democrats.'"[12]

Most scholars who use the congruence approach have focused on two big questions: what kind of political culture is necessary to maintain stable and effective democracies, and how does this kind of political culture emerge? To answer these questions, political scientists rely on carefully structured interviews with representative samples of each country's population to discover what they believe about politics. Gabriel Almond and Sidney Verba's *The Civic Culture,* published in 1963, was the pioneering study using this approach. The researchers surveyed citizens' political attitudes in five democracies: Britain, the United States, Germany, Italy, and Mexico. They concluded that the political cultures of the United States and Britain came closest to approximating the kind of "civic culture" they believed was most suited for stable, effective democracy. Interestingly, Almond and Verba's civic culture did not exhibit the characteristics extolled in civics textbooks of the era. According to the latter, the democratic ideal was one in which every citizen is politically well informed and actively involved. Almond and Verba found that this pattern did not hold true, even in the most developed democracies. Many citizens were "**participants**" who voted, paid attention to politics, and were aware of how politics affected their lives. Typically, however, they read about politics and voted at election time, but did little beyond this. Most participants were not active in politics as family, friends, work, and social activities occupied most of their time and thought. Other citizens in these democracies were "**subjects**" who paid little attention to politics, obeyed laws, and were not politically active. A small number were "**parochials**" who had little or no knowledge of politics, no interest in participating, and were often ignorant of the ways in which politics affected their lives. Almond and Verba concluded that the civic culture with its mix of participants, subjects, and parochials was actually preferable to the ideal political culture of the civics textbooks. The mix of citizens helped maintain a balance between keeping a government responsive to citizens while allowing it to govern without undue disruption.[13]

Recent research suggests the kind of political culture Almond and Powell thought necessary for preserving democracy may not be helpful in creating it or making it effective. Drawing on a much larger base of evidence from data gathered by the World Values Survey over nearly 30 years, Ronald Inglehart and Christian Welzel argue that an activist political culture is necessary to make and maintain effective democracies. In their view, a vigorous democracy requires the development of certain **self-expression values**: valuing freedom of speech, tolerance toward people with different lifestyles, a willingness to voice one's opinion and challenge authorities, and a belief that others can be trusted. These values matter because they ensure citizens' right to speak out even when they say things that are deeply offensive to others' fondest beliefs. They also provide the motivation for citizens to challenge authoritarian regimes by signing petitions, demonstrating, and joining protest movements. Such actions have led to the collapse of authoritarian regimes in many countries in recent decades, including South Korea, the Philippines, and Poland. Finally, self-expression values continue to be important after democracy is achieved by making leaders responsive to public demands. Inglehart and Welzel find a strong correlation between the strength of self-expression values and the level of effective democracy.[14]

At the personal level, according to Inglehart and Welzel, the rise of self-expression values does not bring greater selfishness. Instead, it appears to "widen the circle of others with whom people build up solidarities." The finding is surprising because so many people equate individualism with selfishness. The researchers argue that "individualism does not necessarily destroy solidarity, but leads to a different kind of solidarity.[15] Self-expression values create bridging rather than bonding behavior. **Bonding behavior** occurs when people identify with their in-group based on ethnicity, race, language, or religion and discriminate against outsiders. They belong to a collective. A familiar example of bonding behavior occurs among students during sporting events with a school that is their arch rival. This is epitomized in the title of a recent book about the Duke–North Carolina basketball rivalry, *To Hate Like This Is to Be Happy Forever*.[16] In contrast, **bridging behavior** is based on mutually agreed interests and empathy for others. It requires seeing others as individuals who make choices, not as a community of people who are like others in an in-group.

The congruence approach to political culture differs considerably from the social character approach. The social character approach sets out to *discover* a society's political culture and how its elements fit together to affect political institutions and processes. It attempts to understand a country's political culture as the citizens of the country understand it. In contrast, the congruence approach *constructs* political culture from answers to survey questions about what people believe and value. Scholars can use these answers to construct a profile of an individual country's political culture, to track changes in values and opinions over time, or to test hypotheses using dozens of countries. This approach has two main strengths. It is based on empirical data about what individuals say they believe rather than inferring what people believe from historical studies, reports of country experts, novels, or journalistic accounts. Moreover, the approach has contributed to our understanding of the kinds of beliefs needed to help create and sustain a stable, effective democracy. But the congruence approach does not directly address what has become one of the central issues in political science; namely, why individuals often fail to cooperate to achieve goals that almost all of them agree are desirable.

The Social Capital Approach

The **social capital approach** takes up this challenge. It seeks to explain why people manage to collaborate to attain shared goals in some societies, but find it extraordinarily difficult to do so in others. **Social capital** is the "ability of members of a group to collaborate for shared interests." It is based on "trust among people in a society and their ability to work together for common purposes."[17] "At heart, social capital is a simple concept—that is, relationships matter."[18] Friendship, for example, is an example of one of the most important relationships people have. But relationships can extend beyond friendships to large numbers of people who do not know each other. Trust enables large numbers of people to cooperate to achieve goals that no individual could achieve alone.

Greg Mortenson's best-selling book *Three Cups of Tea* describes the author's promise to build an elementary school in a remote area of Pakistan in return for the villagers' kindness in nursing him back to health after a failed mountain-climbing attempt. He eventually fulfilled his promise not only in this one village, but in dozens of others as well. The schools enabled children to become literate and numerate and go on to higher education. One girl who followed this path sought to become the director of a hospital that would serve the entire region, a goal that would have been unthinkable for her earlier. The schools that helped her and other rural Pakistani children achieve their potential required the cooperation of thousands of people in Pakistan and the United States, who contributed labor, money, or skills to the effort. Much of the book is devoted to explaining how Mortenson was able to motivate and mobilize them to act.

Lack of cooperation, on the other hand, can prevent people from reaching their goals even when everyone agrees on their desirability. In Russia, for example, tax collection agencies are notoriously corrupt. As much as the average Russian may want to end this corruption, doing so is difficult. Most Russian citizens refuse to pay taxes because they think their tax money will go into officials' pockets instead of toward desirable goals such as building schools to educate their children and clinics to keep them healthy. They also refuse to pay taxes because they know most of their fellow citizens are not following suit. Why should they pay if no one else is? The same logic works for tax collection officials. Many might prefer to be honest, but they don't want to be suckers, giving up the extra income that their corrupt counterparts would continue to collect. The result is a stalemate in which Russian citizens continue to refuse to pay taxes and officials continue to be corrupt.[19] As a consequence, only 26 percent of the taxes citizens are supposed to pay is collected. The Russian tax collection problem is an example of a **social dilemma**, a situation in which "even if everyone realizes that cooperation would be beneficial for all, it will only come about if the agents trust that (almost all) others are going to cooperate."[20]

In Sweden, by contrast, 98 percent of the taxes people are supposed to pay actually gets paid. Unlike Russians, Swedes believe other citizens are paying their taxes. They also believe government officials will use their tax money for public purposes and not steal it. These differing perceptions of Russian and Swedish citizens are confirmed by international rankings of public sector corruption. In 2009, Russia was ranked as one of the most corrupt countries in the world, while Sweden was ranked as one of the least corrupt.[21]

The lesson here is that what people do is shaped in part by what they think others are doing. If they think their fellow citizens are cheating, they too are likely to cheat. If they think fellow citizens are honest, they are likely to follow suit. Once these patterns of behavior become established it is very difficult to change them. As one expert on these problems in Latin America put it, "It's a vicious cycle that is very hard to break. People don't want to pay taxes because they say government doesn't deliver services, but government institutions aren't going to perform any better until they have resources, which they obtain when people pay their taxes."[22]

Achieving important goals requiring the cooperation of large numbers of people over a long period of time requires **generalized trust** in a society. Generalized trust is the belief that most people can be trusted, not just one's family members or close friends. It is the most essential element of social capital. It is also an essential part of a democratic political culture because "it clearly indicates an inclusive and tolerant approach to the population at large."[23] Generalized trust is based on the norm of **generalized reciprocity**, or the norm that if one does something for others, they will reciprocate sometime in the future. This is different from an immediate exchange of favors based on the premise, "I'll do this for you now, if you do that for me now."[24] Generalized reciprocity in a society creates large amounts of social capital. This makes it possible for individuals to cooperate to achieve goals that no individual working alone could attain. It also enables them to achieve their goals much more efficiently. Someone who wants to buy a book can give his or her credit card number to Amazon.com, trusting that employees will not steal their credit card information and that the book will arrive in a timely manner. The level of trust required to make internet commerce work can be contrasted with the lack of such trust in Nigeria. In the 1990s, hotel clerks there wrote down the serial number of each piece of paper currency handed to them to pay for a hotel room because they trusted no one. They suspected everyone was out to cheat them by giving them counterfeit money.

Generalized trust in a society can affect how institutions perform, but state institutions and policies also shape levels of trust.[25] Democratic state institutions and policies that were established after World War II in Germany helped reshape its political culture from one supportive of authoritarianism to one supportive of democracy. The behavior of judges, police, and other civil servants dealing directly with the public are especially important in affecting levels of cooperation and trust.[26] Where persons in positions of authority ignore ordinary citizens with impunity, and demand bribes to perform public services that should be done as a matter of course, citizens understandably do not trust their government. This was the case for a young mother in India who had just given birth to her first child in a public hospital. The nurse told her she would have to pay the equivalent of a $12 bribe if she wanted to see her baby. This is a small amount in the United States, but it was a considerable amount for the new mother's family, whose husband earned less than a dollar a day. The woman finally got to see her baby after her mother-in-law promised to pawn a gold earring to pay the bribe. Not surprisingly, many poor people in India do not go to public hospitals to have babies delivered.[27] They prefer to have the least possible contact with government officials. They do not trust officials for good reasons and have low expectations for them.

Recent studies have looked at how the internet and social networking sites such as Facebook and YouTube impact social capital. Some scholars argue that they weaken social capital because individuals spend increasing amounts of time online and have fewer face-to-face contacts. People also spend less time as members of voluntary organizations that in the past were the main institutional bases of social capital. One study found, however, that Facebook helped young people maintain relationships as they moved from high school to college, from college into the working world, and from one area of the country to another. Social networking sites also helped them create new relationships and provided them with the opportunity to join thousands of different online groups.[28]

We have focused on the benefits of social capital and the benefits of bridging behavior in the example of using cooperation and trust to build schools for Pakistani children. Cooperation and trust in the form of bonding behavior can be used for destructive purposes. For example, the solidarity created in high school cliques empowers members to bully and humiliate students who are not part of the group. On a larger scale, organized crime syndicates in Japan and China build cooperation and trust among their members in order to prey on other citizens. And at a political level the Nazis used networks of sympathetic organizations to orchestrate their rise to power in 1933.

IN BRIEF

Social Character, Congruence, and Social Capital Approaches

Social Character
- Societies have prevailing cultural beliefs and values that give them a distinctive character.
- Societies' cultural beliefs and values shape behavior, beliefs, and institutional arrangements.

Congruence Approach
- A lack of congruence between a country's political culture and its institutions is likely to create political instability in the country.
- There is a strong correlation between the strength of self-expression values in a country and the level of effective democracy in the country.

Social Capital Approach
- It seeks to explain how large numbers of people manage to collaborate to achieve desired goals, and why people often find it difficult to do so.
- Achieving desired goals requiring the cooperation of large numbers of people requires generalized trust based on the norm of generalized reciprocity.

POLITICS OF IDENTITY

We have discussed culture and political culture so far without examining the ways in which people living in the same country can have very different ways of distinguishing between "we" and "they." The same person can identify herself as daughter, friend, college sophomore, tennis player, Catholic, Italian-American, and Republican. The relative importance of these various identities differs from culture to culture. In some countries one's family identity looms largest and citizens introduce themselves by telling people who their relatives are. In other countries, occupation looms much larger in defining one's identity, and when making introductions people typically mention what they do for a living.

Three identities play especially important roles in politics: ethnicity, nationality, and religion. All tend to run deep because they provide people with a sense of place and meaning, and a feeling of being part of a larger "we" that distinguishes them from "others." These identities often drive political competition as groups vie for recognition and government resources. Sometimes they even lead to violent conflict. In the 1990s, many political scientists believed that ethnic, national, and religious ties would fade in importance as countries modernized economically and socially. They assumed that as countries became more economically developed people would increasingly focus on their own self-interest and would shift their allegiance to voluntary associations. However, their expectations have not been borne out. Ethnic, national, and religious identities remain extremely important in many countries.

Ethnicity

Ethnic identity is a sense of collective belonging that can "be based on common descent, language, history, culture, race, or religion."[29] Examples of ethnic groups in the United States include Irish-Americans, Chinese-Americans, Mexican-Americans, and Native-Americans. Very few countries are ethnically homogenous. Most have some degree of ethnic diversity and some countries contain dozens of ethnic groups. Ethnic identity is first and foremost a social identity, rather than a political reality. People can take pride in their ethnic background and celebrate ethnic customs and holidays without linking their ethnicity to politics.

▶ IN BRIEF

Ethnicity and Race

Individuals are usually assigned to racial categories on the basis of "observable physical characteristics that do not change over a lifetime," such as skin color, hair type, and facial features. By contrast, ethnic identity is usually based on linguistic

Continued

and cultural practices that can change. These definitions are not very precise and sometimes have been used arbitrarily to assign individuals to racial and ethnic groups. People with power get to make the assignments. For example, in the American South of the 1930s a person was "black" if any ancestor was black. Everyone was said to be either black or white, and there was no category of "mixed race," as there is in Brazil, which allows for many racial gradations.

Elsewhere, however, ethnicity has become linked to politics. This is the case in advanced democracies as well as in less developed countries around the world. Three trends account for the political importance of ethnicity in advanced democracies. First is increasing ethnic diversity. In the United States, Hispanics have attracted most of the attention, but the numbers of other ethnic groups have also increased, whether as a result of immigration or high birth rates. In Europe, the growth of Arab Muslim populations has been at the center of controversy, particularly in France. The second trend is the politicization of ethnic and cultural differences and the rise of identity politics, as ethnic groups demand recognition and government policies that respond to their needs. The final trend is the adoption of multicultural policies to accommodate these demands. The policies include changes in school curriculums, exemptions from dress codes, public funding of ethnic organizations, and affirmative action for immigrant groups.

Multicultural policies have set off an intense debate in a number of countries. In the United States and France many citizens, and some scholars, believe that multicultural policies have gone too far. In their view, increasing ethnic diversity and policies to accommodate ethnic minorities threaten the shared beliefs and values that make countries unique and hold them together.[30] Other countries, such as Australia and Canada, have chosen to embrace multicultural policies as part of a strategy to reduce inherited stereotypes of minority ethnic groups and increase a sense of inclusiveness for all citizens. In Canada, adoption of multicultural policies has become a matter of national pride and identity. "It has become what it means to be a Canadian distinct from an American." Supporters of Canada's multicultural policies argue that they have not led to a loss of Canadian identity, but rather to a different conception of that identity.[31]

Political struggles based on ethnicity can be pursued in peaceful ways using established institutions, or in violent ways outside the normal political process. In many countries the struggle is pursued in peaceful ways using established political institutions. In other countries, however, competition among ethnic groups for recognition and power leads to violence. This violence takes three main forms. One is **mob violence,** in which people from one ethnic group target people from another in response to a perceived grievance. Mob violence occurs suddenly, and although it can be intense while it lasts, it tends to die down quickly. Typically, it is limited to particular cities or regions rather than engulfing the entire country in violence.

▶ THE GOOD SOCIETY IN DEPTH

Kenya—Ethnic Violence and Capabilities

In ethnically divided societies such as Kenya, a common way of winning elections is to appeal to voters belonging to one's own ethnic group. Politicians promise that if they win, members of their ethnic group will benefit. Once in office the politician can then use the politics of patronage to deliver on that promise with roads, schools, clinics, and other kinds of government spending. In Kenya there are particularly strong incentives for politicians to win office, and to hold it at all costs. Members of parliament receive annual salaries of $145,565, or 187 times the income of average Kenyans. If members of the U.S. Congress were paid 187 times the average American income each would earn $8.5 million per year.

The politics of patronage dates back to the time when Kenya was a British colony. The British drew rigid distinctions between ethnic groups, or what they called "tribes." Prior to the arrival of the British, distinctions between ethnic groups were fuzzy and the boundaries between one group and another were loose. The new, rigid distinctions became the basis for electoral competition after Kenya won its independence in 1963. In the first decades after independence, President Jomo Kenyatta favored his own Kikuyu ethnic group. Kenya's second president, Daniel Arap Moi, funneled government resources toward Kalenjin politicians and their business allies. When a Kikuyu, Mwai Kibaki, was elected president in 2002, it was again the Kikuyus' "turn to eat," or to use the resources of government to benefit themselves.

In the December 2007 presidential election, President Kibaki was challenged by Raila Odinga, a Luo, who was also supported by the Kalenjin ethnic group. Even though Odinga appeared to have won the election, election officials rigged the vote in favor of Kibaki. Angry Luo and Kalenjins rioted, and Kalenjin mobs began killing Kikuyus. In one of the worst incidents dozens of women and children who had taken refuge from mobs in a church were burned alive. Friends turned on friends. Government backed mobs retaliated. The killings finally ended when the leaders of the factions agreed to a coalition government in 2008. While the coalition brought a fragile peace, Kenyan politics still revolves around ethnic competition and patronage. Government resources are targeted to benefit narrow groups of supporters rather than to improve the capabilities of all Kenyans.*

For Further Discussion

1. Why does the politics of ethnic patronage make it very difficult to raise capabilities for broad categories of people?

2. How do the concepts of bonding and bridging behavior help explain ethnic violence in Kenya?

*Jeffrey Gettleman, "East Africa: The Most Corrupt Country," *New York Review of Books* (January 14, 2010), p. 35–38.

The second form that ethnic violence takes is **forcible removal** in which one group drives another out of territory that both claim. In the nineteenth century, for example, Native-Americans were herded into reservations in the western United States. A more recent example is the "ethnic cleansing" that occurred during the 1990s when Serbs drove Bosnian Muslims out of territories claimed by the Serbs, killing many of them in the process. The third and most destructive form of ethnic conflict is **genocide**, when it becomes state policy to kill all members of a particular ethnic group. The worst example of genocide in recent history occurred during World War II, when the Nazis tried to exterminate all European Jews. A more recent example occurred in Rwanda in 1994 when Hutu leaders incited members of their ethnic group to murder an estimated 800,000 Tutsis along with any moderate Hutus who helped them.

COMPARATIVE POLITICAL ANALYSIS

Is Ethnic Diversity the Root Cause of Civil Wars?

Problem

In the last 65 years many more people have died in wars fought inside countries than in wars fought between countries. Civil wars have devastating effects on capabilities. They disrupt health care and agricultural production causing more deaths from disease and famine than from combat. Education suffers as well. There are massive violations of civil and political rights, and mass rape is sometimes used to terrorize local populations. What causes these destructive wars?

Methods and Hypothesis

One popular hypothesis is that ethnic and religious diversity are the root cause of civil wars. James Fearon and David Laitin test this hypothesis as well as the alternative hypothesis that attributes civil war to state weakness. State weakness matters because weak states do not have the administrative, military, and policing abilities to control all areas of a country and suppress rebels.

Operationalizing Concepts

The authors use three concepts to test the competing hypotheses:

1. Civil war is defined as "fighting between agents of state and organized non-state groups who seek to take control of a government, take power in a region, or use violence to change government policies." To count as a civil war, the conflict must result in at least 1,000 deaths with a yearly average death toll of at least 100, and at least 100 must have been killed on each side.
2. Ethnic diversity is defined using an index of ethnic fractionalization based on the probability that two randomly drawn individuals in a country come from different ethnic groups.

3. State weakness is defined using per capita income as the indicator for state weakness. The assumption here is that the poorer the country, the more likely it is to have a weak state.

Results

The authors find no support for the hypothesis that ethnic diversity is the root cause of civil war. There is no consistent relationship between a country's degree of ethnic diversity and the outbreak of civil war, once the level of income is taken into account. More ethnically diverse countries have no greater likelihood of civil war than less diverse countries among countries at the same income level. State weakness turns out to be a better explanation for the outbreak of civil war.

For Further Discussion

1. This Comparative Political Analysis box and the final section of the previous chapter both use "weak states" as a variable, but they use different operational definitions of the concept. Why? Is one preferable to the other?

2. Based on the authors' findings what would be the best way for states to prevent civil wars and the devastating consequences they have for citizens' capabilities?

Source: James D. Fearon and David D. Laitin, "Ethnicity, Insurgency, and Civil War," *American Political Science Review* 97 (2003), 75–86.

Nationalism

Political identity can also take the form of **nationalism,** which is a sense of pride in one's nation and a desire to control a state representing that nation. Unlike ethnicity, nationalism is inherently political. A **nation** is a group of people sharing a common identity that derives from either having a state of their own or desiring one. In Benedict Anderson's famous definition, a nation is "an imagined political community" in which "the members of even the smallest nation will never know most of their fellow-members, meet them, or even hear of them, yet in the minds of each lives the image of their communion."[32] The concept of nationalism emerged in the late eighteenth century and has three main components. First, the members of a nation think of themselves as equals united by their common nationality. Second, they see their nation as one among many in a world divided into sovereign nation-states. Finally, in each nation-state legitimate authority is derived from the people.[33] Nationalism is so emotionally compelling that in the last two centuries millions of people have been willing to fight and die for it. In recent years, universities have appropriated the term as way of encouraging fellow feeling and loyalty among current students and graduates of the university. The University of Florida refers to its students and alumni as the "Gator Nation," using the alligator that is the symbol of the school's athletic teams as the symbol of the "Gator Nation." The University of Georgia uses the concept of "the Bulldog Nation" in the same way. The two schools are fierce rivals in sports, though fortunately no alumni are likely to fight and die for their *alma mater.*

Religion

Religious identity is the third major form of identity that can become politicized. Like ethnic identity, religious identity is not inherently political. One can be a Baptist, Catholic, Muslim, or Hindu without connecting one's religious beliefs to political beliefs or political action. In recent years, however, religious beliefs have become the basis of political conflict and political violence in many countries. In India, for example, Hindus and Muslims have fought over religious difference for decades. In 1992, Hindu extremists destroyed a Muslim mosque in the northern Indian state of Uttar Pradesh provoking Muslim retaliation. The ensuing violence resulted in over 2,000 deaths and the incident remains a source of tensions to this day. Religious violence has also been a major problem in Nigeria, where an estimated 3,000 people have been killed in the last decade in fighting between Christians and Muslims.

Why does violence erupt among ethnic, national, and religious groups? Some analysts believe it is the natural result of conflicts with deep historical roots that go back to "time immemorial." This approach to explaining violence among groups is known as **primordialism**. It assumes that intergroup conflict is inherent in human nature. People need enemies to help define who "we" are and who "they" are. Once groups are defined in this way, conflict between them becomes inevitable. The best known proponent of this perspective is the Harvard political scientist Samuel Huntington, who argued in his 1997 book, *The Clash of Civilizations,* that "[i]t is human to hate. For self-definition and motivation people need enemies. . . . They naturally distrust and see as threats those who are different and have the capability to harm them."[34] However, this approach has trouble explaining why Hindus and Muslims in India, Hutus and Tutsis in Rwanda, and Christians and Muslims in Nigeria were able to live alongside each other peacefully for decades before the violence began. Primordial explanations of ethnic conflict also have difficulty explaining why violent conflict breaks out in certain regions or cities in a country and not others.

A second attempt to explain why conflict arises is **instrumentalism**. Its proponents hypothesize that violence is provoked by political leaders who manipulate symbols and beliefs to set groups against each other for political benefit. This argument has been used to explain the attack on the Muslim mosque in India by Hindu extremists in 1992. The attack was provoked by leaders of the BJP, a Hindu nationalist party, to increase their electoral support. The destruction of the mosque, and the violence between Hindus and Muslims that followed, enabled party leaders to portray violent Muslims as a threat to Hindu values. The provocation worked. The party's political support among Hindus increased dramatically in the aftermath of the violence. As a Hindu priest who deplored the destruction of the mosque put it: 'Those Hindu activists did all this for political gains. We had no hassles with our Muslim brothers."[35] It is important to note, however, that there are limits to instrumental explanations of violence. Political leaders cannot manipulate people's identities in any way they desire at any time. Nor can they construct entirely new identities to suit their purposes. They must work within the framework of conditions and identities that already exist.

The approach that currently has the most support in explaining how identities are formed and why they sometimes lead to violence is known as **constructivism**. Its proponents assert that identities are not simply given, but are socially constructed. There are different ways of constructing boundaries among ethnic, racial, and religious groups and deciding who counts and who does not. In the United States, white Americans tend to play down ethnic difference among themselves while drawing attention to racial differences between whites and blacks. In France, by contrast, the difference between white French citizens and Muslims Arabs is the major ethnic division in society. The question of who is "not one of us" is "determined by a cultural script, not by some biological fact about blood and genes."[36] Identities do not derive back to time immemorial or remain eternally fixed, as primordialists argue. Instead, they change over time in a continuing process of refinement and redefinition.[37]

Each society tends to have one socially constructed master cleavage, such as that between whites and blacks in the United States or Muslims and Hindus in India. Extremists can use an incident that happens spontaneously, or manufacture one, to start violence. They do so by placing the incident into the larger context of the master cleavage. This is what BJP politicians did when they placed the destruction of the Muslim mosque in 1992, and the violence it provoked, into a larger narrative of conflicts between Hindus and Muslims.[38] The social constructivist approach suggests both that cultures change more than primordialists assume and that cultures are less easily manipulated than instrumentalists believe. While the social constructivist approach does a better job than the other two of explaining identity formation, it too has trouble explaining why ethnic, national, or religious conflict occurs at specific times in specific locations.

POLITICAL CULTURE, IDENTITY, AND THE GOOD SOCIETY

We conclude the chapter with an examination of how political culture and political identity affect citizens' capabilities. For one thing, political culture affects capabilities when it is used to construct ethnic or racial categories that privilege some people and penalize others. For example, an important political cleavage in many Latin American countries is between the descendants of Spaniards and the descendants of indigenous peoples. Spain colonized large parts of Latin America, and Spaniards used indigenous people as forced laborers. Once established, these kinds of categories are difficult to erase. Latin American countries with the highest percentages of indigenous people still tend to be those with the highest levels of inequality in access to health care and education.[39] Ethnic, racial, and religious minorities have less access to those goods in many other regions of the world as well. A recent study found that some 60 million girls do not attend school. Approximately three-fourths of them belong to ethnic, racial, religious, or other minorities. They are concentrated in ethnically and linguistically diverse countries that are particularly prone to deny girls from minority groups an education.[40]

Another way that countries' political culture affects capabilities is associated with levels of generalized trust. Recent research using both the congruence and social capital approaches suggests that citizens living in countries with high levels of generalized trust are more likely to be tolerant toward people different from themselves. They tend to "believe that various groups in society have a shared fate" and that there is a responsibility to provide those with fewer resources an opportunity to develop their capabilities."[41]

The political scientist Peter A. Hall and the sociologist Michèle Lamont suggest a third way in which culture affects capabilities. They argue that some cultural repertoires are richer and better than others at helping people cope with "the wear and tear of daily life." Such wear and tear comes from many sources, including the challenges of making a living, raising a family, and striving to achieve personal goals. When these challenges outstrip people's abilities to deal with them, they often become prone to "intense feelings of anger, anxiety, depression or stress"[42] that increase the likelihood of chronic illnesses, strokes, and heart attacks. Hall and Lamont argue that dense social networks connecting people to each other, and high levels of generalized trust and reciprocity serve as buffers that protect people and improve their health. Hall and Lamont also found that health improves when societies develop shared narratives that extend a citizen's moral community beyond their immediate family, ethnic, or racial group to include "a wide range of people ... deserving of recognition."[43] Leaders can then draw upon this broader moral vision to mobilize people to act together to improve the health of all citizens.

The findings of authors who stress the importance of generalized trust and shared narrative that extend individuals' moral community in improving capabilities give rise to the following hypothesis: the higher the level of generalized social trust in a society, the higher the level of capabilities. We divide this general hypothesis into four specific hypotheses that we test using scatter diagrams instead of bar charts as in the previous chapters. The strength of bar charts is the ability to present a great deal of data in an easily understood manner. A glance at the height of the bars conveys relationships among variables quickly. But this simplicity can also be a weakness. Bar charts do not allow us to compare individual countries and whether or not they fit the relationship a hypothesis predicts, but scatter diagrams do. When countries do not fit the expected pattern we are led to ask why. That question becomes the basis for further research that will help us get a better understanding of the relationships among variables. Neither bar charts nor scatter diagrams offer a better way to test hypotheses across the board. Each has strengths and weaknesses, but knowing how to use both is very useful.

Physical Well-Being

Our first hypothesis is that the higher the level of generalized social trust in a country (independent variable), the lower the rate of infant mortality (dependent variable). We operationally define the level of generalized trust by using data from the 2005–2008 World Values Survey covering 57 countries. In this survey people were asked whether they agreed with the statement that "Most people can be trusted." The responses varied from 74 percent agreement in Norway to only 4.9 percent in Rwanda. Infant mortality rates are the ones from our data set used in previous chapters.

The independent variable, level of generalized trust, is on the horizontal, or "X" axis in the figure. The dependent variable, infant mortality rate, is on the vertical, or "Y" axis of the figure. Each diamond-shaped point in the figure represents a country. For example, in Figure 4.1 the point at the extreme lower right of the figure stands for Norway. Its trust level, on the X axis, is 74, and its infant mortality rate, on the Y axis, is 3.6.

As the scatter diagram shows, there is modest support for the hypothesis. Infant mortality does tend to be lower in countries where there are higher levels of trust. The line in the scatter diagram helps us see this relationship. It is called a regression line and is drawn so that it fits the points in the scatter diagram as closely as possible. In this scatter diagram, it slopes downward from left to right, showing that the higher the value of the independent variable (trust), the lower the value of the dependent variable (infant mortality). Such a pattern is called negative correlation. It is important to keep in mind that negative correlation does not mean there is no relationship between the variables.

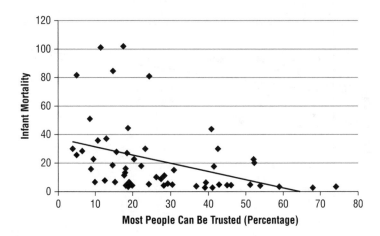

FIGURE 4.1

Generalized Trust and Infant Mortality Rates

Data Source: World Values Survey, 2005–2008
www.worldvaluessurvey.org.
Country Comparison: Infant Mortality Rate
Data Source: CIA World Factbook,
https://www.cia.gov/library/publications/the-world-factbook/rankorder/2091rank.html

Other studies using different sets of countries have found similar results, but not all studies confirm these findings,[44] and the distribution of countries in the figure suggests there are other variables at work, in addition to generalized trust. For example, there are five countries at the top left corner of the figure that stand apart from the other countries with extremely high infant mortality rates of 80 and above. One of the main advantages of using scatter diagrams is they help us to identify **outliers,** or countries that stand far apart from other countries in a scatter diagram. Why are their infant mortality rates so much higher than those of other countries? The outliers encourage thinking about other variables that might affect infant mortality, in addition to generalized trust. The five countries are Zambia, Mali, Rwanda, Burkina Faso, and Ethiopia. They are all very poor African countries. This suggests that another important variable in explaining levels of infant mortality is a country's per capita income.

Informed Decision Making

The literature on social trust suggests that people living in countries with higher levels of generalized trust are more willing to provide all citizens with the opportunities to develop their capabilities. If this is the case, then they should be willing to provide all citizens with the opportunities to become literate. This leads to the hypothesis that the higher the level of generalized trust in a country, the higher the levels of adult literacy. The results of testing this hypothesis can be seen in Figure 4.2.

There is a modest relationship in the expected direction: the higher the level of generalized trust, the higher the literacy rate. Almost all countries

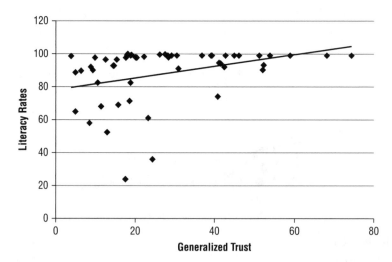

FIGURE 4.2

Generalized Trust and Literacy Rates

Data Source: World Values Survey, 2005-2008.

www.wvsevsdb.com/WVS.AnalizeIndex

The United Nations Human Development Report, 2009. Statistical Index, Table H. Human development index and its components. http://.undp.org/en/reports/global/hdr/2009

where more than 40 percent of the population says other people can be trusted have high levels of literacy. But a number of countries do not fit the expected pattern. There are several countries with low levels of generalized trust that have very high levels of literacy. One of them is Chile, where 96 percent of adults are literate, yet only 13 percent of people say most people can be trusted. There are also countries with very similar levels of trust that vary dramatically in the level of literacy. Two countries are outliers with adult literacy rates below 40 percent. What accounts for these outliers? Identifying them helps suggest an answer. They are Mali and Ethiopia, two of the five outliers we identified in Figure 4.1. They are very poor countries with limited resources to spend on education.

Safety

It seems reasonable to expect that countries with high levels of trust among people will have lower levels of homicides than those with low levels of trust. We can test the validity of this hypothesis by using data on trust from the World Values Survey and operationally defining homicide rates using data on homicides per 100,000 people from the data set for *The Good Society*. The results can be seen in Figure 4.3.

Once again, there is modest support for the hypothesis: the higher the level of trust in a country, the lower the murder rate. But as we have seen in tests of

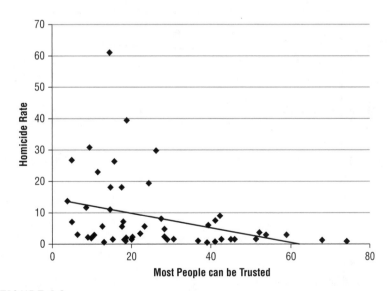

FIGURE 4.3
Generalized Trust and Homicide Rates

Data Sources: World Values Survey, 2005–2008
www.worldvaluessurvey.org.
Murder Rates around the World
United Nations Office on Drugs and Crime http://data.un.org/Data.aspx?d=UNODC&f=tableCode%3a1

the other hypotheses, there are numerous exceptions to this hypothesis. This time we focus on one of the outliers, the country at the top of the scatter diagram with a homicide rate of over 60. It is Colombia. Its exceptionally high level of homicides is explained in large part by conflict between government paramilitary forces and rebels funded by cocaine trade and by ongoing gang warfare to control the trade. Homicide levels in Colombia have declined in recent years.

Democracy

Finally, we test the hypothesis that the higher the level of generalized trust in a country, the higher its level of democracy is likely to be. A country's level of democracy is operationalized using Polity IV data. Twenty is the highest level of democracy and zero is the most extreme level of authoritarianism.[45] The results of the test can be seen in Figure 4.4.

As the scatter diagram demonstrates, there is no relationship between trust and democracy. Countries are randomly distributed around the scatter diagram. Countries with very different levels of trust all receive the highest democracy rating. Norway, in which 74 percent say that most people can

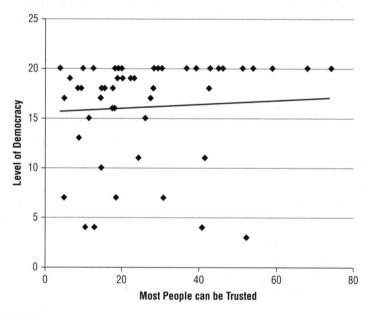

FIGURE 4.4
Generalized Trust and Democracy

Data Sources: World Values Survey, 2005–2008
www.worldvaluessurvey.org.
Polity IV Country Reports, 2007
http://www.systemicpeace.org/polity/polity06.htm

be trusted, has a democracy rating of 20, but so does Cyprus where only 10 percent of the people agree that most other people can be trusted. Countries can achieve high democracy scores without having high levels of generalized trust.

CONCLUSION

We began by noting that cultural analysis is full of traps. They include using stereotypes about what people believe rather than evidence based on careful analysis, assuming that culture is unchanging and monolithic, and imagining that people are not capable of stepping outside accepted modes of thought.

We then discussed three different ways of using culture and political culture in the study of comparative politics: social character, congruence, and social capital approaches. The social character approach assumes that societies have enduring beliefs and values that give them a particular character, and shape their choices about political institutions and appropriate government policies. The congruency approach assumes that long-term political stability requires a good fit between its political culture and its institutions. For supporters of democracy, creating incongruities between political culture and political institutions in authoritarian states is desirable if the results work to provide democracy. Self-expression values contribute to this end. The social capital approach seeks to explain why it is easier for people in some societies to cooperate and organize for collective action. In this view, the reason is that some societies have greater levels of trust among citizens based on norms of generalized reciprocity.

This chapter next focused on three of the most important forms of political identity: ethnicity, nationalism, and religion. In many countries these political identities can be accommodated peacefully. In others, identity politics has led to violence. The three main ways of explaining such violence are primordialism, instrumentalism, and constructivism. Primordial explanations blame the violence on ancient rivalries and hatred. Instrumental explanations assume violence is the result of manipulation by political leaders for political gain. Constructivism argues that conflict results from successful efforts of instigators to link particular incidents or rumors to the country's socially constructed master cleavage.

The final section examines three ways in which political culture might affect capabilities. One is through sustaining categorical differences between groups in society such that some citizens are denied an equal chance to develop their capabilities. A second is the extent to which culture and political culture help people cope with "the wear and tear of daily life." The third is the degree of generalized trust in a society. In general, we found that the higher the level of generalized trust in a society, the higher the level of capabilities. The exception is democracy. There is no correlation between the level of generalized trust and the level of democracy.

EXERCISES

Apply what you learned in this chapter on MyPoliSciKit (www.mypoliscikit.com).

 ASSESSMENT
Review this chapter using learning objectives, chapter summaries, practice tests, and more.

FLASHCARDS
Learn the key terms in this chapter; you can test yourself by term or definition.

 VIDEO CASE STUDIES
Analyze recent world affairs by watching streaming video from major news providers.

COMPARATIVE EXERCISES
Compare political ideas, behaviors, institutions, and policies worldwide.

CRITICAL THINKING QUESTIONS

1. Why do political scientists make a distinction between culture and political culture? Why not simply use culture and dispense with the concept of political culture?
2. Why would the social character approach have difficulty explaining why Mexico and the United States have different political institutions?
3. In *The Civic Culture*, Almond and Verba suggest democratic stability does not require that all citizens be extremely well informed and active in politics. In fact, it is helpful for stability to have a mix of participants, subjects, and parochial. On the other hand, Inglehart and Welzel argue that high levels of self-expression values are essential for healthy democracy. Which set of authors do you believe has a better case and why?
4. What does the social capital approach add to our understanding of politics beyond what the social character and congruence approaches contribute?
5. Why do most political scientists believe primordial and instrumental explanations of ethnic violence are unsatisfactory, and suggest social constructivism as a better explanation?

KEY TERMS

Culture 83
Political culture 83
Social character
 approach 84
Congruence
 approach 85
Participants 86
Subjects 86
Parochials 86
Self-expression
 values 86

Bonding behavior 87
Bridging behavior 87
Social capital
 approach 87
Social capital 87
Social dilemma 88
Generalized trust 89
Generalized
 reciprocity 89
Ethnic identity 91
Multicultural policies 92

Mob violence 92
Forcible removal 94
Genocide 94
Nationalism 95
Nation 95
Religious identity 96
Primordialism 96
Instrumentalism 96
Constructivism 97
Outliers 100

SUGGESTED READINGS

Benedict Anderson, Imagined *Communities: Reflections on the Origins and Spread of Nationalism* (New York: Verso, 1991). A classic exploration of how concepts of nation and nationalism emerged, changed over time, and gained so much emotional attachment that people are willing to die for them.

Peter A. Hall and Michèle Lamont (ed.), *Successful Societies: How Institutions and Culture Affect Health* (New York: Cambridge University Press, 2009). Successful societies are defined as the ones that enhance people's capabilities to lead the kinds of lives they have reason to value. The authors focus on how culture and institutions interact to shape peoples' opportunities to lead healthy lives.

Ronald Inglehart and Christian Welzel, *Modernization, Cultural Change, and Democracy: The Human Development Sequence* (New York: Cambridge University Press, 2005). Argues that social and economic modernization lead to cultural change emphasizing self-expression values and demands for democracy.

Seymour Martin Lipset, *Continental Divide: The Values and Institutions of the United States and Canada* (New York: Routledge, 1990). Use of the comparative method to demonstrate how values contribute to the shaping of political institutions.

Bo Rothstein, "Trust, Social Dilemmas and Collective Action," *Journal of Theoretical Politics* 12:4 (2000), pp. 477–501.

NOTES

1. In Iraq, and everywhere else in the world, what people in the United States call soccer is called football. In the following story the association is referred to as the Iraqi Football Association. "No Promised Land at the End of All This," *The Economist* (March 4, 2010). www.economist.com.

2. Anthony Shadid, "In Iraq, Even a Vote Hints of Violence," *The New York Times*, March 19, 2010.

3. Ronald Inglehart and Christian Welzel, *Modernization, Cultural Change, and Democracy: The Human Development Sequence* (New York: Cambridge University Press, 2005), p. 4.

4. Hazel Rose Markus in *Successful Societies: How Institutions and Culture Affect Health*, ed. Peter A. Hall and Michèle Lamont (New York: Cambridge University Press, 2009).

5. Ronald Inglehart, "The Worldviews of Islamic Republics in Global Perspective," p. 18. www.worldvaluessurvey.org. Accessed September 4, 2009.

6. Howard J. Wiarda, *The Soul of Latin America: The Cultural and Political Tradition* (New Haven, CT: Yale University Press, 2001), p. 3.

7. This summary draws on Wiarda, *The Soul of Latin America*, p. 2.

8. Seymour Martin Lipset, *Continental Divide: The Values and Institutions of the United States and Canada* (New York: Routledge, 1990), p. 17.

9. "The objectives of the good society" is Lipset's phrase. p. xiii.

10. Lipset, *Continental Divide*, p. 21.

11. Inglehart and Welzel, (2005), p. 186.

12. Cited in Christian Welzel and Ronald Inglehart, "Mass Beliefs and Democratic Institutions," in *The Oxford Handbook of Comparative Politics*, ed. Carles Boix and Susan C. Stokes (New York: Oxford University Press, 2009), p. 298.

13. Gabriel Almond and SidneyVerba, *The Civic* Culture: *Political Attitudes and Democracy in Five Nations* (Princeton University Press, 1963), p. 475. p. 475.

14. Inglehart and Welzel (2009), pp. 150–157.

15. Christian Welzel, "Political Culture," in *The Sage Handbook of Comparative Politics*, ed. by Todd Landman and Neil Robinson (Thousand Oaks, CA: Sage Publications, 2009) pp. 308–309.

16. Will Blythe, *To Hate Like This Is to Be Happy Forever: A Thoroughly Obsessive, Intermittently Uplifting, and Occasionally Unbiased Account of the Duke-North Carolina Basketball Rivalry* (New York: Harper Collins Publishers, 2006).

17. Kirk Hamilton, "Where Is the Wealth of Nations? Measuring Capital for the 21st Century," (Washington, D.C.: The World Bank, 2006) p. xvii.

18. Viva Ona Bartkus and James H. Davis, "Introduction: The Yet Undiscovered Value of Social Capital," in *Social Capital: Reaching Out, Reaching In*, ed. Viva Ona Bartkus and James H. (Northhampton, MA: Edward Elgar Publishing 2009), p. 1.

19. Bo Rothstein, "Trust, Social Dilemmas and Collective Memories," *Journal of Theoretical Politics* 12:4 (2000), pp. 477–478.

20. Bo Rothstein and Dietlind Stolle, "The Quality of Government and Social Capital: A Theory of Political Institutions and Generalized Trust," Quality of Government Working Paper Series 2007:2 (March 2005), p. 1. www.qog.pol.gu.se. Accessed November 11, 2009.

21. Bo Rothstein, "Trust, Social Dilemmas, and Collective Memories," *Journal of Theoretical Politics* 12:4 (October 2000), pp. 477–479.

22. Cited in Bo Rothstein, "Trust, Social Dilemmas, and Collective Memories," p. 479.

23. Bo Rothstein and Dietland Stolle, "How Political Institutions Create and Destroy Social Capital: An Institutional Theory of Generalized Trust." Paper prepared for the 98th meeting of the American Political Science Association, August 29 to September 2, 2002, p. 2.

24. Robert Putnam, *Making Democracy Work* (Princeton, NJ: Princeton University Press, 2003), p. 182.

25. Bo Rothstein, "Trust, Social Dilemmas and Collective Action," p. 491.

26. Rothstein and Stolle (2007).

27. Soren Holmberg and Bo Rothstein, "Dying of Corruption," Quality of Government Institute Working Paper Series 2009:16, University of Gothenburg, Sweden, 2009, p. 3. www.qog.pol.gu.se. Accessed June 23, 2010.

28. Nicole Ellison, Charles Steinfield, Cliff Lampe, "The Benefits of Facebook 'Friends': Social Capital and Sudents' Use of Online Social Network Sites," Journal of Computer-Mediated Communication, 12:4 (July 2007), 1143–1168.

29. Ashutosh Varshney, "Ethnicity and Ethnic Conflict," in *The Oxford Handbook of Comparative Politics*, p. 277.

30. Will Kymlicka, "The Multicultural Welfare State," in *Successful Societies: How Institutions and Culture Affect Health*, pp. 226–229.

31. Ibid., pp. 250–251.

32. Benedict Anderson, *Imagined Communities: Reflections on the Origins and Spread of Nationalism* (New York and London: Verso, 1991), p. 6.

33. Liah Greenfeld and Jonathan Eastwood, "National Identity," *The Oxford Handbook of Comparative Politics*, pp. 258–261.

34. Samuel P. Huntington, *The Clash of Civilizations and the Re-Making of World Order* (New York: Touchstone, 1997), p. 130.

35. "The mosque at Ayuthaya: A destructive legacy," *The Economist* (November 26, 2009). www.economist.com.

36. Kymlicka, "The Multicultural Welfare State," p. 245.
37. Liah Greenfeld and Jonathan Eastwood, "National Identity," in *The Oxford Handbook of Comparative Politics*, p. 257.
38. Varshney, "Ethnicity and Ethnic Conflict," p. 287.
39. Patrick Heller and James Mahoney, "The Resilience and Transformation of Persistent Inequality in Latin America." Report Submitted for the World Bank Report on Inequality in Latin America, May 2003, pp. 23–25.
40. Maureeen Lewis and Marlaine Lockhart, "Inexcusable absence: Why 60 Million Girls Still Aren't in School and What to Do about It," Center for Global Development, March 2007, p. 1. www.cgdev.org. Accessed August 31, 2009.
41. Bo Rothstein and Eric M. Uslaner, "All for All: Equality, Corruption, and Social Trust," *World Politics* 58:1(2005), p. 42.
42. Michèle Lamont, "What Makes a Society Successful?" *Perspectives on Europe* 40:1 (Spring 2010), p. 14.
43. Peter A. Hall and Michèle Lamont, "The wear and tear of our daily lives," *The Globe and Mail*, November 13, 2009. See also Peter A. Hall and Michèle Lamont, "Introduction," *Successful Societies: How Institutions and Culture Affect Health* ed. by Peter A. Hall and Michèle Lamont (New York: Cambridge University Press, 2009), pp. 1–22.
44. M. Kamrul Islam, Juan Merlo, Ichiro Kawachi, Martin Lindstrom, and Ulf-G. Gerdtham, "Social Capital and Health: Does Egalitarianism Matter? A Literature Review," *International Journal for Equity in Health* 5:3 (2006).
45. Polity IV ranks countries from 10 (most democratic) to – 10 (most authoritarian). We have added ten points to each country's Polity IV score so that the scores are all positive to make the scatter diagram easier to interpret.

Political Economy

INTRODUCTION

The good society depends upon institutional arrangements that enhance people's capabilities. In Chapter 3, we saw that people who live in strong states that are able to translate demands from below into effective policies enjoyed more life chances than those who lived in weak states that could not produce order or deliver on their policy commitments. In Chapter 4 we observed that some cultures, such as those that promoted generalized trust, led to better results than those in which people were suspicious and felt no sense of obligation to each other. In this chapter we consider the proper sphere or range of state activity. Take the case, for example, of the former Soviet Union, which demonstrated the perils of too much state intervention. State control of the economy, the media, the arts, and civic life in the Soviet Union came at the expense of freedom, initiative, prosperity, and justice. The planned economy led to economic ruin, state censorship led to uninspiring art, political control of the media led to disinformation, Communist Party domination led to bureaucratic inertia, and state control of civic associations led to a spiritless public life.

If the Soviet Union was a cautionary tale about the evils of too much state intervention, then post-Communist Russia is a moral tale about the perils of too little. People now live in fear of thugs and racketeers because the state is unable to protect them, much as they had previously lived in fear of the secret police under communism. Prosperity and initiative are no longer foreclosed by a command economy run by the state but are now beyond reach because the state has difficulty upholding contracts, preventing fraud and extortion by criminal syndicates, or creating a stable, predictable environment for production and exchange. Court decisions that are now for sale are as arbitrary and unfair a way of dispensing justice as when the state told judges how to decide cases. Bribes are now as effective as Communist Party orders had once been in motivating state officials. Thus, Russia's second marriage, in which it suffers at the hands of a negligent and unfaithful state, is no better than its first, when Russia suffered at the hands of a domineering and abusive one.[1]

How much state activity is enough, we might ask, to produce the good society? This question applies most with regard to the role of the state in the economy. "Fundamentally," the economist Milton Friedman writes, "there are only two ways to coordinate the economic activities of millions. One is central planning by the government; the other depends on the voluntary cooperation of individuals—the technique of the marketplace."[2] According to the economist Joseph E. Stiglitz, the struggle between these two alternatives is the defining political question of our age. Stiglitz points out that "[t]he battle of ideas between those who advocate a minimalist role for the state and those who believe that there is a greater need for government . . . is being fought in country after country, in the developing world no less than in the developed, [and] on both sides of the Atlantic and Pacific."[3] What balance between states and markets most enhances people's capability and contributes to the good society? Under communism, as we just saw, citizens in the former Soviet Union suffered from too much state power and not enough markets. Since the fall of communism, Russian citizens have suffered from the opposite disorder, too much market and not enough state control.

According to the political economist Charles Lindblom, markets have always been with us, but market *systems* have not. Records of people, cities, and states engaging in exchange go back to antiquity. But most premodern economic activity was not organized for the market. Households were self-sufficient, producing for their own use, and they infrequently engaged in exchange with others. Today, by contrast, almost all countries use market systems to organize and coordinate production. The term **market system** refers to an economy in which production for profit is intended for and coordinated through private exchanges between buyers and sellers.

European states were intent on shifting from household production to production for the market because the latter was more efficient and would produce more taxable wealth. But the change was fraught with conflict, as peasants at home and natives in the colonies resisted producing for the market. They saw market production as a threat to their welfare because it exposed them to more risk and uncertainty than subsistence production. States interested in increasing their revenue brought their subjects who were interested in defending their security into the market system at the point of a gun.[4]

Since then, the market system has become more extensive in terms of its global reach. Today, countries are engaged in more trade with each other than ever before. Exports and imports make up a larger proportion of their gross national product than in the past. Foreign direct investment, in which firms invest outside their country's borders, has risen even faster than foreign trade. The growth in trade and foreign direct investment, however, pale in comparison to the growth in international financial transactions. International borrowing and lending, as well as currency trading, have increased spectacularly.

The market system has become not only more extensive, diffusing over the entire globe, but also more intensive, involving more social transactions. In developed societies, and increasingly in developing societies as well, people rely on the market to satisfy their needs. Goods and services that families previously provided for themselves, such as caring for their children or cooking their own food, are now outsourced to the market in the form of day care centers and eating at McDonalds. We now go to the market to meet needs that people once satisfied in other ways.

States determine how extensive markets are. For example, they can discourage foreign trade by placing taxes on imported goods or encourage it by permitting imports to compete with domestic goods on a level playing field. Similarly, states can pass laws that discourage foreign investment or adopt laws that encourage it. They can place strict controls on their currency or allow it to move freely across borders. In addition, states sign treaties and join international organizations that set the rules for exchange between countries. These rules can either promote or inhibit the **extensive growth of markets**.[5] Similarly, states also determine how intensive markets are. They can restrict what is for sale, allowing some exchanges but blocking others, such as the sale of sexual favors or body parts.[6] In effect, states can say that there are some things money should not buy. They make these decisions based upon the competing pressures they receive from those who benefit from the extensive and **intensive growth of markets** and those who do not.

In this chapter, we first examine the relationship between states and markets. At the same time that states provide an alternative to markets, markets require states in order to thrive. States set the ground rules without which markets cannot work. We then describe the advantages and disadvantages of market systems. Next, we examine some of the ways states try to manage market systems. Finally, we review whether market-oriented or state-directed forms of political economy contribute most to people's capability.

> **IN BRIEF**

Market Systems
- Commodity production in which goods are produced for sale.
- Productive assets are privately owned and employed to earn profits for their owners.
- Prices are not administered but set through supply and demand.

STATES AND MARKETS

The triumph of market systems, their extensive and intensive growth, has been lauded as the triumph of freedom. In this view, states are about rules and compulsion while markets are about choice and individual expression. But, in fact, while markets may lack the coercive apparatus of courts, jails, and police that states possess, their disciplinary power is just as great. "Like the state," Lindblom writes, "the market system is a method of controlling and coordinating people's behavior."[7] In market systems, production is coordinated not by a central plan but "through the mutual interaction of buyers and sellers."[8] The price at which firms sell their goods or what workers receive in wages obey the unseen imperatives of the market, like iron filings caught in an invisible magnetic force field. The magnet at one end of the force field is called "supply," while the magnet at the other end is called "demand."[9] People respond to shifts in the market, in the balance between supply and demand, but no one controls it. Producers have no choice but to reduce prices when demand is slack and increase prices when demand is high, if they want to remain in business. Those who misread or respond too late to market signals do so at their peril.

But markets require states to function and cannot exist without them. As a congressman from Mississippi once put it: "The free enterprise system is too important to be left in the hands of private individuals."[10] Market systems need states to create a common currency to facilitate trade and exchange; to enforce contracts; and to supply public goods, such as transportation networks and police protection, that markets cannot furnish themselves.[11] The state makes capital viable and promotes economic growth by creating and structuring markets in such a way that creativity and investments pay off. The visible hand of the state supplements the invisible hand of the market. Market freedom requires state compulsion in order to thrive.

The economist John McMillan uses the metaphor of the internet to explain how markets require states to work. Instead of connecting buyers and sellers to each other, the internet connects computers to other computers, without any centralized agency directing its operation. But the anarchic, unplanned quality of the internet rests on a foundation created by the state. The United States subsidized the internet's initial development, created common technical standards so that computers could communicate with each other, managed the assignment of names so that each Web address would be unique, and created and enforced laws against the spread of computer viruses.[12]

Markets, the political economist John Zysman offers, "do not exist or operate apart from the rules and institutions that establish them." Such rules "structure how buying and selling, the very organization of production, takes place."[13] Thus, states make market systems possible, making the ground rules that permit market systems to work at all. Consider, for example, the board game Monopoly, which is intended to replicate a market in real estate that stretches from the low-rent district of Mediterranean and Baltic Avenues to the expensive properties of Park Place and Boardwalk. Players are given money and the opportunity to buy, sell, and trade different properties. Now, consider playing Monopoly if there were no rules stipulating what happened if you landed on someone else's property; no rules about how you could mortgage your property to raise cash; and no rules about how you could build houses and hotels to increase the value of your property. Monopoly is unplayable without rules. Markets are only as good as the rules states make to support them. The historian Jacques Barzun attributed the emergence of Venice as the center of international trade in the mid-seventeenth century to the quality of its regulatory, or rule-making, political institutions,[14] and the historian Niall Ferguson made a similar point in explaining why London, rather than Paris, emerged as the epicenter of world capitalism in the eighteenth century. Ferguson writes, "The key difference between France and Britain in the eighteenth century, then, was not a matter of economic resources. France had more. Rather, it was a matter of institutions."[15] The reason some countries prospered while others did not is explained, the economist John McMillan argues, "by the quality of their institutions," the rules that states design for them.[16] Just as states can create conditions that promote the creation of wealth, they can make rules that impede it.

The balance between political and market forces within a country, or what is referred to as its **political economy**, is critical in determining whether it will meet the minimal conditions of the good society. As Jacob S. Hacker and Paul Pierson explain, "the debate should not be whether government is involved in the formation of markets. It always is. The debate should be over whether it is involved in a manner conducive to a good society."[17] For example, as we saw previously, Russia first suffered from too much state control and then from too much markets. Both forms of economic management failed to produce results that permitted Russians to enjoy flourishing lives.

THE ADVANTAGES OF MARKET SYSTEMS

Security was surprisingly haphazard on July 25, 1959, for a meeting in Moscow between leaders of the two superpowers. Reporters and cameramen jostled with each other amid workers still preparing for the opening of the American National Exhibition. The Exhibition, the first of its kind in the Soviet Union since the Communists took power in 1917, would display the achievements of American capitalism. More than 800 corporations donated exhibits, including color televisions and a model home, extolling the American way of life. Vice President Richard M. Nixon had arrived to cut the ceremonial ribbon officially opening the Exhibition, while his host, Soviet Premier Nikita S. Khrushchev, looked on with satisfaction.

But this trivial effort to build understanding between Cold War rivals quickly took an ominous turn. The two leaders began to argue and debate the relative merits of capitalism and communism. They chided each other as they passed through a model kitchen. Khrushchev complained about its affordability and workmanship. Nixon lauded its durability and technology. The confrontation climaxed when Nixon led Khrushchev into an exhibit of a working television studio and invited him to make some remarks. Khrushchev threw down the gauntlet. He claimed that the United States was three times older than the Soviet Union, but that the Soviet Union, despite its late start, would soon outproduce its rival. Communism would win the battle of the standard of living over capitalism. The Soviet Union would soon surpass the United States in productivity and production and look in its rearview mirror to wave as it sped by.[18]

The "kitchen debate," as this small episode from the Cold War was called, had no apparent winner at the time. But 50 years of subsequent history has given a clear, unequivocal answer to the issue the leaders debated at the opening of the American Exhibition in Moscow. The Soviet model of the planned economy was no match for the dynamism of American capitalism. Far from overtaking the American economy, as Khrushchev confidently predicted, the Soviet Union fell further and further behind, until it collapsed completely. In 1990, the average Soviet living standard was only one-third that of the average American. The Soviet Union lost the Cold War not on the battlefield, but in the war of production between planned economies and market-based economic systems. Market systems were nimble, while planned economies were all thumbs; the former was innovative, while the latter was immobile. "When it comes to the question of which system today is the most effective at generating rising standards of living," *New York Times* columnist Thomas A. Friedman writes, "the historical debate is over. The answer is free-market capitalism."[19] "There Is No Alternative," according to former British Prime Minister Margaret Thatcher. Societies either adopt market systems or suffer—as happened with the Soviet Union—being left behind in poverty and stagnation.

Market systems have many advantages. First, they are extraordinarily dynamic, promoting the development of new products and more efficient production methods and technologies. Competitive pressures and the thirst for profits encourage firms to innovate constantly. Firms that fail to innovate and become more productive lose market share and profits to those who do. The Austrian economist Joseph Schumpeter described the unceasing transformation that market systems create as a process of "creative destruction." New products and more efficient technologies and production methods sweep away old firms, goods, skills, and even whole industries. And what is new today will be seized upon for revision and improvement tomorrow as firms continue to innovate under the pressure of competition and their desire for profits.

Second, market systems are enormously productive. As Marx and Engels acknowledged in *The Communist Manifesto* more than 150 years ago, capitalism developed "more massive and more colossal productive forces than have all the preceding generations put together."[20] The application of science to industry, advances in communication and transportation, and the development of more efficient ways to deploy and motivate labor all contributed to higher levels of labor productivity. Half the number of workers employed could now turn out twice as much as before. The result has been unimaginable wealth: rising per capita incomes, higher standards of living, and larger gross national products.

Finally, it appears that market systems enhance the prospects of democracy and political rights. Michael Mandelbaum writes, "The key to establishing a working democracy, and in particular the institutions of liberty, has been the free-market economy."[21] In contrast to planned economies, where the state determines what is produced, what people are paid, where production takes place, and where profits are invested, the reach of the state within market systems is limited. The potential threat of an all-powerful state is stymied by removing such decisions from the state's purview. Market systems separate economic power from political power, permitting each to offset the other. In contrast, planned economies combine economic and political power in the hands of the state, foreclosing the development of countervailing economic power to it.[22] While market systems are no guarantee of democracy and political freedom—one need only recall how well capitalism functioned in Nazi Germany, or how well the market system has fared in Communist China— liberal democracy has had the most success in societies with market systems, and has been absent from societies without them.

THE DARK SIDE OF MARKETS

The American economic model, based on low taxes, weak unions, and small government, produced results that were the envy of the world in the 1990s. The economy grew, creating new jobs and new wealth. With credit cheap and banks anxious to lend, many people took out mortgages to purchase homes, causing prices to rise. The housing boom attracted more buyers anxious to take advantage of rising property values, pushing up housing prices even more. The market was feeding on itself. But then the music stopped. Investors who provided seed money for housing loans became skeptical of the values underlying the mortgage securities they bought. As the money to finance new mortgages dried up, housing prices began to plummet. In Fort Myers, Fla., the median price of a home, which had risen to $320,000 in 2005, fell to an astonishing $106,000 three years later. People who had taken out mortgages when prices were going up now could not pay their debt as housing prices started to fall. In some cases, prices had fallen so low that people's debt was greater than the value of their home. New homes that had been constructed in anticipation of the boom now stood empty and were joined by an inventory of foreclosed homes, which depressed prices even more. Just as rising demand for housing had pushed prices higher, so did the increasing supply of unsold homes drive prices lower, creating its own momentum in the opposite direction.

Previously, homes sales had contributed to the country's prosperity, filling bank coffers with profits. Now foreclosures threatened lenders with bankruptcy as people could not repay their loans. As quick as they were to loan money in good times, banks were reluctant to do so when the economy soured. Banks would not extend credit, which threatened the entire economy, making it difficult for firms to pay suppliers, meet payrolls, or purchase goods. The economy entered its worst recession since the Great Depression. In a period of 18 months, from the last quarter of 2007 through the first quarter of 2009, about $12 trillion of wealth evaporated as housing prices collapsed and the stock market tumbled. Unemployment rose above 10 percent, the highest it had been in 26 years.

As this example shows, while market systems promote innovation and productivity and provide a hospitable environment for democracy and personal freedom, they are also highly volatile. Markets do not remain in a stable equilibrium but are susceptible to periods of boom and bust. In the former, the economy is buoyant with investment, jobs, and commerce; in the latter, the economy is depressed with bankruptcies, layoffs, and declining sales. The volatility of markets would not be so worrisome if its disconcerting shifts were not so socially destructive. When the economy contracts, plants are idle and workers are unemployed. Vital resources are wasted that could be engaged productively. When markets are unstable, entrepreneurs are reluctant to invest in new plants and workers are unwilling to invest in new skills, because the future is too uncertain and the risks are too great.[23] Market instability also has more personal, more intimate costs. When markets move capriciously they leave people with a sense of powerlessness and insecurity, the feeling that they do not control their own fate.

Market systems, as we have seen, generate extraordinary wealth. But they also generate extraordinary inequality. As the market's range expands, increasing competition for jobs, it tends to depress the bargaining power and hence the earnings of those without valued skills. The growth of the market, however, has the opposite effect on those who enjoy market power. Those who control scarce resources, such as skills or capital, are now able to apply their advantage over a much wider field and thereby recoup bloated rewards from it.[24] Able to extend their market advantage over a bigger playing field, they can capture commensurately bigger rewards. The result of these dynamics is increasing inequality, as the market position of low-skill workers declines while those with market power increases.

Finally, market systems create **harmful spillover effects** or externalities. In market systems, participants tend to perceive their interests narrowly. They do not consider the consequences of their decisions wherever they may fall but only those consequences that may fall on them. If people can avoid the costs of their decisions and pass them on to others, then they are that much better off—although the society onto which the costs have been displaced may not be. For example, firms acting in a self-interested manner will not clean up the pollution they create because it would hurt their profits to do so. Instead, the costs of pollution will be borne by everyone in the form of dirty air and impure water. The firm's financial statement will look better as a result. But society's balance sheet will look worse.[25] Another example of harmful spillover is global warming. The prices people pay to drive their cars or heat their homes do not reflect their true costs in terms of the greenhouse gases they release. These gases create global warming that may be the greatest, most costly harmful spillover of all in terms of its costs on future generations.

IN BRIEF

The Advantages and Disadvantages of Market Systems

Advantages of Market Systems
- Promotes efficiency and productivity.
- Promotes innovation.
- More conducive to democracy than command economies.

Disadvantages of Market Systems
- Promotes inequality.
- Subject to volatile and destructive swings between recession and prosperity.
- Social costs of production are ignored.

THE SHIFTING BALANCE BETWEEN STATES AND MARKETS

Market systems, we argued previously, require rules enforced by the state in order to work at all. Rules reduce uncertainty that contracts will be honored; that money will retain its value; and that consumers will not be cheated. But states do more to assist market systems than simply reassure participants that others will play fair. They try to steer economies to certain goals, actively intervening in the market to alter their results. For example, states try to counteract the three drawbacks of market systems we just reviewed. They create welfare systems to neutralize the natural tendency of markets toward inequality; they create regulations, such as pollution controls, to minimize harmful spillover effects; and they use their budgetary powers and control over the money supply to reduce the swings in the business cycle.

The degree to which states should intervene in the marketplace and impose their priorities on it is a source of tremendous conflict within most societies. To what degree should the welfare state alter market outcomes? To what degree should the state create regulations that require firms to limit harmful spillovers? To what degree should the state use budgetary powers and control over the money supply to reduce the cycle of boom and bust? The boundary between what should be left to markets and what should be determined by states shifts constantly in response to political pressure. Following World War II, state intervention was accepted practice, whether this took the form of nationalized industry in Britain, indicative planning in France, the welfare state in Sweden, state-regulated business in India, or state-owned companies and marketing control boards in Africa. Everywhere, the state extended its reach into the economy "powered by the demands of the public in the industrial democracies for greater security, by the drive for progress and improved living conditions in the developing countries—and by the quest for fairness and justice."[26]

State interference was necessary to correct the all too apparent deficiencies of markets during the Great Depression, which left millions unemployed. After World War II, the benefits of state intervention were perceived to be as obvious as the market's failures had been in the 1930s. States led the reconstruction effort in Europe following the war, laying the groundwork for a new "Golden Age" of prosperity in the West. They created welfare systems that protected people from the ravages of unemployment, sickness, and old age. They managed their budgets and money supply to tame the business cycle so that it would not be so disruptive, and nationalized industries to ensure the production of essential goods and services. The growth of the welfare state, public enterprise, and state efforts to guide private investment were regarded as essential to a prosperous, public-spirited economy.

Working-class voters were the driving force behind the rise of the mixed economy of state intervention and private enterprise. Workers appreciated the security the welfare state offered, as opposed to the precariousness of markets. They valued efforts to smooth out the business cycle as a way to avoid the massive unemployment of another depression, and they supported efforts to nationalize firms and regulate corporate behavior in order to assert public priorities. As a result of these policies, workers' standards of living in the West improved, unemployment declined, the average workday shrank, and unions grew.

State intervention became the new gospel not only in the developed world, but in developing countries as well. Nation-building elites in Africa and Asia assumed that only the state could harness the resources necessary to transform traditional, agrarian societies into modern, industrial ones. The developing countries needed infrastructure—transportation and communication networks, electrical power, water and sewer lines—in order to lay the foundations for development, and only the state could raise the capital and assume the risk for such investments. Private sources of capital, it was believed, were too small and too concerned with narrow self-interest to get the job done. Thus, nationalistic elites in developing countries looked to the state to propel industrialization. They became the advocates of states over markets. In India, this took the form of creating national champions, public enterprises that could meet the consumer needs of a soaring population. In Africa, it took the form of state-run marketing boards to which growers had to sell their produce at fixed prices, and in Asia it took the form of states encouraging firms to cooperate rather than compete.[27] The borders of the market were being rolled back.

But the tide began to shift beginning in the 1970s. Economic growth in the West stalled as developed societies were ravaged by rising energy prices, increasing unemployment, and galloping inflation. Recession created the opportunity for new groups proposing new ideas to challenge the orthodoxy of the mixed economy. Backed by the business community, market supporters such as Prime Minister Margaret Thatcher of Britain (1979–1991) and President Ronald Reagan in the United States (1981–1989) took power, arguing that prosperity was being strangled by state intervention. Previously, advocates of states had pointed to systematic market failures as the reason that state intervention was required. Now, promoters of markets pointed to systematic political failures as the reason that markets needed to be restored. It was argued that growth had slowed because the welfare state had undermined the work ethic; that regulations had constrained entrepreneurial energies; that taxes had diverted too much income; and that public enterprises were inefficient. Market inequalities based on capital and wealth had simply been replaced with new inequalities based on power and privilege, and instead of looking out for the public good, public officials managing the economy looked out only for themselves.

Management of the economy changed to reflect this new consensus. Policies shifted to reflect the new balance between states and markets. But the shift was more qualitative than quantitative. That is, it was not as if the level of state activity declined or that states actually contracted. To the contrary, they continued to grow in terms of their activities and budgets. But their purpose changed, as states were now less inclined to direct markets than to support them. Making markets work better required states to do new things, not fewer things. For example, supporting markets did not mean reducing the welfare state as much as it meant reorienting the welfare state so that it was more employment-friendly, encouraging work. Supporting markets did not mean less regulation but new types of regulations that encouraged competition.[28]

But the global recession of 2007 that began in the United States—the paragon of the market approach—cast doubt on that very model. Financial crisis in the United States spread like a virus throughout the world, forcing governments to rescue failing banks and pump money into their economies to prevent them from collapsing. Faith in the recuperative power of the market gave way to a new belief in the restorative power of states. The U.S. government, first under Republican President George W. Bush and then under his Democratic successor, Barack Obama, intervened dramatically in the economy, bailing out banks, buying shares in car companies, and investing in markets in order to prop them up. Other governments quickly followed suit. The market model was in retreat. In 2010, *The Economist,* a sober and respected newsweekly magazine acknowledged that just when it seemed that "the great debate about the proper role and size of the state had been resolved . . . Big Government is back with a vengeance: not just as a brute fact, but as a vigorous ideology."[29] Even President of France Nicholas Sarkozy, who admired the American model, acknowledged what everyone now recognized: "Laissez-faire is finished. The all-powerful market that always knows best is finished. Self-regulation as a way of solving problems is finished."[30] With the world economy teetering on the brink and governments providing life support to bankrupt companies and banks, it was hard to argue otherwise. In the 1980s, advocates of markets silenced critics by asserting "There Is No Alternative" (or what came to be known as TINA) if the mistakes of the previous period were to be avoided. But in a startling about-face, the critics of markets now invoked TINA against those who had once used it against them. Advocates of more government intervention now claimed there was no alternative if countries were to avoid falling off the precipice to which the free market model had brought them. As Mohammed El-Erain, CEO of the giant bond company Pimco, told investors, "the new normal" is a world in which "the public sector plays a much more influential role."[31]

Shifting paradigms between states and markets reveal that economic models diffuse across the globe. As countries adopt similar policies, their economic fortunes are tied more closely together. Both are evidence of what social scientists refer to as globalization, which we review next.

THE GOOD SOCIETY IN DEPTH

India—From States to Markets

After India gained independence in 1947, its rulers embarked on policies that called for a large degree of state intervention in the economy. They chose this route as one that reflected both their socialist inclinations and their ambitions to create a strong state with which citizens could identify. Statist economic policies included high tariffs that limited imports in order to protect domestic producers from foreign competition; public ownership of the commanding heights of the economy, including steel, power, and telecommunications; and heavy regulation of industry through licensing that would give the state control over investment, competition, prices, technology, and labor policy. Businesses had to appeal to a dense bureaucracy to receive licenses that regulated production, prices, and credit.

But India abandoned statist economic policies in the wake of the economic reversals that it suffered in the 1980s. The industrial licensing system was abolished. Firms were now free to make decisions about investments, prices, and technology. Privatization proceeded alongside deregulation. Where 18 industries had once been in the public sector, their number was now reduced to three. And the economy welcomed foreign trade and investment. Tariffs were cut and foreign firms could now wholly or partially own domestic companies. The Indian economy became more privatized, less regulated, and more open to foreign competition.

As a consequence of this shift from state to market, foreign trade and foreign direct investment grew dramatically, as did GDP. Income has risen for all groups, including the poor. Prior to the reforms in 1991, one-third of all Indians lived on $1 a day; that figure is now down to one-quarter of the populace. The middle class has grown dramatically, to include nearly 200 to 250 million people, and the number of

Continued

very rich citizens has increased as well. But the reforms also exaggerated the income gap between rural and urban India. More than 60 percent of all Indians derive their livelihoods from agriculture, an economic sector that experienced little growth. Thus, while the reforms greatly improved the life chances of many urban Indians, they failed to have much impact on rural residents.

For Further Discussion

1. How can market reforms that have such unequal effects, leaving out the bulk of the population in the countryside engaged in agriculture, maintain popular support in a democracy such as India?

2. Without jeopardizing or undermining the impact of market reforms, what can states do to make their consequences fairer, so that they enhance the capabilities of a larger number of citizens?

GLOBALIZATION

The concept of **globalization** can be captured by looking at a map of the world that compares the number of commercial intercontinental flights in 1960 and 2000. The number of flights per year is displayed as lines of various widths. The map for 1960 shows relatively thin lines connecting the various continents, indicating that there were very few intercontinental commercial flights. In contrast, the map for 2000 shows so many lines that the continents themselves are nearly obscured. What is true of commercial airline flights is also true for trade, investment, crime, culture, labor, technology, and ideas. A few thin lines connecting countries and even continents have been replaced by many thicker ones.

Globalization refers to the increasing flow of money, people, skills, ideas, and goods across borders, or what we referred to earlier as the extensive development of markets. Until the recent global recession, trade between countries grew, as they lowered trade barriers, opening up their markets to foreign competition. Foreign direct investment, in which businesses invest outside their home countries, also increased. That is, firms were both selling more goods outside their home market and manufacturing more products abroad. Indeed, globalization has proceeded so far that different steps in the manufacturing process may now take place in different countries. For example, Barbie dolls, which are sold all over the world, are the product of a **global production chain.** The United States provides the cardboard packaging, paint pigments, and molds; Taiwan refines the oil into plastic for the body; Japan contributes the nylon hair; and all of these parts are then assembled in China where Barbie's clothes are also produced; and the final product is shipped out of Hong Kong. The iPod is also the product of a global supply chain, with its computer chips produced in Taiwan, its display modules made in Japan, and its memory chips manufactured in Korea.[32] Not only is there more economic exchange between countries, but there is also more cultural traffic. Curry has

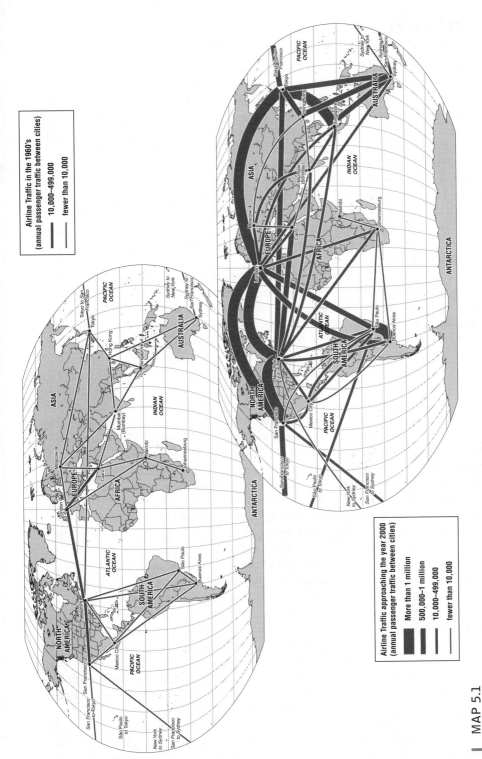

MAP 5.1
Airline Map circa 1960 and 2000

replaced fish and chips in Britain as the most common lunch, while kids in China dress like homeboys, listen to rap music, and do the worm.

There has always been trade, investment, and cultural exchange across borders. What is different today is the volume of international exchange, the breadth of the connections, and the speed with which they occur. Globalization is, in part, the result of technological change. For example, the dramatic increase in intercontinental flights is unimaginable in the absence of powerful jet engines that permit planes to fly long distances in a short amount of time. Huge cargo ships that ply the oceans have reduced transportation costs for goods at the same time the internet has increased the cross-national flow of ideas. But globalization is not simply the result of impersonal forces. It has been actively promoted by multinational corporations, governments, and international agencies.

Prior to the 1980s, many states exercised a great deal of control over their trade through high tariffs, over foreign investment by restricting entry, and over their currency by limiting its movement abroad. But the 1970s recession saw the emergence of a new paradigm to restore growth based on markets called the "**Washington consensus**" by its supporters and "**neoliberalism**" by its critics. This policy package required countries to balance their budgets by cutting spending, open their markets to foreign trade and investment, and sell off nationalized industries to private investors. The Washington consensus was supported by large multinational corporations, the United States, and such international agencies as the **World Bank**, which provides loans and grants to countries for development projects, and the **International Monetary Fund** (IMF), which loans money to countries so they can pay their bills.[33] The World Bank and IMF required countries in financial difficulty to adopt the policies of the Washington consensus as a condition for receiving aid from them.

Critics charged that the Washington consensus hurt the poor by requiring cuts in social services in order to achieve balanced budgets, increased unemployment and drove out small business by requiring countries to open up their markets to imports and foreign competition, and weakened democracy by requiring countries to conform to IMF and World Bank conditions in order to obtain assistance from them.[34] Critics claimed that what they disparagingly referred to as "neoliberalism" merely rationalized policies that justified exploitation of less developed countries by multinational corporations and their political allies. In response, supporters of the Washington consensus accused their critics of espousing "economic rubbish that jeopardizes . . . [advancing the] egalitarian causes" that critics said they valued.[35] Neoliberals argued that balanced budgets were necessary to stabilize a country's currency, that removing trade and investment controls was needed to attract foreign capital, and that privatizing state businesses was vital to increase their competitiveness and efficiency.

The debate between critics and supporters of the Washington consensus captured in microcosm a larger debate between the skeptics and advocates of globalization. In many ways, it reprises the argument between those who see only the benefits of markets and those who see only their dark side. Proponents perceive the economic openness that accompanies globalization as creating the conditions for a "race to the top." Firms in less developed countries that participate in global commodity chains can make profits, pay workers more than they would have earned as farmers, and give them an opportunity to learn new skills.[36] From that point, these firms can grow and employment and wages can increase. For example, Giant Manufacturing in Taiwan began as a low wage manufacturer, producing bicycles for the Schwinn Corporation, based in the United States. Today, Giant is on the cutting edge of high-tech racing and mountain bikes, sells two-thirds of its bicycles under its own name, and boasts the third-highest sales of bicycles in Europe and the United States, while Schwinn's bicycle business recently was sold in bankruptcy.[37]

Detractors of globalization argue that it actually creates a "race to the bottom" in which each country competes to have the lowest wages, lowest taxes, and fewest regulations in order to attract foreign investors who now have the whole world to choose from.[38] For example, corporations like General Electric and General Motors were attracted initially to Mexico because of its low wages and access to American markets, but then moved their businesses to China where production costs were even lower.[39] Countries compete in prostituting themselves, repressing labor, driving down wages, and removing regulations, in order to attract capital investment.

The record of countries that followed the development strategy of the Washington consensus has been uneven, at best. Chile was a success story, but most Latin American countries that opened their markets to foreign investors, balanced their budgets, and deregulated their markets were not. While many countries that followed the rules of the Washington consensus failed to grow, those that diverged from its prescriptions, such as China, South Korea, and Taiwan, often experienced great success. The World Bank now concedes that its one-size-fits-all prescription of balanced budgets, open markets, and privatization, "proved to be theoretically incomplete and contradicted by the evidence."[40]

If embracing globalization was no magic elixir, there is also little evidence that globalization leads to a race to the bottom by depressing living standards and eliminating jobs in less developed countries. Workers in several Asian countries that are deeply enmeshed in the global economy, including South Korea, Taiwan and Thailand, have seen their standard of living improve. Hundreds of thousands of well-educated, young workers in India's information technology industry have dramatically increased their incomes since the country opened this sector to foreign investment and trade. Critics assume that employers are only looking to invest in countries that offer the lowest labor costs and taxes. In fact, investors are often less interested in countries that offer low wages than in those that offer political stability, good infrastructure, and a skilled labor force able to deliver higher levels of productivity. Far from creating a race either to the top or to the bottom for developing countries, globalization has increased the difference between the top and bottom among them. Some developing countries have profited enormously from globalization while others have been victimized by it. Globalization has been the source of wealth and success for some developing countries, such as Thailand, Taiwan and China, while it has been the scourge of countries in sub-Saharan Africa and Latin America.

Globalization has such varied outcomes because it is refracted through different institutions and governing coalitions. Countries that invite globalization by opening their economies to foreign trade and investment will profit only if they have supportive institutions and governing coalitions in place that can take advantage of its benefits and ameliorate its costs. What matters is not how much state activity there is but its quality. As Tina Rosenberg wrote of Haiti, which followed the Washington consensus and saw its economy contract in the 1990s: "if you are a corrupt, and misgoverned nation with a closed economy, becoming a corrupt, misgoverned nation with an open economy is not going to solve your problems."[41] Reaping the benefits of globalization may be less a question of too much state and not enough market, as the Washington consensus imagined it, than a question of how effective states are at putting in place the foundations that enable markets to work well. Such prerequisites include educating workers, constructing a reliable infrastructure, and enforcing the rule of law. What matters are the different tools states use to influence the allocation of resources in the economy and how well they use them. We examine this issue next.

COMPARATIVE POLITICAL ANALYSIS

Does Globalization Help or Hurt Workers in the Developing World?

Problem

Mosley and Uno ask whether globalization contributes to or compromises workers' rights in developing countries? Leftists frequently assert that globalization hurts workers' rights because it leads to a "race to the bottom." Countries compete with one another to repress labor and drive down its cost in order to attract investors. Others argue that globalization offers a "climb to the top." Globalization contributes to workers' rights in developing countries by attracting companies that bring their best practices with them and care more about the quality of their labor than its cost.

Methods and Hypothesis

Mosley and Uno hypothesize that the impact of globalization on workers depends on the way countries participate in global production networks. Workers will benefit when countries attract more foreign direct investment but they will suffer when countries engage in more trade. Foreign direct investment is benign because multinationals urge governments to improve infrastructure and the skills of the native workforce. Trade, on the other hand, compromises workers' interests because low wages are key to increasing exports and winning business for local subcontractors. Mosley and Uno test their hypothesis statistically.

Operationalizing Concepts

The authors operationally define workers' rights, their dependent variable, by counting the number of labor rights violations that countries committed from 1985 to 2002 as recorded by the U.S. State Department, the International Labor

Organization (ILO), and the International Confederation of Free Trade Union (ICFTU). They operationalize one of their independent variables, foreign direct investment (FDI), by looking at annual changes in FDI and the overall level of FDI as a percent of GDP. They operationalize their other independent variable, trade, by looking at the ratio of imports and exports to GDP.

Results

Statistical analysis confirmed Mosley and Uno's hypothesis: The higher the level of FDI as a percentage of GDP, the greater the respect for labor rights. Mosley and Uno also found that growth in FDI as a percentage of GDP had an even more positive effect on labor rights than its overall level. Conversely, trade openness was shown to be detrimental to workers. Countries with higher levels of imports and exports treated their workers less well. It appears that globalization's effect on workers' rights depends on the specific way in which countries are integrated into the global economy. Workers' rights improve in developing countries that are able to attract foreign direct investment, while they deteriorate in those countries that engage in more trade.

For Further Discussion

1. Mosley and Uno looked at labor rights to see whether globalization led to a race to the bottom or a climb to the top. What other criteria might they have investigated to see whether globalization hurts or helps workers in developing countries?

2. What sorts of controls do you think Mosley and Uno should have used in their analysis? What factors do you think they needed to hold constant to accurately determine the effect of foreign direct investment and trade on labor rights?

Source: Layna Mosley and Saiko Uno, "Racing to the Bottom or Climbing to the Top," *Comparative Political Studies* Vol. 40, No. 8, (August 2007), pp. 923–948.

FORMS OF STATE INTERVENTION

Fiscal Policy

States try to influence economic conditions through **fiscal policy**, which involves juggling their budgets, their overall levels of revenues and expenditures. Fiscal policy is often set by the executive branch, which submits a budget, consolidating revenue and spending targets, to the legislature for approval. On the one hand, states can stimulate the economy and reduce unemployment by running budget deficits, which occur when the state spends more than it receives in revenues. Budget deficits put money into circulation that increases the demand for goods that, in turn, encourages businesses to invest and put people to work. On the other hand, states can dampen an economy that suffers from inflation by running a surplus, taking in more money than they spend. A surplus

TABLE 5.1

Government Revenues and Expenditures as a Percentage of GDP, 2006. [1]

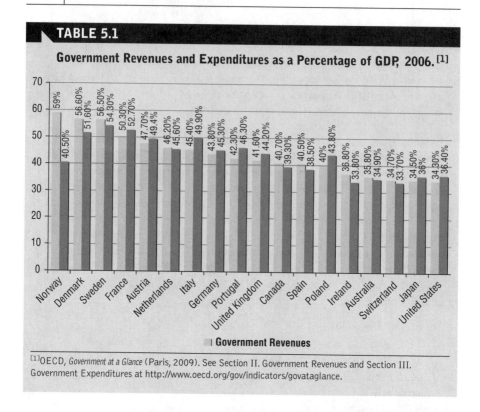

Government Revenues

[1]OECD, *Government at a Glance* (Paris, 2009). See Section II. Government Revenues and Section III. Government Expenditures at http://www.oecd.org/gov/indicators/govataglance.

withdraws money from circulation, which depresses spending and discourages investment, thereby reducing inflationary pressures in the economy.

States differ greatly in the proportion of their economy devoted to taxes and state expenditures. Americans complain frequently that taxes in the United States are too high and the government spends too much. In fact, Americans enjoy a lighter tax burden than citizens in other rich democracies, and the American government is lean compared to others. As Table 5.1 reveals, taxes are a lower proportion of GDP in the United States than in any other country, and state expenditures in the United States are relatively low as well. Only Australia, Ireland, Japan and Switzerland recorded lower state spending as a percentage of their economies than the United States. At the opposite end of the spectrum is Sweden, where state revenues and spending amount to more than half of GDP. The fact that the Swedish government collects more than half the national income in the form of taxes and diverts it in the form of spending gives it enormous power to determine how money is used and distributed within society.

Monetary Policy

Another means by which states influence economic conditions is through **monetary policy**, by manipulating interest rates. Just as the state tries to fine-tune the economy by adjusting its budget, so does it try to manage the economy by regulating how much it costs to borrow money. High interest rates tend to discourage borrowing and spending and are used to counteract tendencies toward inflation. In contrast, low interest rates encourage borrowing and spending by making loans cheap, and are employed to fight recessions.

Interest rates are largely determined by **central banks** that issue currency and manage its value in foreign exchange. One measure of the control that states exert over the economy is the influence they have over the country's central bank. In some countries, central banks are purposely insulated from political control and states have little leverage over their policies. The central bank of the United States, for example, is the Federal Reserve. Neither the president nor Congress have much leverage over Federal Reserve Bank policies. For those European countries that have adopted the Euro as their currency, interest rate targets are set by the European Central Bank (ECB), which is even less transparent and accountable than the U.S. Federal Reserve Bank. The European Central Bank's decisions are not reviewable by any external body, and it does not publish minutes of its meetings, divulge how members voted, or even have to explain its decisions when it announces them.

In other countries, governments enjoy more power over central banks. For example, the People's Bank in China is simply an administrative organ for carrying out decisions made by the governing Chinese Communist Party. Changes in the interest rate or the money supply require the approval of the government and the central bank enjoys little independence.[42] In South Korea, during the 1970s, the state owned every bank in the country and used that leverage to make loans to companies that helped South Korea industrialize rapidly. In return for investing in industries desired by the government, companies were able to borrow money during these years at an interest rate of *minus* 6.7 percent.[43]

Regulatory Policy

States manipulate budgets and central banks manage interest rates with the intent of stabilizing prices and sustaining employment. But states can also use a more direct means to influence economic actors: They can issue regulations that set explicit rules of behavior that firms must follow. States engage in regulation, compel firms to behave in certain ways, in order to manage competition, set industry standards, and require or forbid certain business practices. For example, states may set minimum wages to prevent firms from profiting by paying substandard wages; mandate environmental quality standards to prevent firms from polluting the air and water; and mandate product standards to prevent firms from selling goods that are unsafe or unreliable. Regulation is necessary to channel firms away from destructive forms of competition from which they may profit at the expense of society.[44]

Some states are more committed to regulation than others. The number of procedures and days it takes to start a new business is a standard measure used to compare the thickness of the regulatory environment from country to country. According to the World Bank, it takes nine separate interactions taking an average of 45 days to obtain the necessary licenses and permits to start a business in Germany, and 17 steps lasting 152 days in Brazil, as compared with just five steps lasting five days in the United States.[45] Another gauge of the regulatory environment is available if we examine labor relations. In many European countries, managers are required to negotiate with workers' councils in their shops, companies must follow a tedious and lengthy process prior to firing workers, and employees are entitled to seats on the board of directors. Employers in the United States do not have to adopt any of these practices because there are no laws requiring them. They do not have to negotiate with their employees or let them participate in setting corporate strategy, and they can fire any worker for any reason, except discrimination, without having to justify their decision legally. As two labor relations specialists acknowledged, "By most international standards, American employers . . . are confronted with fewer direct regulations of employment conditions than employers in other countries."[46] Despite frequently heard complaints about "Big Government" and its obtrusiveness, these measures indicate that the U.S. economy is actually one of the least regulated in the world. American entrepreneurs are less burdened in obtaining the necessary permits and licenses they need to get started and they have more autonomy in managing their workforce than their counterparts elsewhere.

Nationalization

Finally, states try to influence economic activity by nationalizing industries in which states own and control public enterprises. Nationalized industries permit the state to control strategic assets through which it can influence the economy. For example, the state owns and controls the oil industry in Mexico, Venezuela and Saudi Arabia, where oil is a major export. Public enterprises also help the state inject social criteria into the economy. While state-owned enterprises in China may be inefficient, the government continues to subsidize them because they provide jobs and services to millions who would be poor and jobless without them.

States differ in the degree to which they nationalize industry. In socialist countries, such as Cuba and North Korea, the state owns and controls all of the means of production. But with the demise of the Soviet Union, such socialist outposts are now few, small, and insignificant. At the opposite end of the spectrum are countries like the United States and Chile, where the few public enterprises that exist contribute a very small percentage to the GDP. Some countries that once had a substantial nationalized industrial sector have divested and sold off their holdings to private investors. By 1992, more than 80 countries had sold off as many as 6,800 public companies. In Britain, the list of privatizations since 1979 has included such industries as gas, coal, electricity, water, steel, telecommunications, and rail. This sweeping privatization reduced the workforce in British nationalized industries by 83 percent, from 1.8 million workers in 1979 to less than 350,000 twenty years later.[47]

Fiscal policy, monetary policy, regulation, and nationalization hardly exhaust the tools states use to influence the economy. In Japan, the state once intervened by promoting mergers and cooperation among firms in order to create businesses that were large and efficient enough to compete in world markets, and in Germany intervention takes the form of the state brokering agreements among union and employer organizations. Each country works out, through political struggle, its own balance between states and markets. And the mix of policy tools that states adopt is different from country to country. Some have a preference for regulation while others rely more on monetary policy to influence the economy. Where markets play a greater role we expect to find that (1) states do not redirect as much of the country's income through taxes and expenditures; (2) states do not exert much influence upon central banks that set interest rates; (3) state regulations are not as copious or intrusive upon managers; and (4) public enterprises contribute little to the GDP. The opposite is the case where states play a powerful role in determining who gets what. The state redirects a larger proportion of the country's income through their budget; states exert enormous influence over central bank policies; state regulations directing firms to do certain things are profuse and pervasive; and public enterprises control the economy's strategic industries.

The political economies of different countries can be placed on a continuum that stretches from the most market-oriented to the most state-directed. The Fraser Institute of Canada has developed a scale, which evaluates political economies according to their degree of market control. Their country rankings take into account such factors as those we enumerated above and measure the different places that countries draw the line between political and market forces in making allocation decisions. Table 5.1 in the Appendix gives the results of the Fraser Institute's survey. The higher a country's rankings, the more their economies are governed by markets, with the most market-oriented economies receiving the highest score of 10 and the most state-directed economies receiving the lowest score of 0.

MARKETS AND THE GOOD SOCIETY

Do countries in which market systems prevail do a better job of enhancing people's capabilities than countries with heavy state intervention? Which form of political economy is most compatible with the good society: meeting people's material needs, helping them make educated choices about their lives, protecting them from harm, and promoting democracy so they may participate in making the rules that govern them?

Physical Well-Being

The good society requires that citizens' basic material needs are met, which we operationally defined in terms of infant mortality rates. As is apparent from Figure 5.1, those countries that receive top scores from the Fraser Institute are also countries in which infant mortality rates are low. It appears that market systems are better able to meet the physical needs of citizens than more state-directed economies.

Informed Decision Making

Another attribute of the good society is the ability of its citizens to make informed decisions. The good society does not stipulate how people should live

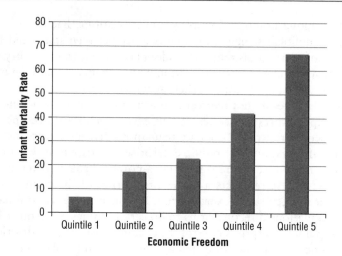

FIGURE 5.1

Capitalism and Infant Mortality Rates

Data Sources: James Gwartney and Robert Lawson, *Economic Freedom of the World: 2009 Annual Report* (Vancouver: Fraser Institute, 2009), p. 10

Country Comparison: Infant Mortality Rate

Data Source: CIA World Factbook, https://www.cia.gov/library/publications/the-world-factbook/rankorder/2091rank.html

but ensures that people can make knowledgeable choices about how they want to live. As we argued earlier, literacy enhances people's ability to do that. According to Figure 5.2, the average literacy rate for countries in the top quintile, or top fifth, of market-based societies was 96.1 percent; in the second quintile it was 92.2; the third quintile was 89.6; the fourth quintile was 77.5; and the average literacy rate for countries in the bottom quintile, which included countries with the most state-directed economies, was 62.3 percent.

Safety

Warfare poses the greatest threat to citizens' safety, and, as we noted in Chapter 2, wars are far more likely to occur within states than between them. Data show that the type of political economy a country has is virtually irrelevant in determining its risk of war. Countries with market-led economies are no less likely to be engaged in hostilities with other countries or erupt into civil war than those where states play a greater allocative role. Unlike democracies, which normally do not fight each other, countries with market-driven economies and those with state-led economies will sometimes fight with their own kind and any other kind. The type of political economy in place has no affect on levels of state aggression.[48]

Aside from warfare, safety can also be assessed by comparing homicide rates. Figure 5.3 below examines the relationship between homicide rates and type of political economy, as measured by the Economic Freedom Index. The average

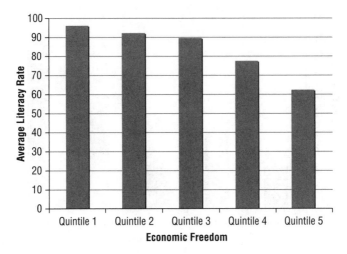

FIGURE 5.2

Capitalism and Literacy Rates

*Data Sources:*James Gwartney and Robert Lawson, *Economic Freedom of the World: 2009 Annual Report* (Vancouver: Fraser Institute, 2009), p. 10

Adult Literacy Rate (% aged 15 and above)

Data Source: Human Development Report 2009, http://hdrstats.undp.org/en/indicators/89.html

homicide rate does rise as we move from the highest to the lowest quintile of market economies. While these figures indicate a correlation between market-based economic systems and low homicide rates, a closer look makes us skeptical of the strength of that relationship. Colombia has the highest homicide rate in the world. It ranks 123 on the Economic Freedom scale, making it one of the most state-led economies in the world. Some countries that rank high on the Economic Freedom scale, such as Singapore, rank low in terms of murder rates, while others that also rank high, such as the United States, have much higher murder rates. There are even quite different homicide rates within countries that share the same economic system. For example, murder rates in 2003 were 33 percent higher in the American South (6.9 per 100,000) than in the Northeast (4.2 per 100,000), even though both shared the same economic system. When we look more closely beyond the averages in our test, and we remember that market-based economic systems do not shy away from state aggression, it is hard to feel confident that market-based economic systems contribute much to citizens' safety.

Democracy

A quick look at the Economic Freedom rankings finds robust democracies in the top quartile and repressive dictatorships at the bottom. These results are reflected in Figure 5.4, which show an apparent correlation between democracy and free markets. Yet, there are some striking anomalies. Number one on the Economic Freedom scale is Hong Kong, which is a special administrative

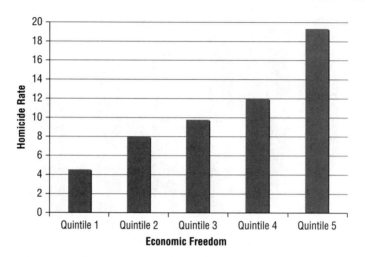

FIGURE 5.3

Capitalism and Homicide Rates

*Data Sources:*James Gwartney and Robert Lawson, *Economic Freedom of the World: 2009 Annual Report* (Vancouver: Fraser Institute, 2009), p. 10

Murder Rates around the World

United Nations Office on Drugs and Crime http://data.un.org/Data.aspx?d=UNODC&f=tableCode%3a1

region of Communist China, a one-party dictatorship. The chief executive of Hong Kong is appointed by and responsible to the Chinese Communist Party in Beijing, while only half of the seats in the legislature are directly elected. This has spawned a popular and assertive pro-democracy movement in Hong Kong, whose very existence confirms democracy's absence there. Second on the list of the most market-friendly economies in the world is Singapore, a one-party state that controls the media, regulates political activity and meetings, and engages in heavy surveillance of its citizens. Or compare the rankings of Israel, which is ranked 78th on the Fraser Institute Economic Freedom scale and Egypt, which follows it next at 79th. Israel has a chaotic, fulsome democratic culture, while the government of neighboring Egypt does not permit free and fair elections and opponents of the government are repressed. Given these anomalies, the best we can say with some certainty is this: market-oriented economic systems may not guarantee liberal democracy, but there are no liberal democracies without them. Although more markets do not translate automatically into more political freedom, the lack of a strong market system does seem to preclude it. While democracies are monogamous and are faithful only to capitalist economies, market systems are known to sleep around and can be found in bed with all sorts of different political systems.

In conclusion, these comparisons tell us that organizing economies more along market lines does improve people's capabilities, but not consistently so. While democracy may be weak among countries that do not rely upon markets to organize production, it is not necessarily strong among those that do.

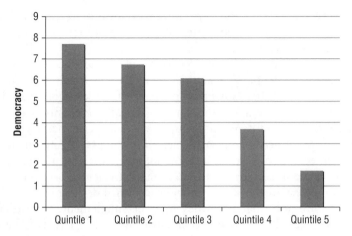

FIGURE 5.4

Capitalism and Democracy

Data Sources: James Gwartney and Robert Lawson, *Economic Freedom of the World: 2009 Annual Report* (Vancouver: Fraser Institute, 2009), p. 10

Polity IV Country Reports, 2007

http://www.systemicpeace.org/polity/polity06.htm

Democracy may require markets but markets do not require democracy. There does appear to be a correlation between market-based systems and high literacy and low homicide rates. But because averages may be obscuring volatility within the data we cannot be confident in the strength of those relationships. Finally, the presence of developed market systems does appear to correlate with low infant mortality rates, our proxy for the ability of societies to meet people's basic material needs.

CONCLUSION

Market systems require states to ensure that property is safe, contracts are enforced, and vital goods that the market cannot supply are available. Laws and regulations set the ground rules that undergird markets, making exchanges predictable, secure, and easy.

Following World War II, the balance between states and markets tilted toward states as developed countries relied on them to manage postwar reconstruction, and developing countries looked to states to promote economic growth following independence. But in the 1970s, states began to concede more space to markets. While there was a strong disposition toward markets leading to a more global economy, countries have moved in that direction to different degrees and in some cases are even swinging back in the other direction. The global recession that struck in the last quarter of 2007 has revived people's faith in states as a necessary and important defense against the volatility of capitalism. In some countries, states continue to have a powerful influence over the economy through levels of taxation and expenditures, central banks, regulations, and public enterprises. In other countries, states are more reluctant to use these levers to interfere with the market.

We then inquired whether market-oriented political economies perform better in increasing people's capabilities than those in which the state plays a larger role. We found that moving up the scale of market economies does not guarantee liberal democracy, although virtually all the countries ranked low on the scale are without it. We also found, with some qualifications, that people's basic material needs tend to be met more successfully in countries with market-oriented economies. We also found, albeit with even more qualifications, that people in countries with more market-oriented economies tend to be safer and have a greater ability to make informed decisions.

Markets are not a panacea; they must be supplemented in order to increase people's capability. As one economist famously advised, "The market has a place but must be kept in its place." The issue, then, is how to develop a balance between states and markets that promotes the best qualities of markets, such as innovation and productivity, while avoiding their worst effects, such as instability and inequality.

mypoliscikit EXERCISES

Apply what you learned in this chapter on MyPoliSciKit (www.mypoliscikit.com).

 ASSESSMENT
Review this chapter using learning objectives, chapter summaries, practice tests, and more.

 VIDEO CASE STUDIES
Analyze recent world affairs by watching streaming video from major news providers.

 FLASHCARDS
Learn the key terms in this chapter; you can test yourself by term or definition.

 COMPARATIVE EXERCISES
Compare political ideas, behaviors, institutions, and policies worldwide.

CRITICAL THINKING QUESTIONS

1. Why do countries differ in their balance between states and markets? What factors determine why some countries depend more on markets while others depend more on states?

2. What sort of activities should be left to the marketplace and what should be insulated from it? What criteria should determine where it is appropriate for markets to operate and where they should be prevented from working?

3. Why have some developing countries benefited from globalization while others have been victimized by it?

4. Many central banks that set monetary policy and influence interest rates are independent of government and, in effect, unaccountable to the people their policies affect. Should central banks be more democratically accountable?
5. We noted that although there are no democracies that are not also capitalist, many capitalist economies operate within authoritarian political systems. Why does democracy seem to require capitalism but capitalism does not seem to require democracy?

KEY TERMS

Extensive Growth of
Markets   110
Intensive Growth of
Markets   110
Market Systems   111
Political Economy   112
Harmful Spillover
Effects   115

Globalization   120
Global Production
Chains   120
"Washington
Consensus"or
Neoliberalism   122
The World Bank   122

International Monetary
Fund (IMF)   122
Fiscal Policy   125
Monetary Policy   126
Central Bank   127

SUGGESTED READINGS

Robert Kuttner, *Everything for Sale: The Virtues and Limits of Markets* (New York: Knopf, 1997). A critical view of markets that acknowledges both their virtues and shortcomings.

Charles E. Lindblom, *The Market System: What It Is, How It Works, and What to Make of It* (New Haven, CT: Yale University Press, 2001). An overview of markets that, like Kuttner's book, assesses the strengths and weaknesses of markets.

John McMillan, *Reinventing the Bazaar: A Natural History of Markets* (New York: Norton, 2002). An engaging, even entertaining, analysis of markets that examines why they are good, under what conditions they function well, and why limits to markets are necessary.

Thomas L. Friedman, *The World Is Flat: A Brief History of the Twentieth Century* (New York: Farrar, Straus, Giroux, 2005). The most accessible treatise in support of globalization. The title reflects Friedman's idea that globalization has leveled the playing field, making the good things in life available to more people.

Daniel Yergin and Joseph Stanislaw, *The Commanding Heights: The Battle between Government and the Marketplace That Is Remaking the Modern World* (New York: Simon & Schuster, 1998). A dutiful history of how the competing paradigms of states and markets have slipped in and out of fashion over the course of recent history.

NOTES

1. These paragraphs borrow heavily from Stephen Holmes, "What Russia Teaches Us Now: How Weak States Threaten Freedom," *The American Prospect* No. 33 (July/August 1997), pp. 30–39.
2. Friedman is quoted in Robert Kuttner, *Everything for Sale: The Virtues and Limits of Markets* (New York: Knopf, 1997), p. 33.
3. Joseph E. Stiglitz, *The Roaring Nineties: A New History of the World's Most Prosperous Decade* (New York: Norton, 2003), p. xi.
4. See Eric Wolf, *Peasant Wars of the Twentieth Century* (New York: Harper & Row, 1969); and James C. Scott, *The Moral Economy of the Peasant: Rebellion and*

Subsistence in Southeast Asia (New Haven, CT: Yale University Press, 1976). For a contrary view, which contends that peasants embrace markets because they permit peasants to increase their incomes, see Samuel L. Popkin, *The Rational Peasant: The Political Economy of Rural Society in Vietnam* (Berkeley, CA: University of California Press, 1979).

5. Richard Whitley, *Divergent Capitalisms: The Social Structuring and Change of Business Systems* (New York: Oxford University Press, 1999), p. 122.
6. On blocked exchanges, see Michael Walzer, *Spheres of Justice: A Defense of Pluralism and Equality* (New York: Basic Books, 1983). See also Judith Andre, "Blocked Exchanges: A Taxonomy," *Ethics* , Vol. 103, No. 1 (October 1993), pp. 29–47.
7. Charles E. Lindblom, *The Market System: What It Is, How It Works, and What To Make of It* (New Haven, CT: Yale University Press, 2001), p. 7.
8. Ibid., p. 3.
9. The metaphor applying the power of the market to invisible magnetic force fields comes from Robert L. Heilbroner, *The Logic and Nature of Capitalism* (New York: Norton, 1985), pp. 17–18.
10. Quoted in John McMillan, *Reinventing the Bazaar: A Natural History of Markets* (New York: Norton, 2002), p. 174.
11. Stephen Holmes and Cass R. Sunstein, *The Cost of Rights* (New York: Norton, 1999), p. 70.
12. McMillan, *Reinventing the Bazaar*, pp. 155–60.
13. John Zysman, "How Institutions Create Historically Rooted Trajectories of Growth," *Industrial and Corporate Change* , Vol. 3, No. 1 (1994), p. 243.
14. Barzun is cited in Dani Rodrik, "Feasible Globalizations," unpublished paper (May 2002), p. 3.
15. Niall Ferguson, *The Cash Nexus: Money and Power in the Modern World, 1700–2000* (New York: Basic Books, 2001), p. 174.
16. McMillan, *Reinventing the Bazaar*, p. 222.
17. Jacob S. Hacker and Paul Pierson, *Winner-Take-All Politics: How Washington Made the Rich Richer—and Turned its Back on the Middle Class* (New York: Simon & Schuster, 2010), p. 82.
18. Three years earlier at a U.S. embassy reception in Moscow Khrushchev challenged, "Whether you like it or not, history is on our side. We will bury you." Although Americans interpreted his boast as a military threat, Khrushchev was instead predicting that the Soviet economy would soon be bigger, wealthier, and more productive than the United States. Khrushchev is quoted in David P. Calleo, *Rethinking Europe's Future* (Princeton: Princeton University Press, 2001), pp. 119–20.
19. Thomas L. Friedman, *The Lexus and the Olive Tree* (New York: Farrar, Straus, Giroux, 1999), p. 86.
20. Robert C. Tucker, ed., *The Marx-Engels Reader*, 2nd ed. (New York: Norton, 1978), p. 477.
21. Michael Mandelbaum, "Democracy without America: The Spontaneous Spread of Freedom," *Foreign Affairs* (September/October 2007), Vol. 86., No. 5. pp. 123–124.
22. Milton and Rose Freedman, *Free to Choose: A Personal Statement* (New York: Harcourt, Brace, Jovanovich, 1980).
23. Ricardo Hausmann, "Will Volatility Kill Democracy," *Foreign Policy*, No. 108 (Fall 1997), p. 55.
24. Timothy J. McKeown, "The Global Economy, Post-Fordism, and Trade Policy in Advanced Capitalist States," in Herbert Kitschelt, et al., *Continuity and Change in Contemporary Capitalism* (New York: Cambridge University Press, 1999), pp. 11–36.

25. Lindblom, *The Market System*, pp. 147–153.
26. Daniel Yergin and Joseph Stanislaw, *The Commanding Heights: The Battle between Government and the Marketplace That Is Remaking the Modern World* (New York: Simon & Schuster, 1998), p. 11.
27. Yergin and Stanislaw, *The Commanding Heights*, pp. 67–92.
28. Jonah D. Levy, ed., *The State After Statism: New State Activities in the Age of Liberalization* (Cambridge: Harvard University Press, 2006).
29. *Economist*, "The Growth of the State: Leviathan Stirs Again," (January 21, 2010).
30. Sarkozy is quoted in Steven Hill, *Europe's Promise: Why the European Way Is the Best Hope in an Insecure Age* (Berkeley: University of California Press, 2010), p. x.
31. El-Erian is quoted in James Surowiecki, "The Age of Political Risk," *The New Yorker*, (May 24, 2010), p. 24.
32. Greg Linden, Kenneth L. Kramer, and Jason Dedrick, "Who Captures Value in a Global Innovation System? The Case of Apple's iPod," (Irvine, Ca.: Personal Computing Industry Center, 2007).
33. The World Bank and IMF are often confused with one another, so it may be helpful to distinguish their different missions through a metaphor. The World Bank loans money to poor store owners so they can make improvements to their businesses, while the IMF loans money to poor store owners who are about to default on their mortgage.
34. Adam Przeworski, "The Neoliberal Fallacy," *Journal of Democracy* 3:3 (1992), p. 56.
35. John Williamson, "Democracy and the 'Washington Consensus,'" *World Development*, 21:8 (1993), p. 1330.
36. Thomas L. Friedman, *The World Is Flat: A Brief History of the Twenty-First Century* (New York: Farrar, Strauss and Giroux, 2005).
37. Russell Flannery, "Tread Ware," *Forbes* Vol. 168, No. 11 (October 29, 2001), p. 118.
38. Jeremy Brecher and Tim Costello, *Global Village or Global Pillage: Economic Reconstruction from the Bottom Up* 2nd ed. (Cambridge, MA: South End Press, 1998), pp. 3–33.
39. William Greider, "A New Giant Sucking Sound," *The Nation* (December 13, 2001).
40. World Bank, "Economic Growth in the 1990s: Learning from a Decade of Growth," (Washington, D.C.: World Bank, 2005), p. 11.
41. Tina Rosenberg, "The Free Trade Fix," *New York Times Magazine Section* (August 18, 2002), p. 31.
42. Bruce Gilley and David Murphy, "Why China Needs a Real Central Bank," *Far Eastern Economic Review* (May 24, 2001), pp. 48–52.
43. Bruce Cumings, *Korea's Place in the Sun: A Modern History* (New York: Norton, 1997), p. 317.
44. Michael Zweig, *The Working Class Majority: America's Best Kept Secret* (Ithaca: Cornell University Press, 2000), p. 164.
45. World Bank, *2005:World Development Indicators* (Washington, DC: The World Bank, 2005), Table 5.3 "Business Environment," pp. 278–280.
46. Paul Osterman, Thomas A. Kochan, Richard Locke, and Michael J. Piore, *Working in America: A Blueprint for a New Labor Market* (Cambridge, MA: MIT Press, 2001), p. 47.
47. Chris Howell, *Trade Unions and the State: The Construction of Industrial Relations Institutions in Britain, 1890–2000* (Princeton, NJ: Princeton University Press, 2005), p. 154.
48. Morton H. Halperin, Joseph T. Siegle, and Michael M. Weinstein, *The Democracy Advantage: How Democracies Promote Prosperity and Peace* (New York: Routledge, 2005), p. 12.

Authoritarianism

INTRODUCTION

In 1994 members of the Hutu ethnic group in Rwanda slaughtered nearly 800,000 Tutsis and moderate Hutus. In the immediate aftermath of the killings Rwanda's future looked grim. Ethnic groups feared and distrusted one another. Establishing a stable government seemed unlikely. Despite these gloomy prospects, the government of President Paul Kagame, who came to power in 2000, has made considerable progress. It has increased economic growth, reduced corruption, cut infant mortality, improved children's chances of getting an education, lengthened citizens' life expectancy, and promoted equality for women. In short, the government has had considerable success in improving capabilities—with one crucial exception: it has restricted civil and political liberties and retained power by authoritarian means. In the guise of preventing "divisionism" that might lead to renewed ethnic violence, the government has stifled criticism of its policies and intimidated its political opponents. The government gets to decide when opponents are practicing "divisionism" and can jail them when they cross the fuzzy line between what they are permitted to say and what they are not.[1]

President Kagame's success in improving citizens' capabilities while maintaining authoritarian rule raises uncomfortable questions for supporters of democracy. Is democracy appropriate for all countries? Is it possible that in some circumstances, such as those in Rwanda, authoritarian rule is necessary? Is it sometimes necessary to limit civil and political rights to achieve improvements in education, health, and safety? If so, are some kinds of authoritarian rule more successful than others at improving capabilities?

Authoritarianism is a type of political system in which a single individual or small elite rules without constitutional checks on their use of power. They can use their power to change rules when it is to their advantage and to decide who gets to participate in politics. They also set the penalties for breaking the rules they have made. Citizens in authoritarian systems cannot hold rulers accountable. They have no recourse to independent courts of law or constitutional guarantees to free and fair elections.[2]

Authoritarianism has been the main form of government through most of recorded history. Czars, emperors, kings, and sultans have assumed the right to rule with no restraints on their power from ordinary people. Louis XV, the absolute monarch of France from 1715 to 1774, proclaimed without any hint of humility:

> In my person alone resides the sovereign power . . . and it is from me alone that the courts hold their existence and their authority. That . . . authority can only be exercised in my name. . . . For it is to me exclusively that the legislative power belongs. . . . The whole public order emanates from me since I am its supreme guardian. . . . The rights and interests of the nation . . . are necessarily united with my own and can only rest in my hands.[3]

Although absolute monarchs like Louis XV have disappeared, new forms of authoritarianism have taken their place. Like their premodern predecessors, modern forms of authoritarianism continue to concentrate state power in the hands of a small elite. What is new is their claim to have popular support and represent the will of the people.[4] Authoritarian leaders now feel obliged to make a show of ruling by democratic means. They live in an age when democracy has become a universal value, even though it is not universally practiced.[5] But these modern forms of authoritarianism have two features that make them authoritarian rather than democratic. First, power is concentrated in the executive branch of government, and within that branch it is concentrated further in the office of the chief executive. The legislature lacks power to influence government policies and the judiciary lacks power to assert the law independent of the executive. Second, governments are not accountable to citizens. Civil and political rights are restricted or denied.

Authoritarian governments were on the defensive between 1974 and 2000. The number of authoritarian governments in the world fell dramatically during these years. By the 1990s, especially after the fall of the Soviet Union, many political scientists believed there was no credible alternative to democracy. They assumed it was only a matter of time until democracy triumphed in countries still under authoritarian rule. The transition to democracy might take longer in some countries than in others, but liberal democracy would eventually become "the final form of human government."[6]

More recently, however, that optimism has ebbed. A number of authoritarian regimes have displayed impressive staying power. This is especially true in the Middle East where not a single Arab country is a democracy. Authoritarianism is also prevalent in some parts of Africa and Asia, including China, the world's most populous country. To make matters worse, some countries that once appeared to be on their way to democracy have slipped back into authoritarian rule. Russia is the most significant example.[7] Democracy specialist Larry Diamond acknowledged in 2008: "In a few short years, the democratic wave has been slowed by a powerful authoritarian undertow, and the world has slipped into a democratic recession."[8]

Authoritarian leaders are now on the offensive. Some of them can claim considerable success in improving their citizens' lives. China's Communist Party leaders can take credit for one of the fastest economic growth rates of any country in history, which has raised more people out of abject poverty in a shorter time than any country in history. China is also a leader in terms of adopting green technologies.[9] Its leaders attribute their success to their ability to make decisions quickly and to make policy for the long run. They criticize the United States and other democracies for getting bogged down in endless arguments and for thinking no further into the future than the next election cycle. Democracies, they charge, are reluctant to change ineffective and outdated policies supported by entrenched interest groups in fear of offending them.[10]

This chapter begins by distinguishing between authoritarianism and its extreme form, totalitarianism. It then turns to a description of different kinds of authoritarian rule: monarchy, military, one-party, electoral authoritarian, and personal rule. A **regime** is "a set of rules and procedures for choosing leaders and policies that exists in a country during a period of time, and the government that embodies these rules, not individual leaders."[11] The chapter next examines how leaders of numerous authoritarian regimes have managed to persist in an age of democratization, focusing on why there are no Arab democracies. The chapter ends with a comparison of how different forms of authoritarianism fare in promoting capabilities. The question of how authoritarianism fares in comparison to democracy, in terms of increasing citizens' life chances, is deferred until Chapter 7.

AUTHORITARIAN AND TOTALITARIAN REGIMES

Political scientists distinguish between authoritarianism and the extreme version of authoritarianism known as **totalitarianism**. **Totalitarian regimes** seek to gain total control over citizens' behavior and thoughts and to transform societies in accord with ideological goals. Totalitarian regimes have five things in common. First is an encompassing ideology that offers a critique of existing society, a vision of a radically different and supposedly better society, and a program for realizing that vision. Second, they have a single political party usually led by one dominant leader. Third, the state controls newspapers, radio, television, and book publishing to promote its views and stifle alternatives. Fourth, totalitarian regimes make continuous efforts to mobilize enthusiastic mass support for the party and leader through the media, rallies, and propaganda. Finally, they use terror and violence on a massive scale to intimidate or destroy not only political opponents but entire categories of people. These regimes do not necessarily achieve their goals, but they go farther in trying to control citizens' private lives than any other type of regime. Examples of totalitarian regimes include the Soviet Union under the leadership of Joseph Stalin from the early 1930s until his death in 1954, China under the leadership of Mao Zedong from the late 1950s until 1976, and Germany under the leadership of Hitler from 1933 until 1945. The only current example is North Korea.

Authoritarian regimes differ from totalitarian governments on each of these points. Authoritarian regimes use ideologies to justify their rule, but these are not as elaborate or ambitious as those of totalitarian regimes. While some authoritarian regimes have been ruled by one party, they do not seek total control over citizens' behavior and thoughts or a total transformation of societies. Authoritarian regimes also sometimes allow limited freedom of the press, as long as the media do not directly criticize the regime's top leadership. Nor do authoritarian regimes try to mobilize fervent mass support. They prefer politically apathetic citizens who obey the regime and do not challenge it. Finally, while they use torture, violence, and even murder to intimidate opponents and eliminate perceived threats to their rule, authoritarian rulers do not use those methods on the massive scale of totalitarian regimes.

TYPES OF AUTHORITARIAN REGIMES

In this section, we examine five types of authoritarian rule: monarchy, military, one-party, electoral authoritarian, and personal rule.[12] We focus only on "pure" regime types. For each regime type we discuss who rules, how rulers justify their domination, and how they stay in power.[13]

Monarchies

In 2005, there were more ruling monarchies in the world than there were one-party or military regimes. This is surprising, since monarchy is an ancient form of rule that seemed unlikely to survive into the twenty-first century. Indeed, monarchies have not just survived, but—measured by length of tenure in office—have been the most successful of all authoritarian regimes. In a **monarchy**, the person who rules is someone of royal descent who inherits "the position of head of state in accordance with accepted practice or the constitution."[14]

Monarchs are not just symbolic heads of state like the Queen of England or the King of Sweden, but make major policy and personnel decisions. Most of them rule Arab countries, including Saudi Arabia, Oman, the United Arab Emirates, and Jordan. Some, such as Saudi Arabia, have abundant oil reserves. Others, such as Jordan, do not. All of these monarchies, however, rule countries in an area of the world of great strategic interest for Western Europe and the United States.

Contemporary ruling monarchs are challenged to justify their right to rule and claim legitimacy. **Legitimacy** is the willingness of citizens to acknowledge that a regime rightfully holds and exercises political power.[15] In democracies, governments claim legitimacy by being elected. Since monarchs are not elected, they need other ways of making their rule legitimate. One way is to claim legitimacy on the basis of long-standing tradition. In Arab countries, they can link their rule to traditional Islamic practices. Monarchs can also seek legitimacy by presenting themselves as effective rulers who promote the well-being of their subjects. Huge oil deposits have provided several of the Arab monarchies with the means to do so. These monarchies can use oil revenues to provide free health care, education, and housing for citizens, as well as government jobs.

Monarchies stay in power not just by appealing to traditional religious practices or providing citizens with welfare state benefits, but through fierce repression. All of them have large security forces. Their secret police and intelligence agencies are well funded, and have been very effective at disrupting movements critical of the monarchy and crushing dissent.

Military Regimes

Military regimes were one of the most common forms of rule from the end of World War II through the 1980s. During these decades the military intervened in politics in nearly two-thirds of the less developed countries of Africa, Asia, Latin America, and the Middle East. Nowhere was the entry of the military into politics as extensive as in Latin America. In 1960, nine out of ten countries in Latin America were democracies. A dozen years later, that number had fallen to just two.

In **military regimes**, "a group of military officers decides who will rule and exercises some influence on policy."[16] Officers take and hold power, using or threatening to use force. The sudden, violent use of force to overthrow a government is known as a **coup d'état**. In a coup d'état armed troops converge on the office of the civilian president or prime minister, arrest or kill him, and seize control of key government ministries. In some coups, such as the one that occurred in the West African country of Niger in 2010, only a small number of troops are involved and few people are injured or killed. In others, such as the coup that overthrew the elected government of Chile in 1973, several thousand people are killed.[17]

One of the immediate challenges facing military leaders following a coup d'état is to consolidate their hold on power. While they use violence to take over the government, trying to rule by relying on force is costly and inefficient. The military leaders need to convince people that they have a right to hold office.[18] Leaders often try to assert their legitimacy by promising a quick return to democratic rule after they clean up problems created by the civilian government. For example, the leaders of the Niger coup signaled that intention by calling themselves "the Supreme Council for the Restoration of Democracy."[19] Military leaders also try to gain legitimacy by holding elections. In such elections the military establishes a political party, which is given considerable advantages over competing civilian parties. The most important is that "the incumbents have guns, whereas the opposition does not."[20] Finally, some military regimes seek legitimacy by claiming to defend the nation from domestic or foreign threats. In the 1960s and 1970s, military regimes in Asia and Latin America frequently invoked the menace of communism to secure support from the population. In South Korea, Thailand, and Indonesia military regimes pointed to the threat posed by China. Military regimes in Latin America in the 1970s and the 1980s pointed to the threat posed by Cuba.

Seeking legitimacy goes only so far in helping military governments consolidate control. Officials of the ousted civilian government and many other citizens are unlikely to accept the legitimacy of a military government that seized power illegally. These critics often protest the illegal seizure of power by organizing mass protests and criticizing the military government in newspapers and journals. Military governments control such opponents by declaring **martial law,** which gives them the authority to set curfews, ban protests, and public assemblies. They also use spies and informants to find dissidents and arrest them. The military governments of Chile and South Korea even had spies in the United States to inform on citizens living there who were critical of the military. Military governments also ban opposition newspapers and journals. Suspected opponents are arrested, imprisoned, and tortured. Military regimes in Argentina, Brazil, and Chile killed thousands of people, never informing friends and relatives who they had murdered or where they were buried. The Indonesian military was responsible for the deaths of an estimated 500,000 people in the two years following its seizure of power in 1965.

Military regimes do not rule by martial law and coercion alone. They also attempt to build support by crafting policies that benefit particular groups in society. In a few cases, these policies benefit a large cross section of the population. The military regime that ruled South Korea in the 1970s and 1980s enacted land reform policies that helped poor farmers and educational policies that helped the sons and daughters of workers. In other cases they benefit a small number of cronies of the military rulers or narrow constituencies. Military governments in Latin America, such as those in Brazil and Chile, enacted policies that benefited narrow constituencies. The main beneficiaries of their rule were big businesses and commercial farming interests. In many sub-Saharan African countries military leaders pursued policies that benefited a still narrower clique of supporters at the expense of the populace as a whole.

Single-Party Regimes

In **single-party regimes,** one party controls access to political office and policy making. According to political scientist Barbara Geddes, in these regimes the party organization "exercises some power over the leader at least part of the time, controls the selection of officials, organizes the distribution of benefits to supporters, and mobilizes citizens to vote and show support for party leaders."[21] In many single-party regimes, no other parties are permitted to exist. If other parties are allowed, they serve a purely symbolic function and cannot challenge the rule of the dominant political party.[22] The three main types of single-party regimes have been communist, fascist, and nationalist. All three led mass movements, and once in power, legitimized their rule with ideologies promising a better future for their followers. Single parties can be used to construct either totalitarian or authoritarian regimes. For example, Joseph Stalin used his control of the communist party in the Soviet Union to construct a totalitarian regime, but subsequent leaders of the party eased totalitarian controls to create authoritarian regimes. Communist parties ruled 16 countries in the 1980s,[23] but are now found only in China, North Korea, Vietnam, Laos, and Cuba. Fascist parties ruled Germany and Italy from the 1930s until the end of World War II, but there are now no countries with ruling fascist parties. Finally, nationalist parties led successful independence movements against colonial powers in the 1950s and 1960s and became the ruling parties of these newly independent countries. Most of these single-party regimes were located in Africa. A number of them have been overthrown by military coups d'état, but a dozen remained in 2009.[24] In the remainder of the section, we focus on communist and fascist political parties because these two types of political parties have had enduring effects on the lives of hundreds of millions of people.

In communist regimes, leadership positions are staffed by members of the communist party. Internally **communist parties** are hierarchically organized, with real power concentrated in the hands of a small number of leaders who determine public policy. In theory these leaders are elected by lower-ranking party organizations, but in reality such elections are a façade to legitimize the rule of the leaders. Communist parties have five main features. First, their avowed goal is to lead workers and peasants in revolution to take power and build communism. Second, they are vanguard parties. Their members form an elite group that provides leadership for working class and peasant movements. Third, there is an elaborate ideology based on Marxism-Leninism. Fourth, communist parties ruthlessly eliminate opposition political parties and independent associations in society. Finally, communist parties penetrate deeply into society with party branches in local governments, factories, schools, and organizations of all kinds.

Communist parties have come to power in two ways. First is through **revolution,** which "is a rapid, fundamental, and violent domestic change in the dominant values and myths of a society, in its political institutions, social structure, leadership, and government activity and policies."[25] This is how communist parties came to power in the Soviet Union, China, Cuba, and Vietnam. Communist parties also achieved power by being imposed on neighboring countries. The Soviet Union imposed communist rule on a number of countries in Eastern Europe at the end of World War II.

Traditionally, communist parties have sought legitimacy by appealing to ideology, nationalism, and protection from internal and external threats. Communist ideology is based on **Marxism**. According to Karl Marx, all societies rest on the exploitation of one social class by another. What slaveholding, feudal, and capitalist societies share is an economic structure in which one class owns the means of production and lives off the surplus produced by others. The state and legal system reinforce these relations of exploitation. Just as slavery was replaced by feudalism, which, in turn, was replaced by capitalism, so will capitalism be replaced by communism. Capitalism, according to Marx, cannot help but produce a revolutionary working class that will overthrow it and institute a new order dedicated to economic equality and the ability of all individuals to develop their creative capacities. Marx assumed that communist societies will have highly developed industrial economies. They will have no specialization of labor in which some persons are privileged because of the kind of work they do. Social classes will disappear and with them so will the state, a tool of the ruling class to dominate other classes. Communist societies will be societies of abundance in which the criterion for the production and distribution of goods and services will be "from each according to his ability; to each according to his needs." This vision of communism might be an improbable fantasy to readers today, but it attracted many workers and intellectuals in the nineteenth and twentieth centuries.

Communist parties have also appealed to nationalism to legitimize their rule. Soviet leaders won support from their population by leading the country to victory over Nazi Germany in World War II, and by transforming it into one of the two "super powers" of the Cold War period. Soviet citizens took pride in their country's rise to the status of a world power. China's leaders have similarly won support for transforming China from an impoverished country in 1949 to a major economic and military power today. The 2008 Summer Olympics in Beijing, which showcased China's achievements, was a source of great national pride.

Finally, communist parties claim legitimacy on the basis of defending their countries from foreign attack and preventing domestic instability. Communist parties' allegations that their countries were threatened by foreign attack were credible to citizens. Soviet leaders could point to U.S. troops in Europe and ballistic missiles armed with nuclear warheads targeted at Soviet cities, and China can make similar assertions about U.S. intentions today. In addition, both the Soviet and Chinese communist parties claimed that their tight control over society was necessary to prevent political instability and turmoil.

Where the velvet glove fails, communist parties can rely on the iron fist. Communist parties have not been reluctant to use massive force against their opponents. Mao Zedong gave a classic description justifying the use of such force when he wrote,

> A revolution is not a dinner party, or writing an essay, or painting a picture, or doing embroidery; it cannot be so refined and so leisurely and gentle, so temperate, kind, courteous, restrained and magnanimous. A revolution is an insurrection, an act of violence in which one class overthrows another.[26]

Communist party repression has been used to destroy the economic and political power of entire social classes, such as capitalists in cities and large landholders in the countryside. Their assets and land were seized, many were killed, and millions of others were sent to prison or to labor camps. After communist parties were firmly in power, they continued to use security forces to control societies through the use of surveillance, informants, and arrests.

State ownership of the economy provided another means of control. Every worker worked in a state-owned factory. Workers' housing and health care, and their children's schooling were tied to the firm where they worked. Similarly, rural citizens' lives were controlled by forcing them to live on state-organized cooperative or collective farms and placing tight restrictions on their ability to move from one part of the country to another.

Another means of control has been state-sponsored organizations for workers, youth, women, and intellectuals. These organizations were controlled by the communist party rather than by leaders selected by their members.

Finally, communist parties have enacted social and economic policies that benefit particular social classes and groups in society in order to win and maintain their support. In the initial decades of communist control, urban workers benefited from guaranteed jobs in state-owned firms, state-provided housing, and state-sponsored health care. The jobs paid low wages, living quarters were cramped, and the quality of health care was often low. On the other hand, workers never lost their jobs, they had roofs over their heads, and low-quality health care was better than none at all. Peasants received some benefits in the form of education and health care, but communist parties gave them lower priority than urban workers. In recent decades communist parties have reversed some of these policies and begun to pursue policies that benefit businesspeople in the private sector. Workers do not receive the same priority they did from the 1950s through the 1970s. China has closed hundreds of state enterprises, throwing tens of thousands of people out of work. Today, high-ranking communist party officials and their children are among the main beneficiaries of communist rule. Every economic transaction offers opportunities for party officials to demand payoffs and bribes. As David Remnick writes in *Lenin's Tomb: The Last Days of the Soviet Empire*, "the communist party apparatus of the Soviet Union "was the most gigantic mafia the world has ever known."[27] Corruption is also pervasive in China, where party officials use their power to enrich themselves.

The second major type of one-party regime is rule by a **fascist party**. In 1922, Benito Mussolini's Fascists marched on Rome and successfully deposed

Italy's fragile democracy. In 1933, Adolf Hitler became Chancellor of Germany and proceeded to create the Third Reich on the ashes of the beleaguered Weimar Republic. Fascism was on the move elsewhere in Central Europe as Austria succumbed to the fascists a year after Germany and powerful fascist movements contended for power in Romania and Hungary.

Fascist political parties were organized differently from communist political parties. While communist parties retain the façade of elected leaders who are responsible to party members, fascist parties are distinguished by "unadorned centralization with overall command exercised by an individual leader figure." This leader was called *der fuhrer* in Germany and *il Duce* in Italy. Fascist parties copied the hierarchical structure of military organization complete with military-style uniforms and salutes.[28]

Fascist parties use ideology, the façade of democracy, and charismatic leaders to gain legitimacy. Ideologically, they presented themselves as anticommunist mass movements drawing support from all social classes. Their popular appeal was rooted in ultranationalism. Instead of emphasizing class struggle as communist parties do, fascists emphasized the importance of a cohesive, "organic" nation. The harmony of the nation allegedly permitted them to transcend the kinds of social conflicts that afflicted other societies such as the conflict between labor and capital.[29] On the other hand, fascist political parties drew clear boundaries between those who were part of the nation and those who were not. Ethnic, religious, and cultural minorities threatened the unity of the nation and were defined as "others." The most destructive outcome of such policies was the Nazi regime's murder of six million Jews.

Fascist political parties in Germany and Italy also claimed the mantle of democracy to shore up their legitimacy. Citizens were stripped of civil and political rights, and free elections were ended, but the Nazi Party in Germany claimed to represent the will of the people in a "German democracy." Mussolini described Italy as an "authoritative," "organized," and "centralized" democracy representing the will of the Italian people.[30] In both cases, the leaders presented their version of democracy as superior to that of parliamentary democracy in Western Europe and North America. They claimed to speak for all of the people who were part of the "organic" nation, unlike leaders in other democracies who represented the narrow interests of particular groups in society.

Finally, fascist parties relied heavily on **charismatic leaders** for legitimacy. Supporters of Adolf Hitler and, to a lesser extent, Benito Mussolini, saw them as extraordinary, superhuman beings with abilities far beyond those of ordinary politicians. They inspired fanatical support that was cultivated through mass rallies of tens of thousands of people, featuring martial music, and elaborate pageantry. They embodied the promise of an integrated, organic nation led by "a single, cohesive will."[31] The state was the institutionalized expression of the unified nation, and within the state, the unity of the nation was expressed in the authority of the supreme leader.

Fascist political parties used a combination of violence, restrictions on civil and political rights, informants, and party-led organizations to control their populations. The Nazi party used paramilitary thugs to intimidate its electoral opponents. Mussolini became the leader of Italy in 1922 by having the Fascist militia march on Rome and intimidate the king into naming him as the prime minister. Once in office, fascist parties use security forces to terrorize citizens and strip them of rights and due process of law. "There are no citizens in the Fascist state," one observer commented, "there are only subjects."[32] Citizens had no way to select or remove their leaders, who ruled through charisma and intimidation. Fascist parties in Germany and Italy made extensive use of informants to report citizens who did not support party policies. Finally, the fascist state commandeered autonomous civic organizations, such as labor unions and social clubs, in an effort to create and express the organic community. An independent public sphere outside the state was suppressed. As Mussolini proclaimed, "Everything in the State, nothing against the State, nothing outside the State."[33] The boundary between the public and private spheres collapsed. "The only private individual" under fascism, it was quipped, "was someone asleep."[34]

Fascist regimes permitted business owners to retain their property, but they also reserved the right to control how that property was used. Private interests were protected but subordinated to the national interest. While differences between labor and capital were supposed to be subordinated to the interests of the nation as a whole, the interests of capitalists prevailed over the interests of labor.

The fascist regimes in Germany and Italy ended with crushing defeats in 1945, and their leaders met ignominious ends. Hitler committed suicide in his bunker. Mussolini was killed by Italian guerilla fighters who hung his body upside down from a meat hook in Milan and left it to be ridiculed and abused by passersby. The failure of these regimes was so complete that no current authoritarian regime is based on fascist principles.

Electoral Authoritarian Regimes

In the 1980s and 1990s, large numbers of authoritarian regimes were washed away by the wave of democratization sweeping across Latin America, Africa, and Asia. The remaining authoritarian rulers learned to adjust to pressures for democratization coming from the United States, Western Europe, and from their own societies. The main form this change took was for leaders of dominant ruling parties to make opposition parties legal and permit regular elections. These regimes "institute the *principle* of popular consent, even as they subvert it in *practice*."[35] They are now the most common form of authoritarian rule in the world.[36]

Electoral authoritarian regimes hold regularly scheduled elections for chief executives and members of national parliaments, and allow multiple political parties to vie for power. The elections are not free and fair, and election rules are tilted strongly in favor of the ruling political party. Opposition parties do win seats in parliament, and in some countries, such as Mexico, opposition parties have even managed to win the presidency, transforming an electoral authoritarian system into a democracy.[37] In most of these regimes, however, winning leadership position requires being a member of the ruling party or faction, and opposition parties have little chance of gaining power. Prominent examples of such regimes include Russia, Malaysia, and Egypt.[38]

Electoral authoritarian regimes are not unique in holding elections. Some monarchies, many military regimes, and one-party regimes have also done so. Two features make electoral authoritarian regimes distinctive from the other types of authoritarian regimes. One is that multiparty elections determine who holds powerful leadership positions in the country. In monarchies and communist party regimes, voters never get to vote for or against the monarch or leader of the communist party. Second, elections can be meaningful in electoral authoritarian regimes. While it is highly unusual for leaders of these regimes to lose office as a result of elections, it does happen.

Holding regularly scheduled multiparty elections is the main way that electoral authoritarian regimes seek legitimacy. Some of them, such as the ones in Malaysia and Russia, have also relied on economic growth and raising citizens' standard of living as means of gaining legitimacy. Rising incomes in those countries have enabled urban middle class citizens to wear trendy clothes, rent nice apartments, and drive luxury cars. Leaders can even add restoring national pride to their list of accomplishments. The current leaders of Russia take credit for reinstating Russia as a world power following the collapse of the Soviet Union.

Electoral authoritarian regimes in Asia and the Arab world pursue broadly similar economic and social policies. They have implemented market-oriented economic reforms, privatizing firms and permitting more foreign investment, but the state still plays a considerable role in the economy. Market-oriented policies have both economic and political goals. They are designed to promote faster economic growth and win the support of business-people who benefit from such growth.[39]

Leaders of these regimes use coercion to control groups in society, but make less use of open violence and terror than military and one-party regimes. Security forces intimidate political opponents and arrest citizens who cross the often fuzzy line between what is politically permissible and what is not. Courts apply laws in ways that allow the regime to shut down human rights groups and labor unions. Election commissions manipulate voting results in favor of the ruling elite.[40] The commissions decide which opposition candidates are allowed to run for office, control access to media needed to publicize opposition parties' policies, and alter vote counts to ensure the victory of the ruling party.[41]

This uneven playing field creates dilemmas for leaders of opposition parties. They know they are competing in a rigged game. If they choose to participate they run the risk of legitimizing the rules of the game. If the ruling party wins elections with large majorities, the results confirm its leaders' claims that it is popular and has wide support. Repeated losses by large margins can demoralize leaders of opposition parties and convince them that it is useless to challenge the regime. Such losses also demoralize citizens who voted for the opposition parties and cause them to drop out of politics. If this happens, the regime wins by default.

Allowing multiple political parties to compete for offices also creates dilemmas for ruling elites. It means the regime must give up any pretence that there is a generally agreed upon common good that the ruling elite embodies, and concedes that there are cleavages in society.[42] Regime leaders have to decide which particular means of manipulating the election they will use and to what degree. Which opposition candidates will they allow or disallow? What restraints will they place on candidates' abilities to have rallies and move about the country? There is the risk that even with all of these restraints an opposition candidate for the chief executive will prove more popular than anticipated.[43] Then they face the question of how to manipulate vote totals without sparking public outrage and mass demonstrations. The Iranian presidential election of 2009 provides an example of how a ruling elite can misgauge an opposition candidate's popularity. When the opposition candidate did unexpectedly well, the Iranian leadership clumsily rigged the vote totals so their candidate, Mahmoud Ahmadinejad, won the presidency by an implausible margin. The announcement of Ahmadinejad's victory ignited massive street demonstrations by supporters of the losing candidate, and growing divisions and struggles within the regime itself.

◤ COMPARATIVE POLITICAL ANALYSIS

Why Do Some Authoritarian Regimes Survive Elections While Others Do Not?

Problem

Even when authoritarian regimes hold elections, they are not free and fair. Political scientists disagree on whether such elections can lead to full democratization. Some political scientists believe such elections can be used to build support for more democratic rights and thereby destabilize authoritarian regimes. Others believe they strengthen authoritarian regimes by acting as a safety valve for dissent. In *Authoritarianism in an Age of Democratization* Jason Brownlee suggests a third possibility. Whether elections lead to instability or not depends on regimes' capacity for weakening and marginalizing candidates from opposition political parties in elections.

Hypothesis and Method

Brownlee hypothesizes that authoritarian regimes with a ruling political party are likely to face less serious opposition challenges to their rule and remain more durable than

Continued

authoritarian regimes without such a party. Ruling parties lead to greater durability for two reasons. First, they provide party elites with benefits for themselves and their followers that make it worthwhile to stick with the ruling party rather than defecting to the opposition. Ruling parties also provide a forum for working out differences among leaders. Countries without a ruling party are much more likely to experience serious disagreement between members of the governing elite and defectors, which strengthens the opposition. Brownlee uses the comparative case study method to test the hypothesis, comparing half a century of historical experiences in Egypt, Malaysia, the Philippines under authoritarian rule in the 1970s and 1980s, and Iran.

Operationalizing Concepts

Brownlee defines the two central concepts as follows:

- A ruling party is a "national organization with mass membership and a sustainable decision making structure."
- A regime's capacity to marginalize the opposition is measured by the percentage of seats won by the regime's principal party or factions in legislative elections and its percentage of the popular vote in presidential elections.

Results

The comparative case studies confirm Brownlee's hypothesis. Egypt and Malaysia differ from each other in many ways. What they share is a strong ruling party and durable authoritarianism. Iran and the Philippines are likewise different in many ways. What they have in common is the lack of a strong ruling party. The authoritarian regime in the Philippines, led by Ferdinand Marcos, was overthrown in 1986 and followed by an unstable, fragmented democracy. The Iranian regime is still in power, but Brownlee's analysis helps us understand why it has been less stable than the regimes in Egypt and Malaysia. His analysis also helps explain why the regime's candidate for president in 2009 faced such strong opposition and why protests and political unrest continued after the election.

For Further Discussion

1. How can Jason Brownlee's analysis be used to project which electoral authoritarian regimes are likely to survive and which are not?
2. Would it be desirable to have an electoral authoritarian regime, such as the one in Egypt, collapse, even if radical Muslim parties won ensuing free elections and gained control of the government?

Personal Rule

The leaders of monarchies, military, single-party, and ruling parties in electoral authoritarian regimes rule in consultation with supporters in the regime who helped them come to power. There have been numerous cases, however, when individual leaders in each of these types of regime have been able to concentrate power in their own hands and loosen organizational restraints on what they can do. When they accumulate so much power that they can impose their decisions without significant constraints from other leading members of the regime, the result is **personal rule**. It can emerge from any of the four regime types discussed previously.[44] Personal rulers gain control over personnel as well as policy decisions and tend to stay in power for life. They "range from vicious psychopaths to benevolent populists."[45]

Personal rule usually emerges from power struggles in a ruling political party or military regime after it has seized control of the state. Joseph Stalin came to power in the Soviet Union through such a struggle, as did Mao Zedong in China. In both cases, Stalin and Mao continued to have the support of the communist party, but were able to make decisions without being accountable to it.[46] The best current example of personal rule is North Korea, where the leader controls the Korean Workers' Party rather than being controlled by it.

Personal rulers can come to power in countries with strong state institutions as well as weak ones. In the Soviet Union and China, dictators commanded relatively strong states that were capable of enforcing policies throughout the territory they claimed to control. This has also been the case with Mahathir Mohamad of Malaysia, who transformed "a semidemocratic one-party regime into something more closely resembling personalized authoritarian rule" during the 1990s.[47] But most cases of personal rule occur in very poor countries with weak political and economic institutions. The political scientist Barbara Geddes lists 22 countries governed by personal rule in 2009. Twelve of them were in sub-Saharan Africa where weak institutions prevail.[48]

Weak party and state institutions also shape the ways in which personal rulers hold on to power. These countries do not have strong and capable civil services that rulers can depend on to implement policies, nor do they have strong institutional protection from attempts to overthrow them. In these circumstances, personal dictators seek loyalty by using patronage to fill posts in the military, police, and civilian bureaucracy with members of their extended family, or people from their region, religious group, or ethnic group. In return for their loyalty, these officials are given the opportunity to enrich themselves through corruption. Recent examples of personal rule in Africa include Sese Seko Mobutu, the onetime dictator of Zaire (now renamed the Democratic Republic of the Congo) and the current president of Chad, Idris Derby, who took power in 1990.

Personal rulers sometimes appear to have overwhelming power, but that appearance can be misleading. They do have strong despotic power, but infrastructural power is weak. **Despotic power** is power to make decisions without having to follow organizational procedures or consult with groups in society. Personal rulers can decide to remove officials from office, intimidate journalists, and have opponents arrested. Despotic rulers use their security forces to abduct, torture, and murder opponents. But most of these rulers have weak infrastructural power. **Infrastructural power** is the ability to implement decisions effectively. This requires effective bureaucracies[49]. Leaders of democracies can have much stronger infrastructural power than personal rulers. For example, democratic Costa Rica has much stronger infrastructural power than authoritarian Chad. As we saw earlier, Costa Rica has an extremely effective health care delivery system in rural areas for expectant mothers and their newborns. In contrast, a 2004 study in Chad that tracked what happened to government money intended for rural health clinics found that "only 1 percent of it reached the clinics."[50] The rest was siphoned off by corrupt officials. The consequence is that in Costa Rica only 9 infants die in their first year of life, compared with 99 in Chad.

◤ THE GOOD SOCIETY IN DEPTH

Zimbabwe: How Personal Rule Wrecked an Economy and Lowered Capabilities

Zimbabwe won its independence in 1980 after a prolonged civil war. At the time it was one of the most economically promising countries in sub-Saharan Africa, with its fertile soil, thriving commercial agriculture, and strong export earnings. It also had a major problem. During British colonial rule, white farmers took control of 70 percent of the arable land, leaving black farmers with arid plots that were ill-suited for agriculture. President Robert Mugabe, whose picture is at the beginning of the chapter, has used controversies over how to correct this imbalance in land distribution to consolidate and perpetuate his power. The result has been economic disaster and falling capabilities for Zimbabwe.

Mugabe initially supported gradual reforms predicated on the willingness of whites to sell farm land to blacks. This policy achieved little. By the 1990s thousands of poor black Zimbabweans, including veterans of the civil war, pressed for faster transfers of land, and began to invade land owned by white farmers. To sustain their support, Mugabe proposed a new constitution in 1999 that would allow the government to seize white farmers' land without payment and give it to blacks. The proposed constitution would also extend his term in office well beyond what was allowed at the time. These proposed constitutional changes were rejected in a referendum in 2000.

Mugabe retaliated for this defeat in two ways. One was by going after the white farmers. He accused them of stirring up and financing opposition to his rule, and he encouraged veterans and landless blacks to occupy their land. The second was by ruthlessly attacking the opposition. Newspapers were closed, leaders were arrested, and demonstrators were beaten.

These decisions set off a downward spiral. Agricultural production plummeted, resulting in lower export earnings and lower government revenues. To make up for the lost revenue, Mugabe printed money, which led to accelerating inflation. By

Continued

2007, a beer cost one million Zimbabwe dollars. In late 2008, citizens were restricted to borrowing a maximum of $100,000,000 from their bank account each week. Although that figure sounds like a huge amount, it was the equivalent of only $2.50 in U.S. currency.

The economic problems have had devastating consequences for capabilities. Many hospitals and rural clinics lack basic supplies. Infant mortality rose from 54 per 1,000 in 1990 to 69 in 2000 before declining to 56 in 2009.[*] Life expectancy, which stood at 61 years in 1990, had plummeted by 2005 to just 41.5 years.

For Further Discussion

1. How does Mugabe fit the characteristics of personal rule?
2. Mugabe argues the land seizures were justified. Whites took the land from Africans during the colonial era and blacks are now taking the land back. Do you agree?

[*] World Development Indicators. www.google.com/public data.

IN BRIEF

Types of Authoritarian Rule

- Monarchy—the ruler is someone of royal descent who inherits the position of head of state in accordance with accepted practice or the constitution. The king of Saudi Arabia is an example
- Military—rule by a military officer or group of officers backed by a country's military. Prototypical examples include military rule in Brazil and Chile in the 1970s and 1980s and Burma (Myanmar) currently.
- One-party—Rule by a single political party with no other party having a real chance of gaining control of state institutions. The three main variants are:
  - Communist—a vanguard political party based on Marxism claiming to represent the working class. The prototypical example is the Communist Party of China
  - Fascist—a political party claiming to represent an organic nation of citizens led by a charismatic leader. Prototypical examples were the National Socialist German Workers Party (Nazi) in Germany and National Fascist Pary in Italy in the 1930s and 1940s.
  - Nationalist—a political party that began as the leading party of a nationalist movement and continues as a country's dominant political party. An example was the Revolutionary Party of Tanzania from the early 1970s until the mid-1990s.
- Electoral authoritarian—These kinds of regimes hold regular elections for chief executives and members of national parliaments, and allow multiple political parties to participate in the elections. The election rules are so tilted in favor of the regime that it is extremely difficult, if not impossible for opposition parties to win the most important leadership positions. Malaysia and Russia are prototypical examples.
- Personal rule—rule by a single leader who controls decision without organizational constraints.

Finally, leaders can reach beyond their borders to seek support from powerful countries. During the Cold War personal rulers made efforts to win support from either the United States or the Soviet Union. Both superpowers supported a number of repressive regimes. The United States gave substantial economic aid to the Mobutu regime in Zaire, in part to keep the country out of Soviet hands and in part to ensure access to its valuable mineral wealth. Mobutu used this aid to enrich himself and his supporters and help maintain the patronage network he used to keep control of the state and society.

EXPLAINING AUTHORITARIAN PERSISTENCE

The late twentieth century was particularly auspicious for democracy. Between 1974 and 1995, the number of democracies rose from 40 to 117. Yet many authoritarian regimes survived—some types more than others. The number of military and one-party regimes declined dramatically, but the number of monarchies remained largely unchanged, while the number of electoral authoritarian regimes increased. Not only did the democratic wave remove some forms of authoritarianism more than others, but its geographic reach was uneven as well. Democracy swept away numerous authoritarian regimes in Latin America, Africa, and Asia. In contrast, the Middle East remained a solid rock of authoritarian resistance. Israel was the only liberal democracy in the region in 1974, and this remained the case in 2010.

▶ IN BRIEF

Distinguishing between Middle Eastern and Arab Countries

The Middle East is a geographical concept. It usually refers to the countries located between Turkey and India including those on the Arabian Peninsula. There are differing opinions about which specific countries belong to the region. The countries included by most authors are Bahrain, Iran, Iraq, Israel, Jordan Kuwait, Lebanon, Oman, Qatar, Saudi Arabia, Syria, Turkey, United Arab Emirates, and Yemen. Some authors include Egypt in the region, but because it is located in North Africa it is often omitted from the list.

The term *Arab* is a linguistic and cultural concept, referring to people who speak Arabic and practice Arab customs. Arabic countries include Algeria, Bahrain, Egypt, Iraq, Jordan, Kuwait, Lebanon, Libya, Morocco, Oman, Qatar, Saudi Arabia, Syria, Tunisia, the United Arab Emirates, and Yemen. It is important to bear in mind that not all Middle Eastern countries fall into this category. Two notable exceptions are Israel and Iran. The population of Israel is predominantly composed of Jews who speak Hebrew. The population of Iran is largely composed of Persians, who speak Farsi. Although ethnically and linguistically different from Arabs, most Iranians do share their Muslim faith.

The persistence of authoritarianism in the Arab world remains a puzzle in an "age of democracy."[51] Some scholars attribute the failure of democracy to take root in the Middle East to Islam. The political scientist Samuel P. Huntington maintains that authoritarianism in the Arab world "has its source at least in part to the inhospitable nature of Islamic culture and society to Western liberal concepts."[52] Those who agree with Huntington believe that democracy requires a willingness to challenge political authority and the acceptance of pluralism, competition among ideas, equality of rights, and different lifestyles. They argue Islam rejects these values. Democracy also requires vesting authority in secular government rather than religious authority, whereas Islam supposedly regards God as "the sole source of political authority and from whose divine law must come all regulations governing the community of believers."[53]

Others scholars reject the assertion that Islam is incompatible with democracy. They point out that there is no single interpretation of Islam that is accepted by all Muslims, as the previous authors imply. Citizens living in predominantly Muslim countries differ greatly in their attitudes toward political authority, rights for women, and acceptance of different lifestyles. This is the case even in Iran, the only country in the world where Islamic clerics control the state.

Until recently, the debate about whether Islam is compatible with democracy was based on a selective reading of Islamic texts and on impressionistic views of what citizens in predominantly Muslim countries believe. Empirical research based on carefully conducted interviews allows us to correct a number of misconceptions. One of the main findings of this research is that Muslim populations can strongly support democracy. World Values Surveys in 1995–1996 and in 2000–2002 in six Arab countries asked interviewees whether they agreed with the statement, "Democracy may have problems, but it's better than any other form of government." A higher percentage of respondents in Arab countries expressed agreement than did those in European countries.[54] A Pew Foundation survey of Muslim populations in 2003 likewise found that large majorities supported Western-style democracy.[55] These findings contradict assertions that Islamic publics are hostile to democracy.

At the same time, the surveys discovered other, less encouraging results. High levels of popular support for democracy are not a good predictor of whether a country will become and remain a democracy. People living in countries with authoritarian regimes may like what they take to be the results of democracy but not like its procedures. Some may associate democracy with the economic wealth of the United States and Europe and believe it will bring similar prosperity to their country. Others imagine that in a democracy people like themselves will have more influence over government policies, but do not like the idea of people with different values having more influence. It turns out that a better predictor of whether a country will become a democracy is its population's support for self-expression values.[56] As we discussed in Chapter 4, these values include a willingness to challenge political elites, and support for both free speech and freedom in choice of lifestyles. Surveys find lower levels of enthusiasm for these values in predominantly Muslim countries than in Europe and North America. Over half of the citizens surveyed in five Arab countries favor "men of religion" having influence "over government decisions" and in another set of countries half of the respondents believed Islamic *shari'a* law should be the law of the land.[57]

In summary, the evidence concerning whether Islamic values are compatible with democracy is inconclusive. There is a problem, however, with using only Arab countries to test the hypothesis. To test the hypothesis adequately, we need to examine *all* predominantly Muslim countries, not just ethnically Arab ones.[58] It happens that eight countries in which Muslims comprise a majority of the population are electoral democracies that use "free and fair elections to determine who rules."[59] One of them is Indonesia, the fourth most populous country in the world and by far the most populous Muslim country. Indonesia was ruled by a military regime from 1965 until 1998. After the military regime collapsed, the first democratically elected president was Abdurrahman Wahid, the leader of the country's largest Islamic organization. Wahid was a prankster and joker who loved Western classical music. He once teased a friend by suggesting that Christians must be closer to God than Muslims because Christians only have to whisper for God to hear them, while Muslims have to shout from loudspeakers. Wahid supported the right of people of all religions to worship as they chose. Indonesia, and the other seven Muslim majority countries that have free and fair elections, are evidence that Islam is not an insuperable obstacle to democracy.

But this leaves the question of why so many Muslim countries in the Middle East are autocratic. One possible explanation has to do with low levels of economic and social development. A strongly supported generalization in the social sciences is that the higher the level of a country's economic development, the higher the chance that it will be a democracy. That explanation is not persuasive in this case. While Yemen is a low-income country, Iran, Iraq, Jordan, and Syria are lower-middle-income countries, and Bahrain, Kuwait, Qatar, Saudi Arabia, and the United Arab Emirates are wealthy countries. In 2009 Qatar enjoyed the second highest GDP per capita in the world and Kuwait the seventh highest.[60]

An alternative explanation for the persistence of authoritarian rule in Arab countries has to do with state dependence on oil revenues. Eleven of the sixteen Arab countries derive the bulk of their revenues in that manner. Oil is a scarce and valuable natural resource that produces high incomes, or rents, for the states that own rights to the oil. States that benefit from abnormally high profits from such natural resources are called **rentier** states. Governments use oil rents to buy support by providing extensive public services and large numbers of government jobs without having to tax their citizens. The revenues also pay for large and powerful state security institutions used to stifle dissent. At first glance this appears to be of great benefit to citizens, but the cost of not having to pay taxes is a lack of government accountability. In Samuel P. Huntington's words, "'No taxation without representation' was a political demand; 'no representation without taxation' is a political reality."[61] States that get their revenues from taxes have to be responsive to citizens who want a voice in how their money is spent. The *rentier* phenomenon may explain why authoritarian regimes in the Middle East, with oil and gas reserves, such as Saudi Arabia, stay in power. However, this is not the whole answer, since autocratic governments persist in Arab countries like Jordan, which lacks such resources.

The final explanation for the persistence of authoritarianism in the Middle East is that many of the region's leaders have learned how to "upgrade authoritarianism" to keep pace with changing economies and societies.[62] There is no single formula that fits all of the countries, but the essence of upgrading authoritarianism has been to combine looser political controls with selective repression. Leaders allow controlled elections that have electoral rules designed to ensure regime victories. They split their opposition by convincing secular opponents that they dare not risk allowing radical Islamic parties to come to power.

In conclusion, Islam has been used to help establish and legitimize authoritarian regimes in the Middle East. Like many major religions, its religious texts can be interpreted to support authoritarian rule. Rulers such as the Ayatollah Ruhollah Khomeini, who led the 1979 revolution in Iran that installed the Islamic Republic of Iran, promote versions of Islam that are antidemocratic, but that does not prove that Islam is antidemocratic or that it cannot be interpreted in ways supportive of democracy. Leaders such as Abdurrahman Wahid of Indonesia have shown that it can.

AUTHORITARIANISM AND THE GOOD SOCIETY

While some authoritarian regimes such as China's have had success in promoting economic growth and improving citizens' capabilities, many have not. In this section we assess the records of the four different kinds of authoritarian regimes and how well they do at improving capabilities.

Physical Well-Being

Several Middle Eastern monarchies have had considerable success in lowering infant mortality rates. Oman has had the greatest success, lowering rates from nearly 100 infant deaths for every 1,000 births in 1975 to only 11 deaths in 2007. The United Arab Emirates has also had considerable success with only 7 deaths per 1,000.[63] These statistics approach those achieved by some European countries. Other Middle Eastern monarchies have not had this level of success, but all have lowered infant rates. Bhutan and Morocco have been the least successful monarchies with much higher infant mortality rates than the Middle Eastern monarchies.[64]

While the Arab monarchies have all succeeded in lowering infant mortality rates, military regimes vary dramatically in their level of success. South Korea had one of the most successful military regimes in the world from 1961 to the late 1980s. During these years the regime sharply reduced infant mortality rates, from nearly 100 to just 8 infants per 1,000. Other military regimes were not as successful as South Korea, but nevertheless lowered infant mortality rates significantly. These include the military regimes in Brazil (1964–1985), Chile (1973–1988), and Indonesia (1965–1998). All three countries had high infant mortality rates when military regimes came to power. In 1970 Brazil's infant mortality rate was nearly 100 per 1,000, while Indonesia's was even higher. Indonesia still had a relatively high rate of 40 per 1,000 when the military was forced out of office in 1998. The Chilean military regime reduced the infant mortality rate to 18 per thousand during the years it ruled. In contrast to the successes of the military regimes in South Korea and Latin America, military regimes in sub-Saharan Africa have failed to promote sustained economic development or measurably improve citizens' well-being. The military governments that controlled Nigeria from the early 1970s until the late 1990s provide a striking example. Infant mortality rates remained at 120 per 1,000 from 1975 until 1995 near the end of military rule.

Communist one- party regimes have also had very different levels of success in improving infant mortality rates. Cuba has a lower infant mortality rate than the United States, despite having a much lower per capita income. China, Laos, and Vietnam have all succeeded in bringing down infant mortality, but infant mortality rates in Laos were still 48 per 1,000 in 2008, which is only slightly lower than Haiti's rate. North Korea is one of the few countries in the world to have rising infant mortality rates since 1980. In short, communist party rule is no guarantee of great success in lowering infant mortality.

Electoral authoritarian regimes also vary dramatically in infant mortality rates. This is true in large part because they are found in countries with very different levels of economic development. Mozambique in sub-Saharan Africa is among the poorest countries in the world, while Malaysia in Southeast Asia has a much higher income per capita. It is not surprising to find that infants in Malaysia have a much higher probability of living past their first year of life than those in Mozambique. Malaysia's infant mortality rate is 16 per 1,000 while Mozambique's stands at 106.[65]

Informed Decision Making

The different types of authoritarian regimes have the same general patterns for informed decision making that they do for infant mortality. The Middle Eastern monarchies have relatively high rates of adult literacy, ranging from 83 per cent in Saudi Arabia to 94.5 percent in Kuwait. Bhutan and Morocco do much worse, with the literacy rate in Bhutan being only 52 percent.

The literacy record of military regimes tracks their record with infant mortality. South Korea had a relatively high literacy rate at the beginning of military rule and the rate was even higher by the time the military stepped down from power. Brazil and Chile also raised literacy rates, but with big differences among income groups. The African military regimes lag well behind, as they did with infant mortality. When the military stepped down from power in Nigeria in the late 1990s, literacy rates were only 55 percent.

Communist one-party regimes also have literacy rates that parallel their records in reducing infant mortality. According to the United Nations Development Programme, Cuba has the highest literacy rate of any country in the world. Other communist regimes do not have such stellar records, but China and Vietnam have literacy rates over 90 percent. Laos lags behind, as it did with infant mortality rates.

Electoral authoritarian regimes vary greatly in literacy as they did in infant mortality. Very poor ones tend to have very low literacy rates, such as Mozambique's 54 percent, while wealthier ones such as Malaysia have literacy rates above 90 percent.

Safety

In this category of capabilities, monarchies are the clear winners. Even Bhutan with the highest homicide rate of 4.3 per 100,000 has a lower homicide rate than the United States. Most of the Middle Eastern monarchies have homicide rates matching those of advanced European democracies. The average homicide rate for the nine monarchies for which such data are available is only 1.7 per 100,000.[66]

Military regimes have some of the lowest and highest homicide rates of any type of authoritarian regime. Some, such as Syria, have homicide rates as low as many advanced democracies, while others such as Rwanda, have among the highest homicide rates in the world. Homicide rates are a misleading indicator of safety in many military regimes. Military regimes threaten, beat, and jail suspected opponents, and some kill thousands of people as they take power and consolidate their control. Military rulers in Brazil and Chile killed thousands of suspected opponents, while the Indonesian military killed hundreds of thousands in the 1960s.

Communist party regimes generally have low homicide rates, although we lack data for homicide rates in North Korea. Of today's other four communist party regimes, only Cuba has a higher homicide rate than the United States, and this is by the slim margin of 6 per 100,000 compared with 5.9 in the United States. As with the case in military regimes, homicide rates can be a misleading indicator of safety. These regimes also use intimidation, mass campaigns against class enemies, and prison sentences to punish their enemies or suspected enemies. They also killed many more people while taking power and consolidating it than have military regimes. The highly respected China scholar Andrew Nathan puts the human cost of communism in China in the tens of millions.[67]

Electoral authoritarian regimes tend to have either very low or very high homicide rates. Several, including Egypt, Malaysia, Singapore, and Tunisia have homicide rates below 2 per 100,000. Others, including Mozambique, Russia, Tanzania, and Zambia, have rates over 20 per 100,000, placing them among countries with the highest homicide rates in the world. No single variable seems to explain the differences. For example, Singapore has a very high income per capita and a very low homicide rate, but Egypt's rate is almost identical to that of Singapore, and Egypt is a much poorer country.

Democracy

While monarchies were the winners in having the lowest average homicide rates, they are losers in democracy ratings. The most authoritarian rating used by Polity IV is – 10 and both Qatar and Saudi Arabia receive a – 10. Most other monarchies do little better, with the exception of Jordan, which receives a – 3. The average for nine contemporary monarchies is – 7.2. This makes them the most authoritarian regime type, even more authoritarian than communist single-party regimes. They rule without constitutional checks on their power, and citizens do not have recourse to independent courts of law or constitutional guarantees to free and fair elections to change leaders. In addition, some of the Arab monarchies—Saudi Arabia in particular—severely restrict women's freedom to make decisions about their lives. Women are not allowed to drive cars in Saudi Arabia, and the sexes are strictly separated in public places. Women are not so restricted in other Arab monarchies. In Kuwait, for example, women can drive cars and serve as members of parliament.

Most military regimes are less authoritarian than monarchies. Four current military regimes average a – 4 in Polity IV rankings, but this average hides extremes.[68] At the most repressive extreme is Myanmar (Burma) in Southeast Asia—with a ranking of – 8—where the military has been in power since 1962 and has ruthlessly beaten down resistance to its rule. The authors of the Polity IV Country Report on Myanmar for 2008 point out, "There are few institutional constraints on the executive, particularly as the unicameral legislature has never convened."[69] Algeria practices a less authoritarian form of military rule and has a Polity IV ranking of 2. It allowed several candidates to compete for the presidency in 2004, but real power remains in the hands of the military rather than in the hands of voters.

Communist one-party regimes all receive a – 7 ranking from Polity IV. They are among the most authoritarian types of regimes along with monarchies, and like monarchies rule without constitutional checks on their power. Their citizens do not have recourse to independent courts of law or constitutional guarantees to free and fair elections to change leaders. China has initiated some limited experiments with democratic elections at the local level but has no intention of extending them to the national level, or allowing challenges to the communist party's hold on power.

Finally, electoral authoritarian regimes are the most democratic of the types of authoritarian rule. As we have noted, they allow competitive elections for major executive offices and for national legislatures, and in some extremely unusual cases have even stepped down from power after losing elections. Nevertheless, they remain authoritarian regimes whose leaders intend to maintain their hold on power. Egypt is one of the best known examples of such a regime, and receives a Polity IV rating of only – 3. Its presidential and parliamentary elections are tightly controlled to eliminate any real opposition from gaining power. Russia is another example of an electoral authoritarian regime, but has a higher Polity IV rating of 5.

CONCLUSION

The resilience of authoritarian regimes has forced political scientists to reassess their assumption of the 1990s that in the post-Cold War era authoritarian regimes were relics that would be replaced by democracies. In the past 10 years, political scientists have devoted considerable attention to explaining why they have survived.[70] Their findings lead to four conclusions. First, the types of feasible authoritarian regimes have been narrowed. Fascism—one of the main forms of authoritarian rule in the twentieth century—has been completely discredited. Communist regimes have either collapsed as in the case of the Soviet Union, or been forced to make substantial changes. They have moved away from economic models based on state ownership and central planning and toward a significant role for markets. They have also given their citizens greater freedom to decide where to live, what to buy, and what to believe. Leaders of nearly all authoritarian regimes, excepting North Korea and Cuba, assume that the only effective economic system is one that relies extensively on markets.

Second, democracy today is the only widely accepted way of gaining political legitimacy. Amartya Sen writes, "While democracy is not yet universally practiced, nor indeed universally accepted, in the general climate of world opinion, democratic governance has now achieved the status of being taken to be generally right."[71]

Third, there are no ideologies comparable to Marxism that have appeal for large numbers of people in different parts of the world. Fundamentalist forms of Islam might gain some traction in a few countries outside the Middle East, but even if regimes based on fundamentalist Islam can be established, it remains to be seen how effective and enduring such regimes can be. Iran, the only country governed by Islamic clerics, is badly divided between supporters of the Iranian theocracy and supporters of a more secular regime. The country has lacked political stability for several years.

Finally, while electoral authoritarianism is the most prevalent kind of authoritarianism, it does not ensure authoritarian persistence. The political scientist Andreas Schedler suggests that electoral authoritarianism represents the last and weakening "line of authoritarian defense in a long history of struggle that has been unfolding since the invention or modern representative institutions"[72] As the 2009 presidential elections in Iran demonstrated, elections have the potential to destabilize authoritarian control. Some electoral authoritarian regimes with strong party and state institutions will be able to remain in power for the foreseeable future. But without strong party and state institutions, these regimes are vulnerable. This is especially true of *rentier* states that use revenues from valuable natural resources sales to stay in power by buying off support. Falling resource prices could threaten their stability. In summary, while authoritarian regimes proved more resilient than many political scientists predicted in the 1990s, many of them may be more vulnerable than they appear.[73]

EXERCISES

Apply what you learned in this chapter on MyPoliSciKit (www.mypoliscikit.com).

 ASSESSMENT
Review this chapter using learning objectives, chapter summaries, practice tests, and more.

 VIDEO CASE STUDIES
Analyze recent world affairs by watching streaming video from major news providers.

 FLASHCARDS
Learn the key terms in this chapter; you can test yourself by term or definition.

COMPARATIVE EXERCISES
Compare political ideas, behaviors, institutions, and policies worldwide.

CRITICAL THINKING QUESTIONS

1. Why are rulers of authoritarian regimes more hopeful about their prospects today than they were in the 1990s?
2. Is authoritarian rule justified if a leader can achieve improvements in citizens' capabilities, as President Paul Kagame has done in Rwanda?
3. How do communist and fascist regimes differ, and why have communist regimes been more enduring?
4. Why do electoral authoritarian regimes present dilemmas for both rulers and opposition?
5. Is one form of authoritarianism better than another?

KEY TERMS

Authoritarianism 139
Regime 140
Totalitarianism 140
Monarchy 141
Legitimacy 142
Military regime 142
Coup d'état 142
Martial law 143

Single-party regimes 144
Communist party 144
Revolution 144
Marxism 145
Fascist party 146
Charismatic leader 147
Electoral authoritarian
   regime 148

Personal rule 152
Despotic power 152
Infrastructural
   power 152
Rentier states 157

SUGGESTED READINGS

Paul Brooker, *Non-Democratic Regime*, 2nd Edition (New York: Palgrave MacMillan, 2009). Excellent overall introduction to the types of authoritarian regimes, how they consolidate power, and seek legitimacy.

Jason Brownlee, *Authoritarianism in an Age of Democratization* (New York: Cambridge University Press, 2007). Argues that the strength and coherence of ruling parties determine which regimes survive holding elections and which do not. An excellent example of using the comparative cases method.

Larry Diamond, "Why Are There No Arab Democracies?" *Journal of Democracy* 21:1 (January, 2010), pp. 93–104. A brief, clear examination of the competing explanations of why there are no Arab democracies.

Steven Levitsky and Lucan Way, *Competitive Authoritarianism: The Origins and Evolution of Hybrid Regimes in the Post-Cold War Era* (New York: Cambridge University Press, 2010). Finds that competitive authoritarian regimes with close links to Western countries are most likely to democratize. In those without such links, democratization is most likely where regimes lack cohesive political parties.

Andreas Schedler, editor. *Electoral Authoritarianism: The Dynamics of Unfree Competition* (Boulder, CO: Lynne Rienner Publisher, 2006). Chapters by leading authorities defining electoral authoritarianism and discussing how rulers use elections to remain in power.

NOTES

1. "Divisionists beware," *The Economist* (March 4, 2010). www.economist.com. Accessed April 8, 2010.
2. Steven Levitsky and Lucan A. Way, "Why Democracy Needs a Level Playing Field," *Journal of Democracy* 21:1 (January 2010), pp. 57–58.
3. Quoted in David Held, *Models of Democracy*, 2nd ed. (Stanford: Stanford University Press, 1996, p. 71.
4. Paul Brooker, *Non-Democratic Regimes*: Theory, Government and Politics (New York: St. Martin's Press, 2000), pp. 3–4
5. Amartya Sen, "Democracy as a Universal Value,' *Journal of Democracy* 10 (July 1999) cited in Marc Plattner, "Populism, Pluralism, and Liberal Democracy," *Journal of Democracy* 21: 1 (January 2010), p. 82.
6. Francis Fukuyama, *The End of History and the Last Man* (New York: Simon and Schuster, 2006), p. xi.
7. Jason Brownlee, *Authoritarianism in an Age of Democratization* (New York: Cambridge University Press, 2007), p. 25.
8. Larry Diamond, "The Democratic Rollback: The Resurgence of the Predatory State," *Foreign Affairs* (March/April 2008. www.foreignaffairs.com, accessed. March 5, 2010.
9. Keith Bradsher, "China Leading Global Race to Make Clean Energy," *The New York Times* (January 31, 2010).
10. Michael Wines, "As China Rises, Fears Grow on Whether Boom Can Endure," *New York Times* (January 12, 2010).
11. Barbara Geddes, "Why Parties and Elections in Authoritarian Regimes?" Revised version of paper prepared for presentation at the annual meeting of the American Political Science Association, Washington, D.C. 2005.

12. This typology with the exception of personal rule draws upon Axel Hadenius and Jan Teorell, "Pathways from Authoritarianism," *Journal of Democracy*, 18:1 (January 2007), pp. 145–149. Andreas Schedler, "Electoral Authoritarianism," in Todd Landman and Neil Robinson (eds), The Sage Handbook of Comparative Politics (Thousand Oaks, CA: Sage Publications, 2009), pp. 381–394.

13. These categories are adapted from Hadenius and Teorell, "Pathways from Authoritarianism."

14. Hadenius and Teorell, p. 146.

15. Bruce Gilley, "The Meaning and Measure of State Legitimacy: Results for 72 Countries," *European Journal of Political Research* 45 (2006), pp. 500–503.

16. Barbara Geddes, *Paradigms and Sand Castles: Theory Building and Research Design in Comparative Politics* (Ann Arbor, MI: University of Michigan Press, 2003), p. 51.

17. Adam Nossiter, "Niger Capital Is Calm After Coup," *New York Times* (February 20, 2010 and Paul Brooker, *Non- Democratic Regimes* (New York: Palgrave Macmillan, 2000), p. 69.

18. Paul Brooker, *Non-Democratic Regimes*, p. 100.

19. Nossiter, "Niger Capital is Calm after Coup."

20. Richard Snyder, "Beyond Electoral Authoritarianism: The Spectrum of Nondemocratic Regimes," in Andreas Schedler, editor, *Electoral Authoritarianism: The Dynamics of Unfree Competition* (Boulder, CO: Lynne Rienner Publishers, 2006), p. 219.

21. Geddes, *Paradigms and Sand Castles*, p. 52.

22. Axel Hadenius and Jan Teorell, "Pathways from Authoritarianism," *Journal of Democracy* 18:1 (January 2007), p. 147.

23. Paul Brooker, *Non-Democratic Regimes*, p. 81.

24. This figure is from Barbara Geddes' updated and revised dataset for authoritarian governments 1946–2009. We gratefully acknowledge her willingness to make the dataset available to us.

25. Samuel P. Huntington, *Political Order in Changing Societies* (New Haven: Yale University Press, 1968), p. 264, cited in Steven Pinkus, "Rethinking Revolutions: A Neo-Tocquevillian Perspective in *The Oxford Handbook of Comparative Politics*, ed. Carles Boix and Susan C. Stokes (New York: Oxford University Press, 2009), p. 398.

26. Mao Zedong, "Report on an Investigation of the Peasant Movement in Hunan, March 1927." www.fordham.edu/halsall/mod/1927/mao, accessed December 6, 2010.

27. David Remnick, *Lenin's Tomb: The Last Days of the Soviet Empire* (New York: Vintage Books, 1994), p. 183.

28. Paul Brooker, *Non-Democratic Regimes*, p. 92.

29. Michael Mann, *Fascists* (New York: Cambridge University Press, 2004), p. 13.

30. Paul Brooker, *Non-Democratic Regimes*, p. 104.

31. Mann, *Fascists*, p. 14.

32. Sherri Berman, *The Primacy of Politics: Social Democracy and the Making of Europe's Twentieth Century* (New York: Cambridge University Press, 2006), p. 132.

33. Quoted in Mann, *The Fascists*, p. 7.

34. Quoted in Robert O. Paxton, *Anatomy of Fascism* (New York: Knopf, 2004), p. 144.

35. Andreas Schedler, "Electoral Authoritarianism," in, *The SAGE Handbook of Comparative Politics*, eds. Todd Landman and Neil Robinson (Thousand Oaks, CA: Sage Publications, 2009), 388.

36. Axel Hadenius and Jan Teorell, "Authoritarian Regimes Dataset 2.1. Updated from Axel Hadenius and Jan Teorell, "Pathways from Authoritarianism," *Journal of Democracy* 18:1 (January 2007), pp. 143–156. The authors are grateful to Jan Teorell for providing the data to us.

37. Different authors have different names for variants of this type of regime. They include "limited multiparty regimes" and "competitive authoritarian regimes."

38. Hadenius and Teorell, "Pathways from Authoritarianism," *Journal of Democracy* 18:1 (January 2007), pp. 149–150.

39. Steven Heydemann, "Upgrading Authoritarianism in the Arab World, " Brookings Institution,The Saban Cener for Middle East Policy. Analysis Paper Number 13 (October 2007) pp. 5–17. www.brookings.edu, accessed January 6, 2010.

40. Heydemann, "Upgrading Authoritarianism in the Arab World," p. 11.

41. Schedler, "Electoral Authoritarianism," pp. 383–387; and Hadenius and Teorell, "Authoritarian Regimes: Stability, Change, and Pathways to Democracy, 1972–2003," p. 27.

42. Schedler, "Electoral Authoritarianism," p. 389.

43. Ibid., pp. 383–389.

44. Dan Slater, "Iron Cage in an Iron Fist: Authoritarian Institutions and the Personalization of Power in Malaysia," Comparative Politics 36:1 (October 2003), p. 86 and Paul Brooker, *Non-Democratic Regimes*, 2nd Edition (New York: Palgrave Macmilland, 2009), pp. 125–129.

45. Geddes, *Paradigms and Sand Castles*, p. 53.

46. Barbara Geddes, "What Do We Know About Democratization After Twenty Years?" *Annual Review of Political Science* 2 (June 1999), p. 123.

47. Dan Slater, "Iron Cage in an Iron Fist: Authoritarian Institutions and the Personalization of Power in Malaysia," pp. 81–101.

48. This number is from Barbara Geddes' updated and revised dataset for authoritarian governments 1946–2009 provided by the author.

49. Michael Mann, "The Autonomous Power of the State: Its Origins, Mechanisms, and Results," *European Archive of Sociology* 25 (1984), pp. 185–212.

50. Paul Collier, *The Bottom Billion* (New York: Oxford University Press, 2007), p. 66.

51. The phrase is Jason Brownlee's from *Authoritarianism in an Age of Democratization* (New York: Cambridge University Press, 2007).

52. Samuel P. Huntington, *The Clash of Civilizations and the Remaking of World Order* (New York: Touchstone, 1997), p. 114.

53. Mark Tessler, "Islam and Democracy in the Middle East: The Impact of Religious Orientations on Attitudes toward Democracy in Four Arab Countries" *Comparative Politics* Vol. 34, No. 3 (April, 2002), p. 340.

54. Ronald Ingelhart, "The Worldviews of Islamic Republics in Global Perspective," *Worldviews of Islamic Publics, ed. Mansoor Moadell.* www.worldvaluesurvey.org. Accessed September 4, 2009.

55. "Views of a Changing World 2003," The Pew Research Center for the People and the Press (June 3, 2003). http://people-press.org/report/185/views-of-a-changing-world-2003, accessed February 8, 2010.

56. Ronald Inglehart and Christian Welzel, *Modernization, Cultural Change, and Democracy*, pp. 119–120, 253–254.

57. Larry Diamond, "Why Are There No Arab Democracies?" *Journal of Democracy* 21:1 (January 2010), p. 96.

58. Geddes, *Paradigms and Sand*, pp. 89–93.
59. Diamond, "Why Are There No Arab Democracies," p. 94.
60. CIA *The World Fact* Book. www.cia.gov. Figures based on purchasing power parity. Accessed December 6, 2010.
61. Samuel P. Huntington, *The Third Wave: Democratization in the Late Twentieth Century* (Norman, OK: Oklahoma University Press, 1991), p. 65. Quoted in Diamond, "Why Are There No Arab Democracies?" p. 98.
62. Steven Heydemann, "Upgrading Authoritarianism in the Arab World," The Saban Center for Middle East Policy at the Brooking Institution, Analysis Paper Number 13, October 2007.
63. All data on capabilities in this section are from the World Bank's World Development Indicators available at www.google.com/publicdata unless otherwise noted. The site allows tracking changes in capabilities over time.
64. Monarchies include Bahrain, Bhutan, Jordan, Kuwait, Morocco, Oman, Qatar, Saudi Arabia, and the United Arab Emirates.
65. Infant mortality rates are from World Bank, World Development Indicators. www.google.com/publicdata, accessed August 3, 2010.
66. Homicide rates are from the Data Set for *The Good Society,* 2e.
67. Andrew J. Nathan, *China's Transition* (New York Columbia University Press, 1997), pp. 15–16.
68. These military regimes are Algeria, Myanmar, Rwanda, and Syria.
69. Polity IV Country Report 2008: Myanmar (Burma). www.systemicpeace.org. Accessed May 5, 2010.
70. Marc Plattner, "Populism, Pluralism, and Liberal Democracy," *Journal of Democracy* 21:1 (January 2010), pp. 81–82.
71. Amartya Sen, "Democracy as a Universal Value,' *Journal of Democracy* 10 (July 1999), cited in Marc Plattner, "Populism, Pluralism, and Liberal Democracy," p. 82.
72. Andreas Schedler, "Authoritarianism's Last Line of Defense," *Journal of Democracy* 21:1 (January 2010), p. 69.
73. Reported in Bruce Gilley, "Democratic Triumph, Scholarly Pessimism," *Journal of Democracy* 21:1 (January, 2010), p. 165.

Democracy

INTRODUCTION

9/11 is a date of mourning and sorrow, especially for Americans. On September 11, 2001, Islamic terrorists attacked the United States causing death and destruction. But while 9/11 looms large and invokes a tragedy, 11/9, refers to a joyous and remarkable occasion that is celebrated in many countries throughout the world. On November 9, 1989, the Berlin Wall, a symbol of oppression, came down. Early that night, Gunter Schabowski, the leader of East Berlin's Communist Party, declared the border that divided the city would be opened. Following his announcement, hundreds of people converged on the wall and jubilant East Germans surged through the border to meet cheering West Germans on the other side. Crowds proceeded to clamber up the wall and hack large chunks out of it. The border separating East and West Germany was finally open. Democracy had triumphed in Europe at last.

The fall of the Berlin Wall in 1989 was part of a larger, worldwide democratic surge. In country after country, from Eastern Europe to Latin America, authoritarian states were replaced by democracies. Of course, as the preceding chapter made clear, authoritarianism still exists and displays both vigor and variety. But for a period of time it was noticeably in retreat. "For the first time in history," the Institute for Democracy and Electoral Assistance noted in 1998, "more people are living in democracies than under dictator-ships."[1] In 2001, Freedom House judged that 121 out of the world's 192 governments— 63 percent—qualified as constitutionally democratic systems with competitive, multiparty elections, the most ever in history.[2] According to the political scientist Valerie Bunce, "mass publics today have a higher probability than they ever had of living in a democratic system."[3] Desperate measures such as intimidation, torture, violence, and even sexual titil-lation could not prevent democratic transitions. In 1990, Soviet leaders programmed a tel-evision movie featuring nudity called "The Sex Mission" in order to distract people from pro-democracy demonstrations scheduled that night in many cities. Like many less amus-ing ploys, this one failed to stem the democratic tide, and the Soviet Union fell a year later.[4] The allure of democracy was so great that even governments that were not democratic needed to justify themselves by reference to it. For example, the so-called Democratic People's Republic of Korea—or what we are familiar with as North Korea—is a ruthless police state in which opposition is not tolerated and the ruler, Kim Jong Il, has absolute authority. The Democratic People's Republic of Korea has as much to do with real democ-racy as the National Socialist Party—the Nazis—had to do with real socialism.

This chapter first reviews the remarkable growth of democracy. It examines the tran-sition to democracy and the reasons behind it. Next, it will survey the two predominant forms democracy takes, parliamentary and presidential democracy. Third, it will review electoral rules and the different ways party competition is organized in democracies. Finally, it will assess whether Winston's Churchill's conviction that democracy is the worst form of government except for all the others is true. Do democracies have a better record of promoting people's capabilities than their authoritarian counterparts?

TRANSITIONS TO DEMOCRACY

The term **democracy** is derived from the Greek word *demokratia*, from the roots *demos* (people) and *kratos* (rule). Democracy, then, means rule by the people. Some take this quite literally. In classical times, democracies were states in which people participated directly in making the laws that governed them. Although direct democracy is still practiced within intimate small group settings, such as local town meetings, it is unworkable for large, complex societies. Modern democracy depends on having our interests and views represented by others. Participatory democracy must of necessity give way in contemporary societies to representative democracy.

According to the economist Joseph Schumpeter, a realistic standard of democracy is one in which virtually all citizens are eligible to vote on who will represent them in free, fair, and periodic elections. The role of citizens in this version of democracy resembles that of consumers in an open marketplace. Just as consumers can choose among competing products offered by firms, citizens can choose among competing candidates offered by political parties.[5] While Schumpeter's standard is less demanding than the **classical definition of democracy**, some countries still have not met it, and those that have done so found it surprisingly hard to achieve.

The transition from autocracy to democracy proceeded in three waves, according to the political scientist Samuel P. Huntington.[6] The first wave had its roots in the American and French revolutions of the eighteenth century. The United States and some countries in Europe gradually began to expand the vote to citizens who previously had been excluded, and chief executives and their cabinets became responsible to elected assemblies. By 1930, about 30 countries worldwide met this minimal standard of democracy. Barrington Moore, Jr., attributed the transition to democracy in those countries where it was established to the presence of an independent, self-confident, vigorous commercial middle class. The formula was plain, according to Moore: "No bourgeois, no democracy."[7] Where the middle class was weak, its members feared that democracy would empower the lower classes to take their property and redistribute their wealth. Believing that authoritarian governments would better serve their interests, they tended to ally with others, including landlords and aristocrats, who shared their qualms about the lower orders' latent power under democracy. For example, in Germany, where commercial and manufacturing interests were small and late in developing, the bourgeoisie allied with the landed upper class and royal bureaucracy. By contrast, where the urban, moneyed middle class was strong and assured, according to Moore, they did not find it necessary to join with antidemocratic elites in order to achieve political power. Instead, the middle class allied with the lower orders to press for democracy, which they believed they could still control to serve their own interests. Thus, the size, independence, and vigor of the middle class explain why some countries took the democratic road during this first wave while others did not.

The first wave began to recede in the 1930s. The newest democracies were the first to crumble. Military coups in Latin America and fascism in Europe reversed the democratic tide. But the defeat of fascism in World War II inaugurated a second wave of democratization. Germany, Austria, and Japan emerged from Allied occupation as democracies, and the fight against fascism provided the rhetoric and ideology that third world independence movements used to make democratic claims against European colonial rule. As the Ghanian nationalist Kwame Nkrumah explained, "all the fair brave words spoken about freedom that had been broadcast to the four corners of the earth [in the fight against fascism] took seed and grew where they had not been intended."[8] Many former European colonies in Africa and Asia contributed to the second wave by taking anti-fascist rhetoric to heart and adopted democratic constitutions on achieving independence.

Social scientists were optimistic about the democratic future of the newly independent countries in Africa and Asia. They argued that modernization, in the form of increasing education, urbanization, and the weakening of traditional loyalties to tribe and village, would result in more tolerant attitudes and more democratic expectations.[9] But the second wave began to recede in the 1960s. Military coups beset countries in Latin America, and one-party dictatorships emerged in many African and Asian countries. Third world tyrants dismissed critics, claiming that democracy was a Western luxury their countries could not afford. Some social scientists attributed the turn to authoritarianism to the realities of Cold War politics, in which the United States supported dictators so long as they were sufficiently anticommunist. Others turned the conventional wisdom on its head and saw authoritarianism, not democracy, as the natural product of modernization. Guillermo O'Donnell argued that modernization activated lower-class groups, whose economic policies led to inflation and budget deficits that required authoritarian intervention to resolve.[10]

▶ THE GOOD SOCIETY IN DEPTH

Mauritius—A Democratic Enigma

Mauritius, an island nation of over one million located off the southeast coast of Africa, hardly seemed ripe to be the poster child for democracy in the developing world. Authoritarian governments predominate throughout Africa, especially in countries like Mauritius that are ethnically and religiously diverse. But Mauritius confounds such expectations. The country has been a stable democracy since gaining independence in 1968. The rule of law obtains, elections are free and fair, citizens enjoy civil and political rights, and parties alternate in power. Mauritius's democratic record is so good that it is the only African country to earn a perfect ten on the Polity IV democracy index.

Scholars attribute Mauritius's democratic success to a "vibrant and healthy civil society that cuts across ethnic cleavages."[11] The island nation boasts an extraordinary number of civic organizations for a country its size, everything from soccer clubs to seniors groups to trade unions. Many of these are bridging organizations that cross religious and ethnic boundaries. They connect Chinese, Indians, Creoles, whites, Christians, Muslims, and Hindus to each other, "creating transethnic 'common denominators' that solidify national unity," according to the

Continued

political scientist William F. S. Miles.[12] Participation in a multitude of nongovernmental organizations that bridge ethnic and religious identities, Miles writes, "has been a big factor in maintaining interethnic harmony."[13]

The bridging role that civic organizations play in helping people transcend exclusive ethnic identities is supplemented in Mauritius by political institutions that promote the inclusion of all groups. Checks and balances proliferate, making it hard for any one group to obtain too much political power. There is no standing army, the judiciary is independent, the civil service is professional, supermajorities are required to make constitutional changes, all of the constitutionally recognized ethnic and religious groups (Hindus, Muslims, Chinese, and the "general population," composed of whites and Creoles) are guaranteed seats in parliament, and the Constitution even provides for an office of Leader of Opposition whom the president must consult on some issues. In other words, political institutions are designed so that no group is left out and policy making requires their broad inclusion.

Democracy is no panacea. Mauritius has ethnic conflict and suffers from corruption, but its democratic record is the best in Africa and among the best in the developing world.

For Further Discussion

1. The case of Mauritius suggests that a robust civil society is vital to the success of democracy. How can a vigorous civil society be promoted or created?

2. Why haven't Mauritius's political rules that divide power so that no group can ever get too much led to stalemate and deadlock, as opposed to successful governance?

The third wave of democracy appeared even before the second had fully receded. In 1974, Portugal emerged from a half-century of dictatorship, followed soon after by the collapse of the ruling military regime in Greece and of despotism in Spain. The democratic wave then crossed the ocean to Latin America, where democratic civilian governments replaced military juntas in Ecuador, Peru, Bolivia, Argentina, and Brazil. Asia also felt its effects as democracy was restored in India and the Philippines, and new elections were held in Korea, Turkey, and Pakistan. The global tide of democracy next touched down in Eastern Europe as the Berlin Wall fell and one country after another—Poland, Hungary, Czechoslovakia, Bulgaria, Romania, and finally the Soviet Union itself—deposed their ruling communist parties and held democratic elections. Only countries in the Middle East and Africa resisted the democratic surge. The growth of democracy is evident in the rising dashed line in Figure 7.1.

Why have some countries succumbed to the appeal of democracy while others successfully resisted it? Some analysts offer cultural and sociological explanations. For example, countries with large Muslim populations are less

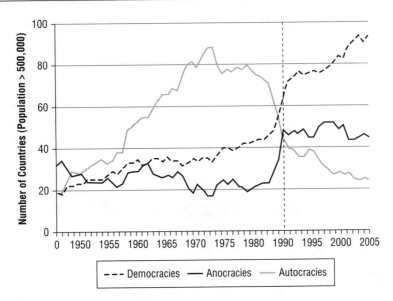

FIGURE 7.1
Global Trends in Governance, 1946–2008[14]

Data Source:
Polity IV Country Reports, 2007
http://www.systemicpeace.org/polity/polity06.htm

likely to be democratic, while those with higher levels of education are likely to be more democratic. Other analysts find economic explanations more persuasive, arguing that economic development promotes democracy across the board or that only certain kinds of economic development foster democratic government. For example, oil-producing countries in the Middle East are wealthy but not democratic. They suffer from the so-called curse of oil, with authoritarian rulers using oil revenues to pacify their citizens with low taxes, subsidized essentials, and reinforced security forces. Still other scholars argue that economic development causes democratic stability, not democratization. They contend that rich democracies are simply more stable than poor ones. Poor democracies are more likely to collapse into authoritarianism, leading "over time to a high proportion of rich countries among democracies."[15]

It is difficult to isolate a single determining factor that would account for why some countries take a democratic path and others do not. Wealth, education, and the existence of a self-confident middle class are the seeds of democracy, but whether they take root depends on the soil in which they are planted. Some preceding forms of authoritarianism may be more amenable to democratization than others. For example, military regimes are far more likely to give way to new democracies than personalized dictatorships that are often simply replaced by another personalized dictatorship.[16]

But even this precaution does not expand our view of the issue far enough because it looks for the answer only in domestic politics. Democratic transitions are also influenced by the international environment. For example, the European Union has helped promote and consolidate democracy among countries that want to join it. In addition, political scientists have also noticed a **diffusion effect** in which countries surrounded by democracies find it in their interest to emulate their neighbors. As two political scientists report, "There is a strong association between a country's institutions and the extent of democracy in the surrounding regional context."[17] External circumstances can promote or discourage the transition to democracy as much as internal conditions.

COMPARATIVE POLITICAL ANALYSIS

Does Diversity Undermine Democracy?

Problem

Is it true that diversity poses an obstacle to democracy? Do ethnic, religious, and linguistic differences make compromise and consensus more difficult? Do competing political parties tend to exacerbate such differences instead of bridging them? Authoritarian leaders often claim that if they did not rule with an iron fist over ethnically divided societies they would collapse in civil conflict. Is this argument valid or simply provide an excuse for authoritarian leaders of diverse societies to deprive people of their rights?

Methods and Hypothesis

M. Steven Fish and Robin S. Brooks used Freedom House rankings (similar to our use of the Polity IV index discussed in Chapter 1) in order to scale countries from democratic to authoritarian and thereby establish their dependent variable. They then used another data set for their independent variable that assessed the fractionalization, or degree of diversity, within each country. Next, they did a statistical analysis to determine whether fractionalization affected the type of regime. To ensure that their results caught only the effects of fractionalization, they controlled for four other variables often regarded as determinants of democracy: economic development and British colonial heritage (which are presumed to promote democracy) and the predominance of Islam and oil production (which are reputed to retard it). Fish and Brooks then tested the hypothesis that diversity hinders democracy.

Results

The authors found that, contrary to prevailing wisdom, diversity or fractionalization did not hinder democracy. Fish and Brooks' results "provide grounds for doubt that monoethnic societies have an edge when it comes to founding and preserving democratic rule." Holding constant other factors that might affect their results,

Continued

Fish and Brooks found that fractionalization or diversity had little impact on the prospects for democracy.

For Further Discussion

1. How is it possible for democracy to survive ethnic conflicts when it gives free rein to their expression? How can democracies contain centrifugal forces that threaten to tear them apart?

2. If Fish and Brooks are correct in claiming that diversity does not reduce people's capabilities in terms of democracy, might it reduce their life chances in other ways, such as posing increased risks to their safety?

M. Steven Fish and Robin S. Brooks, "Does Diversity Hurt Democracy?" *Journal of Democracy*, (January 2004), Vol. 15, No. 1., p. 164.

PRESIDENTIAL AND PARLIAMENTARY DEMOCRACY

Democracy, like authoritarianism, comes in many different forms. Adam Przeworski writes, "Systems of representation, arrangements of division and supervision of powers, manners of organization of interests, legal doctrines, as well as bundles of rights and obligations associated with citizenship differ significantly across regimes that are generally recognized as democratic."[18] The different models of democracy can be arrayed along a continuum of presidential and parliamentary forms, with all sorts of hybrids in between. The United States is an example of a presidential system. In **presidential systems**, the executive and legislative branches are separated from each other.[19] That is, presidents do not owe their office to the legislature and do not require supportive legislative majorities to continue in it. Presidents are popularly elected and they serve for a fixed term. In addition, presidents often have some lawmaking authority; otherwise, they would be mere figureheads.[20]

▌IN BRIEF

Presidential Systems

Presidential systems have some of the following properties:

- Sovereignty is shared between the legislature and the president, creating checks and balances between them.
- Presidents are directly elected by the people.
- Presidents serve for fixed terms in office.
- Presidents do not require legislative support to remain in office.

In contrast, in parliamentary democracies the legislature is the only institution directly elected by voters. As a result, the legislature embodies the will of the people and its power is supreme. Legislatures then delegate power to the executive, which they elect. The government, which is composed of the prime minister and his or her Cabinet, is an elected committee of the legislature. The legislature and executive are not separate branches, as in the presidential model, but are fused together, with the former empowering the latter.

The leader of the government in **parliamentary systems** is the prime minister, who is indirectly elected by the legislature. The prime minister's job is to form and direct the government—that is, to select a cabinet composed of ministers to run the various executive departments and direct and coordinate the government's activities. Rather than serving for a fixed term, prime ministers govern for as long as they maintain the confidence of the legislature. They may be removed from office and forced to resign when their party loses its parliamentary majority in national elections, when they no longer enjoy support among parliamentary members from their own party, or when coalition partners from other parties that helped create a legislative majority defect.

Relations of power between the executive and legislative branches are a bit different in parliamentary than in presidential regimes. In the former, the government is much more confident of having its proposals accepted by the legislature where, after all, it enjoys a majority of support. Unlike presidents, prime ministers don't need to worry much about having their policies rejected by the legislature because they have a majority within it. On the other hand, presidents don't have to fear the legislature dismissing them from office as prime ministers do. The nature of legislative power is also different between the two models. In presidential systems, the legislature is more likely to develop its own bills and alter those proposed by the government. But it cannot make or break governments, as legislatures in parliamentary systems are able to do. The legislature in a parliamentary regime wields power through the government that it elected, as opposed to checking governments elected independently.[21]

The dispersion of power within democratic states occurs in presidential systems through checks and balances between the legislative and executive branches. Presidents and legislators are elected independently, and because each branch can check the other the passage of bills requires the consent of both. In parliamentary systems, the fusion of the executive and legislative branches tends to concentrate power in the prime minister. But prime ministers are not all-powerful, because they must constantly look over their shoulder to ensure that they retain the confidence of the legislature. In addition, the checks and balances that exist between the legislative and executive branches in presidential systems may take the form of checks and balances among the different parties that comprise the ruling coalition in parliamentary systems. Prime ministers may not have to negotiate with obstreperous legislatures, but they may have to negotiate with defiant parties in their ruling coalition that can block policies they propose.

IN BRIEF

Parliamentary Systems

Parliamentary systems have some of the following qualities:

- The legislature is directly elected by the people and is sovereign.
- Prime ministers are selected by the legislature.
- Prime ministers can be removed when they lose the confidence of the legislature.
- While prime ministers rule only with the approval of the legislature, that support also assures them of legislative support for their policies.

Most new democracies created in the third wave chose to take a presidential, as opposed to parliamentary, form. Did they make the right choice? Presidential systems are said to suffer from gridlock that results when the legislative and executive branches, which are independent of one another, disagree. According to the political scientist Juan Linz, their impasse may be so paralyzing that it undermines support for democracy itself.[22] Presidential systems are also often criticized for being unrepresentative. The president may have only won a narrow plurality of the vote but gets to assume all the power. For example, following the very close 2000 U.S. presidential election, Republicans took complete control of the executive branch. Despite winning almost half the votes in the Electoral College, the Democrats were completely deprived of any executive power. Critics claim that presidential systems are unrepresentative because election results are divisible while executive power is not.

Although presidential systems may offer less in terms of representation than parliamentary regimes, they may offer more in terms of accountability. Voters can hold presidents accountable for their performance because they directly elect them, in contrast to parliamentary systems where the chief executive is selected by the legislature. In addition, voters have a more difficult time in parliamentary systems assigning responsibility for performance. The core executive in parliamentary systems is often composed of a ruling coalition of officials from different political parties, whereas the core executive in presidential systems is typically drawn from the same party, thus making it easier for voters to assign credit and blame. Finally, voters in presidential systems can more easily target their votes in support of, or opposition to, a particular chief executive, because control of the executive in parliamentary systems often depends on postelection negotiations among political parties. Voters in presidential systems can take better aim at their intended target, making their vote a more potent weapon than in parliamentary regimes.

ELECTORAL RULES AND PARTY SYSTEMS

Democracies differ not only in how power is distributed between the legislative and executive branches but in their **electoral systems**, which determine how elections are conducted. For example, democracies differ in the average number of seats or representatives they assign to each election district. Some countries, such as the United States, have **single-member districts** where only one legislator is elected from each district. Other countries, such as Sweden, have **multimember districts**, in which the number of legislators from each district depends upon their size. The voting district that includes Stockholm County, the county's capital, has 36 seats to represent 800,000 residents, while the less populated Gotland County, an island in the Baltic Sea with just 44,000 people, is accorded only two seats. In Israel and the Netherlands, the entire country is one multimember electoral district. In single-member districts, there is only one winner. The losing candidates return to the obscurity of their former line of work. Not so in multimember districts. Not only does the winner who is selected from a list of candidates that parties submit to voters get seated, but so does the runner-up—and so on down the line, depending upon the number of seats accorded to that district.

Electoral systems also differ in the way votes are allocated: that is, how votes obtained by candidates and parties in elections are translated into legislative seats. Some countries run elections according to plurality, or whoever-gets-the-most-votes-wins, rules. Such rules govern elections in the United States, Canada, and the U.K., where the candidate receiving the most votes in a district is declared the winner. Americans tend to confuse pluralities, in which candidates receive the most votes, with majorities in which candidates receive more than 50 percent of the vote because the two major parties in the United States virtually monopolize political competition. In a two-party race, the candidate who receives the most votes must necessarily receive a majority. But countries that use plurality voting rules may have more than two effective parties. In this circumstance, it is unusual for the candidate who wins the most votes to also achieve a majority. In Canada and the U.K., where the two major parties are not as dominant compared to the United States, it is unusual for the winning candidate who obtains a plurality to also win a majority. In the 2010 election in Britain, not one candidate elected to Parliament won a majority of the vote in their district.

Other countries, such as France, guarantee that winning candidates must have majority support by running **double-ballot elections**. If no candidate wins a majority in the first election, a run-off is held between the two candidates who received the highest number of votes in the first round. In the 2007 French presidential election, for example, 12 candidates competed in the first round, with Nicholas Sarkozy placed first with 31 percent of the vote and Segolene Royal finishing second with 26 percent. Two weeks later, when the top two candidates faced off against each other, Sarkozy managed to obtain an absolute majority of 53 percent, against Royal's 47 percent. Double-ballot electoral rules are not unique to France, but have been adopted by many former communist countries in Eastern Europe, as well as some countries in Africa, such as Chad, Gabon, and Mauritania.[23] They are even used in the United States, where many southern states require candidates to win a majority of the vote. In the 2008 election for a Senate seat in Georgia, a third party "spoiler" candidate was able to attract enough votes so that neither the Democratic nor the Republican candidate was able to obtain a majority on Election Day in November. This precipitated a run-off four weeks later when the Republican was finally able to obtain the majority required for election.

A third alternative is to run elections according to **proportional representation** (PR) rules. Once parties attain a certain threshold of votes, they are awarded seats in the legislature based on the percentage of the vote they receive. For example, in the Netherlands, 10 parties competed in the 2006 parliamentary election and seats were awarded to each party in the legislature based on the percentage of the vote they received. The largest party, the Christian Democratic Appeal, won 27 percent of the vote and received 27 percent of the seats in Parliament; Labour, the next largest party, garnered 21 percent of the votes and was awarded 21 percent of the seats, and so on down to the Reformed Political Party, the smallest party, which received 1 percent of the vote and was given one percent of the legislative seats. Advocates of proportional representation argue that it is preferable to district-based, plurality, winner-takes-all electoral rules because it offers voters "a broader range of candidates who have a real chance of being elected, and who talk about a greater breadth of issues that attract more voters to the polls."[24]

Electoral rules matter greatly. How votes are counted matters as much as how many votes candidates receive. Winners can become losers and losers turn into winners depending on how votes are counted. Take the case of the 2000 presidential election in the United States. Democratic candidate Al Gore received 550,000 more votes than his Republican opponent, George W. Bush, but Bush was declared the winner because he received the most votes in the Electoral College. The election turned on Florida where, even though Bush won by just 550 votes out of almost 6 million cast statewide, or 0.0001 percent of the vote, he received 100 percent of Florida's Electoral College vote, giving him the majority in the Electoral College he needed to become president. If the outcome had been determined according to the rules that govern all other federal elections where the popular vote decides the winner, Al Gore and not George Bush would have been elected president. Likewise, if states had split the votes awarded them in the Electoral College in proportion to the percentage of the vote each candidate received, then Al Gore would again have been elected president. Different ways of counting votes produce different results.

Political actors began to think strategically about electoral rules as democracy took root and the franchise was extended to working-class voters. Groups and parties wanted rules that worked to their advantage. For example, ethnic and regional minorities that could win elections locally supported proportional representation as a way to ensure that their interests were represented in the national legislature. But the most powerful supporters of PR were elites who were frightened by the prospect of working-class mobilization that might propel socialist parties to victory. Elites feared that bourgeois parties would suffer if elections were decided by plurality or majority rules in single-member districts. According to Andrew McLaren Carstairs, as "universal suffrage rendered it increasingly likely that the social democrats would achieve the status of a major or dominant party, it was bourgeois and nonsocialist parties that inclined toward a reform of the electoral system."[25] Elites believed that proportional representation would blunt the power of socialist parties, requiring them to share power in order to govern.

Electoral rules are not neutral; inevitably they advantage some parties at the expense of others. For example, in Britain, the Liberal Democrats have been a victim of whoever-gets-the-most-votes wins, or plurality, electoral rules, while the Labour Party has benefited from them. In the 2010 election, the Labour Party received 29 percent of the vote but won 40 percent of the seats in Parliament, while the Liberal Democrats received 23 percent of the vote but won only 9 percent of the seats because their voters were not geographically concentrated enough to win many districts outright. Not surprisingly, the Liberal Democrats propose to change electoral rules in Britain from the current plurality system to proportional representation. If that reform was enacted, it would reward the Liberal Democrats with seats in Parliament equal to their popular support, which current rules deprive them of.

With so much at stake, parties sometimes try to change the electoral system so as to compete under electoral rules that are more advantageous to them. In Britain, when no party received a majority in Parliament following the 2010 elections, the Liberal Democrats, who have been disadvantaged by electoral rules, made it a condition of their parliamentary support to change them. Similarly, in France, the ruling Socialist Party anticipated defeat in the 1986 legislative elections and sought to minimize its losses by changing electoral laws. They switched from double-ballot electoral rules to proportional representation, believing the latter would give a radical right-wing party a better chance to draw off votes and seats from the Socialists' chief opponent, the Republican Right. When the Republican Right coalition took office following the election, they switched rules back to the old electoral system that offered them more protection. A popular radical right-wing party that could obtain enough votes to earn seats in the legislature under PR would have a harder time obtaining a majority in any district under double-ballot election rules.

Even though parties have an incentive to manipulate electoral rules in order to maximize their advantages, electoral systems rarely change. Winners under existing rules are unlikely to alter a system that benefits them. In the 1970s, the Parti Quebecois (PQ) in Canada held only a handful of seats in the provincial legislature, even though they received about 25 percent of the vote. Feeling cheated of the seats they deserved by plurality electoral rules, the PQ promised to enact proportional representation if elected. But when the PQ came to power in 1976, it failed to carry out its promise because PR might jeopardize the success the party now enjoyed. PQ deputies thought they stood a better chance of winning in the district where they were well known than competing as part of party list in a proportional representation election.[26] If the Liberal Democrats were to somehow prevail in Britain, it is likely they, too, would lose their appetite for electoral reform once they were in office.

Electoral rules shape **party systems** or recurring patterns of party behavior resulting from political competition. The number of legislative seats accorded to each district and the way that votes are translated into seats affect the number of effective parties that compete. Single-member districts in which winners are selected by simple plurality voting rules create a bias toward two-party systems. Voters fear wasting their votes on small third parties that cannot win and tend to choose candidates from those that can, a calculation that works to the advantage of the two largest parties. By contrast, countries with multimember districts selected by proportional representation tend to have multiparty systems. Voters can vote their consciences for minor parties that will lose knowing they will be awarded some seats anyway. Just as electoral rules have a ripple effect on the number of parties, so does the number of parties influence other aspects of the political system. The advantage of multi-party systems is that they accurately reflect the diversity of opinion within the country. The disadvantage is that they may be so representative of diverse opinions that countries become ungovernable. If, for example, many parties compete and receive seats, it becomes difficult to construct a majority coalition and form a government. And such governments are not likely to last: The smaller the share of seats held by the largest party, the more fragile the government will be.

Electoral systems affect not only the degree of party competition but the internal life of parties as well. For example, **party discipline** in the legislature is greater in PR systems. Legislators want to increase their chances for reelection and move higher up on the party list by proving their loyalty to party leaders who make those lists. Electoral rules also influence the number of female legislators. Plurality-based, single-member electoral systems tend to reinforce the advantages of incumbency that is often enjoyed by men who already hold elected office. With only one candidate to offer for each seat, underrepresented groups, such as women, find it difficult to get into the game. In contrast, in multimember PR systems, where there are more seats to fill in each election district, parties have greater scope to offer more women as candidates. In addition, more parties use quotas under these rules to reserve a certain number of spots for women on their lists. Consequently, women comprise a higher proportion of legislators under PR than they do in other electoral systems.

No electoral system is perfect. The economist Kenneth Arrow developed a set of requirements that any reasonable voting system should satisfy and found that none could meet them all. When the Royal Swedish Academy of Sciences gave Arrow a Nobel Prize for this work in 1972, it called his result "a rather discouraging one as regards the dream of a perfect democracy."[27] Electoral systems require one to choose among flawed options. Some promote accountability at the expense of choice. Others do the opposite. While some may find it disheartening that the best electoral system is a choice among lesser evils, this is still better than the greater evil of having no choice at all.

DEMOCRACY, AUTHORITARIANISM, AND ECONOMIC DEVELOPMENT

When it comes to soccer, past performances in the World Cup indicate that teams from fascist countries have better records than those governed by party dictatorships, teams representing military dictatorships have a higher winning percentage than those ruled by fascists, and teams fielded by West European democracies have the best record of all.[28] But that's soccer. Do democracies perform as well at enhancing the capabilities of their citizens as they do on the soccer field? Are they better at meeting their citizens' basic physical needs, ensuring their safety, and promoting their ability to make informed decisions than authoritarian political systems? Are people better off under democracy than authoritarianism? In Chapter 1, we described democracy as one of the elements that comprise a good society, but we also warned that all good things do not necessarily go together. Perhaps the provision of health care, safety, education, and democracy are at odds with one another, so that some conditions that permit people to lead lives they value come at the expense of others.

One of the indices that is frequently used to compare the performance of different types of states is economic growth. But as we argued in Chapter 1, economic growth is not a good indicator of how well states perform because all, or even most, citizens may not benefit from it. The fruits of economic growth may flow disproportionately to a rich few while the living standards of the majority decline. Still, although economic growth is hardly a panacea, it is a necessary, though not a sufficient condition to reduce poverty in extremely poor countries. Redistribution from the rich to the poor will not do much good where there is little wealth to redistribute. Growing the economy, increasing the wealth it produces, is the only way to raise the standard of living in countries that are very poor.

Is democracy or authoritarianism more conducive to generating economic growth? According to some political scientists, authoritarian regimes can better invest society's limited resources where they will do the most good. They will not succumb to the temptation of democracies to invest in low-yield projects in return for votes. Another alleged benefit of authoritarianism is that it permits the government to ignore demands to spend money that will be consumed immediately (bigger pensions, better schools, and more health care) and instead direct the country's limited savings toward investments that will pay off in the future. Party competition, it is argued, also makes democracies susceptible to expensive bidding wars in which candidates try to win elections by pandering to citizens' short-term welfare needs instead of making the long-term investments that are the key to future growth. Finally, authoritarianism supposedly can create a more consistent, stable, orderly environment that is more favorable to investment and long-term growth. While democracies are beset by racial, tribal, religious, and ethnic conflicts that result in stalemate or worse, authoritarian regimes are decisive and strong enough to rise above such conflicts and get things done. In brief, the argument is that authoritarian states produce better economic results because their policies are not distorted by crass political concerns.

Other political scientists challenge this account. They argue that democracy is an advantage, not a handicap, in promoting economic growth. Democracies, they claim, enjoy the rule of law that creates a predictable environment. Where the state wields power arbitrarily, insecurity discourages entrepreneurs from investing. In addition, democracies benefit from more debate, more access to information, and more responsiveness, enabling them to act effectively when things go wrong. The openness and adaptability of democracies permit them to recognize and reverse policy mistakes more quickly and easily than authoritarian regimes. Finally, democracies give their citizens more freedom, which encourages them to be more creative and innovative.

When evaluated according to the standard of promoting economic growth, the record of democracies and dictatorships is quite mixed. In the ranks of democracies and dictatorships, we can find countries that are remarkable economic successes and others that are massive failures. For example, in the 1970s and 1980s, many Latin American countries experienced stagnant and even negative growth rates following their transition from military rule to democracy. Some authoritarian regimes have performed no better. Many African economies went into free fall following their transition to one-party dictatorships. On the other hand, supporters of democracy and authoritarianism can both boast of economic successes. Supporters of democracy can celebrate the prosperity of the West compared to the collapse of communist one-party states, while admirers of authoritarianism can point to the superior growth of the People's Republic of China compared to democratic India. Indeed, it is difficult to attribute better or worse economic performance to either democracy or authoritarianism. As the Nobel Prize-winning economist Amartya Sen puts it, "The selective anecdotal evidence goes in contrary directions, and the statistical picture does not yield any clear relationship at all."[29] Another analysis by Adam Przeworski and Fernando Limongi confirmed Sen's judgment. They write, "It does not seem to be democracy or authoritarianism per se that makes the difference but something else. What that something else might be is far from clear."[30]

Although neither democracy nor dictatorship can take credit for economic growth, democratic systems do have two important advantages. First is the greater range of choices open to women under democracies. When women have more opportunities, they tend to have fewer children. As the fertility rate falls, so does the number of citizens competing for the national income. Although the pot itself is not any bigger in democracies, it is divided among fewer people, thereby raising the country's per capita income. Second, democracies have a better record of steady economic performance and avoiding calamitous outcomes. "Democracies," Halperin and his associates found, "regardless of income level, rarely let the bottom fall out of their economies."[31] When economic disaster strikes in the form of hyperinflation or massive unemployment, people have to sell off their assets in order to survive. Because democracies are more likely to avoid economic catastrophes, their citizens are better able to accumulate assets over time than their counterparts in dictatorships.

Overall, the results of our inquiry about which type of state better promotes economic growth are inconclusive, with democracies, perhaps, earning the benefit of the doubt. But regardless of the outcome, higher economic growth does not translate automatically into higher capabilities for citizens, which is our standard for measuring state performance. How do democracies and authoritarian political systems compare when we look at capabilities?

DEMOCRACY, AUTHORITARIANISM, AND THE GOOD SOCIETY

Physical Well-Being

We used Polity IV scores (see Table 1.4 in the Appendix) to distinguish democratic from authoritarian countries. Taking into account various criteria such as the openness and competitiveness of the political system, how chief executives are selected and the constraints on their power, and how open and competitive political participation is, the most democratic countries were given a 10, while the most authoritarian states were given a value of –10. We then assigned countries on this scale into one of four groups: democracies were those countries that received either a 9 or 10 on the Polity IV index; semi-democracies were those countries that received from 8 to 0; semi-authoritarians received a –1 to –6; and authoritarian states received –7 to –10.

In order to assess the relative ability of democracies and authoritarian countries to meet their citizens' basic physical needs we will again look at infant mortality rates. As we noted previously, experts often use this indicator to gauge material well-being because it "reflects a multitude of conditions, from access to food, health care and housing to the availability of schools for girls."[32] When we compare the performance of democracies and authoritarian states, the results are inconclusive as Figure 7.2 reveals: democracies had average infant mortality rates of 12.53 per 1,000 live births; semi-democracies recorded an average infant mortality of 45.52; semi-authoritarians 57.48; and authoritarian political systems 27.57. While the most democratic states had the best average infant mortality rates, the most authoritarian states had the second best.[33]

Informed Decision Making

The results are the same when we turn from satisfying basic needs to enhancing the capability of citizens to make informed decisions about their lives. In Figure 7.3, democracies performed the best with an average literacy rate of 94.24; authoritarian states were the next best at 87.39, semi-democracies scored 76.44; with semi-authoritarian countries bringing up the rear at 66.68.

Safety

Finally, as Figure 7.4 reveals, the most authoritarian states had the best record when it came to safety, as measured by average homicide rates, with 5.43 murders

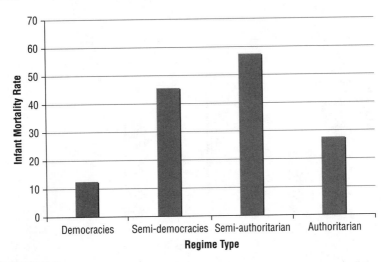

FIGURE 7.2
Democracy and Infant Mortality Rates

Data Sources:
Polity IV Country Reports, 2007
http://www.systemicpeace.org/polity/polity06.htm

Country Comparison: Infant Mortality Rate
Data Source: CIA World Factbook, https://www.cia.gov/library/publications/the-world-factbook/rankorder/
2091rank.html

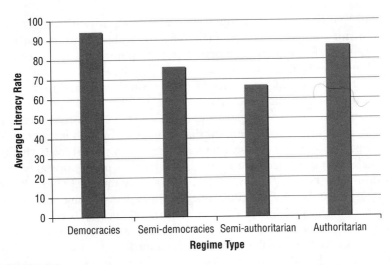

FIGURE 7.3
Democracy and Literacy Rates

Data Sources:
Polity IV Country Reports, 2007
http://www.systemicpeace.org/polity/polity06.htm

Adult Literacy Rate (% aged 15 and above)
Data Source: Human Development Report 2009, http://hdrstats.undp.org/en/indicators/89.html

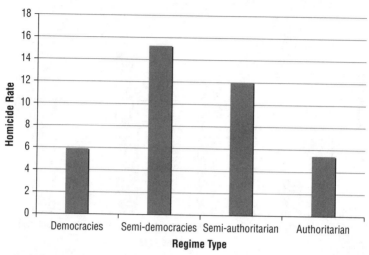

FIGURE 7.4
Democracy and Safety

Data Sources:
Polity IV Country Reports, 2007
http://www.systemicpeace.org/polity/polity06.htm

Murder Rates around the World
Data Source: Guardian.co.uk, http://www.guardian.co.uk/news/datablog/2009/oct/13/homicide-rates-country-murder-data

per 100,000 citizens. Democracies were close behind with an average of 5.91 homicides, with semi-democracies (15.28) and semi-authoritarian systems (12.04) performing much worse than the "purer" forms of democracy and authoritarianism.

While the most democratic states scored best on two out of three of our performance tests, semi-democratic states did not perform on average better than semi-authoritarian states, and pure authoritarian states performed better than both of them. Thus, it does not appear that democracy by itself is the answer for all public problems. Some democracies have a relatively poor record. After more than a half-century of democratic rule, India had an infant mortality rate of 30.15 deaths for every 1,000 live births, an illiteracy rate of 39 percent, and a homicide rate of 5.5 per 100,000 citizens. In contrast, some authoritarian regimes have performed remarkably well on certain indices. It is hard to think of a country that has been more successful than China at reducing poverty, or that has done more to wipe out illiteracy than Cuba, or that is safer than the United Arab Emirates. All of them are closed societies. The results of our tests thus confirm our earlier warning that all good things do not go together. More democracy only matters in terms of improving people's life chances at the highest level. Otherwise, it does not appear to improve people's life chances very much in terms of making them safer, healthier, or more literate. Of course, this says nothing about whether democracy should be valued for its own sake, as opposed to the effect it may or may not produce on other aspects of life.

CONCLUSION

We saw in this chapter that more people than ever before live under democratic rules that permit citizens to choose their political leaders in free, fair, and periodic elections. Political scientists attributed the rise of democracy to domestic factors, such as economic development, and to external forces, such as regional diffusion effects. Historically, democratization proceeded in waves. The American and French Revolutions launched the first wave, in which monarchies were overthrown and replaced by republican forms of government. Voting rights were extended to workers and chief executives and their cabinets were now responsible to elected assemblies. The second wave occurred following World War II, as many former colonies in Africa and Asia drafted democratic constitutions when they became independent. The third wave began in 1975, with democratic transitions occurring first in Portugal, Spain, and Greece, and then traveling across the ocean to remove military dictatorships in Latin America, passing through Asia where elections were held in formerly autocratic countries, and finally cresting in Eastern Europe, where communist parties were forced to give up their monopoly of power.

As democracy spread, it took two predominant forms, presidential and parliamentary democracy. In the former, presidents are directly elected for fixed terms and serve independently of the legislature. In the latter, the legislature selects and empowers the executive. Democracies differ not only in how authority is distributed between the legislative and executive branches, but in how elections are conducted. Countries use different formulas to translate votes into legislative seats. These election rules, in turn, shape party behavior and competition.

Finally, the chapter examined whether democracies have a better record of improving people's life chances than authoritarian political systems. We found that only at the highest levels does democracy actually improve the quality of people's lives in terms of safety, subsistence, and literacy. But our analysis looks only at the consequences of democracy for various aspects of citizens' lives. It begs the question of whether democracy may have value in and of itself, even in those countries where its effect on other aspects of people's lives is not evident.

EXERCISES

Apply what you learned in this chapter on MyPoliSciKit (www.mypoliscikit.com).

 ASSESSMENT
Review this chapter using learning objectives, chapter summaries, practice tests, and more.

 VIDEO CASE STUDIES
Analyze recent world affairs by watching streaming video from major news providers.

FLASHCARDS
Learn the key terms in this chapter; you can test yourself by term or definition.

 COMPARATIVE EXERCISES
Compare political ideas, behaviors, institutions, and policies worldwide.

CRITICAL THINKING QUESTIONS

1. How would you define democracy? Should democracy be judged simply by process without regard to results?
2. Why has democracy been so elusive for developing countries? Why did so many developing countries fall prey to authoritarianism?
3. What social conditions are conducive to democracy?
4. Did many new emerging democracies make the right choice in adopting presidential as opposed to parliamentary democratic forms?
5. What are the advantages and disadvantages of different electoral rules? Which set of electoral rules is most compatible with democracy?
6. If democracy is so beneficial, why didn't it appear to enhance people's capabilities when we ran our tests? While the most democratic countries performed better, more democracy did not correlate with higher capabilities outside this select group of countries.

KEY TERMS

Democracy   169
Classical definition of democracy   170
Diffusion effects   174
Presidential systems   175

Parliamentary systems   176
Electoral systems   178
Single-member districts   178
Multimember districts   178

Double-ballot elections   178
Proportional representation   179
Party systems   181
Party discipline   181

SUGGESTED READINGS

Andrew McLaren Carstairs, *A Short History of Electoral Systems in Western Europe* (London: George Allen & Unwin, 1980). As the title suggests, the book is a good introduction to the origins and effects of different electoral systems.

Morton H. Halperin, Joseph T. Siegle, and Michael M. Weinstein, *The Democratic Advantage: How Democracies Promote Peace and Prosperity*, (New York: Routledge, 2005). A careful analysis that argues democracy produces beneficial economic and social results.

Samuel P. Huntington, *The Third Wave: Democratization in the Late Twentieth Century* (Norman OK: University of Oklahoma Press, 1993). A concise history that probes the cycles of democratization and how each new wave leaves more democracies before receding again.

Michael Meyer, *The Year That Changed the World: The Untold Story behind the Fall of the Berlin Wall* (New York: Scribner, 2009). One of the best narrative histories of the end of communism in Eastern Europe.

Fareed Zakaria, *The Future of Freedom: Illiberal Democracy at Home and Abroad* (New York: Norton, 2003). An accessible and lively argument that democracy depends on the level of economic development.

NOTES

1. Quoted in Niall Ferguson, *The Cash Nexus: Money and Power in the Modern World* (New York: Basic Books, 2001), p. 353.

2. Barbara Crossette, "As Democracies Spread, Islamic World Hesitates," *New York Times*, (December 23, 2001).

3. Valerie Bunce, "Comparative Democratization: Big and Bounded Generalizations," *Comparative Political Studies* (Aug.–Sept. 2000), p. 704.

4. Bruce Gilley, *China's Democratic Transition* (New York: Columbia University Press, 2004), p. 113.

5. Ira Katznelson, Mark Kesselman, and Alan Draper, *The Politics of Power: A Critical Introduction to American Government* (New York: Norton, 2010).

6. Samuel P. Huntington, *The Third Wave: Democratization in the Late Twentieth Century* (Norman OK: University of Oklahoma Press, 1993).

7. Barrington Moore, Jr., *The Social Origins of Dictatorship and Democracy* (Boston MA: Beacon Press, 1993), p. 418.

8. Quoted in Johann Hari, "The Two Churchills," *New York Times Book Review* (August 15, 2010), p. 11.

9. Seymour Martin Lipset, "Some Social Requisites of Democracy: Economic Development and Political Legitimacy," *American Political Science Review* 53 (1959), pp. 69–105.

10. Guillermo O'Donnell, *Modernization and Bureaucratic Authoritarianism: Studies in South American Politics* (Berkeley, CA: Institute of International Studies, 1973).

11. William F. S. Miles, "The Mauritius Enigma," *Journal of Democracy* 10.2 (1999), p. 99.

12. Ibid. p. 99.

13. Ibid.

14. From Polity IV home page at: http://www.systemicpeace.org/polity/polity4.htm

15. Barbara Geddes, "What Causes Democratization," in *The Oxford Handbook of Political Science*, ed. Robert E. Goodin (New York: Oxford University Press, 2009), p. 596.

16. Geddes, "What Causes Democratization."

17. Kristian Skrede Gleditsch and Michael D. Ward, "Diffusion and the Spread of Democratic Institutions," in *The Global Diffusion of Markets and Democracy*," ed. Beth A. Simmons, Frank Dobbin, and Geoffrey Garrett (New York: Cambridge University Press, 2008), p. 295.

18. Adam Przeworski, *Sustainable Democracy* (New York: Cambridge University Press, 1995), pp. 12–13.

19. William Bagehot, the British political journalist, wrote that "the independence of the legislative and executive powers is the specific quality of presidential government, just as their fusion and combination is the precise principle of cabinet [parliamentary] government." Quoted in Percy Allum, *State and Society in Western Europe* (Malden, MA: Blackwell, Publishers, 1995), p. 304.

20. This particular definition is drawn from Mathew Soberg Shugart and John M.Carey, *Presidents and Assemblies: Constitutional Design and Electoral Dynamics* (New York: Cambridge University Press, 1992).

21. Michael Gallagher, Michael Laver, and Peter Mair, *Representative Government in Europe*, 3rd edition (New York: McGraw-Hill, 2001), p. 69.

22. Juan Linz, "The Perils of Presidentialism," *Journal of Democracy* 1 (Winter 1990), pp. 51–69.

23. Sarah Birch, "Two Round Electoral Systems and Democracy," *Comparative Political Studies*, (2003) Vol. 36, pp. 2–27.

24. Steven Hill, *Europe's Promise: Why the European Way is the Best Hope in an Insecure Age* (Berkeley: University of California Press, 2010), p. 265.

25. Andrew McLaren Carstairs, *A Short History of Electoral Systems in Western Europe* (London: George Allen & Unwin, 1980), p. 215.
26. Henry Milner, "Obstacles to Electoral Reform in Canada," *American Review of Canadian Studies* 24 (1), pp. 39–55.
27. Quoted in Anthony Gottlieb, "Win or Lose," *The New Yorker* (July 26, 2010), p. 76.
28. Franklin Foer, "Political Pitch," *The New Republic* (June 19, 2006), pp. 15–17.
29. Amartya Sen, "Human Rights and Economic Achievements," in Joanne R. Bauer and Daniel A. Bell, eds., *The East Asian Challenge for Human Rights* (New York: Cambridge University Press, 1999), p. 91.
30. Adam Przeworski and Fernando Limongi, "Political Regimes and Economic Growth," *Journal of Economic Perspectives*, Vol. 7 (Summer 1993), p. 65.
31. Morton H. Halperin, Joseph T. Siegle, and Michael M. Weinstein, *The Democratic Advantage: How Democracies Promote Peace and Prosperity*, (New York: Routledge, 2005), p. 34.
32. Halperin, Siegle, and Weinstein, *Democratic Advantage*, p. 38.
33. For further support that democracy has little effect on infant mortality rates (and life expectancy), see Michael Ross, "Is Democracy Good for the Poor?," *American Journal of Political Science* (October 2006), Vol 50, No. 4, pp. 860–874.

Development and Underdevelopment

INTRODUCTION

On January 12, 2010 a powerful earthquake shook Haiti, destroying most of the buildings in the capital of Port Au Prince, killing over 200,000 people, and leaving hundreds of thousands homeless. People set up makeshift shelters using sheets, cardboard, and pieces of rubble. Business owners lost the stores and inventories that were their sources of income. Public buildings and records were destroyed, weakening the government's ability to respond to the crisis.

Conditions were bad enough for Haitians before the earthquake. The poorest country in the Western Hemisphere, its GDP per person is approximately $1,200, as compared to the Caribbean and Latin American average of about $10,000. Haitian infant mortality rates are nearly 55 per 1,000 children born, versus 20 in Latin America as a whole.[1] As grim as these statistics are, there are several countries poorer than Haiti.

Differences in per capita incomes among countries have enormous consequences for people's lives. Being born in a wealthy country such as Sweden gives an infant a high probability of surviving to adulthood, receiving an advanced education, having excellent health, being safe from violence, exercising civil and political rights, and enjoying a long life. Being born in a very poor country such as the Democratic Republic of the Congo in sub-Saharan Africa gives newborns a greater than one in ten chance of dying before their first birthday. If they survive, they are likely to have poor health care, little better than a 50 percent chance of finishing primary school, few civil and political rights, and dying before reaching their fiftieth birthday. These differences between Sweden and the Democratic Republic of the Congo raise one of the biggest questions in the social sciences: Why are some countries much more developed than others?

The first section of the chapter addresses the issue of how to define development and discusses the difference between economic development and human development. The second turns to the question of why there are such differences in development among countries. We examine five major explanations: imperialism, geography, culture, institutions, and political leadership. The chapter ends with a discussion of how differences in levels of economic development affect citizens' capabilities.

ECONOMIC DEVELOPMENT AND HUMAN DEVELOPMENT

Social scientists distinguish between economic development and human development. **Economic development** is the process of increasing a country's wealth by diversifying the goods and services it produces and making that production more efficient. In less developed countries, the path to economic development often leads from production of a few major crops to the production of a greater range of crops, and the development of industries outside the agricultural sector. As countries continue to develop economically, agriculture usually begins to make up a smaller percentage of the economy and manufactured goods become more important. Countries gradually shift from products that involve relatively simple manufacturing processes, such as textiles and garments, to products that require more sophisticated production methods, such as steel and automobiles. As countries move up the development ladder, skilled labor replaces unskilled labor, complex technologies replace simple machines, quality replaces quantity as the standard of production, and per capita income rises. Eventually, industrial production becomes a smaller percentage of a country's GDP, losing ground to service, professional, and managerial activities that characterize postindustrial economies.

Most developed countries began this process in the middle to late 1800s. By the middle of the twentieth century they became industrialized countries, and subsequently completed their postindustrial transformation. Less developed countries got a much later start in this process. Most of them had been colonies of industrialized countries, and their economic development was stunted by the policies of their colonizers. Typically, the main products the colonizers extracted from them were agricultural goods or minerals. Most had little, if any, industrialization. Real industrialization did not get underway in many of these countries until the 1950s and 1960s when they won their independence. The exceptions were countries in Latin America that had achieved independence and began to industrialize much earlier.

By the 1980s, several less developed countries in Asia and Latin America had made considerable economic progress. These so-called **newly industrialized countries**, or **NICs**, included South Korea, Taiwan, and Brazil. Their economies had become advanced enough to make a wide range of industrial products that are competitive in global markets, including steel, automobiles, and semiconductors. These countries have their own multinational corporations that produce and market goods around the world.[2] For example, Hyundai, Samsung, and LG are all South Korean multinationals. Achieving rapid economic development requires a combination of economic factors: skilled workers, capable managers, and effective banking and financial institutions. It also requires political leaders who support sound economic policies and a state bureaucracy that can implement them.

Other less developed countries have made some economic progress, but have not had the kind of success the NICs have had. They include countries such as Botswana, Mexico, and Thailand. Still other less developed countries have languished. Between 1981 and 1998, the poorest 60 percent of less developed countries had "nearly zero or slightly negative growth of income per person."[3] Most of these countries are located in sub-Saharan Africa, but they also include Haiti in the Americas, Laos, Cambodia, and Burma (now Myanmar) in Southeast Asia and North Korea in East Asia. Several of these countries have had some economic growth since 2000, but they remain very poor.

THE GOOD SOCIETY IN DEPTH

South Korea—From Least Likely to Succeed to Most Successful in Its Class

In the 1950s, South Korea was "a terribly depressing place where extreme privation and degradation touched everyone." The Korean War had just ended and much of the country's infrastructure had been destroyed. Beggars roamed city streets, "often traveling in bunches of maimed or starved adults holding babies" and searching through garbage dumps to find food."* An American official called South Korea an economic "basket case," and yet by 2005, South Korea had become one of the World Bank's high-income countries as well as one of the United Nation's high human development countries. No other country has managed to come so far so fast.

The military regime that assumed power in 1961 set out to make South Korea an industrialized country as rapidly as possible. In contrast with military regimes in other less developed countries, it succeeded at its task. Government-controlled banks funded the development of privately owned industrial conglomerates, enabling them to become competitive in international markets. The puzzle is why this way of building an industrial society did not result in the creation of large numbers of inefficient firms and the massive theft of state funds. Several factors come into play here. South Korea's very existence was threatened by two hostile neighbors, North Korea and China. Its leaders believed the country had to industrialize rapidly to survive. Second, the military needed capitalist support to achieve this goal. Militaries cannot build dynamic industrial economies, but capitalists can. Third, the government inherited a relatively competent state bureaucracy and a good infrastructure of roads and electricity from South Korea' years as a Japanese colony. Finally, it received considerable economic aid from the United States.

Although the military government placed less emphasis on developing citizens' capabilities than on industrialization, it turned out to be successful in both endeavors. The educational system was expanded, improving basic literacy and numeracy, and increasing the numbers of engineers and scientists. Health care was expanded too, although mainly for the benefit of the regime's political allies. On the negative side of the ledger, the regime restricted citizens' civil and political rights and ruthlessly suppressed the rights of workers at the behest of corporate elites.

After the fall of the military regime in 1987 and the emergence of democracy, the government began to expand civil and political rights and pushed for broad-based improvements in capabilities. In 2008, South Korea had lower infant mortality rates, longer life expectancies, and higher graduation rates than the United States.

For Further Discussion

1. Why has South Korea been so much more successful than many other poor countries?

2. What caused its military regime to behave so differently from military regimes in other countries, such as Nigeria?

* *Source:* Bruce Cumings, *Korea's Place in the Sun: A Modern History* (New York: W.W. Norton and Company, 1997), p. 303.

Some scholars prefer to focus more broadly on human development as opposed to economic development. The United Nations Human Development Programme defines **human development** as "the process of expanding the choices people have to lead lives that they value."[4] Aspects of human development include being well fed and healthy; being safe from violence; being literate and numerate; and enjoying political participation. In other words, human development means improving people's capabilities. The Human Development Programme has developed a **Human Development Index (HDI)** to measure progress on this score. The index has three components: how healthy people are in a country, as measured by life expectancy at birth; how knowledgeable they are, as measured by adult literacy rates and school enrollments; and whether they have a decent standard of living, as measured by their purchasing power. The value of the index ranges from 0 to 1.[5] In 2007, Norway had the highest HDI score with a value of 0.971 and Niger had the lowest at 0.340. The United States ranked thirteenth at 0.956.

In the best of circumstances, economic development and human development reinforce each other. Economic development can generate more choices for people by creating jobs that increase their incomes. It also provides resources that can be used to pay for clinics and hospitals, medicines, schools, and universities. In turn, better educated, healthier people can perform better as workers, which promotes economic development. Generally speaking, the more economically developed a country is as measured by GDP per capita, the higher is citizens' capability as measured by HDI scores. There is a positive correlation between the two. Norway and the United States are wealthy countries with very high HDI scores, while Niger is one of the poorest countries in the world, and its HDI score reflects this. But the correlation between income per person and HDI scores is not perfect. Countries can have identical per capita incomes and very different HDI scores. For example, the per capita incomes of both Afghanistan and Nepal are approximately $1,100, yet Nepal's HDI score is 0.55 while Afghanistan's is only 0.35. The difference between a country's GDP rank and its HDI rank shows how successful, or unsuccessful, it has been in using whatever wealth it has to improve citizens' health, education, and income.[6] Table 8.1 shows the differences between GDP per capita and HDI rank for the countries we use as case studies in Chapters 9, 10, and 11. Countries with positive figures have been more successful in converting their wealth into capabilities than those with negative figures.

It is important to keep in mind that these HDI values are averages for entire countries. Whether economic growth improves the lives of most citizens in a country or only those of a small elite depends "on how the fruits of economic growth are used."[7] This, in turn, depends on the country's political economy, or the balance between political and market forces in making decisions about who gets what, and the balance of power among competing groups and social classes. India is an example of a country that has made considerable economic progress in recent decades, as reflected in its rapidly growing and well-educated middle class. But its rural population has languished. A survey of public schools in 16,000 rural villages in 2007 found that large numbers of students could not read and write. Teachers regularly came late to class or did not show

TABLE 8.1

GDP per Capita Rank versus HDI Rank 2007

Country	GDP Rank	HDI Rank	GDP Rank minus HDI Rank
Sweden	18	9	9
United States	9	13	−4
Germany	24	22	2
Nigeria	141	158	−17
Brazil	79	75	4
Iran	71	88	−17
Russia	55	71	−16
China	102	92	10

Source: *Human Development Report 2009; Overcoming Barriers: Human Mobility and Development* (New York: Human Development Programme 2009), pp. 171–175.

up at all.[8] In his award-winning novel *The White Tiger*, whose main character is a charming and unscrupulous young man who managed to make it out of his village and succeed in the city, Aravind Adiga divides India into two countries: an urban India of Light, with many well-educated citizens, successful entrepreneurs, and wealthy corporations, and a rural India of Darkness, with failing schools, abject poverty, and oppressive strongmen.[9]

IN BRIEF

Economic Development and Human Development

- Economic development is the process of increasing a country's wealth by diversifying the goods and services it produces and increasing the efficiency with which it produces them. The progress of economic development is measured in two ways: (1) changes in the predominant economic structure, from agriculture, to industry, to services and (2) increasing per capita income.
- Human development is the process of "expanding the choices people have to lead lives that they value." These choices depend on whether the society in which they live gives them the opportunity to be well fed and healthy, safe from violence, literate and numerate, and able to participate in politics.

DIFFERENCES BETWEEN DEVELOPED AND LESS DEVELOPED COUNTRIES

Having discussed the meaning of economic development and human development, and the relationship between them, we can now turn to the ways in which developed and less developed countries differ. Any attempt to categorize countries on the basis of the level of economic or human development requires some degree of arbitrariness. For example, in 2008 the World Bank grouped countries into four categories on the basis of per capita income: low income ($975 per capita or less), lower-middle income ($976 to $3,855), upper-middle income ($3,856 to $11, 905), and high income ($11, 906 or more). Using this scheme, Panama with a per capita income of $11, 650 was an upper-middle-income country, while Bulgaria at $11, 950 was a high-income country along with the United States, which had a per capita income of $46,970. Likewise, the United Nations Human Development Programme divides countries into four categories: low, medium, high, and very high human development. The result is that countries with very similar HDI scores end up in different categories.

Where does one draw the line between "developed" and "less developed" countries, or between different degrees of development? We follow the lead of the World Bank and the United Nations Human Development Programme by employing four categories of development ranging from highly developed, to high, medium, and least developed. We call countries that are in both the World Bank's and Human Development Programme's highest development category "highly developed." Countries that are in both organizations' next highest category are in our "developed" category. We use the same procedure to place countries in our "moderate" and "least developed" categories. While most countries fit into one of the four categories, some do not. For example, Saudi Arabia is in the World Bank's highest income category, but in the Human Development Programme's second highest category. Table 8.2 lists representative countries for each of our categories. We have included all of the countries we use for case studies in Chapters 9–11 (listed in boldface), and several countries featured in the In-Depth Boxes. The number beside each country is its HDI rank in 2009.

TABLE 8.2

Countries Categorized by Level of Development in 2009

Highly Developed (38 Countries)	Developed (45 Countries)	Moderately Developed (75 Countries)	Least Developed (24 Countries)
1. Norway	41. Poland	87. Thailand	159. Togo
7. **Sweden**	44. Chile	88. **Iran**	167. Rwanda
8. France	53. Mexico	92. **China**	169. Liberia
13. **United States**	54. Costa Rica	134. India	171. Ethiopia
21. United Kingdom	66. Malaysia	141. Pakistan	175. Chad
22. **Germany**	71. **Russia**	147. Kenya	180. Sierra Leone
26. South Korea	75. **Brazil**	149. Haiti	181. Afghanistan
27. Israel	81. Mauritius	158. **Nigeria**	182. Niger

Source: "Human Development Report 2009—HDI Rankings. www.hdr.undp.org/en/statistics

Rather than discussing countries in all four of our development categories, we focus on countries at the two extremes: the highly developed and the least developed. We compare those extremes in regard to the capabilities of their citizens, the resilience of their economies, and the viability of their governments. Citizens in more highly developed countries tend to have higher and more secure capabilities; the economies of more highly developed countries tend to be more productive and less vulnerable to economic shocks; and more highly developed countries tend to have stronger and more democratic states. By and large the differences become more pronounced as one moves from highly developed countries to least developed countries.

Lower and Less Secure Capabilities

As one ascends the scale of development, citizens' capabilities increase. The difference in capabilities is particularly stark between the most and least developed countries. Table 8.3, which compares these countries' average infant mortality and adult literacy, illustrates the point.

Most of the least developed countries are located in sub-Saharan Africa. In the poorest sub-Saharan African countries, such as Niger, 176 of every 1,000 children died before their fifth birthday in 2007, and the adult literacy rate was only 29 percent.[10] But while sub-Saharan Africa has the highest *percentages* of citizens with low capability, the region with the largest *numbers* of persons with low capability is South Asia, which includes India, Pakistan, and Bangladesh.

Poorer and More Vulnerable Economies

Low capability is directly linked to **absolute poverty** so extreme as to be life threatening. Absolute poverty means that individuals and families have a difficult time buying food to keep them nourished or medicine to combat disease. Unable to afford adequate housing, they often live in squalid shacks made of tin or cardboard. They often lack access to clean water and cannot afford school fees for their children. The United States has poor people, but their poverty is usually not so severe that it threatens their lives. They are poor in relation to other people, thus they experience **relative poverty**.

TABLE 8.3

Capabilities in Countries with Highest and Least Development

	Infant Mortality	Adult Literacy
Highly Developed Countries	4.1	98.8
Least Developed Countries	111.5	41.1

Source: Data set for *The Good Society* and *Human Development Report 2009*.

According to the World Bank, people suffer from absolute poverty when their income is less than $1.25 a day, adjusted for purchasing power differences among different countries. World Bank figures reveal that the *number* of people living in absolute poverty has been declining since the 1980s. That number fell from about 1.9 billion people in 1981 to about 1.4 billion in 2005. However, there are substantial regional differences. China has had the greatest success in reducing absolute poverty. Absolute poverty rates there dropped from 84 percent of the population in 1981 to only 16 percent in 2005. Absolute poverty rates also dropped in South Asia during these decades, though not as spectacularly as in China. They were slightly lower in sub-Saharan Africa, falling from 54 percent to 51 percent, which still leaves half of the population living in extreme poverty. To make matters worse, while the *percentage* of those in poverty dropped, the actual *numbers* of absolutely poor sub-Saharan Africans nearly doubled because of rapid population growth.[11]

Less developed countries not only have lower incomes per capita than wealthier countries do. They also tend to be more vulnerable to sudden shocks created by changes in the world economy. Outside shocks have included dramatic increases in the cost of oil, increases in interest rates on loans, falling prices for key export crops, and sudden withdrawals of capital by foreign investors. Each new shock slows economic growth and shrinks government tax revenues. Take the case of the so-called oil shocks of the 1970s. In the period between 1960 and 1973, when the first shock hit, 42 countries enjoyed extremely fast growth rates exceeding 2.5 percent per person per year. When the Organization of Petroleum Exporting Countries (OPEC) raised oil prices in 1973–1974 and again in the late 1970s, this growth slowed dramatically. Large numbers of less developed countries had to borrow money to finance their oil imports. When the United States raised interest rates in the early 1980s to curtail its domestic inflation, the unintended effect on the less developed countries was to increase the amount of debts they owed. Many had great difficulty paying back their loans, and a number of them never fully recovered from the twin shocks of the oil price increases and large debt burdens. Only 12 of the 42 countries averaging growth rates of more than 2.5 percent per year between 1960 and 1973 managed to recover the same growth rate in the following decade.[12]

Rapid changes in prices for crops and minerals in the world market are another source of economic woes. Countries dependent on a small number of export crops are particularly vulnerable. Coffee price fluctuations provide an instructive example. Almost 25 million farmers grow coffee, most of them cultivating small plots in Africa, Asia, Latin America, and the Caribbean. An increase in the supply of coffee between 1997 and 2002, coupled with slower growth in consumption, caused international prices to fall by two-thirds. The result was decreasing incomes for poor farmers, who only receive a very small percentage of the sales price of their product. For each dollar spent on roast ground coffee in the United States in 2002, a nickel went to the grower and eight cents went to the farmworkers who had harvested the coffee. Sixty-seven cents went to processors in the United States and eleven cents went to the retail store.[13] By 2006, the price of coffee had recovered to twice what it was in 2002, but the drop in prices caused great hardship for many of the smallholders who grew coffee.

The most recent world economic crisis was the deep recession of 2007–2009 created by the meltdown of the financial sector in the United States. It hit the United States and Europe harder than any downturn since the Great Depression of the 1930s. In a change from past world economic crises, however, many developed and moderately developed countries rode out the recession better than the United States did. China continued to have rapid economic growth, and Brazil's economic performance was stronger than expected. The economic growth of most developing countries slowed only a bit, and then began to resume in 2009. The less developed countries that were most affected by the crisis were Mexico and those Caribbean countries that are heavily dependent on exports to the United States.

Weaker and Less Democratic States

While some less developed countries have strong, effective states that have promoted economic development and distributed the fruits of development equitably, many do not. Strong states are able to defend their territory from outside attacks, maintain order within their borders, and implement policies effectively throughout the country. They can collect the taxes necessary to pay for defense, health programs, and education. They can do so because they have competent, well-trained state bureaucracies, and high levels of legitimacy.

Typically, states in the least developed countries are weak. Their constitutions give state agencies formal power, but they are unable to translate that power into action and implement policies effectively. This incapacity can have lethal results. Drinking water that is supposed to be clean carries dysentery, and garbage that is supposed to be collected attracts vermin. Millions of people in Africa have died from AIDS because governments cannot effectively administer antiretroviral drugs.[14]

Not only are weak states unable to implement policies, but many cannot even do the bare minimum of what defines a state, namely maintain law and order. Some extremely weak states have little authority beyond the immediate vicinity of the capital city. Local strongmen, criminal gangs, or warlords rule large parts of their countries. Afghanistan provides an example. The United States was able to crush the Taliban government that ruled the country between 1996 and 2001, but the U.S.-backed government that replaced the Taliban has little control of much of the country. Some areas are ruled by warlords and the Taliban has reasserted control over large areas of the country. Several West African countries also have extremely weak states.[15]

In the highly developed countries, civil servants are recruited on the basis of merit and generally have a strong sense of professionalism. They usually implement decisions on the basis of clearly defined rules and responsibilities. In the least developed countries government officials often sell decisions to the highest bidder for their services.[16] One way to think about this is to imagine a university in which professors had no sense of commitment to their profession but were willing to hand out grades to students who bid the most for them. This way of distributing grades would destroy the usefulness of grades as a measure of how hard and how well students had worked. It would also destroy the educational objectives of the university. In some less developed countries, getting college grades by paying for them is not unusual. A case in point comes from the Philippines, where the son of a wealthy sugarcane planter paid the registrar to record grades for classes he never attended. The scheme was discovered when the registrar died unexpectedly.[17]

This story highlights the problem of corruption that afflicts many developing countries. **Corruption** is behavior by government officials "which deviates from the formal duties of a public role" for the sake of private gain in the form of money or status. The behavior can help friends, family members, or political allies,[18] and can take many forms. Presidents and prime ministers can use their offices to become very wealthy by confiscating foreign aid. One estimate suggests that corrupt officials stole up to one-third of $30 billion the World Bank provided for Indonesia between 1965 and 1998.[19] Corruption percolates all the way down through the state to the level of teachers, police officers, and mail carriers. At all levels it weakens the state, and the consequences are felt most strongly by poor citizens who cannot afford to pay bribes or who lack the power to defend themselves from arbitrary actions by officials.

Table 8.4 provides a more precise way of measuring relative levels of corruption among countries. It is a ranking of selected countries from the least corrupt, New Zealand, to the most corrupt, Somalia. The number to the left of

TABLE 8.4

Corruption Perceptions Index 2009

Rank	Country
1	New Zealand (least corrupt country)
2	Sweden
14	Germany
19	United States
42	Mauritius
43	Costa Rica
75	Brazil
79	China
130	Nigeria
146	Russia
168	Iran
179	Afghanistan
180	Somalia (most corrupt country)

Source: Transparency International, "Corruptions Perceptions Index 2009." www.transparency.org

the country is its rank among the 180 countries ranked. Countries that are used as case studies in subsequent chapters are in bold face.

Different degrees of corruption among countries are also revealed in a fascinating study of diplomatic abuse of parking privileges. All foreign diplomats in New York City, where the main offices of the United Nations are located, can park their cars illegally without incurring fines because they enjoy immunity from local laws. Diplomats from countries with reputations for high levels of corruption in Table 8.4, such as Nigeria, were more likely to violate local parking laws than diplomats from countries that were regarded as less corrupt, such as Sweden. The latter played by the rules even when they did not have to, whereas the former did not. Researchers concluded that norms about corruption are so engrained that a country's diplomats will follow them even when they are posted abroad.[20]

Economic development can coexist with corruption. South Korea has had a great deal of economic success over the past few decades, despite substantial levels of corruption. This paradox can be explained in part by South Korea's practice of keeping corruption out of government agencies responsible for managing the economy. There has also been a balance of power between business and political elites that prevented political elites from preying on relatively weak businesspeople, as they do in many poor countries.[21] When corruption is pervasive in weak states such as Nigeria, achieving sustained economic development is extremely difficult. These states are not able to make and enforce policies that are essential for economic growth. They cannot build needed infrastructure, such as roads and bridges, because much of the money budgeted for such projects disappears into the pockets of officials. They often fail to utilize the best talent because people are hired on the basis of their political connections, rather than their competence. Contracts are awarded on the basis of political loyalty, not performance.

Weak, extremely corrupt states cannot effectively promote either economic development or citizens' capability. They have difficulty collecting taxes because they do not control large areas of the country. Without adequate tax revenues they cannot adequately finance education, public health, or law and order. Extremely weak states can make life difficult even for well-educated citizens. A citizen of Angola with a Ph.D. in political science told a reporter in 2000 that "human excrement splatters day and night" on the balcony of his apartment. His neighbors "toss it by the bucketful from above."[22] This man lived in Angola's capital city, Luanda, in an apartment building that had "no electricity, no telephones, no elevators, no windows, no garbage pickup and no plumbing."[23] Garbage filled a lagoon next to the building. Children living in the apartments often got dysentery from polluted water and malaria from mosquitoes that bred in the lagoon. This was not an isolated case: Only 20,000 of the capital's estimated four million residents had running water.

States in less developed countries tend to be both weaker and less democratic than states in the advanced industrial countries. While there has been a trend toward democratization among less developed countries, many have only the façade of democracy. That is, they lack contests in which candidates compete for votes in fair elections. Candidates who are not from the government's party are intimidated along with the voters who would like support them. Candidates are sometimes killed. This has been a substantial problem in some parts of India, as well as other less developed countries, including Iraq. In addition to this kind of intimidation, landlords, business owners, and local strongmen can make real citizenship impossible for extremely poor citizens who depend upon them for their livelihood.[24] Finally, as we saw in Chapter 6, despite the rise in the number and percentage of democracies there are still a number of authoritarian regimes in Africa, Asia, and the Middle East that allow no meaningful participation in politics. The Middle East has the worst record in this respect.

WHY DID SOME COUNTRIES BECOME MORE DEVELOPED THAN OTHERS?

In the sixteenth, seventeenth, and eighteenth centuries, knowledgeable Europeans believed that South America had better economic prospects than North America. Mexico's per capita income was nearly identical to that of the thirteen colonies that would become the United States. Even more surprisingly, in 1790, Haiti was possibly "the richest society in the world on a per capita basis."[25] Yet by 2008, the per capita income of the United States, adjusted for purchasing power, was 3.5 times that of Mexico and 42 times that of Haiti. The economist Lant Pritchett calls this widening gap between the incomes of today's high-income and low-income countries "divergence, big time."[26] This section examines five ways of explaining this divergence: Western imperialism, geography, culture, institutions, and leadership.

Imperialism

One explanation attributes the growing differences in incomes worldwide to the effects of Western imperialism and colonialism. **Imperialism** is the economic or political domination of one region or country by another. It involves a relationship of inequality in which powerful countries subjugate others and control their behavior.[27] **Colonialism**, on the other hand, is a less inclusive concept. It refers to formal political rule of one country over another. Colonial powers define the boundaries of their colonies, set up administrations to manage them, and exercise sovereign power within them.[28] Imperialism existed long before modern times, but no prior imperialist movement controlled so much of the world's territory, or had so much of an impact on so many people as Western imperialism.

European countries began to exert their control over larger and larger parts of the world in the sixteenth and seventeenth centuries, when the Spanish and the Portuguese established colonies in Latin and Central America. By the eighteenth century, Britain and France had colonies in North America and the Middle East, and in the nineteenth and early twentieth centuries, along with the Netherlands, they established colonies throughout Asia. China was never colonized, but

European powers managed to divide it into European spheres of influence. Sub-Saharan Africa was the last major area to be colonized in the late nineteenth century. The United States and Japan joined in the rush for colonies around the turn of the twentieth century, with the United States gaining control of the Philippines and other Pacific islands and Japan colonizing Taiwan and Korea.

Some scholars argue that imperialism and colonialism enabled European powers to fund their own economic development while stripping their colonies of wealth and blocking their economic potential. Haiti provides an example of this sort of exploitation. As noted previously, Haiti was perhaps the richest society in the world in 1790 because of its lucrative sugar exports. But almost all of the profits went to the French colonialists, not to the African slaves who grew and harvested sugarcane. Haitian slaves won their independence from France in 1804 after an uprising that lasted 12 years. In exchange for independence, France demanded reparations that went on for decades. By one estimate, Haiti was still spending 80 percent of its national budget on those reparations in 1900.[29] These reparations increased France's income while impoverishing Haiti. Some critics of Western imperialism and colonialism argue that the Haitian case is representative of the broader pattern of relationships. European countries enriched themselves by using forced labor to grow lucrative cash crops for world markets. These profits funded their economic development while impoverishing their colonies and leaving them with overwhelming economic and political problems that persisted even after independence.

The debate over the effects of colonialism and imperialism on less developed countries has been intense. Those who disagree with the argument that Haiti is representative of the broader pattern of relationships between colonizers and colonies advance three main criticisms. First, they argue that the profits European countries made from colonialism were not sufficient to account for why they became so much wealthier than the rest of the world.[30] Second, the profits do not explain why the wealth was put to such productive use in Europe. Wealth in and of itself does not insure sustained economic growth. Nigeria has earned billions of dollars from oil sales in recent decades, yet the country remains extremely poor. Third, not all former colonies are poor today. Indeed, some are among the wealthiest countries in the world, including Australia, Canada, New Zealand, the United States, and South Korea. In addition, there are a number of former colonies that have achieved substantial economic growth, even though they have not reached the income levels of the previous set of former colonies. They include Botswana in sub-Saharan Africa, Malaysia in Southeast Asia, and Chile in Latin America, all of which are much wealthier than Haiti. A successful explanation of the differences in income among countries must be able to explain these different levels of development. The following four explanations attempt to do so.

Geography

A number of authors suggest that geographic location is the most important variable in explaining differences in levels of economic development. Jared

Diamond's book *Guns, Germs, and Steel* proposes that some regions of the world became much more powerful and wealthy than others largely because of advantages conferred on them by their location. The most favored continent was Eurasia, the huge landmass that reaches from Western Europe across the Middle East to China. Eurasia had a climate that allowed the development of many species of domesticated plants, including wheat and rice. Its east–west orientation with only limited differences in growing conditions between regions allowed crops developed in one area to spread rapidly to others. For example, wheat, which was originally domesticated in Southwest Asia, eventually arrived in Europe, where it flourished. The continent was also the home of large mammals, such as horses, cows, and pigs that could be easily domesticated. Cows gave milk, meat, and manure for fertilizer, pigs supplied meat and manure, and horses provided power for pulling plows and mobility for warfare. The combination of these advantages in crops and animals led to food surpluses, which in turn allowed for the development of "large, dense, sedentary, stratified societies."[31] Although many people remained farmers, these societies could also support spiritual leaders who founded religions, and political leaders who founded kingdoms and empires. They could also support artisans and fund the development of new technologies, including steel, swords, guns, cannons, and oceangoing ships.[32] These advantages contributed to Western Europe's eventual dominance of other societies in Latin America and Africa. By the early 1500s, European innovations in ship design helped European explorers reach Latin America, and superior weapons helped them conquer that continent. Germs were the other advantage European conquerors had over the native peoples of Latin America. Living in close proximity to domestic animals for thousands of years had given Europeans immunity to many diseases spread by animals. The native peoples of the Americas had no such immunity, and more natives were killed by diseases carried by Europeans than by their weapons.[33]

Other authors believe that geography continues to explain why many less developed countries have difficulty making progress. Some countries have rich natural resources, while others have none. Some have fertile soils, while large parts of other countries are deserts. Some of the poorest countries in the world are located in the interior of Africa. This geographical location creates several obstacles to development. For example, landlocked countries have no direct access to seaports to export their products abroad. They must ship goods across the territory of other countries that often lack adequate road and railway networks. Several of these countries are bad neighbors wracked by civil wars and predatory governments that make transportation across them especially difficult. In short, it is difficult for landlocked countries to develop because the costs of transportation are too high. They are "condemned to small internal markets, an inefficient division of labor, and continued poverty."[34] Finally, some countries have to deal with deadly and debilitating diseases. Their climates are ideal for the spread of malaria, which infects and kills large numbers of people every year. Endemic diseases, along with small local markets and poverty, discourage foreign trade and investment.[35]

Geography alone, however, does not work as an all-purpose explanation for why some countries have achieved much greater economic and human development than others. While Eurasia had special advantages over other areas of the world, many countries in this vast region have very different levels of economic development. China is poorer than Western European countries. Some countries in the region remain very poor. They include Myanmar (formerly known as Burma) and Bangladesh, neither of which is landlocked. Several African countries with access to the sea are also among the poorest countries in the world. Nor is the presence of rich natural resources a guarantee of economic success. Oil riches are often a curse rather than an aid to economic development. In addition, some of the most economically successful less developed countries, such as South Korea, have no valuable mineral deposits or oil reserves.

Culture

Another group of scholars attributes the success of the highly developed countries not to the hard materialism of geographic endowment, but to the soft intangibles of cultural values. These scholars argue that the progress of different societies is determined by what is in people's heads, not by what is under their feet. The presence of certain values and beliefs is said to dispose some societies to be more productive and democratic than others. For example, the German social scientist Max Weber contended that the Protestant ethic's emphasis on steady, disciplined hard work, thriftiness, honesty, and effective use of one's time helps explain why economic development took off in Europe, where that ethic was most prevalent. Contrary to popular belief, the capitalist spirit was not dominated by greed, or motivated by a desire for comfort or pleasure.[36] Greed and a desire for comfort and pleasure were not new in human history. What fueled economic development in Europe was an ethic that promoted steady, systematic work, effective use of one's time, and reinvestment of earnings into one's business rather than spending them on immediate gratifications. Weber did not claim the Protestant ethic was the sole cause of the economic development of Europe. Rather, he argued it was one in a constellation of other factors that came together to support dynamic, sustained economic growth.[37]

A number of contemporary authors have drawn on Weber's work to try to explain why some countries are economically developed and others are less developed. The Harvard historian David Landes writes, "If we learn anything from the history of economic development, it is that culture makes almost all the difference."[38] Landes acknowledges the importance of geography and institutions in explaining economic development.[39] Nevertheless, he believes that in the end the key to European economic success was "the making of a new kind of man—rational, ordered, diligent, productive."[40] Landes notes that this ethic does not have to be Protestant. He attributes Japan's success in catching up to Europe to a Japanese version of the work ethic.[41] In contrast, China, Islamic societies, and other parts of the world fell behind because they did not develop values conducive to promoting economic growth.

While some scholars explain economic development in terms of character traits, others emphasize social capital and trust. Francis Fukuyama argues, "A nation's well-being, as well as its ability to compete economically, is conditioned by a single, pervasive cultural characteristic: the level of trust inherent in the society."[42] Economic activity, from running a factory to international trade, depends on social cooperation. If a factory depended mainly on penalties to prevent workers from stealing goods, and if firms depended mainly on lawsuits to enforce contracts, economic transactions would be very inefficient.[43] Trust "acts like a kind of lubricant that makes any group or organization run more efficiently."[44] The dearth of social capital is one of the factors contributing to Nigeria's poor record of economic development. Many businesses refuse to extend credit to customers because they cannot be sure of getting reimbursed. Stores do not accept personal checks, or even credit cards.[45] Such pervasive lack of trust slows economic development.[46]

Like geography, culture cannot serve as an all-purpose explanation of why some countries have more economic and human development than others. Cultural explanations have a difficult time explaining why countries with similar cultural backgrounds have different records of economic performance. For instance, North Korea and South Korea were part of the same country for hundreds of years and have the same cultural background. Yet South Korea has experienced extraordinary economic development, while North Korea remains a poor country. Cultural explanations also have difficulty in explaining sudden changes in economic performance. In the late 1950s, one scholar attributed Thailand's lack of economic development to its Buddhist religion and Thais' love of fun rather than hard work.[47] This study was published just as Thailand began several decades of rapid economic development that made it the fastest-growing country in the world for a while in the 1990s. Finally, cultural arguments have trouble explaining history's winners and losers. For example, some scholars contend that Islam is responsible for the fact that the Arab world has fallen so far behind the West. But the alleged "backwardness" of Islam did not prevent Arab civilization from being more dynamic, innovative, and technologically advanced than Europe during the Middle Ages. Technological advances and scientific discoveries that now flow from the West to the Middle East used to go in the other direction.

Institutions

The fourth way of explaining differences in economic performance among countries uses institutions as the main independent variable.[48] The economist Dani Rodrik argues that "the quality of institutions overrides everything else" in explaining the huge differences in incomes between the richest and the poorest countries.[49] Economic institutions matter because they shape individuals' incentives for investment, whether to expand crop production, build new firms and factories, develop new technologies, or train workers in useful skills. Economic and political institutions also determine how the benefits of growth are divided among individuals and groups in society.[50]

According to institutionalists, three sets of economic institutions are particularly important: market creating, market stabilizing, and market legitimizing institutions. First, there must be *market-creating institutions* that protect property rights. Without property rights markets work poorly or do not work at all. Property rights reassure entrepreneurs that they will be able to reap what they sow. They will be loath to invest in countries where rulers or warring factions indiscriminately seize property and earnings. Entrepreneurs are more secure when they know what the rules are and that they will be enforced. This is not to say that property rights cannot be infringed upon, only that any abridgment of rights should be according to the due process of law.

Property rights help initiate economic development, but sustained development requires additional kinds of institutions. There must also be *market-stabilizing institutions* that prevent markets from careening out of control because of runaway inflation or excessive budget deficits. Developed countries in North America and Europe typically run inflation rates of 2 to 10 percent. In comparison, the inflation rate in Zimbabwe was approaching 1,000 percent in 2006. Toilet paper cost the equivalent of $417 in Zimbabwe—not for the roll, but for a single two-ply sheet! Inflation worsened in subsequent years. With prices increasing daily, even hourly, survival depends on keeping up with rising prices for basic necessities—a race that many citizens were losing.[51]

The institutions that play the most important role in controlling inflation and prudently managing the budget are ministries of finance, budgetary agencies, and central banks. Such institutions must be staffed by competent civil servants who are recruited on the basis of merit, not by political cronies.[52] In addition, they must be independent from groups and politicians who want to keep printing money regardless of its consequences for inflation or keep borrowing money regardless of its consequences for the public debt.

Finally, as economic development proceeds and more and more people become dependent on the market for jobs, food, and housing, countries also need *market-legitimating institutions.*[53] These are institutions that soften the harsh consequences of markets. Such institutions are necessary because markets, left to themselves, can produce results that do not meet people's needs and that violate their sense of what is fair. To paraphrase Sheri Berman, markets make great cooks, but lousy hosts. They are good at creating lush, full meals, but bad at making sure everyone gets enough to eat.[54] Markets generate too much inequality, too much instability, too many harmful spillovers, and too few public services. Consequently, market-legitimating institutions are necessary to reduce the inequality that markets naturally create. Regulations such as pollution controls are necessary to protect citizens from spillovers that markets ignore. Programs that protect people from risk, such as unemployment insurance, are necessary to cope with the instability that is endemic to markets. And public goods such as schools for all children are necessary to provide services that markets won't create on their own because it is not profitable to do so. Market systems without market-legitimating institutions can be desperate places in which to live for poor citizens.[55]

Considering the importance of market-creating, market-stabilizing, and market-legitimating institutions, the puzzle is why some countries managed to establish them while others did not. Acemoglu, Johnson, and Robinson suggest that the type of economic institutions that emerge in a country "depends on who is able to get their way—who has political power."[56] In their view the distribution of political power in a country is the main determinant of the kind and the quality of economic institutions that develop there. European countries with access to the Atlantic Ocean that were heavily engaged in trade and colonialism were the first to begin sustained economic growth. The authors suggest this was because profits from trade gave their merchants the economic and political power "to demand and obtain the institutional changes necessary for economic growth." Changes in economic institutions offered "secure property rights to a broad cross-section of society" and made it possible for citizens to enter a wide variety of businesses freely. Changes in political institutions restricted the power of monarchs and "groups allied with the monarchy."[57]

Social scientists who favor the institutional approach also have an explanation for the large differences in income among former colonies. They contend that colonies in which European settlers became the majority of the population adopted the same growth-promoting institutions that developed in their home countries. By contrast, colonies where Europeans were few in number and relied primarily on slave labor to support them established very different kinds of institutions. European elites in these colonies designed institutions to protect their economic and social privileges. Land-holding laws ensured that they maintained their profitable rights to mines or plantations. Voting laws allowed them to monopolize their stronghold on political power. Education was restricted to the children of the elite and denied to the broad masses of the population.

This is not to say that the colonies in which Europeans constituted the majority of the population were democratic or egalitarian. For example, in the United States the franchise was limited to white men with significant property holdings until the early 1800s. But meaningful voting rights emerged much earlier in the United States and Canada than they did in Central and South America. So did public primary schools. And while Canada and the United States were not societies of equals, they were generally more egalitarian than societies in Latin America, with the major exception being the American South before the Civil War. The key point is that once institutions are in place, they tend to persist because privileged groups defend institutions that benefit them. Former colonies with institutions that were designed to sustain economic and social privilege continue to exhibit extreme economic and political inequality.[58]

Two factors, above all others, determined whether Europeans settled thickly or thinly in colonized areas. One was disease. Europeans were less inclined to settle in places where they were vulnerable to tropical illnesses like malaria, typhus, and yellow fever. The other factor was the suitability of soils and climates for growing cash crops like tobacco and sugarcane that could be grown profitably with forced labor. Thus, institutionalists do affirm that geography matters. They also affirm that imperialism and colonialism matter—not so much because of the wealth that Europeans took from their colonies, however, but because of the institutional legacy they left behind.

Colonial powers also left other obstacles to development for newly independent countries. They sometimes left an economy that was highly vulnerable to market fluctuations because of its dependency on a single export crop. They sometimes drew the borders of a country arbitrarily, so as to encompass many different ethnic, linguistic, and religious groups. Such extreme diversity creates strains that even strong political institutions would have difficulty handling. Finally, colonial powers sometimes introduced racial cleavages. This was particularly the case in Latin America and the Caribbean countries where most workers in the sugar plantations were African slaves or their descendants. During Brazil's "first 250 years, roughly 70 percent of the immigrants to this Portuguese colony arrived in chains."[59]

Leadership

Interestingly, none of the four explanations for development and underdevelopment that we have considered—imperial history, geography, culture, and institutional structure—address the issue of leadership. Yet leadership clearly plays an important role in promoting or hindering development. Granted, some leaders of less developed countries face particularly difficult obstacles. Yet development is determined not only by a country's past and its position in the international division of labor, but also by its leaders' will and skill in choosing successful policies, constructing coalitions of supporters for these policies, and establishing effective economic and political institutions.[60] While South Korea had advantages that sub-Saharan Africa lacked, it is unlikely that the former would have achieved its current level of development as rapidly as it did without the leadership provided by General Park Chung Hee. Likewise, President Paul Kagame has also made a difference in Rwanda, and political leaders in Mauritius and Costa Rica have managed to improve the capabilities of many citizens while sustaining effective democracies.

IN BRIEF

Five Explanations for Different Levels of Development among Countries

- Imperialism increased the wealth of European countries and impoverished colonies. It also created numerous obstacles for newly independent countries, including dependence on a single crop for export earnings, extreme ethnic diversity, and racial cleavages.
- Geography favored countries in Eurasia over countries in Africa and Latin America by providing native plant and animal species that were suitable for domestication and adaptable to different environments. Today, geography

Continued

inhibits trade and development in poor landlocked countries with bad neighbors.

- Cultures that emphasize disciplined work and investment over self-gratification contribute to economic development. So do ones with high levels of social capital and trust.
- Institutions matter for development because they can create incentives for productive investment or destroy them. The reason that Western European countries outpaced the rest of the world in development was that they were first to establish economic institutions that support sustained growth and political institutions to complement them.
- Leadership matters because of the policies leaders choose, the kinds of coalitions of supporters they create, and the quality of institutions they help create.

COMPARATIVE POLITICAL ANALYSIS

Institutions as the Main Cause of Development and Underdevelopment

Problem

Citizens who live in wealthy countries have a much higher probability of developing their human potential than those who live in poor countries. Social scientists disagree about why some countries are rich while others are poor. The economists Daron Acemoglu and Simon Johnson, and the political scientist James A. Robinson, believe the answer lies in differences in economic and political institutions.

Hypothesis and Method

The authors hypothesize that economic institutions protecting property rights and relying on markets are most likely to sustain economic growth. The authors use the comparative case studies method to test their hypothesis by comparing the development experiences of North Korea and South Korea. These countries were chosen because they were one political entity for hundreds of years. They have the same geography, culture, and experience of being a Japanese colony. They differ in economic and political institutions as a result of being separated after World War II. The communist party that ruled North Korea abolished private property and markets, and introduced a state- planned economy. The military government that ruled South Korea from 1961 to 1987 maintained private property and promoted the development of internationally competitive industries. It used government-owned banks to fund the growth of corporations and decided which firms would receive priority for funding.

Continued

Operationalizing Concepts

The authors operationalize their central concepts as follows:

- The independent variable is the presence or absence of private property rights and market incentives.
- The dependent variable is economic growth defined as GDP growth per capita

Results

The results confirm the authors' hypothesis. They write, "By the late 1960's South Korea was transformed into one of the Asian 'miracle' economies, experiencing one of the most rapid surges of economic prosperity in history while North Korea stagnated. By 2000 the level of income in South Korea was $16,100 while in North Korea it was only $1,000. . . . There is only one plausible explanation for the radically different economic experiences on the two Koreas after 1950: their very different institutions led to divergent economic outcomes."

For Further Discussion

1. If private property, markets, and political institutions that constrain political elites are essential for creating sustained development, how can the authors explain China's development success?

2. What are the limits of using the comparative cases method to confirm the hypothesis?

Source: Acemoglu, Johnson, and Robinson, "Institutions as a Fundamental Cause of Long-Run Growth," p. 406

DEVELOPMENT, UNDERDEVELOPMENT, AND THE GOOD SOCIETY

Economic development can make a big difference in people's capabilities. Wealthier countries have more income to spend on health care, education, and safety. Higher levels of income per capita are also associated with higher levels of democracy. In this section, we test the hypothesis that higher income per capita is associated with higher capabilities.

Physical Well-Being

We begin with the hypothesis that higher income per capita is associated with lower infant mortality rates. We use income per capita adjusted for purchasing power in 2008 from the World Bank's World Development Indicators.[61] We take the data for infant mortality from the database for *The Good Society*. We test the hypothesis using the 32 countries in Table 8.2, whose incomes range from very high to low. The results can be seen in Figure 8.1.

The relationship is generally what we expect to find. Higher income countries do tend to have lower infant mortality rates than low income

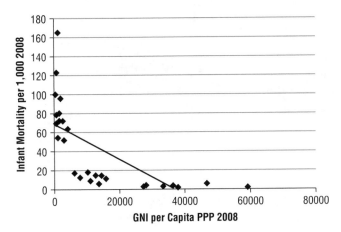

FIGURE 8.1

Income per Capita and Infant Mortality Rates, 2008

Data Sources:

World Development Indicators
www.worldbank.org/indicator

Country Comparison: Infant Mortality Rate
Data Source: CIA World Factbook, https://www.cia.gov/library/publications/the-world-factbook/rankorder/
2091rank.html

countries. But it is not the case that each increase in income per capita brings a similar decrease in infant mortality. Countries with per capita incomes ranging from approximately $30,000 to $60,000 have nearly identical infant mortality rates. It is possible to achieve low levels of infant mortality even in the absence of extremely high per capita incomes. A second conclusion is that very poor countries differ profoundly in infant mortality levels. The country with the highest infant mortality rate is Afghanistan, which is located at the top of the vertical axis. Its infant mortality rate is over 160 per 1,000, and its per capita income in 2008 was $1,100. Haiti, with a per capita income of only $180 more per capita than Afghanistan, has a much lower infant mortality rate of 54. This is still a tragically high infant mortality rate, but it demonstrates that Haiti does a better job than Afghanistan of converting meager resources into fewer infant deaths.

Informed Decision Making

The second hypothesis we test is that higher income per capita is associated with higher adult literacy rates. We use the same sources as for Figure 8.1.[62] The results are shown in Figure 8.2.

Here again, the hypothesis is borne out. Higher income per capita countries do have higher adult literacy rates. But the results resemble those for the relationship between income per capita and infant mortality. Countries at very different levels of income can achieve nearly 100 percent literacy. The literacy

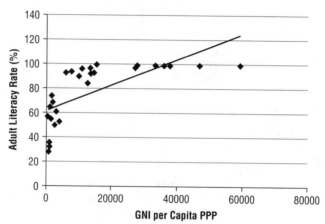

FIGURE 8.2

Income per Capita and Adult Literacy Rates, 2008

Data Sources:

World Development Indicators
www.worldbank.org/indicator.

Adult Literacy Rate (% aged 15 and above)
Data Source: Human Development Report 2009, http://hdrstats.undp.org/en/indicators/89.html

rate in Russia, with a per capita income of $15,460, matches those of countries with a per capita income several times as high. And we find the same pattern of very wide differences among the poorest countries'. Despite the fact that Haiti and Chad have similar per capita incomes, Haiti's literacy rate is 55 percent, while Chad's stands at only 32 percent.

Safety

The next hypothesis we test is that higher per capita income is associated with lower homicide rates.. Admittedly, homicide rates can be a very misleading gauge of citizens' feelings of safety in many less developed countries. In sub-Saharan Africa some very poor countries are embroiled in civil wars in which civilians die and combatants often perpetrate mass rapes. Yet neither deaths nor rapes associated with warfare are reflected in homicide figures, which can sometimes conceal more than they reveal about citizens' safety. Take, for example, the case of Iraq. That country's reported homicide rate is lower than that of Costa Rica, but it is highly unlikely that citizens feel safer from physical violence in Iraq than in Costa Rica. Despite this caveat, we include a test of the hypothesis that higher income is associated with lower rates of homicide, to see if there is a relationship between per capita income and one particular kind of threat to safety. The results are in Figure 8.3.[63]

As expected, homicide rates are lower in higher income countries. But the scatter diagram reveals several discrepancies from the overall pattern. All of the countries with an income per capita over $20,000 have a homicide rate

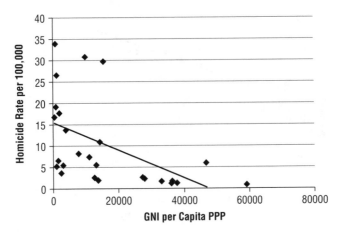

FIGURE 8.3
Per Capita Income PPP and Homicide Rates

Data Sources:

World Development Indicators
www.worldbank.org/indicator.

Murder Rates around the World
United Nations Office on Drugs and Crime http://data.un.org/Data.aspx?d=UNODC&f=tableCode%3a1

lower than 5 per 100,000 except the United States. Even Haiti and India have lower homicide rates than the United States, despite the latter's far greater wealth. The scatter diagram also shows that poor countries vary wildly in outcomes. Rwanda has the highest homicide rate at 34 per 100,000, but rates in countries with only slightly higher incomes are much lower. In summary, per capita income is associated with all three capabilities in the way we hypothesized. But in and by itself, it is far from a complete explanation for variations in capabilities.

Democracy

The final hypothesis we test is that higher per capita income is associated with higher levels of democracy. We use income per capita adjusted for purchasing power in 2008 from the World Bank's World Development Indicators.[64] We take the data for the level of democracy from the Polity IV indicators in the database for *The Good Society*.[65] The results can be seen in Figure 8.4.

The results confirm the hypothesis. This is not surprising, because as we saw in the previous chapter there is a strong relationship between higher levels of per capita income in a country and democracy. Rising income in a country is accompanied by increases in the size of the middle class and higher levels of education, which are the seeds of democracy. But as we also saw, the relationship between higher levels of per capita income and democracy is far from perfect. As can be seen in Figure 8.4, countries with very different levels of income per capita have the highest Polity IV score possible. Also, countries with very

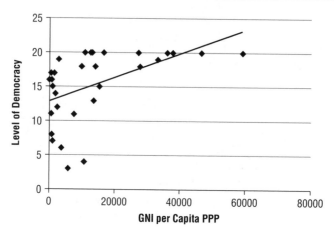

FIGURE 8.4
Per Capita Income PPP and Democracy

Data Sources:

World Development Indicators
www.worldbank.org/indicator

Polity IV Country Reports, 2007
http://www.systemicpeace.org/polity/polity06.htm

similar income levels have very different levels of democracy. There are other variables that help account for these differences. They include internal conditions such as high government revenues from oil exports and regional factors, including whether a country is located close to other democracies.

CONCLUSION

This chapter has focused on the major development gaps between developed countries and less developed countries. It began by distinguishing between economic development and human development and suggesting that the two often, but not always, go together. Some countries have much more success in promoting human development than might be expected from their level of economic development, while in others, human development lags well behind.

The chapter then discussed three main ways in which the less developed countries differ from the developed countries. First, a higher percentage of citizens in less developed countries have lower and less secure capabilities, as measured by infant mortality rates, life spans, and literacy. Second, the economies of less developed countries are less productive. They have lower per capita incomes, and tend to be more vulnerable to economic shocks. Finally, less developed countries tend to have weaker, less democratic states. They are often unable to collect taxes effectively to pay for dedicated and skilled teachers, health care workers, and police officers. Weak states are also unable to enforce policies throughout the country, with the result that many poor people and minorities continue to be dominated by powerful local elites. The lack of effective democracy makes it difficult to change these patterns of domination.

The following section of this chapter examined five explanations for differences in development among countries. The first says that imperialism and colonialism are the main causes of the gap. European countries grew wealthy by exploiting and impoverishing their colonies in other parts of the world. The second emphasizes the effect of geography, which gave Eurasia advantages over Africa and South America, and continues to hamper countries that lack access to ports and trade routes. The third suggests that some cultural values are more conducive to economic development than others. The fourth focuses on institutions as the main cause of developmental differences. In this context, we identified those institutional differences that appear to be most important and tried to show why they emerged in some countries rather than others. Finally, we suggested a fifth explanation: leadership can make a difference. Men and women can act as agents of their own destiny, although this is much easier in some times and places than others. Some leaders are successful in using new policies and approaches to put together coalitions of supporters to set their countries on favorable paths.

mypoliscikit EXERCISES

Apply what you learned in this chapter on MyPoliSciKit (www.mypoliscikit.com).

 ASSESSMENT
Review this chapter using learning objectives, chapter summaries, practice tests, and more.

 VIDEO CASE STUDIES
Analyze recent world affairs by watching streaming video from major news providers.

 FLASHCARDS
Learn the key terms in this chapter; you can test yourself by term or definition.

 COMPARATIVE EXERCISES
Compare political ideas, behaviors, institutions, and policies worldwide.

CRITICAL THINKING QUESTIONS

1. What is the difference between economic development and human development?
2. Why are there sometimes discrepancies between a country's level of economic development and its level of human development?
3. How do differences in state strength between developed and less developed countries make a difference for citizens' capabilities?

4. How would supporters of imperialist, geographical, cultural, and institutional explanations, respectively, explain why Haiti changed from being one of the richest societies in the world in 1790 to one of the poorest today?
5. What variables in addition to per capita income might account for the big differences in infant mortality rates among very poor countries in Figure 8.1?

KEY TERMS

Economic
   Development   192
Newly Industrialized
   countries (NICs)   193
Human Development   195

Human Development
   Index (HDI)   195
Absolute Poverty   198
Relative Poverty   198
Corruption   201

Imperialism   203
Colonialism   203

SUGGESTED READINGS

Daron Acemoglu, Simon Johnson, and James A. Robinson, "Institutions as a Fundamental Cause of Long-Run Growth," in *Handbook of Economic Growth*, edited by Philippe Aghion and Steven N. Durland (Elsevier B.V. 2005), pp. 385–472. An influential explanation of the role of institutions in promoting economic growth and why they emerged in some countries and not others.

Jared Diamond, *Guns, Germs, and Steel: The Fates of Human Societies* (New York: W.W. Norton and Company, 1999). A Pulitzer Prize-winning best seller explaining why geography determines the economic fate of nations.

John Isbister, *Promises Not Kept: Poverty and the Betrayal of Third World Development, 7th edition* (Kumarian Press, 2006). Provides a very useful overview of the literature on the consequences of imperialism and colonialism for less developed countries.

Lawrence E. Harrison and Samuel P. Huntington, *Culture Matters: How Values Shape HumanProgress* (New York: Basic Books, 2000). Includes chapters by several well-known scholars who believe culture makes all the difference in determining whether a country develops or not.

United Nations Development Programme, *Human Development Report 2003: Millennium Development Goals: A Compact Among Nations to End Human Poverty* (New York; Oxford University Press, 2003). Provides an excellent overview of the human development perspective and goals for eliminating poverty.

NOTES

1. "Scrabbling for Survival," *Economist*, January 28, 2010 and World Bank, *World Development Report 2010* (Washington, D.C.: World Bank, 2009), pp. 378–379.
2. Adrian Woolridge, "The World Turned Upside Down," *The Economist* (April 15, 2010).
3. William Easterly, *The Elusive Quest for Growth: Economists Misadventures in the Tropics* (Cambridge, MA: MIT Press, 2001), p. 60.
4. United Nations Human Development Programme, "What Is Human Development?" *Human Development Report 2002*, http://hdr.undp.org.
5. While the component parts of the HDI overlap with the ways of functioning that make up an individual's capability, it is not identical with capability. The HDI is an

average for all people in a country, while the capability approach emphasizes all individuals. As we noted in Chapter 1, countrywide averages can hide large discrepancies. A second difference is the HDI has no indicator for civil and political rights or individuals' abilities to have a say in the political decisions that affect their lives.

6. World Bank, *Beyond Economic Growth: Introduction to Sustainable Development*, 2nd ed., www.worldbank.org/depweb/english/beyond/global.

7. Amartya Sen, *Development as* Freedom, p. 44.

8. Somini Sengupta, "Education Push Yields Little for India's Schools," *New York Times* (January 37, 2008).

9. Aravind Adiga, *The White Tiger* (New York: Free Press), 2008.

10. *World Development Report 2010* (Washington, DC: World Bank, 2009), pp. 379, 383.

11. World Bank, "2008 World Development Indicators: Poverty Data." A supplement to World Develoment Indicators 2008 (Washington, D.C.: The World Bank, 2008), p. 10.

12. Dani Rodrik, The *New Global Economy and Developing Countries: Making Openness Work* (Washington, D.C.: Overseas Development Council, 1999), pp. 68–75.

13. Jorge Ramirez-Vallejo, "A Break for Coffee," *Foreign Policy 132* (September/October 2002), pp. 26–27. The remaining nine cents is for processing in the producing country, transport and loss.

14. Patrick Heller, *The Labor of Development* (Ithaca, NY: Cornell University Press, 1999), p. 28. The examples are from Francis Fukuyama, *State Building* (Ithaca, NY: Cornell University Press, 2004), p. x.

15. William Reno, *Warlord Politics and African States* (Boulder, CO: Lynne Rienner Publishers, 1999).

16. Peter Evans, *Embedded Autonomy: States and Industrial Transformation* (Princeton, NJ: Princeton University Press, 1995), p. 12.

17. Alan Berlow, *Dead Season: A Story of Murder and Revenge on the Philippine Island of Negros* (New York: Pantheon Books, 1996), pp. 137–138.

18. J. S. Nye, "Corruption and Political Development: A Cost-Benefit Analysis," in A. J. Heidenheimer, M. Johnston, and V. T. Levine, eds., *Political Corruption: A Handbook* (New Brunswick, NJ: Transaction Publishers, 1989). Cited in Paul D. Hutchcroft, "Obstructive Corruption: The Politics of Privilege in the Philippines," in Mushtaq H. Khan and Jomo K. S., eds., *Rents, Rent-Seeking and Economic Development: Theory and Evidence from Asia* (New York: Cambridge University Press, 2000), p. 213.

19. Jeffrey Winters, "World Bank Must Face the Corruption Music," *Jakarta Post*, September 23, 1998. Cited in Morton Halperin, Joseph T. Siegle, and Michael M. Weinstein, *The Democracy Advantage: How Democracies Promote Prosperity and Peace* (New York: Routledge, 2005), p. 163.

20. Raymond Fisman and Edward Miguel, "Cultures of Corruption: Evidence from Parking Tickets," NBER Working Paper No. 12312, June 2006.

21. David C. Kang, *Crony Capitalism: Corruption and Development in South Korea and the Philippines* (New York: Cambridge University Press, 2002), pp. 1–17.

22. Blaine Harden, "Angolan Paradox: Oil Wealth Only Adds to Misery," *New York Times*, April 9, 2000.

23. Ibid.

24. Patrick Heller, "Degrees of Democracy: Some Comparative Lessons from India," *World Politics* 52:4 (July 2000), pp. 491–493.

25. Kenneth L. Sokoloff and Stanley L. Engermann, "History Lessons: Institutions, Factor Endowments, and Paths of Development in the New World," *Journal of Economic Perspectives* 14:3 (Summer 2000), p. 217.

26. Lant Pritchett, "Divergence, Big Time," *Journal of Economic Perspectives,*" 11:3 (Summer 1997), pp. 3–17.

27. Benjamin J. Cohen, *The Question of Imperialism: The Political Economy of Dominance and Dependence* (New York: Basic Books, 1973), pp. 15–16.

28. Cohen, p. 10.

29. Alex von Tunzelmann, "Haiti: The Land Where Children Eat Mud," *London Times* (May 17, 2009). Cited in http://chrisblattman.com, January 14, 2010.

30. Patrick O'Brien, "European Economic Development: The Contribution of the Periphery," *The Economic History Review* 35:1 (February 1982), pp. 1–17.

31. Jared Diamond, *Guns, Germs, and Steel: The Fates of Human Societies* (New York: W. W. Norton and Company, 1999), p. 87.

32. Ibid., p. 78 .

33. Ibid, pp. 29, 210–212.

34. Jeffrey D. Sachs, "Institutions Matter, but Not for Everything," *Finance and Development* 40:2 (June 2003), p. 39.

35. Ibid.

36. Gianfranco Poggi, *Calvinism and the Capitalist Spirit: Max Weber's Protestant Ethic* (Amherst, MA: The University of Massachusetts Press, 1983), pp. 40–47.

37. Randall Collins, *Weberian Sociological Theory* (New York: Cambridge University Press, 1987), pp. 23–37.

38. David S. Landes, "Culture Makes Almost All the Difference," in Lawrence E Harrison and Samuel P. Huntington, *Culture Matters* , p. 2.

39. David S. Landes, *The Wealth and Poverty of Nations: Why Some Nations Are So Rich and Some So Poor* (New York: W. W. Norton and Company, 1998), pp. 217–218, 274–275.

40. Ibid., p. 177.

41. Ibid., p. 383.

42. Francis Fukuyama, "The Economics of Trust," *National Review* (August 14, 1995), p. 42.

43. Francis Fukuyama, "Social Capital and the Global Economy," *Foreign Affairs* 74:5 (September/October 1995), p. 90.

44. Francis Fukuyama, "Social Capital," in Lawrence E. Harrison and Samuel P. Huntington, *Culture Matters*, p. 98.

45. Robert Guest, "Striving Amid Chaos," in "Survey of Nigeria," The *Economist* (January 13, 2000).

46. Robert Putnam with Robert Leonardi and Raffaella Y. Nanetti, *Making Democracy Work: Civic Traditions in Modern Italy* (Princeton: Princeton University Press, 1993).

47. Eliezer B. Ayal, "Value Systems and Economic Development in Japan and Thailand," *Journal of Social Issues* 19:1 (January 1963), pp. 35–51.

48. Peter Evans, "The Challenges of the Institutional Turn," in *The Economic Sociology of Capitalist Institutions*, ed. Victor Nee and Richard Swedberg (Princeton, NJ: Princeton University Press, 2005); and Daron Acemoglu, Simon Johnson, and James A. Robinson, "Institutions as a Fundamental Cause of Long Run Growth" in *Handbook of Economic Growth, Volume IA,* ed. Philippe Aghion and Steven N. Durlauf (Maryland Heights, MO: Elsevier 2005).

49. Dani Rodrik, "The Primacy of Institutions," *Finance and Development* (June 2003), p. 31.

50. Daron Acemoglu, Simon Johnson and James A. Robinson, "Institutions as a Fundamental Cause of Long-Run Growth," pp. 389–390.
51. Michael Wines, "Zimbabwe's Prices Rise 900%, Turning Staples into Luxuries," *New York Times* , May 2, 2006, p. 1.
52. Peter Evans and James E. Rauch, "Bureaucracy and Growth: A Cross-National Analysis of the Effects of 'Weberian' State Structures on Economic Growth," *American Sociological Review* (October 1999) Vol. 64, No. 5, pp. 748–765.
53. This discussion of the kinds of institutions needed to initiate and sustain growth is from Dani Rodrik and Arvind Subramanian, "The Primacy of Institutions," *Finance and Development* (June, 2003), pp. 31–34.
54. Sheri Berman, *The Primacy of Politics: Social Democracy and the Making of Europe's Twentieth Century* (New York: Cambridge University Press, 2006), p. 210.
55. The above discussion on market-creating, generating, and legitimating institutions draws on Dani Rodrik and Arvind Subramanian, "The Primacy of Institutions (and What This Does and Does Not Mean)," *Finance and Development* (June 2003), p. 32; Dani Rodrik, "Institutions, Integration, and Geography: In Search of the Deep Determinants of Economic Growth," in Dani Rodrik, editor, *In Search of Prosperity: Analytic Country Studies on Growth* (Princeton, NJ: Princeton University Press, 2003).
56. Daron Acemoglu, Simon Johnson, and James A. Robinson, "Institutions as a Fundamental Cause of Long-Run Growth," p. 446
57. Daron Acemoglu, Simon Johnson, and James Robinson," The Rise of Europe: Atlantic Trade, Institutional Change, and Economic Growth." *American Economic Review* 95:3 (June 2005), pp. 549–551.
58. Kenneth L. Sokoloff and Stanley L. Engerman, "Institutions, Factor Endowments, and Paths of Development in the New World," *Journal of Economic Perspectives* 14:3 (Summer 2000), pp. 220–228.
59. David D. Ferranti, Guillermo D. Perry, and Francisco Ferreira., *Inequality in Latin America: Breaking with History?* (Washington, D.C.: World Bank, 2004), p. 110.
60. Peter Evans and John D. Stephens, "Studying Development since the Sixties: The Emergence of a New Comparative Political Economy," *Theory and Society* 17:5 (1988), p. 725.
61. World Development Indicators, www.worldbank.org. This source uses GNI per capita instead of GDP. GNI adds a country's net income from earnings abroad to GDP, accessed August 1, 2010.
62. Afghanistan is not included because literacy data are not available.
63. China and Niger are not included because homicide rates are not available.
64. World Development Indicators, www.worldbank.org. This source uses GNI per capita instead of GDP.
65. We have added 10 points to each Polity score to avoid using negative figures for countries with authoritarian regimes.

Developed Countries and the Good Society

INTRODUCTION

Ingrid Sorensen lives in Stockholm, Sweden. Her distant cousin, Anna Erickson, lives in Minneapolis, Minnesota where her great-grandfather settled after arriving from Sweden in 1920. Ingrid's younger sister, Stephanie, moved to Germany when her husband got a job with the multinational Bosch Corporation at their headquarters near Stuttgart. Ingrid has one child. So do Anna and Stephanie. After her pregnancy, Ingrid took the legal maximum in Sweden of nine months paid leave, amounting to about 75 percent of her salary before returning to work. Following her pregnancy, Anna also took the most time off that federal law in the United States allows, 12 weeks of unpaid leave, before returning to work. Stephanie in Germany did the same, taking the maximum of 14 months paid leave at 100 percent of her former salary that German law permits.[1]

All three women made child care arrangements upon returning to work. Ingrid returned to work full-time, leaving her son at a state-run preschool on her way to the office in Stockholm. Anna in Minneapolis also returned to work full-time, dropping off her daughter at the home of an accredited caretaker, while Stephanie was lucky to find full-time care for her daughter because it is so rare in Germany. Child care fees for Ingrid were heavily subsidized by the Swedish government, amounting to only 4.5 percent of her salary, while they were 19.5 percent of Anna's paycheck, and 9.1 percent of Stephanie's earnings.[2]

When Ingrid retires, she will receive a basic pension from the Swedish government that will replace about 61.5 percent of her salary. Anna will also receive a pension from the state, but Social Security in the U.S. will cover only 38.7 percent of her salary. Anna has to supplement her anticipated income from social security by deducting money from her paycheck each week and investing it in a private, tax-free retirement account. Stephanie will receive less than her sister Ingrid but more than her cousin Anna, as she will draw 43 percent of her former salary from Germany's pension system when she retires.[3]

Although Ingrid, Anna, and Stephanie each receive the same salary, Anna takes home more money each month because taxes are much lower in the United States than in Sweden and Germany. Ingrid and Stephanie envy how much Anna has left over each week after taxes are deducted. But Anna has to pay more for child care, and contribute to her pension out of her own pocket. She envies the state-provided services that Ingrid receives in Sweden and the state-financed benefits available to Stephanie in Germany.

Ingrid, Anna, and Stephanie are fictitious. They do not exist. But a comparison of their circumstances highlights the differences between citizens in Sweden, the United States, and Germany. Sweden, the United States, and Germany are all capitalist economies. Production is privately controlled and carried on for sale or profit in each country. All of them use market systems to coordinate production. But Sweden devotes 29 percent of GDP to welfare state expenditures, Germany spends 27 percent on welfare, and the United States just 16 percent.[4] This is evident in the type of state services that are available to Ingrid, such as day care, or are paid for by taxes for Stephanie, which are not available to Anna. It is also evident in the higher taxes that Ingrid and Stephanie pay to receive these social services. In fact, when one compares what Anna spends in the market and pays in taxes for social welfare in the U.S., it comes out pretty close to what Ingrid and Stephanie pay in taxes for the same bundle of social services in Sweden and Germany, respectively. The average family in Sweden, the United States, and Germany each spend about 40 percent of their expenses on welfare provision.[5] What is true of average families is true of states. When public and private expenditures for welfare are added together the difference between countries turns out to be relatively minor.[6] What matters is not how much countries spend on welfare but how it is financed and the mix of private and public spending within them. [7] In Sweden and Germany money for social programs is taken out of the taxpayer's pocket, whereas in the United States money to pay for private health insurance and pensions ''is taken out of the consumer's pocket.''[8] Private welfare expenditures contribute more than one-third to welfare expenses in the United States compared to one-tenth of total welfare costs in Germany and Sweden. Some countries, such as the United States, leave their citizens' welfare—such as health care, day care, and pensions— largely to the marketplace, expecting citizens to purchase these items privately out of their own income. Other countries take these issues out of the market and provide them to their citizens. They either provide them as services, as they do in Sweden, or publicly finance them through various insurance funds, as they do in Germany.

Even though the average family in Sweden, Germany, and the United States spend about the same amount for welfare when taxes and private spending are included together, Esping-Andersen reminds us that ''all families are not average.'' This is where the particular mix of public and private spending within countries becomes especially relevant.[9] When welfare is financed privately, as in the United States, access to it depends upon a family's income. Some families can afford to purchase health insurance and contribute to a private pension to supplement inadequate social security payments, while others cannot. Where welfare is financed publicly and taken out of the market, as in Sweden and Germany, even families whose earnings are below average can access welfare in the form of health care, day care, and pensions. Thus, even though total public and private spending on welfare may be similar in Sweden, Germany, and the United States, the *distributional consequences* may be very different depending on the mix of public and private spending in each country.[10]

Sweden, the United States, and Germany represent different types of political models, or families of nations, found among affluent democracies. By the term *political model* we mean countries that share similar institutions, politics, and policies. Certain forms of politics, particular kinds of political institutions, and specific types of policies have an elective affinity for one another; they tend to fit together in predictable ways to form distinctive political models. For example, rich democracies in which social democratic parties are dominant (politics) also tend to have proportional representation electoral systems (institutions) and be high welfare state spenders (policy).[11] We can thus speak of political models in which countries cluster together in terms of their politics, institutions, and policies, which reinforce and complement each other.

Affluent democracies include the countries of Western Europe, such as France, Germany, and Britain; North America, including the United States and Canada; as well as Japan, Australia, and New Zealand.[12] Politically, they are all democracies. Elections are regular, competitive, and open in the sense that citizens are free to organize, express, and exchange their views. Economically, they are all fairly wealthy, with high per capita GPD. Wealth is a result of high levels of labor productivity, which has been supported by large infusions of capital and technology. Sociologically, these countries have moved furthest along the path of a **postindustrial** occupational structure. Industrial jobs in manufacturing have been replaced by the growth of white-collar professional, managerial and service sector jobs.

The aforementioned is a select group of countries. Some countries, such as the oil sheikdoms in the Middle East, may be wealthy and have high per capita GDPs but are not democratic, postindustrial, or even industrial for that matter. Other countries, such as those in Eastern Europe, may be democratic but are not rich. What separates this select group of countries, which is sometimes referred to as the West, from the rest are greater labor productivity, higher per capita incomes, more technologically advanced production methods, a higher percentage of postindustrial workers in the labor force, and a democratic political system. Some countries outside the West may have some of these qualities, but it is only the affluent democracies that rank high on all these measures.

This chapter outlines the characteristics of the social democratic, extreme market, and Christian democratic political models found among Western countries and then offers case studies of countries that represent each of them. Sweden exemplifies the social democratic model; the United States is an archetype of the extreme market model; and Germany embodies the Christian democratic model. Finally, we compare which of these countries performs best in meeting the criteria of the good society.

SOCIAL DEMOCRACY

Social democracy first emerged in the nineteenth century to represent the political interests of a growing and newly enfranchised working class. Although many of these parties had radical Marxist origins, they quickly shed them in favor of an electoral road to socialism. Socialism, they argued, could be achieved through the ballot box by means of a working-class majority. In order to attract voters, these parties dropped all revolutionary pretenses and instead proposed reforms—incremental improvements that would ameliorate the worst aspects of capitalism. Socialism would be reached gradually, as each elected socialist government would build upon reforms of those that preceded it.

The social democratic model is best exemplified in the Scandinavian countries of Denmark, Norway, and Sweden, where social democratic parties are dominant: larger than their rivals, frequently part of the ruling coalition, and often at the head of the government. Social democratic parties have been unusually successful in Scandinavia because their opponents on the right have been divided, workers who share common ethnic and religious roots have been united, and middle-class voters have been attracted to the welfare state benefits these parties offer. Their success has made them the natural party of government in these societies.

Despite their reputation as socialist countries, Scandinavian societies are thoroughly capitalist. Private ownership of the means of production prevails. The state does not dictate prices or production levels, nor does it own and control many firms. Although Scandinavian countries are not socialist, their reputation for big government is well deserved. Taxes and state spending each account for around 50 percent of total GDP, the highest percentage among all affluent democracies. In addition, public sector employment is high, with over 20 percent of the workforce employed by the state. The public sector workforce is so large because they deliver an array of welfare state services.

The social democratic welfare state is distinctive in many respects. First, eligibility for welfare state programs is universal, that is, available to all citizens. Second, the welfare state is comprehensive, providing cradle to grave protection. Third, it is generous. Replacement rates for income lost due to pregnancy, sickness, injury, and unemployment are high. By way of comparison, income replacement ratios for the unemployed varied between 80 percent for up to 260 weeks in Denmark and 85 percent for up to 60 weeks in Sweden, as opposed to just 60 percent for only 26 weeks in the United States.[13] Fourth, not only does the welfare state set high benefit levels, but it also provides an extensive array of services such as health care, day care, elder care, job training, and after-school programs. Finally, social democratic welfare states are redistributive, reducing inequality between the rich and the poor. The effect of these policies is to detach a citizen's quality of life from their job. Their standard of living does not depend so much on how well they perform in the labor market and the paycheck they draw from it.

Critics contend that social democracy needs to be rethought because its program of high taxes, large welfare states, and deficit spending to support employment no longer works. High taxes punish entrepreneurial risk taking. Large welfare states undermine the work ethic. The decline of unions and industry subverts the working-class base of the party, and the introduction of new issues, such as immigration and environmentalism, threaten to crosscut and weaken class identification.

But social democracy has been resilient in response to these challenges. The economist Martin Wolf reports, "There is no sign that highly taxed countries [such as those in Scandinavia] . . . suffer from a huge unrequited outflow of corporate capital. . . . The conclusion is that lack of competitiveness is nowhere to be found in these highly taxed countries. Particularly important is the finding that they are not suffering a hemorrhage of capital or of skilled people."[14] Large welfare states may actually contribute to these countries' economic success by permitting women to enter the workforce in unprecedented numbers. And far from shirking work, Scandinavian societies have some of the highest labor force participation rates among all affluent democracies. Detaching workers' standard of living from the labor market makes them less fearful of change, since society socializes these costs and they do not fall directly on workers themselves. Consequently, there is less resistance to technological innovation and moving resources from declining sectors to rising new industries in response to shifting markets. The welfare state also helps moderate wage demands by offering compensating benefits in place of higher wages that might hurt competitiveness, and **active labor market policies** offer retraining, job placement, and relocation assistance to unemployed workers in order to assist their transition back into the labor force. Scandinavian welfare states offer employment security as opposed to job security. The result is highly competitive economies alongside large and redistributive welfare states. Far from acting as a drag on the economy, the welfare state has permitted women to contribute to the economy through labor force participation, moderated wage demands, improved workers' skills and productivity, and aligned the interests of workers with economic change by removing the threats it posed to workers' standard of living. As former Swedish Prime Minister Goran Persson explained, the size of the Scandinavian welfare state is presumed to prevent the economy from growing just as the bumblebee "with its heavy body and frail wings shouldn't fly. Yet it does. . . . We have high taxes and a big public sector—and yet Sweden flies. And we fly in a way that many look upon with envy."[15] In 2009, the World Economic Forum, a group of world business and political leaders, ranked Sweden fourth, Denmark fifth, and Norway the fourteenth most competitive economies in the world. Welfare states have made Scandinavian economies more, not less, competitive. Instead of being undermined by globalization, the welfare state has eased adjustment to it.

SWEDEN

Historical Background

Sweden has 9 million people, 1 million more than the population of New York City, who live in a country of 174,000 square miles, about the size of California. Although Sweden is small in size and has few strategic assets, it attracts considerable attention. The mainstream press has lampooned it as the country of sex, suicide, socialism, and spirits (the alcoholic kind). But within the field of comparative politics, Sweden has received disproportionate attention because nowhere else has the working class been so successfully organized through labor unions and the Swedish Social Democratic Party (SAP). Sweden boasts the highest proportion of workers who belong to unions among all affluent democracies and, according to the political scientist Goran Therborn, the SAP "has occupied a position of parliamentary power during this [20th] century without parallel in the history of modern democracy."[16] Political analysts have ranked Sweden first, where the working class has been able to attain the most power, among all affluent democracies.[17]

Sweden got a late start on the road to working-class power. Industrialization did not begin until the 1880s, but its growth and development from that point was speedy and thorough. From 1870 to 1914, the value of manufactured goods in Sweden increased twenty-fold and the industrial workforce quadrupled.[18] Farmers, who comprised about three-quarters of the workforce in 1870, composed less than half by the end of World War I, while the number of persons engaged in manufacturing and commerce grew during that period from 20 to 50 percent. With industry advancing rapidly, proletarianization of the workforce proceeded faster in Sweden than anywhere else in Europe. Democracy also got a late start in Sweden. It was not until the end of World War I, when the government was threatened by disturbances at home and the example of the Russian Revolution abroad that universal suffrage was granted and parliamentary democracy was established.

The State

According to the political scientist Arend Lijphart, Sweden is an example of a "consensual democracy," whose political institutions promote "inclusiveness, bargaining and compromise."[19] The consensual character of Swedish democracy

Country	Population	Infant Mortality	Life Expectancy	Adult Literacy	Capital City	GDP Per Capita (PPP)	Labor Force by Occupation
Sweden	9,100,000 (2006)	2.75 deaths under 1 year old per 1,000 live births (2005)	80.9 (2006)	99% (2003)	Stockholm	36,800 (2005)	Agriculture: 1.1% Industry: 28.2% Services: 70.7% (2000)

MAP 9-1
Sweden

is evident, first, in the extent to which governing requires sharing power. Coalition governments are the norm, requiring even dominant parties, such as the Social Democrats, to obtain the support of other parties in order to enact their policies. Second, consensus is apparent in the inclusiveness of the policy-making process. Interest groups are routinely invited to comment on and suggest amendments to bills under consideration. Third, the views of nongovernmental parties are often taken into account in parliamentary committees, where compromises are forged in order to obtain these parties' support. Finally, proportional representation electoral rules ensure that parties with only modest support win some parliamentary seats, and thus the views of even small currents of opinion are heard.[20]

Sweden is a parliamentary democracy. Prime ministers and their cabinets are accountable to the *Riksdag*, the country's unicameral legislature. Elections to the *Riksdag* are held every four years, unless parliament is dissolved before then, which is rare. Elections are conducted according to proportional representation rules in Sweden's 29 **multimember election districts**, with larger election districts being awarded more seats. The *Riksdag* engages in policy making through a strong committee system. Committees review and amend bills, and their recommendations often prevail. The *Riksdag* also performs oversight of the government. Deputies submit written and oral questions to government officials in order to elicit information, and further oversight is performed through the office of the parliamentary **Ombudsman.** The Ombudsman investigates state agencies for malfeasance, either in response to complaints by citizens or upon its own initiative.

The executive branch in Sweden is separated between the head of state and the head of the government. The King is the head of state, but he merely performs ceremonial duties, such as opening parliament and awarding Nobel Prizes. Real power resides within the core executive, composed of prime ministers and their cabinets that administer and direct executive agencies and set the agenda of government. They develop and submit bills to the *Riksdag*, almost all of which become law due to the way the government builds consensus for them. Before proposing a bill, the government will often seek advice from Commissions of Inquiry composed of academic experts, interest group representatives, *Riksdag* deputies and administrative officials, and then when a bill is prepared will invite interest groups to comment on it.

The executive branch dominates policy making in Sweden, as it does in all parliamentary democracies. But the process is more inclusive and permeable than it is in countries with similar political systems. Executive power is tempered by a limited form of judicial review. A similar type of balance is evident when we examine Swedish federalism. The Swedish state is unitary, with political power concentrated at the national level. For example, the Cabinet appoints the governor to each of Sweden's 24 regional, provincial units. Provincial and municipal governments largely carry out policies decided at the top, delivering such services as health care, child care, and education. But regional and local governments now enjoy an increasing amount of discretion in how they perform these tasks. One Swedish political scientist notes that "the autonomy of local and regional governments has increased dramatically" so that the services they provide can be more responsive to their users' demands.[21] Decentralization has given provincial and municipal governments more discretion in how they deliver public services.

State and Society

Following democratization, the SAP emerged as the single largest party in the 1920s but "was unable to govern for more than brief and typically traumatic interludes."[22] In order to break through politically, the SAP dropped its image as a workers' party and instead began to promote itself as the "people's home," which implied reaching out to other social groups and building broad coalitions. To appeal to groups beyond its working class base, the party dropped its program of nationalization, which frightened potential allies, and instead began to articulate a more reformist program. The new strategy, which replaced demands to socialize production with appeals to socialize its distribution, propelled the SAP into power and made it the dominant, governing party in Sweden for the rest of the century and beyond.

The new orientation was first evident in response to the Depression of the 1930s, when the SAP formed a government with the Agrarian Party. Relations with the Agrarian Party, however, began to wane in the 1950s because farmers were losing political influence, being replaced by a burgeoning white-collar, salaried middle-class. In order to attract middle-class support, the SAP proposed to add a second-tier pension, which would be related to earnings, to the very modest pensions already in place. The supplementary pension bound middle-class voters to the SAP, transforming it from a party based on workers and farmers to a modern, wage-earners party based on traditional blue-collar and new middle-class voters.[23]

The new wage earners' coalition of blue- and white-collar workers permitted the Social Democrats to form majority governments from 1958 to 1976. But this was the high-water mark of Social Democratic success. Inflation in the 1970s undermined faith in the party's management of the economy. Citizens also began to question the safety and appropriateness of the party's energy policy based on nuclear power. Finally, business devoted vast resources to defeating the Social Democrats following their proposals to give workers more power at work and the state more power over investment. In the 1976 elections, support for the Social Democrats slipped to its lowest level since 1932, and they were thrown out of office for the first time in 44 years. A coalition government composed exclusively of nonsocialist parties took power for the first time since the establishment of democracy in Sweden at the end of World War I.[24] But when the new government was beset by unemployment, budget crises, and instability among the nonsocialist coalition parties, voters returned the Social Democrats to power in 1982.

Although the Social Democrats returned to their accustomed place as head of the government, the ground had shifted permanently. Social Democratic support became more volatile in ensuing elections, reflecting a general instability in the Swedish party system. New parties emerged and the balance among existing parties shifted. The Social Democrats still remain the dominant, governing party. But they are no longer able to achieve either a majority of votes in elections or of seats in the legislature. The Social Democratic vote fluctuated between 30 and 40 percent and was now concentrated among women, public sector employees, and a declining blue-collar proletariat. Consequently, the Social Democrats needed to depend more on the cooperation of other parties to govern. From 1994 through 2006, the Social Democrats ruled as a single-party minority government. They relied on the Left and Ecology parties' votes in the legislature but ruled them out as formal coalition partners with seats in the Cabinet because of these parties' opposition to Swedish participation in the European Union (EU).

Most of the change within the Swedish party system occurred among the nonsocialist or right-wing bloc of parties. The Agrarian Party changed its name to the Centre Party, signaling its intent to shift its shrinking base among farmers and appeal instead to the growing middle-class. But rebranding could not forestall the party's decline from what had once been the largest nonsocialist party to what is now one of the smallest. Its losses have been captured by the rising fortunes of the Moderate and Christian Democratic Parties. The former denounces the tax-and-spend policies of the Social Democrats and wants to reduce the size of the public sector, while the latter is critical of the Social Democrats' social policies and wants to defend family values. A populist right-wing, anti-immigrant party, New Democracy, was able to pass the 4 percent barrier required for parliamentary representation in 1991, but it quickly passed from the scene. But in the 2010 elections, its successor, the Sweden Democrats, received 5.7 percent of the vote, won 20 seats in the legislature, and is likely to be a permanent fixture in future elections.

Politically, Sweden exhibits much change without change. New parties, such as the Ecology Party on the left and the Sweden Democrats on the right, have emerged, and the distribution of votes among all the parties has shifted. The Social Democrats and the Centre Party, for example, have lost votes, with other parties on the left and the right picking them up. Class voting has declined a bit and new issues, such as immigration, relations with the European Union, family values, and ecology, are now represented within the party system. The party system is no longer exclusively defined by the traditional left–right cleavage reflective of class divisions.[25] But even with the introduction of new sources of party division and more electoral instability among voters, the balance between the right (Conservative/Moderate, Liberal, Christian Democrat, and Center parties) and left (Social Democratic, Left, and Green parties) blocs has not changed much.

But the 2010 election may have signaled a decisive break with the past. For the first time in nearly a century, a right-leaning government finished a full term in office and was reelected by the voters. The Conservative/Moderates won 30 percent of the vote, pulling even with the Social Democrats who continued to decline and suffered their worst result since 1914. But the election was also noteworthy because of the success of the Sweden Democrats, a populist

> ### TABLE 9.1
>
> **Sweden Votes**
>
> | Parties | 1998 Seats % | 1998 Votes % | 2002 Seats % | 2002 Votes % | 2006 Seats % | 2006 Votes % | 2010 Seats % | 2010 Votes % |
> |---|---|---|---|---|---|---|---|---|
> | Social Democrats (S) | 37.5 | 36.6 | 41.3 | 40.2 | 37.2 | 35.2 | 32.3 | 30.9 |
> | Conservative/ | | | | | | | | |
> | Moderates (M) | 23.5 | 22.7 | 15.8 | 15.2 | 27.8 | 26.1 | 30.6 | 30.0 |
> | Liberals (FP) | 4.9 | 4.7 | 13.8 | 13.3 | 8.0 | 7.5 | 6.8 | 7.1 |
> | Christian Democrats | | | | | | | | |
> | (KD) | 12.0 | 11.8 | 9.5 | 9.1 | 6.8 | 6.6 | 5.4 | 5.6 |
> | Left Party (V) | 12.3 | 12.0 | 8.6 | 8.3 | 6.3 | 5.8 | 5.4 | 5.6 |
> | Centre Party | 5.2 | 5.1 | 6.3 | 6.2 | 8.3 | 7.9 | 6.3 | 6.6 |
> | Greens (MP) | 4.6 | 4.5 | 4.9 | 4.6 | 5.4 | 5.2 | 7.1 | 7.2 |
> | Sweden Democrats | | | | | | | | |
> | (SD) | — | — | — | — | — | — | 5.7 | 5.7 |
> | Others | 0 | 2.6 | 0 | 3.1 | 0 | 2.7 | 0 | 1.4 |
> | Turnout | — | 81.4 | — | 80.1 | — | 82.8 | — | 82.1 |

right-wing, anti-immigrant party that was able to enter the legislature for the first time with 5.7 percent of the vote. With the Sweden Democrats on the scene and considered a pariah that no party will ally with, it is now more difficult for both right- and left-wing coalitions to put together a majority in parliament that is necessary to govern. Recent election results that track the shift in support among Swedish political parties is evident in Table 9.1 above.

Political Culture

When a Russian expressed admiration for Sweden, he despaired that his own country could ever achieve the same results because Russia did not have "enough Swedes" to make it work there.[26] Sweden was a compelling but unattainable goal to this Russian observer because his own country lacked the trust, democratic values, pragmatism, and egalitarianism that characterize Swedish political culture.

Swedish political culture is, paradoxically, one in which individualism and statism are not only respected but perceived as augmenting one another. Since Swedish peasants were never serfs, Swedes believe individualism, democracy, and freedom are birthrights, part of their history as a people. But these precious legacies can only be realized through the state, not against it. The state creates an egalitarian community that protects its members from the injustice of social inequality and liberates them from degrading ties of dependency.[27]

Alongside what Lars Tragadh referred to as "statist individualism," Swedes are also quite equalitarian. For example, Swedes are less tolerant of wage differentials between high and low earners that citizens in other countries find morally acceptable. Surveys find that Swedes believe the highest paid occupations should receive 250 percent more than the lowest paid jobs, while Americans thought a pay gap twice that amount would be fair and just, with British and German scores much closer to the American than Swedish ideal.[28] Not only are Swedes less tolerant of gross inequality but they are also more approving of government efforts to reduce it. Public opinion in Sweden is more supportive of government programs that redistribute income than is the case in most other affluent democracies.

In addition, Swedish political culture values consensus and pragmatism: that policy making should be inclusive and consultation should be promoted in order to find solutions to specific problems. The consensual and pragmatic aspects of Swedish political culture are reflected in the policy-making process through Commissions of Inquiry. These Commissions routinely include members from opposition parties, as well as affected groups, to review the government's legislative proposals. According to Thomas J. Anton, broad consultation occurs through the Commissions where "finding workable solutions to specific problems structures a consensual approach to policy-making."[29] The inclusion of political opponents and affected interests in the policy-making process builds consensus for its results.

Finally, Sweden is considered a "high-trust" society in which citizens act virtuously because they believe their fellow citizens are acting virtuously, too. Or, put another way, in high-trust societies, people are not afraid of being considered a chump for not trying to game the system. They don't cheat on their taxes and instead pay their fair share because they are confident that others are not cheating and are paying their fair share as well. High trust is attributed to the high amount of social capital Swedes have that results from a vibrant associational life. Swedes are joiners. Whereas organizational life in many affluent democracies has declined, "voluntary organizations" in Sweden "have been growing in size, level of activity and financial resources."[30] "In terms of membership, activity and financing," the Swedish political scientist Bo Rothstein writes, "the voluntary sector in Sweden is as large, or larger than those in most other Western industrialized democracies."[31] The average Swede belongs to 3.2 private organizations, and only 6 percent of Swedes belong to none. Far from displacing or crowding out trust and voluntary work, the universal welfare state promotes it. Where everyone is included within the welfare state, citizens don't stigmatize those who receive support from the government as "others," and since programs are not means-tested to decide who is eligible, people are less likely to suspect others of cheating in order to qualify for benefits they don't deserve.[32] Universal welfare states take issues that could potentially breed distrust off the table.

But social trust in Sweden is being challenged today by the arrival of immigrants who have different values and customs. Sweden has been transformed from one of the most homogeneous countries in Europe to one of its most diverse, with 17.8 percent of all Swedes being either first- or second-generation immigrants. Maureen A. Eger found that immigration and the proportion of foreign born in Sweden has reduced support for the Swedish welfare state.[33] As one Swedish union official explained, "Sweden is a small country. . . . Up to 10 years ago it was a very homogenous country. Everything was very alike. Up until then all Swedes looked the same; almost all thought the same. Because we are all so equal, we can share the pain of the problems. . . . As Sweden gets more divided, it's more difficult to keep this idea of sharing the pain."[34] Einhorn and Logue explain that since many new immigrants had larger families, received lower wages, and included fewer working women, they also received a disproportionate share of welfare state benefits, which produced a backlash among natives.[35] Whether Sweden will remain a high-trust society, with a high stock of social capital, depends on how positive the experience of immigrants is with other Swedes, public authorities, and their integration into existing organizations. Whether a "minority culture of distrust" takes root as a result of prejudice directed against immigrants or dissipates as a result of tolerance towards them depends on the quality of contact between immigrants and Swedish society.[36]

Political Economy

The SAP wage earners' coalition of blue- and white-collar workers made it "the most successful political party in the world," having governed up to 2006 for 61 of the past 70 years, "a record without equal among democratic societies."[37] The SAP was so successful because it developed a generous, universal, service-oriented welfare state that both middle- and working-class citizens had a stake in defending. Good policy turns out to be good politics. About 50 percent of all Swedish citizens are said to derive their income from the state either as clients who depend on welfare state programs or public-sector workers who deliver them. Both these groups, public sector clients and workers, have an incentive to vote for the Social Democrats in order to protect their benefits or jobs.[38]

A welfare state that was originally designed in the 1930s to eliminate poverty and squalor was transformed in the 1960s into one that would "provide a lifelong middle-class standard of living for all" and redistribute income. Income lost due to sickness, disability, and unemployment was raised from "roughly 30 to 40 percent to 60 to 90 percent of average workers' wages."[39] Maintaining generous, high-quality welfare state programs was possible only as long as full employment and steady growth could generate the tax revenue to pay for them.[40] But in the early 1990s, Sweden experienced the sharpest recession in its history. The economy contracted by 6 percent, and unemployment soared from 2 to 12 percent, creating a severe budget deficit. The budget crisis required Sweden to trim unemployment compensation, sick pay, and parental leave benefits, and charge health care and day care clients higher fees. In response to an explosion in the number of workers receiving sick pay benefits in a country that is one of the healthiest in the world, eligibility rules were tightened in order to rein in costs and pensions were tied more closely to contributions, making them less redistributive. Finally, privatization and markets were introduced. Individuals could now invest some of their pension contributions into individualized accounts that they managed themselves and there was now market competition in the field of education. Instead of a public school monopoly, parents were free to choose whether to send their child to a public school or have the state pay tuition for their child to attend an independent school (which, unlike American private schools, cannot charge private tuition or select their students).[41]

Despite these reforms, one analyst notes, the Swedish welfare state's "major attributes when compared to other countries—e.g. its generosity, universality, and developed welfare state services—are almost as prominent as before."[42] Sweden continues to make more welfare effort than other countries, which produces egalitarian results to offset market-generated inequalities.

Economically, Sweden has also undergone some adjustment. Although, people mistakenly describe Sweden as socialist because of its large welfare state, its economy is thoroughly capitalist. The means of production are privately owned and the market rules. The economist Mike Marshall writes, "Public ownership of industry has always been very rare in Sweden, economic planning has never been undertaken, [and] state intervention in production has not taken place."[43] Not only is Sweden capitalist, but it has also developed a very successful model of capitalism based on three precepts: full employment, **centralized wage bargaining**, and **wage solidarity**. Full employment not only sustains workers' incomes but also keeps the welfare state afloat financially. When people are employed, they require less from the welfare state in the form of benefits and they contribute more to it in the form of taxes on their earnings. But full employment also has a tendency to encourage inflation, which is restrained by centralized wage bargaining. Centralized bargaining prevents workers from bidding up wages that could price goods out of the market. Consequently, the federation of blue-collar unions, the LO, and the employers organization, the SAF, negotiated wage agreements for basic industry, which then set the pattern for white-collar and public-sector workers.[44]

The third principle of the Swedish Model, wage solidarity, was embedded within centralized bargaining. At first, the concept of wage solidarity was captured in the principle of equal pay for equal work: that workers doing the same job at different firms should be paid the same. Over time, however, the concept of wage solidarity was redefined from standardizing pay across industries to equalizing pay within them, that is, narrowing pay differences between high- and low-wage workers. Alongside the old wage solidarity principle of "equal pay for equal work" was now the new principle of "equal pay for all work."[45]

But, like the Swedish welfare state, the Swedish Model fell on hard times in the 1980s. Full employment, the first pillar of the model, collapsed in the recession of the early 1990s, when unemployment hit 12 percent. Centralized bargaining also eroded. In 1990, SAF simply closed its bargaining department, signaling that employers were no longer interested in peak-level negotiations with the LO anymore. Employers instigated a shift to decentralized bargaining at the industry and even firm level in order to disrupt the model's third pillar, wage solidarity. "Equal pay for all work," the more radical meaning of wage solidarity, had inflationary consequences that were unacceptable to Swedish firms that competed in world markets. Giving less productive workers in service and public sector work the same wage increases that more productive skilled, industrial workers received contributed to inflation.[46]

The current Swedish Model may only be a shadow of its past but it produces very similar results. Since the deep recession of the early 1990s, Swedish rates of unemployment have been among the lowest in Europe. Labor force participation rates remain high at 70 percent of all working age adults, while long-term unemployment rates remain low. While both unions and employers retreated from decentralized bargaining and the wage spiral it might have precipitated, this has not brought a return to national-level bargaining. Instead, sector level bargaining now prevails, and wage bargaining in the sheltered or public sector of the economy is no longer coordinated with wage bargaining between labor and capital in the export manufacturing sector of the economy.[47] Even with the demise of wage solidarity, however, pay differentials between the top and the bottom are still the smallest within all of Western Europe.[48]

The Swedish Model has had to adapt in order to address new challenges. In doing so it has shown that economic growth and social equality can go together. It can offer the best of both worlds in which the dynamism and productivity of capitalism is coupled with the security and welfare of social democracy.

EXTREME MARKET DEMOCRACY

Extreme market democracies also form a distinctive type of political model, characterized by roughly similar politics, institutions, and policies. Extreme market democracies are found in the former British colonies of Canada, Ireland, and the United States. Politically, left-wing parties are either completely absent in these countries, as is the case in the United States, or have been outsiders in the political process, as is true in Canada and Ireland. Part of the reason socialist parties have not fared well in these countries is because **class identification** is so weak within them.[49] Other cleavages in these societies crosscut and weaken class identification. In the absence of left-wing parties to aggregate and articulate working-class demands, business has been politically dominant in extreme market democracies. In addition, the electoral system in these regimes is afflicted with low voter turnout, which is due to working-class voters dropping out because the class divide within them is so subdued.[50] As a result, politicians appeal to core wealthy voters who are likely to vote and ignore the demands of peripheral, working-class voters who are less likely to do so.

The politics of extreme market democracies distinguishes them from other Anglo-American democracies, such as Britain, Australia, and New Zealand, with which they otherwise share many features.[51] For example, all these countries share a similar policy profile. But Britain, Australia, and New Zealand all have labor parties that are viable contenders for power. Such parties are absent in our extreme market democracies. And class is a much more significant cleavage and basis of economic and political organization in the other Anglo-American democracies than in those countries we designated as extreme market democracies.

The price of a cup of coffee reveals policy differences between social democratic and extreme market democracies. Coffee costs $3 in a café in Stockholm, Sweden, while it is half that price in Stockholm, Maine. Higher taxes and wages make a simple cup of coffee cost twice the price in Sweden as it does in the United States. But the cost of affordable coffee comes in the form of a lower standard of living for coffee servers and fewer public services for everyone in the United States.[52]

All affluent democracies, including Sweden and Germany, are market democracies. But we describe countries such as Canada, the United States, and Ireland as extreme market democracies because they are more likely to leave the production and allocation of goods to the market than is the case in either social democratic or Christian democratic countries. The public sector is relatively small among extreme market democracies, with these countries clustered near the bottom when it comes to state spending and revenues as a proportion of GDP. One consequence of a small state sector is that extreme market democracies rank low in terms of **welfare effort**—the proportion of GDP devoted to social spending. Social democratic countries devote about a third of their spending to welfare; Christian democratic countries spend about 30 percent; while extreme market democracies spend less than 20 percent.[53]

Like their social democratic counterparts, welfare states among extreme market democracies have certain properties. They are not universal but targeted to the poor. Benefit levels are typically stingy. Consequently, people are more apt to go to the market and pay for welfare services out of their own pocket, as Anna our fictional mother from Minneapolis who we introduced at the beginning of the chapter has to do.[54] As a result of a small state sector and few public services, people's life chances depend greatly on their performance in the labor market. In other words, their standard of living is tied to their job.

Extreme market democracies display a great deal of institutional variety. Both Canada and the United States are federal systems, with power divided between national and regional governments, while Ireland is a unitary state. Both Canada and Ireland are parliamentary regimes, while the United States has a presidential system. All three have bicameral legislatures, with a Senate as the second legislative chamber. But the Senate is weak in both Canada and Ireland, while it is quite strong in the United States. Ireland has a form of proportional representation, while Canada and the United States require successful candidates to win a simple plurality in federal elections. Finally, while judicial review is common to all three countries, it is much stronger in Canada and the United States than in Ireland.

While extreme market democracies exhibit a diversity of state institutions, their interest group structures are quite similar. They all have pluralist systems in which interest groups compete for members, membership is voluntary and highly fluid, and power is decentralized. While unions loom large in the institutional landscape of social and Christian democracy, they are peripheral in extreme market democracies. **Union density** in the latter is relatively low and unions are decentralized, making coordination among them difficult. The same is true of employer organizations. Many businesses are unaffiliated and employer organizations lack the power to direct their members.

THE UNITED STATES

Historical Background

According to Karl Marx, capitalism developed more "shamelessly," in an undiluted form, in the United States than elsewhere.[55] Because capitalists enjoyed great political influence and American workers displayed little class consciousness, unions and working-class political parties tended to be weak and overmatched. Marx's generalization remains true today. Nowhere else is the gap between the power of business and the power of labor as large. According to Seymour Martin Lipset and Gary Marks, "When one compares the United States with other western democracies, the picture that emerges . . . is one of continued lower-class weakness—in politics and in the labor market. No other western democracy remotely approximates America in this regard."[56]

The relative weakness of workers in the United States has been attributed to a host of factors: the success of American capitalism that seduced them; ethnic and racial tensions that divided them; capitalist values of competition and individualism that distracted them; and repression that intimidated them. As powerful as these obstacles may have been, the history of class struggle in the United States has not been a recurring story of working-class defeat. For example, in the midst of the Depression of the 1930s, workers successfully took to the picket lines and the ballot box in order to obtain political power and extract reforms. A New Deal coalition of urban immigrant workers, Southerners, and blacks brought to power the Democratic Party, which proceeded to lay the foundation of the American welfare state, encourage union organizing, and increase state regulation of the economy. The market was peeled back and the state grew, as taxes, government spending, and public employment all increased.

The State

Paradoxically, the United States has been an inspiration to people struggling for democracy, but very few democracies have actually copied its institutional design, which is quite distinctive because of the fragmentation of authority within it. The United States has a federal system, with power divided vertically between national and state governments. The Constitution also divides power horizontally among the executive, legislative, and judicial branches to create a system of checks and balances. The Founders who drafted the Constitution created a complex system of checks and balances because they believed in democracy but wanted to avoid what they regarded as its egalitarian consequences.[57] Checks and balances would not prevent majority rule but would make it much more difficult to achieve by requiring majorities to win three

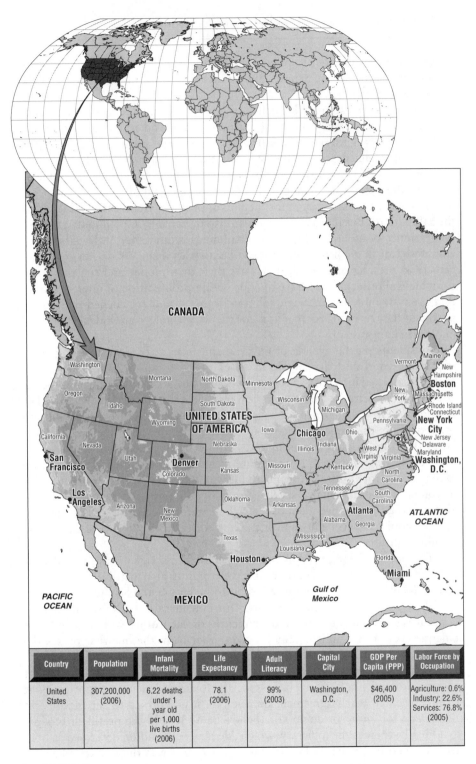

CANADA

UNITED STATES
OF AMERICA

Washington

Montana

North Dakota

Minnesota

Oregon

Idaho

South Dakota

Wisconsin

Michigan

Wyoming

Iowa

Chicago

Ohio

Pennsylvania

Vermont

Maine

New Hampshire

Boston

Massachusetts

Rhode Island

Connecticut

New York

New York
City

New Jersey

Delaware

Maryland

Washington,
D.C.

California

Nevada

Utah

Nebraska

Illinois

Indiana

West
Virginia

Virginia

San
Francisco

Denver

Colorado

Kansas

Missouri

Kentucky

North
Carolina

Los
Angeles

Arizona

New
Mexico

Oklahoma

Arkansas

Tennessee

South
Carolina

Atlanta

Alabama

Georgia

ATLANTIC
OCEAN

Texas

Mississippi

Louisiana

Houston

Florida

Miami

PACIFIC
OCEAN

MEXICO

Gulf of
Mexico

Country	Population	Infant Mortality	Life Expectancy	Adult Literacy	Capital City	GDP Per Capita (PPP)	Labor Force by Occupation
United States	307,200,000 (2006)	6.22 deaths under 1 year old per 1,000 live births (2006)	78.1 (2006)	99% (2003)	Washington, D.C.	$46,400 (2005)	Agriculture: 0.6% Industry: 22.6% Services: 76.8% (2005)

MAP 9-2
United States

different contests in order to prevail: nationally at the presidential level, at the level of the states in the Senate, and by district based on population in the House of Representatives.

Although the different branches of government may check and balance each other, they are far from equal partners. The president is the "energy center" of the federal government, setting its agenda and providing leadership to it. Unlike parliamentary regimes, where prime ministers are head of the government and others perform ceremonial duties as head of state, U.S. presidents combine these two roles, embodying both real and symbolic power. The presidents' powers are vast enough for them to appear like Gulliver towering above the Lilliputians. But just as Gulliver was also tethered by the Lilliputians, presidents must contend with robust challenges from other political actors. Congress can be a formidable obstacle because its members do not owe their careers to presidents. Instead, they raise their own money and run their own campaigns. Presidents also have to cope with a proliferation of interest groups that are now more confrontational, autonomous, and entrenched than in the past, and they have to worry about courts, whose judges are independent and may rule against them.

Presidents set the agenda of government, in part, by default. Congress is too fragmented and decentralized to compete for leadership with them. Members of the House of Representatives, the lower chamber of Congress, are elected by district based on population in each state, for two-year terms. The Founders believed that a popularly elected House of Representatives with small districts and frequent elections "would be the driving force in the system [and] that the people's representatives would be turbulent and insistent."[58] The Senate was supposed to be a more intimate and dignified chamber, with each state awarded just two seats, and it was supposed to be less accountable to voters, with each Senator serving for a six-year term. According to George Washington, the first president of the United States, the Senate was designed to be "the cooling saucer into which the hot coffee from the cup of the House should be poured."[59]

The policy-making process involving the House, Senate, and president is tortuous and filled with innumerable **veto points** at which bills can be defeated. Identical bills are submitted to both the House and Senate and then referred to committees in each chamber for consideration. House and Senate committees can amend a bill independently of each other so that a bill that emerges from one chamber may look different from the one that passes the other. If a bill passes both the House and the Senate, it is then sent to Conference, where members of the two chambers try to reconcile the different versions of the bill they each passed. If House and Senate negotiators at Conference can reach agreement on one bill, it is returned to the House and the Senate for an up-or-down vote before being sent to the president to sign.

Finally, there is the judiciary, which Alexander Hamilton described as "the least dangerous branch" of government because it was the weakest. Federal courts must depend on the other branches of government to implement their decisions. In addition, they lack democratic legitimacy. Rather than being elected, federal judges are appointed by the president and confirmed by the Senate. But the significance of the judiciary should not be dismissed. Federal courts interpret the Constitution and their judgment is final. As Chief Justice of the Supreme Court Charles Evans Hughes once remarked, "We are under a Constitution and the Constitution is what the judges say it is."[60] In addition, federal judges enjoy lifetime tenure, insulating them from political pressure, and the courts have the power of judicial review, giving them the authority to nullify and overturn laws as incompatible with the Constitution.

State and Society

The New Deal coalition that took shape in the 1930s thrust the Democratic Party into the majority and made it the ruling, governing party in the United States for the last two-thirds of the twentieth century, from 1932 to 1994. During that period, the Democrats maintained a majority in the House of Representatives for all but four years, and in the Senate, for all but ten. The welfare state matured and new programs, like **Medicare**, were added to it. Unions grew and were now grudgingly accepted by employers. Through the 1960s, workers' standards of living rose and inequality declined.

But the New Deal coalition began to unravel in the 1960s under the pressure of internal strains and external events. The Southern wing left the Democratic Party over its championing of civil rights for blacks. Northern working-class whites also began to desert the party over civil rights because they believed that black advances came at their expense. Cultural issues also divided the coalition, as traditional working-class Democratic voters came into conflict with more socially liberal middle-class Democrats over such issues as gay rights and feminism. Finally, the New Deal coalition became a victim of policy failure, as its tax-and-spend policies could not revive an economy that suffered in the 1970s from both unemployment and inflation.

As the Democratic majority lost ground, the Republican Party gathered momentum and changed direction. It turned right and moved south. The resurgent Republican Party was first evident at the presidential level, with Republicans holding the presidency for almost twice as long as the Democrats since 1952. Success at the national level eventually filtered down to Congress, when Republicans swept the House and the Senate in the 1994 mid-term elections. The revival of the Republican Party was caused by the South's defection from the Democrats over civil rights; an infusion of money from members of the business community who wanted to rollback government regulations; the mobilization of the Christian Right, which was upset by policies it believed promoted moral decay; and the conservative values of white males, who were threatened by the dismantling of racial and gender hierarchies.

It is unclear at this point whether the Democratic sweep in the 2008 elections augurs a new period of Democratic Party rule reflecting deep changes in the electorate or whether Democratic gains simply reflected surface changes in which voters vented against the failed policies of the Republican President George W. Bush. The base of the Democratic Party today is found among low-income, female, liberal, nonwhite, and unmarried voters. The Republican Party depends on white male, rural, conservative, Southern, and high-income voters. While the two parties are now almost equal in strength, their differences are more profound. Political differences within each party have declined, while the differences between them have grown. The moderate center in American politics has disappeared. Consequently, American politics is coarser and more ideological, with more party discipline, and it is now harder to forge bipartisan compromises.[61] Recent results from presidential elections are given in Table 9.2.

Political Culture

The American state was designed by people who were deeply suspicious and skeptical of it. The Founders constructed a state in which authority was fragmented and checks and balances proliferated because they believed in limited government. Distrust of the state was reflected not only in its design but in the resources devoted to it. The American state, as we describe below in the next section, is smaller as a proportion of GDP than it is in other affluent democracies and plays a more limited role in the United States *"because Americans, more than other people, want it to play a limited role"*[62] (emphasis in original).

In Europe, capitalism and democracy were contested principles. Socialism and authoritarianism competed with liberal democracy. In the United States, on the other hand, liberal capitalism was unchallenged because the United States never had a feudal past that nourished alternatives. Americans were born liberal democrats and knew nothing else. Since alternatives outside the liberal democratic consensus rarely emerge, ideological struggles do not occur over competing principles but over the interpretation of common liberal democratic values.

Americans are also strong individualists. They believe that people should be independent and self-reliant, and are responsible for their own fate in life. People who are poor have no one to blame but themselves while those who are rich are morally deserving of their good fortune as it reflects their effort and talent. But individualism is morally legitimate only in tandem with another core value, equal opportunity. The rich deserve their good fortune and the poor their distress only if they began from the same starting line.

Finally, American political culture also includes political equality and democracy. The government should be accountable to the governed and all citizens are equal in the eyes of the law. Few countries have more frequent elections and none offer more offices to be filled through election than the United States—even to the extent of electing coroners who do autopsies to determine the cause of death.

President Obama gave voice to these values in his victory speech on election night in 2008 when he attributed America's strength to "the enduring power of our ideals: democracy, liberty, opportunity and unyielding hope." These creedal values have bound together an ethnically, racially, and religiously diverse society and have defined what it means to be an American.

TABLE 9.2

America Votes

	1992		1996		2000		2004		2008	
	% Vote	% Electoral College	% Vote	% Electoral College	% Vote	% Electoral College	% Vote	% Electoral College	% Vote	% Electoral College
Dem	43.01	68.8	49.23	70.4	48.38	49.4	48.27	46.7	52.87	67.8
Rep	37.45	31.2	40.72	29.6	47.87	50.4	50.73	53.2	45.6	32.3
Perot/Reform	18.91		8.4		2.73					
Nader/Green			0.71				0.38		0.56	

Political Economy

Class differences in political participation are greater in the United States than in other affluent democracies. The wealthy are more likely to vote, contact public officials, and contribute money to political campaigns than the less privileged. The cumulative effect of these political inequalities led Jacob S. Hacker and Paul Pierson to conclude, "In no other rich democracy has the playing field become so sharply tilted against citizens of modest means."[63]

The gap in political participation and power between the top and the bottom is reflected in public policy. The United States is distinctive in the extent to which it lets markets rule. As we have seen, the public sector is comparatively small in the United States. It collects less in taxes and spends less as a proportion of GDP than almost any other rich democracy. The state does not try to redirect the flow of money through high taxes or high spending, or intrude on corporate decision making. American business executives enjoy more autonomy and less interference from unions or the state regarding the management of their firms than their counterparts elsewhere. A smaller percentage of workers are covered by collective bargaining agreements negotiated between unions and employers than in any other rich democracy. In the absence of such agreements, employers are free to set wages and working conditions. Employers are also freer from work rules imposed by the state. Beyond some antidiscrimination laws and some health and safety standards, state regulations governing the workplace are minimal and those rules that do exist are not vigorously enforced. Unfettered by union contracts or state laws, private employers in the United States, according to two labor experts, "have more authority in deciding how to treat their workers than do employers in other countries."[64]

Letting markets rule has encouraged innovation and wealth. The United States is a leader in developing new technology and has high per capita GDP. But free markets have also contributed to more inequality and greater volatility than in other affluent democracies. The result of its political economy, according to Lipset and Marks, is that "the United States combines an extremely high standard of living with exceptionally low levels of taxation and social spending, and exceptionally high levels of income inequality and poverty."[65]

CHRISTIAN DEMOCRACY

Christian Democracy is "the most successful western European political movement since 1945," according to the respected magazine *The Economist.*[66] The Christian democratic family of nations includes Austria, Belgium, the Netherlands and Germany, where Christian democratic parties are often the largest though not dominant political party. But the influence of these parties is not due to their popularity as much as it is attributed to their frequency in government. Their size and location in the middle of the political spectrum make them frequent partners in any ruling coalition.

Christian democratic parties first arose in the nineteenth century in reaction to state efforts to take over activities, such as education and family policy that churches believed properly belonged to them. Today, Christian democratic parties have only the most extenuating links to the church. They are now fairly secular parties and present themselves more as defenders of Christian values than of church dogma.[67] They seek to moderate class cleavages at the same time they defend class differences. But they are most concerned with safeguarding the strength of the family and the moral authority of the church from threats posed to them by divisive class conflict, an intrusive market, and an encroaching state.[68]

Christian democracy believes in capitalism but also wants to mute its inegalitarian effects. It supports the welfare state and even unions, which compensate for market failure and promote social order through class reconciliation. Christian democracies tend to be high tax-and-spend states due to their welfare effort, which is almost as big as that found in social democratic countries. However, Christian democratic welfare states do not offer the array of collective services that social democrats do; instead they provide generous **transfer payments** in order to ensure income security to families. While the state sector is large, its purpose is limited. Christian democracy is distrustful of too much state intervention that threatens to rule over the moral lives of their citizens and displace civic institutions through which Christian principles are instilled. A basic Christian democratic tenet is that state intervention should "repair society, not replace it."[69]

Institutionally, Christian democratic countries are all parliamentary democracies in which legislative majorities empower the executive and select ruling governments. But there are still notable differences among Christian democracies. All of them have bicameral legislatures, but only Germany invests its second chamber, the *Bundesrat*, with real power. While the Netherlands has no judicial review, and Belgium and Austria only mild forms of it, the German Federal Constitutional Court can nullify laws it finds unconstitutional. Finally, Germany is a federal state in which powers are reserved to the *lander*, or states, which elect their own officials and raise their own revenue. Belgium also has a high degree of federalism, followed closely by Austria and then the Netherlands.

But the most important institutional feature of Christian democratic countries, with the exception of Belgium, is the high degree of corporatism found within them. Austria, for example, "is widely regarded as the 'paradigm' case of corporatism."[70] Groups are organized into a limited number of hierarchically structured associations, and these organizations are recognized by the state and invited to participate in the policy-making process affecting their interests. The state, for its part, plays an unobtrusive role, content to provide a broad legal framework in which social partners can find mutually agreeable settlements.

GERMANY

Historical Background

Germany has had a volatile history. In the space of 100 years, it has been beset by victory and defeat, scarcity and prosperity, and its state has taken a variety of forms, including fascism, communist party dictatorship, and parliamentary democracy. In addition, its borders have been in flux. They have expanded and contracted, been divided and united. It is the biggest country in Europe, with 82 million people, and it has the fourth largest economy in the world, one-third larger than its nearest European competitor.

Germany got a late start politically when the Prussian military leader Otto von Bismarck united small independent principalities in central Europe to form the modern German state in 1871. Germany also had to play catch-up economically. At the beginning of the nineteenth century, Germany was largely an agrarian feudal society that bore few marks of industrial capitalism. However, by the end of the century Germany rivaled such leading economic powers as Britain, France, and the United States. Germany's rapid transformation has been attributed to Bismarck's strategy of imposing high tariffs to protect German producers, capturing colonies to open new markets and obtain raw materials, and creating welfare state programs to co-opt workers and bind them to the state. But Germany's economic ambitions clashed with those of more established European powers, leading it to World War I. Defeat in the greatest mass slaughter the world had seen to that point brought an end to the Second Reich.

With defeat, the authoritarian Second Reich was replaced by Germany's first democracy, the Weimar Republic, named after the city in which Germany's new constitution was drafted. But the new, fledgling Republic lacked legitimacy in the eyes of many Germans. Right-wing parties blamed defeat in the war on democrats who had allegedly stabbed Germany in the back, while left-wing Communists attacked Weimar as a devious attempt to restore German capitalism on a new democratic basis. In addition, onerous war reparations, hyperinflation, and growing unemployment further eroded Weimar's legitimacy. The Nazi Party, led by Adolf Hitler, emerged during this time of crisis and as its electoral success peaked at 37 percent of the vote in 1932 President Hindenberg appointed Hitler as chancellor. When the Reichstag, the home of the German legislature, was destroyed by fire under suspicious circumstances, Hitler was given broad powers by emergency decree that he used to ban political parties and eliminate political opponents.

World War II began when German armies invaded Poland in 1939. Initially, the German army experienced rapid and stunning success, occupying much of Europe. But by May 1945, with Soviet troops advancing from the east and American and British troops from the west, German hopes of creating the "Thousand Year Reich" lay in rubble and defeat. With its surrender, Germany was occupied and the Allies—Britain, France, the Soviet Union, and the United States—partitioned it into four zones. But as the Cold War heated up, the four zones were reduced to just two: the area occupied by the Soviet Union became the German Democratic Republic (GDR) or what was known colloquially as East Germany, and the three zones occupied by France, Britain, and the United States became the Federal Republic of Germany (FRG), or what was commonly called West Germany. The front lines of the Cold War, the line separating capitalism from communism, now ran right through Germany, dividing it between West and East, respectively.

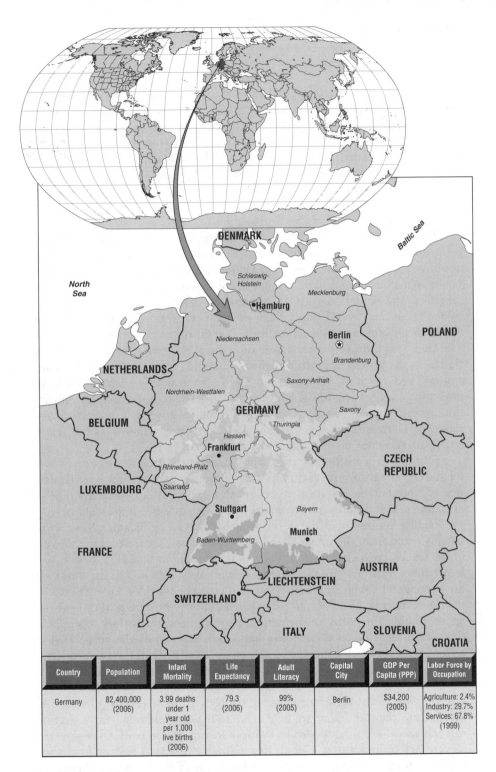

Country	Population	Infant Mortality	Life Expectancy	Adult Literacy	Capital City	GDP Per Capita (PPP)	Labor Force by Occupation
Germany	82,400,000 (2006)	3.99 deaths under 1 year old per 1,000 live births (2006)	79.3 (2006)	99% (2005)	Berlin	$34,200 (2005)	Agriculture: 2.4% Industry: 29.7% Services: 67.8% (1999)

MAP 9-3
Germany

The State

In 1987, the political scientist Peter Katzenstein described Germany as a "semi-sovereign state" in which authority is so divided and shared among institutions that the national government's ability to govern is constrained and circumscribed.[71] Katzenstein attributes the semi-sovereign character of the state, first, to its federal character in which authority is divided between the central government and 16 federal states, or *länder*. The *länder*, not only raise their own taxes and elect their own governments but select members to the *Bundesrat*, the upper house of the national legislature, which has veto power over bills that affect their jurisdictions.

The authority of the national government is not only constrained from below in the form of sharing power with the *länder*, but it is also squeezed from above in the form of the **European Union** (EU). The government has ceded power to the European Union in some policy arenas, such as trade, environmental policy, and border controls. In addition, monetary policy is now performed by the **European Central Bank**, fiscal policy is constrained by EU agreements, and laws are subject to judicial review by the European Court of Justice.

Third, the semi-sovereign nature of political power in Germany is also reflected in the power of judicial review granted to the Federal Constitutional Court. The Constitutional Court has the power to nullify laws passed by the government that it regards as contrary to the Basic Law, Germany's constitution. The Court has not been shy about using its powers of judicial review, requiring German governments to make policy in its shadow as they try to anticipate and take its reactions into account.

Fourth, policy-making by the central government is constrained by powerful and encompassing interest groups that cannot be ignored. This is particularly true of labor and employer organizations that expect to be consulted on policy affecting them if the government wants their cooperation in implementing it.

Finally, the power of the government is stymied by bicameralism. As we already mentioned, the upper chamber, the *Bundesrat*, represents the interests of the *länder*. Each *länd* is given votes in the *Bundesrat* based on its size, with larger states awarded more votes than smaller ones. Deputies to the *Bundesrat* are appointed by their state legislature and vote as a block on instruction from their government. Thus, if one party has a majority in state governments but another holds a majority in the national government, the former can appoint deputies to the *Bundesrat* who can block bills favored by the latter. **Divided government**, in which different parties enjoy a majority in the two legislative houses, is becoming more prevalent, limiting the decision-making capacity of the government.

The *Bundestag*, the lower house of the legislature, selects the government. Elections to the *Bundestag* are held every four years, although early elections can also be called, as happened in 1983, following the no-confidence vote that elevated Helmut Kohl to Chancellor. Citizens cast two ballots in electing deputies to the *Bundestag*. On the left-hand side of the ballot, candidates are listed by name with their party affiliation. Voters select the candidate they want to represent their election district. On the right-hand side of the ballot is a list of the major parties within each state. Here, voters select which party they prefer. The intent of these electoral rules is to permit voters to select the candidate they want to represent them and to apportion seats among the parties in the *Bundestag* according to proportional representation. Each party gets to keep the seats its candidates won in the first vote and then each party is awarded additional seats so that the percentage of seats it holds is equivalent to the support it received on the second, party list vote. In order to prevent small, extremist parties from gaining seats through proportional representation, Germany requires parties to win at least 5 percent of the vote before they are awarded representation.[72]

The head of state is the president, who performs ceremonial functions and selects a party leader to form a government. The head of government is the chancellor, who commands majority support in the *Bundestag*. While chancellors hold the most powerful position in the German political system, they are less powerful than chief executives in other countries. Their powers are limited by coalition treaties they negotiate with their partners in government and by ministers they appoint who are pretty independent in managing their departmental responsibilities.[73]

The semi-sovereign state has been a great success in terms of building a "political and party system that would prove more stable than the Weimar Republic had been, while avoiding the centralization and lawlessness of the Nazi dictatorship."[74] The constraints on the exercise of power by the national government that we just described have fostered consensual decision making and incremental change. Mild reform of current policies is all that can be achieved when so many players have to be accommodated. But Germany now confronts problems on which it may be very hard to attain consensus and incrementalism may be insufficient in providing solutions to them. The semi-sovereign state that was an asset previously when the German state was young may now be a liability in confronting the challenges it faces today.[75]

State and Society

Like the rest of Eastern Europe during the Cold War, East Germany was a one-party state under the control of the Communist Party. It was a "People's Democracy" where the people experienced very little democracy. Economically, the state provided substandard living conditions and, in return, workers produced substandard goods. People pretended to work and the state pretended to pay them. Social life was dreary and spiritless, and the political system was rigid and coercive.

While East Germany strained under the inefficiencies of the planned economy and the lack of freedom under Communist Party domination, West Germany thrived under capitalist democracy. The first election put a coalition consisting of the Christian Democratic Union (CDU), its sister party in the south, the Christian Social Union (CSU), and the centrist party, the Free

Democrats (FDP) into power, which they were able to maintain until 1966. Germany prospered under Chancellor Konrad Adenauer of the CDU and its pro-West, pro-welfare, and pro-market orientation. Between 1950 and 1961 the economy grew at a rapid average rate of 8.3 percent. The social democrats (SPD) were reduced to a perpetual opposition. In order to expand their appeal, they became more reformist, now advocating "as much competition as possible, as much planning as necessary," and adopting a more pro-western foreign policy in the hope of attracting middle-class voters.

Reinvention brought revival. The SPD became a junior partner in government when it participated in the "Grand Coalition" with the CDU in1966, and then took power for the first time in 1969 in coalition with the Free Democrats. Under the SPD leadership of Chancellors Willy Brandt (1969–1974) and Helmut Schmidt (1974–1982), the FRG established diplomatic ties to its Eastern bloc neighbors. But the two-and-a-half party system, composed of the CDU, FDP, and SDP that had dominated German politics to that point, was eroding. Party membership, party identification, turnout, and support for all three governing parties declined. New groups articulating new issues, such as highly educated young people concerned about ecology, emerged to form the Green Party which finally broke through to be represented in the legislature in 1983.

In 1982 the SPD lost a vote of confidence in the legislature when FDP deputies switched sides and gave their support to the CDU. The new parliamentary majority selected CDU leader Helmut Kohl as Chancellor who then called for early elections and was confirmed by voters the following year. Chancellor Kohl ruled Germany from 1982 to 1998, the longest tenure of any elected European leader in the postwar period. German unification occurred in 1990 under his chancellorship as the former East Germany was incorporated into the FRG as five new federal states. Unification accelerated **dealignment** of the party system, as a new party emerged, the Party of Democratic Socialism (PDS), to attract votes from disgruntled East Germans.

In 1998, the CDU-FDP ruling government that Kohl led was finally defeated by a coalition of the SDP and the Greens. The SPD-Green coalition headed by Chancellor Gerhard Schroeder (1998–2005) did not substantially depart from policies followed by Kohl, except it did chart a more independent course in foreign policy, as Schroeder was reluctant to support the United States in the Iraq War. The September 2005 election results between the CDU and SPD were so close that pundits declared nobody won. Angela Merkel of the CDU emerged as Chancellor, but not before she had to make many policy concessions and appoint many Social Democrats to cabinet posts in her government. The inconclusiveness of the 2005 elections was resolved in 2009 when the CDU allied with the FDP to form a government.

But what is noteworthy about recent elections was how both the CDU and SPD have lost ground to other, smaller parties, such as the FDP in the center, the Greens who are now a permanent fixture in the legislature, and to the Left Party, which is composed of disgruntled voters from former East Germany and disaffected leftists from the SPD. **De-alignment**, precipitated by new unattached voters from the east and the emergence of new destabilizing issues in the west, has disrupted the crusty and incestuous two-and-a-half party system in which the CDU on the right and the SDP on the left used to compete for the affections of the FDP in the center. More parties are now seated in the legislature, more cleavages beyond religion and class now divide voters, and more potential combinations of parties to form a government now make ruling coalitions less stable and predictable, as is apparent from recent election results presented in Table 9.3.

Political Culture

Defeat in war and the crimes of the Holocaust required Germans to "create a new life, not just materially, but also intellectually and spiritually."[76] A new German political culture that repudiated a past glorifying militarism, nationalism, and anti-Semitism would have to be constructed. This occurred as much through contrition—Germans deciding to repudiate their shameful past—as it did through imposition, the Allied occupying forces preventing any effort to revive the ideological foundations of Nazism. Germans were anxious to absorb the lessons of defeat as a way of moving beyond the crimes of the Nazis. But the occupying powers were also intent on making sure that those were the only lessons that would be available. For example, Allied efforts to outlaw militarism dovetailed with the sense Germans now had that all war was futile, and Allied efforts to ban Nazis and other antidemocratic elements fit well with German feelings of guilt over Nazi war crimes.

The new political culture was based on a different set of principles. First, German culture was demilitarized. Defeat had tarnished the luster of war and the barbarism with which the Nazis waged it had stained the reputation of the military. The military lost its allure as an institution and war was condemned as a futile exercise. The demilitarization of German society succeeded so well that subsequent attempts at rearmament were opposed by the public, "even to the extent of deploying German troops under the multilateral leadership of the U.N. or NATO." A new "culture of anti-militarism," in which peace "is an absolute, incontestable, and always valued good," has replaced the old culture in which the military was respected and war was glorified.[77]

Similarly, German nationalism was delegitimized as thoroughly as German militarism. German nationalism was suspect because of how the Nazis had used it to justify racism and deceived Germans to follow them. The Fatherland was no longer a source of pride but of shame. In response, Germans became post-nationalist and supporters of European unity. They became enthusiastic supporters of the European Union as an alternative to a national identity that was burdened by a disreputable past.

Finally, the reorientation extended to the new respect given to democracy. The Basic Law, or German Constitution, guaranteed civil and political rights, political parties rotated in office, and government responded to grievances and processed demands successfully. The success of democratic values could be attributed to the comparison between the negative example of East Germany's

TABLE 9.3

Germany Votes

	1998		2002		2005		2009	
	% Vote	% Seat	% Vote	% Seat	% Vote	% Seat	% Vote	% Seat
CDU/CSU	38.1	35.1	38.5	41.1	35.2	36.8	33.8	38.4
SDP	40.9	40.9	38.5	41.6	34.2	36.2	23	23.5
FDP	6.2	6.2	7.4	7.8	9.8	9.9	14.6	15.0
Left Party	–	–	–	–	8.7	8.8	11.9	12.2
Greens	6.7	6.7	8.6	9.1	8.1	8.3	10.7	10.9
PDS	5.1	5.1	4.0	0.3	–	–	–	–
Others	3.0	5.9	3.0	0.0	4.0	0.0	2.1	–

Source: At www.electionresources.org/de/bundestag.php?election=1998;2002;2005;2009, accessed October 31, 2010.

dictatorship and the attractive model the West provided in which democracy and economic success went together. Germans came to believe in democracy because it proved itself in practice.

But the greatest challenge to the reorientation of German political culture took the form of unification and immigration. East Germans learned different lessons of defeat under the rule of the Communist Party in the German Democratic Republic than were absorbed by West Germans living in the Federal Republic of Germany. The cultural walls separating East and West Germans were harder to bring down than the physical ones that separated them. Immigration posed similar cultural challenges when workers from Turkey and other foreign countries came to Germany to relieve labor shortages. They were followed by their dependents and then by asylum seekers from foreign countries who were allowed to settle in Germany as victims of political persecution. By 2009, about 9 percent of the people living in Germany were foreigners. Their different values, religions, and cultural practices tested the tolerance of native Germans who sometimes responded with racist attacks and xenophobic outbursts. The new German political culture will be tested by how it responds to the cultural challenge that unification and immigration pose to it.

Political Economy

German revival following World War II was nothing short of extraordinary. Germany enjoyed steady and fast economic growth, high wages, low inflation, and generous welfare benefits. It became renowned as a producer of high-quality manufactured goods to the extent that, until the recent recession, Germany exported more goods on a per capita basis than any country in the world.

The postwar German model of the **social market economy** called for "as little state intervention as possible" and "as much state intervention as necessary."[78] The state's role was not to intervene in competitive markets but to promote cooperation among its different actors. It would provide broad guidelines and empower private groups, such as employers and unions, to administer programs as opposed to performing those tasks itself or giving them detailed instructions on how to do so. In addition, the state would ensure people's needs were met by creating a generous welfare state and guarantee that workers' demands were heard by requiring the formation of works councils within firms.

The German Model—Modell Deutschland—of the social market economy delivered high-quality products, high wages, high fringe benefits, high levels of worker representation, and high levels of time off work.[79] The model rested upon the consensus and coordination of well-organized and powerful private actors, including employer associations, unions, and banks, that the state helped bring together. Banks provided patient capital that permitted managers to think about the long-term welfare of their business. Employer associations underwrote vocational training, increasing the skills and productivity of the workforce, which no single firm would have done on its own. And unions bargained on behalf of the workforce, moderating wage claims and resolving disputes with employers.

But growth rates began to decline from 2.3 percent in the 1980s to 1.3 percent in the 1990s to almost no growth at the beginning of the twenty-first century. As growth rates waned, so did the economy's ability to create new jobs. The German labor market was increasingly divided between insiders who had good jobs that paid good wages and benefits, and outsiders composed of the long-term unemployed for whom there were no job prospects because the economy was not robust enough to create them. Rising social expenses for pensions, health care, and unemployment insurance, as well as the costs associated with the unification of East Germany—about 1 billion euros ($1.34 billion) invested in East Germany per year—created budget deficits so large that Germany was in violation of the European Monetary Union's deficit rule (3 percent of GDP) and debt rule (60 percent of GDP).

What were previously perceived as the advantages of the German Model—consensus, patience, coordination, and incremental change—are now regarded more suspiciously. As the economy's performance declined, the model began to show signs of erosion. Banks became less patient in seeking a return on their domestic investments, and industry became less willing to pay high payroll taxes that financed a high level of benefits. Both unions and employer associations are now less encompassing as union membership declines and firms defect. Both works councils and individual firms have sought more labor flexibility by ignoring industry-wide agreements and adjusting wages to suit local conditions. With regard to the deficit, political parties are reluctant to impose welfare state cuts in fear of retaliation by voters.

Germany looks more confident and decisive from the vantage point of foreign policy, where it has finally shed its reputation as an economic giant and a political dwarf. Previously, Germany was reluctant to assert itself in world affairs in fear of the suspicions this would provoke given its past. It was an advocate of European integration in order to show that it wanted to be a good neighbor and was a dependable ally of the United States in return for the protection it provided during the Cold War. But a new generation of leaders has emerged who have no direct memory of the Nazi era and feel less constrained by it. In addition, the end of the Cold War has freed Germany from its dependence on the military protection of the United States. As a result, it has begun to punch its weight. Germany is the largest member of the European Union and now feels it is entitled to influence within it that matches its size. In addition, it no longer feels like it has to defer to the United States and was clear in opposing the U.S.-led war in Iraq.

COMPARING CAPABILITIES AMONG SWEDEN, THE UNITED STATES, AND GERMANY

We profiled Sweden, the United States, and Germany because they each typify different political models found among affluent democracies. Sweden represents the social democratic model, the United States is an archetype of extreme market democracies, and Germany typifies the Christian democratic model. A comparison of how these countries perform in terms of our criteria for the Good Society is important because it provides clues as to which of these models better meets its standards. But comparing capabilities among developed countries is more difficult than comparing capabilities between developed and less developed countries. The gap between developed and developing countries is often glaring. That is not the case with Sweden, the United States, and Germany. They are all democracies, literacy rates are high, and infant mortality rates are low. In order to compare capability meaningfully among our three countries that represent different models we need more subtle and discerning measures than those commonly used to compare developed and less developed societies.

Physical Well-Being

We have used infant mortality rates to assess physical well-being in previous chapters. Since we are not worried about finding a measure that applies to such a large number of countries here, we can use poverty rates that provide a better, more discriminating, and more accurate measure. Poverty rates measure the percentage of households who fall below some income threshold. For example, the poverty line for a family of four in 2008 in the United States was $22,025. We will take the income threshold the United States uses to define who is poor, estimate what the poverty rate would be in Germany and Sweden if they adopted the same threshold, and then equalize purchasing power among them. The figures are given in Table 9.4 below.[80]

Sweden and Germany, representing the social democratic and Christian democratic models, respectively, performed similarly, and each performed better than the United States, which typified extreme market democracies, when it came to meeting the physical needs of its citizens. Differences between the two top performers and the United States are actually greater than they appear at first. Poverty rates only measure income and do not include public services or welfare benefits available to the poor. Since these are greater in social democratic and Christian democratic models, Sweden and Germany perform better than appears in comparison to the United States, when one looks only at income.

TABLE 9.4

Poverty Rates

Poverty Rates	
Sweden	7.5%
United States	8.7%
Germany	7.6%

TABLE 9.5	
Literacy Skills	
Performance on IALS Tests	
Sweden	23%
United States	46%
Germany	42%

Informed Decision Making

We require a more demanding measure of this standard than literacy rates since 99 percent of all citizens in Sweden, the United States, and Germany are literate. Consequently, we will use the more discerning International Adult Literacy Survey (IALS), which examines the ability of citizens "to understand and employ printed information in daily activities, at home, at work, and in the community— to achieve one's goals, and to develop one's knowledge and potential."[81]

The IALS assessed literacy skills in three areas and then citizens were graded according to five levels, with level one including people who were functionally illiterate and levels four and five, including respondents who were very proficient at processing information. Table 9.5 above gives the proportion of citizens in Sweden, the United States, and Germany whose average scores across the three literacy skills placed them into either level one or two.[82]

A larger percentage of adults in Sweden performed higher than level II than was the case in the U.S. and Germany, indicating more Swedes were successful at processing and comprehending information than Americans and Germans.

Safety

Unlike some developing societies, where political violence and civil war pose real threats to safety for their citizens, Sweden, the United States, and Germany do not suffer from such turbulence. Citizens in our sample of countries have little to fear from political persecution or civil strife on a massive scale. But physical safety remains an issue nonetheless, due to the prevalence of violent crimes, such as homicides, sex offences, and serious assaults. We will again use homicide rates, which are the most reliable statistic, to assess performance on this criterion. Homicide rates for Sweden, the United States, and Germany are given in Table 9.6.

Just as we found with regard to poverty rates, Sweden and Germany performed similarly and the United States performed the worst according to this measure of safety.

Democracy

Aside from meeting the basic physical needs of citizens, helping them gain the skills to make informed decisions about their lives, and protecting them from

TABLE 9.6	
Safety	
Homicide Rates per 100,000	
Sweden	1.2
United States	5.9
Germany	1.0

harm, the good society, we argued, also guarantees political and civil rights. These are available in all our countries—all of them were rated 10, the highest possible score as democracies—in the Polity IV data set. We need to compare the quality of these rights within them, not whether they exist or not. We propose to do so by measuring the quality of their democratic practice.

Measuring the quality of democracy is even more controversial than measuring crime. *The U.N. Human Development Report*, however, ventured into this delicate area and graded the quality of democracy in different countries, using five criteria. On four of them, no noteworthy differences were found among our countries: all of them scored similarly on press freedoms, political rights, civil liberties, and competitive elections. The fifth measure, which is a composite of various indicators that includes some of those already mentioned, is "Voice and Accountability." This measure was compiled from a variety of sources by the World Bank Governance Indicators Dataset, and aggregates "several indicators of the political process, including the selection of governments, with indicators of civil liberties and political rights, and press freedom and independence." This will be our measure of the quality of democracy among our three countries. Countries were scored on a −2.50 to 2.50 scale on this index. The higher a country's score, the more its citizens were deemed to have "voice and accountability." Results using this measure of democracy are given below in Table 9.7.

According to this measure, the quality of democracy is better in Sweden than in Germany or the United States, and in the loser's bracket, it is better in Germany than in the United States.

In conclusion, it appears some political models are better able to create conditions that enhance the capabilities of their citizens more than others.

TABLE 9.7	
Quality of Democracy[83]	
Voice and Accountability	
Sweden	+1.53 (99.5)
United States	+1.12 (86.1)
Germany	+1.34 (92.8)

Specifically, social democracy, in the form of Sweden, generally performed better in meeting the standards of the Good Society than either Christian democratic or extreme market democracies, represented by Germany and the United States, respectively. The quality of democracy was higher in Sweden and its citizens were more likely to possess the skills they needed to make informed decisions about their lives. When it came to meeting the physical needs of their citizens and providing for their safety, Sweden and Germany performed similarly and both did better than the United States.

CONCLUSION

This chapter described three types of political models, or families of nations, found among affluent democracies: social democracies, extreme market democracies, and Christian democracy. They differ in their politics, institutions, and policies. We then provided case studies using countries that serve as paradigmatic models of each model: Sweden as representative of social democracies; the United States as emblematic of extreme market democracies; and Germany as an example of Christian democracies. Finally, we examined which of these countries—and thereby the models they represent—came closest to meeting the criteria of the Good Society: promoting their citizens' capabilities. According to our tests, Sweden representing social democracy performed best, followed by Germany, and then the extreme market model represented by the United States.

EXERCISES

Apply what you learned in this chapter on MyPoliSciKit (www.mypoliscikit.com).

 CHAPTER MENU ICON
Review this chapter using learning objectives, chapter summaries, practice tests, and more.

 VIDEO CASE STUDIES
Analyze recent world affairs by watching streaming video from major news providers

FLASHCARD ICON
Learn the key terms in this chapter; you can test yourself by term or definition.

 COMPARATIVE EXERCISES
Compare political ideas, behaviors, institutions, and policies worldwide.

CRITICAL THINKING QUESTIONS

1. How would you operationalize the four criteria we used to assess the different political models found in the West. Using your measures, which countries enhance the capabilities of their citizens most and come closest to the standard of the Good Society?

2. Do you think the different Western political models are converging, becoming more alike, in any of the areas we investigated: politics, political institutions,

political culture, or political economy? Or have their differences in all of these arenas remained profound?

3. What would have had to be different for the United States to end up like Germany or Sweden?

4. What do you believe is the greatest challenge social democratic, extreme market democracies, and Christian democratic models face today? In what respect are their challenges similar to each other or specific to each model?

5. What do you see as the strengths and weaknesses of each political model?

KEY TERMS

Postindustrial (society) 224
Active labor market policies 226
Multimember election district 229
Ombudsman 229
Centralized wage bargaining 235

Wage solidarity 235
Class identification 236
Welfare effort 237
Union density rate 237
Veto points 240
Medicare 241
Transfer payments 245

European Union 248
European Central Bank 248
Divided government 248
De-alignment 250
Social Market Economy 253

SUGGESTED READINGS

Ira Katznelson, Mark Kesselman, and Alan Draper, *The Politics of Power: A Critical Introduction to American Government,* 6th edition (New York: Norton, 2011). A critical, introductory text covering American politics.

Gosta Esping-Andersen, *Social Foundations of Postindustrial Economies* (New York: Oxford University Press: 1999). A good elaboration and extension of the three political models offered in this chapter.

Eric S. Einhorn and John Logue, *Modern Welfare States: Scandinavian Politics and Policy in the Global Age,* 2nd ed. (Westport, CT: Praeger, 2003). Offers comprehensive coverage of Scandinavian politics.

Pol O'Dochartaigh, *Germany since 1945* (New York: Palgrave, 2004). A short text covering German politics.

Jonas Pontusson, *Inequality and Prosperity: Social Europe vs. Liberal America* (Ithaca: Cornell University Press, 2005). Offers interesting comparisons among Western democracies.

NOTES

1. Andrea Mahony, "Paid Maternity Leave Entitlements around the World," APESMA Professional Women's Network at: http://www.apesma.asn.au/women/articles/paid_maternity_leave_june_01.asp.

2. These figures are from OECD, *Babies and Bosses: Reconciling Work and Family Life,* p. 151. Chart 6.4 Childcare fees per two-year-old attending accredited early-years care and education services as a percent of the average wage, 2004.

3. This was calculated by using the OECD "Pensions at a Glance: Pension Calculator, 2006," available from their Directorate for Employment, Labour and Social Affairs, presuming each earns average wages.

4. W. Adema, and M. Ladaique, "How Expensive is the Welfare State?: Gross and Net Indicators in the OECD Social Expenditure Database (SOCX)," *OECD Social Employment and Migration Working Papers*, No. 92 (2009), p. 23, Chart 4.1: "The Public Social Spending-to-GDP Ratio Has Been Rising Again since 2000."

5. Gosta Esping-Andersen, *Social Foundations of Post-Industrial Economies* (New York: Oxford University Press, 1999), p. 177.

6. Net total social expenditures for Sweden, the United States, and Germany were 30.6 percent, 24.5 percent, and 30.8 percent of GDP respectively. See Willem Adema and Maxine Ladaique, "Net Social Expenditure," OECD ELSA Working Paper 8, (2005 edition), Table 9.6.

7. Jacob S. Hacker, *The Divided Welfare State: The Battle over Public and Private Social Benefits* (New York: Cambridge University Press, 2002.

8. Gosta Esping-Andersen, *The Incomplete Revolution: Adapting to Women's New Roles* (Malden, Ma: Polity Press, 2010), p. 109.

9. Ibid.

10. Ibid.

11. Alberto Alesina and Edward L. Glaeser, *Fighting Poverty in the US and Europe: A World of Difference* (New York: Oxford University Press, 2004), pp. 81–87.

12. The complete list of rich democracies includes Australia, Austria, Belgium, Canada, Denmark, Finland, France, Germany, Ireland, Italy, Japan, Netherlands, New Zealand, Norway, Portugal, Spain, Sweden, Switzerland, United Kingdom, and the United States.

13. Eric S. Einhorn and John Logue, "Can Welfare States Be Sustained in a Global Economy? Lessons from Scandinavia," *Political Science Quarterly* (Spring 2010), Vol. 125, No. 1, p. 9.

14. Wolf is quoted in Andrew Glyn, *Capitalism Unleashed* (New York: Oxford University Press, 2006), p. 167.

15. Perrson is quoted in Jenny Anderson, "The People's Library and the Electronic Workshop: Comparing Swedish and British Social Democracy," *Politics & Society* Vol. 34, No. 3, (September 2006), p. 439.

16. Goran Therborn, "A Unique Chapter in the History of Democracy: The Social Democrats in Sweden," in Klaus Misgeld, Karl Molin, and Klas Amark, eds., *Creating Social Democracy: A Century of the Social Democratic Labor Party in Sweden* (University Park, PA: Pennsylvania State University Press, 1992), pp. 1–2.

17. See Table 8.2, "Lower-Class Power," in Seymour Martin Lipset and Gary Marks, *It Didn't Happen Here: Why Socialism Failed in the United States* (New York: Norton, 2000), p. 280. Walter Korpi developed a similar, though more complex (and more dated) working-class "power resources" index in which Sweden also ranked first. See Table 3.6, "Patterns of Working Class Mobilization and Political Control in Eighteen OECD Countries, 1946–76," in Walter Korpi, *The Democratic Class Struggle* (London: Routledge & Kegan Paul, 1983), p. 40.

18. Timothy A. Tilton, "The Social Origins of Liberal Democracy: The Swedish Case," *American Political Science Review* 68 (June 1974), p. 563.

19. Arend Lijphart, *Patterns of Democracy: Government Forms and Performance in Thirty-Six Countries* (New Haven: Yale University Press, 1999), p. 2.

20. Eric S. Einhorn and John Logue, *Modern Welfare States: Scandinavian Politics and Policy in the Global Age,* 2nd ed. (Westport, CT: Praeger, 2003), p 42.

21. Rune Premfors, "Reshaping the Democratic State: Swedish Experiences in a Comparative Perspective," *Public Administration* Vol. 76 (Spring 1998), p. 154.

22. Gosta Esping-Andersen, "The Making of a Social Democratic Welfare State," in Klaus Misgeld, Karl Molin, and Klas Amark, eds., *Creating Social Democracy: A Century of the Social Democratic Labor Party in Sweden* (University Park, PA: Pennsylvania State University Press, 1992), p. 41.

23. Esping-Andersen, "The Making of a Social Democratic Welfare State."

24. Bo Sairlvik, "Recent Electoral Trends in Sweden," in Karl H. Cerny, ed., *Scandinavia at the Polls: Recent Political Trends in Denmark, Norway, and Sweden* (Washington, D.C.: American Enterprise Institute for Public Policy Research, 1977), pp. 115–129.

25. David Arter, "Sweden: A Mild Case of 'Electoral Instability Syndrome,' " in David Broughton and Mark Donovan, eds., *Changing Party Systems in Western Europe* (London: Pinter, 1999), pp. 143–163.

26. John Logue, "The Swedish Model: Visions of Sweden in American Politics and Political Science," *The Swedish-American Historical Quarterly*, (July 1999), Vol. 50, no., 3, p. 167.

27. Lars Tragardh, "Sweden and the EU: Welfare State Nationalism and the Spectre of Europe," in *European Integration and National Identity: The Challenge of the Nordic States*, ed. Lene Hansen and Ole Waever (New York: Routledge, 2002), pp. 130–182.

28. Stefan Svallfors, *The Moral Economy of Class: Class and Attitudes in Comparative Perspective* (Stanford: Stanford University Press, 2006), p. 59.

29. Thomas J. Anton, "Policy-Making and Political Culture in Sweden," *Scandinavian Political Studies* (January 1969), Vol. 4, No. 4, p. 99.

30. Bo Rothstein, "Social Capital in the Social Democratic State," in *Democracies in Flux: The Evolution of Social Capital in Contemporary Society*, ed. Robert Putnam (New York: Oxford University Press, 2002), p. 303.

31. Ibid., p. 319.

32. Bo Rothstein and Eric M. Uslaner, "All for All: Equality, Corruption and Social Trust," *World Politics*, Vol. 58, No. 1 (2005), pp. 41–72.

33. Maureen A. Eger, "Even in Sweden: The Effect of Immigration on Support for Welfare State Spending," *European Sociological Review,* Vol. 26, No. 2 (2010), pp. 203–217.

34. Quoted in Eger, "Even in Sweden," p. 203.

35. Einhorn and Logue, "Can Welfare States Be Sustained in a Global Economy?," p. 12.

36. Staffen Kumlin and Bo Rothstein, "Questioning the New Liberal Dilemma: Immigrants, Social Trust and Institutional Fairness," *Comparative Politics* (October 2010), Vol. 43, No. 1.

37. Robert Taylor, quoted in John T. S. Madeley, "*The Swedish Model is Dead! Long Live the Swedish Model: The 2002 Risksdag Election*," West European Politics, 26:2 (January, 2006), p. 165.

38. Gosta Esping-Andersen, *Politics Against Markets: The Social Democratic Road to Power* (Princeton, NJ: Princeton University Press, 1985).

39. Einhorn and Logue, *Modern Welfare States*, p. 197.

40. Esping-Andersen, "The Making of the Social Democratic Welfare State," p. 50.

41. Richard Clayton and Jonas Pontusson, "Welfare State Retrenchment and Revisited: Entitlement Cuts, Public Sector Restructuring and Inegalitarian Trends in Advanced Capitalist Societies," *World Politics,*Vol. 51, No. 1 (1998), pp. 67–98. See also Karen M. Andersen, "The Politics of Retrenchment in a Social Democratic Welfare State," *Comparative Political Studies,* Vol. 34, No. 9 (November 2001), pp. 1063–1091.

42. Anders Lindblom, "Dismantling the Social Democratic Welfare Model? Has the Swedish Welfare State Lost its Defining Characteristics?" *Scandinavian Political Studies*, Vol. 24, No. 3, (2001), p. 17.

43. Mike Marshall, "The Changing Face of Swedish Corporatism: The Disintegration of Consensus," *Journal of Economic Issues*, Vol. 30 (September 1996), p. 858.

44. LO stands for *Landsorganisationen i Sverige*, while SAF stands for *Svenska Arbetsgivareforeningen* in Swedish.

45. Douglas A. Hibbs, Jr., and Hakan Locking, "Wage Dispersion and Productive Efficiency: Evidence from Sweden," *Journal of Labor Economics* Vol. 18, No. 4 (2000), pp. 755–782.

46. Jonas Pontusson and Peter Swenson, "Labor Markets, Productions Strategies, and Wage Bargaining Institutions," *Comparative Political Studies* Vol. 29, No. 2 (April 1996), pp. 223–250.

47. Kathleen Thelen and Ikuo Kume, "Coordination as a Political Problem in Coordinated Market Economies," *Goverance* Vol. 19., No. 1. (January 2006), pp. 11–42.

48. Robert Taylor, *Sweden's New Social Democratic Model* (London: Compass, 2005).

49. Paul Nieuwbeerta, "The Democratic Class Struggle in Postwar Societies: Class Voting in Twenty Countries, 1945–1990," *Acta Sociologica* Vol. 39, No. 4 (1996). See especially Table 9.3, p. 356.

50. Mark Gray and Miki Caul, "Declining Voter Turnout in Advanced Industrial Democracies, 1950 to 1997," *Comparative Political Studies* Vol. 33, No. 9 (November 2000), pp. 1091–1122. In terms of turnout, the United States had the second-lowest average turnout in federal elections from 1990–2000 (45 percent), followed by Canada with the third-worst record (60 percent), followed next by Ireland (71 percent), which was tied with Finland for the fourth-worst record over the course of the 1990s out of 16 rich democracies listed in the Table "International Voter Turnout, 1991–2000," which can be accessed at www.fair-vote.orgiturnoutlinturnout.html.

51. Others make the same distinction among Anglo-American democracies as we do, arguing that Britain, Australia, and New Zealand follow a discrete model that is different from that adopted by Canada, Ireland, and the United States, despite the significant affinities among them. See Francis G. Castles and D. Mitchell, "Worlds of Welfare and Families of Nations," in Francis G. Castles, ed., *Families of Nations: Patterns of Public Policy in Western Democracies* (Aldershot, UK: Dartmouth, 1993), p. 107. Evelyn Huber and John D. Stephens also distinguish Australia and New Zealand from the other conservative regimes, claiming these countries adopted a wage earners' welfare state—"social protection by other means"—that is qualitatively different from that found in Canada, Ireland, and the United States. See Evelyne Huber and John D. Stephens, *Development and Crisis of the Welfare State* (Chicago: University of Chicago Press, 2001).

52. David Brook, "How Sweden Tweaked the Washington Consensus," *Dissent* (Fall 2004), pp. 24–29.

53. Christopher Howard, "Is the American Welfare State Unusually Small?" *PS: Political Science* (July 2003), Table 9.1 Column A, p. 414.

54. Jacob S. Hacker, *The Divided Welfare State: The Battle Over Public and Private Benefits in the United States* (New York: Cambridge University Press, 2002), p. 19.

55. Marx is quoted in Eric Foner, "Why is There No Socialism in the United States?" *History Workshop Journal*, Vol. 17, No. 1 (1984), p. 57.

56. Seymour Martin Lipset and Gary Marks, *It Didn't Happen Here: Why Socialism Failed in the United States* (New York: Norton, 2000), p. 279.

57. Robert Dahl writes that the Founders were alarmed by the prospect "that democracy, political equality, and even political liberty itself would endanger the rights of property owners to preserve their property and use it as they please." Robert Dahl, *A Preface to Economic Democracy* (Berkeley, CA: University of California Press, 1985), p. 2.

58. Quoted in Robert Dahl, *Democracy in the United States: Promise and Performance*, 2nd ed., (Chicago: Rand McNally, 1973), p. 151.

59. Quoted in William F. Connelly, Jr., and John F. Pitney, Jr., "The House Republicans: Lessons for Political Science," in *New Majority or Old Majority: The Impact of Republicans on Congress*, eds. Nicol C. Rae and Colin C. Campbell (Lanham, MD: Rowman & Littlefield, 1999), p. 186.

60. Hughes is quoted in Bernard Schwartz, *A Basic History of the U.S. Supreme Court* (Princeton: D. Van Nostrand Co., 1968), p. 9.

61. This section draws heavily on Ira Katznelson, Mark Kesselman, and Alan Draper, *The Politics of Power: A Critical Introduction to American Government* (New York: Norton, 2011).

62. Anthony King, "Ideas, Institutions and the Policies of Governments: A Comparative Analysis: Part III," *British Journal of Political Science*, (October 1973), Vol. 3, No. 4, p. 418.

63. Jacob S. Hacker and Paul Pierson, *Off Center: The Republican Revolution and the Erosion of American Democracy* (New Haven, CT: Yale University Press, 2005), p. 194.

64. Richard B. Freeman and Joel Rogers, *What Workers Want* (Ithaca, NY: Cornell University Press, 1999), p. 1.

65. Lipset and Marks, *It Didn't Happen Here*, p. 284.

66. Quoted in Stathis N. Kalyvas, *The Rise of Christian Democracy in Europe* (Ithaca: Cornell University Press, 1996), p. 2.

67. Kalyvas, *The Rise of Christian Democracy in Europe*, pp. 222–265.

68. An early statement of Christian Democratic principles is Gabriel Almond, "The Political Ideas of Christian Democracy," *Journal of Politics* Vol. 10 (November 1948), pp. 734–763; for more current analyses, see David Hanley, ed. *Christian Democracy in Europe: A Comparative Perspective* (New York: St. Martin's Press, 1994); and Kees van Kersbergen, *Social Capitalism: A Study of Christian Democracy and the Welfare State* (New York: Routledge, 1995).

69. van Kersbergen, *Social Capitalism*, pp. 180–181.

70. Emmerich Talos, "Corporatism—The Austrian Model," in Volmar Lauber, ed., *Contemporary Austrian Politics* (Boulder: Westview Press, 1996), p. 104.

71. Peter G. Katzenstein, *Policy and Politics in West Germany: The Growth of a Semisovereign State* (Philadelphia, PA: Temple University Press, 1987).

72. Charles Lees, *Party Politics in Germany: A Comparative Politics Approach* (New York: Palgrave 2005), p. 128–137.

73. Simon Green and William E. Paterson, "Introduction: Semisovereignty Challenged," in *Governance in Contemporary Germany: The Semisovereign State Revisited*, ed. Simon Green and William E. Paterson, (New York: Cambridge University Press, 2005), p. 3.

74. Ibid., p. 6.

75. Mark I. Vail, "Rethinking Corporatism and Consensus: The Dilemmas of German Social-Protection Reform," *West European Politics* Vol. 26, No. 3, (July 2003), pp. 41–66.

76. Hans Fuchs, newly appointed president of the North Rhine province under the Allied occupation, quoted in Konrad H. Jarausch, *After Hitler: Recivilizing Germans, 1945–1995* (New York: Oxford University Press, 2006), p. 20.

77. Jarausch, *After Hitler*, p. 45.

78. Pol O'Dochartaigh, *Germany since 1945*, (New York: Palgrave, 2004), p. 41.

79. Lowell Turner, *Democracy at Work: Changing World Markets and the Future of Labor Unions* (Ithaca, NY: Cornell University Press, 1991).

80. See Timothy Smeeding, "Poor People in Rich Nations," *Journal of Economic Perspectives*, Vol. 20, No. 1 (2006), pp. 69–90. See Table 9.2: Absolute Poverty Rates Using Official US Poverty Standards in Nine Rich Countries at the Turn of the Century.

81. OECD/HRDC, *Literacy in the Information Age: Final Report of the International Adult Literacy Survey"* (Paris: Organization for Economic Cooperation and Development; and Ottawa: Human Resources Development Canada, 2000), p. x.

82. *Literacy in the Information Age*, p. xiii.

83. *Governance Matters 2009* at info/worldbank.org/governance/wi/sc_chart.asp. Accessed January 30, 2009.

Less Developed Countries and the Good Society

INTRODUCTION

Almost a quarter of the 541 members of the lower house of India's national parliament elected in 2004 had criminal charges against them. Criminals also run for office in some of India's states on the assumption that once they are elected they can use their authority to conduct criminal activities without interference from the police. In some states "corruption, criminality, murder, and kidnapping" are regular occurrences during election campaigns. In large parts of rural India and in urban slums, poor Indians cannot count on judges, police, or politicians to defend them and "the rule of law means little."[1] They are at the mercy of powerful landlords or gangs. India is the world's most populous democracy, but the quality of its democracy is much lower than in advanced democracies such as Sweden or less developed countries such as Costa Rica.

In these circumstances, poor Indians cannot use elections to choose political leaders who will improve their capabilities or those of their children. Public elementary and secondary schools are often spectacularly bad. Teachers do not come to class or come late, sell rice that is meant for children's lunches, and do not teach basic skills in reading and arithmetic. Public schools "have become reserves of children at the very bottom of India's social ladder," whose parents cannot afford to pay for private schools.[2]

The state of Indian democracy is a reminder that there are degrees of democracy. Individuals' ability to use competitive elections to improve their capabilities and those of their children varies greatly from country to country, and within countries. This chapter examines differences in degrees of democracy among less developed countries and the consequences for citizens' lives.

The affluent democracies discussed in the previous chapter have many things in common. They are all wealthy, highly urbanized societies with high labor productivity and postindustrial occupational structures. Developing countries in Africa, Central and South America, the Middle East and Asia are more diverse. Some, such as Chile, have per capita incomes approaching those of lower-income Western democracies. Others, such as Iran, are middle income countries, while still others, such as Nigeria, are mired in deep poverty and many of their citizens live on less than two dollars per day. Developing countries also vary greatly in levels of labor productivity and technology. In some developing countries, modern conveniences such as electricity and indoor plumbing are common, whereas in other countries many people live much as their ancestors did. In some countries, many people commute to their job at an office in the city, while in others a majority of people still make their living toiling in the fields growing crops. Finally, developing countries differ in levels of urbanization. In some upper-middle-income countries, over 80 percent of the population lives in cities while in most low-income countries less than 50 percent do so.[3]

As might be expected from all this economic and social variety, less developed countries are also highly diverse politically. In some countries their political systems reflect the various types of authoritarianism we reviewed in Chapter 6. Some are governed by monarchies, others by military juntas, a few by political parties that have no opposition, and many by ruling elites that allow multiparty elections that the opposition has no real chance of winning. Just as less developed countries have adopted different models of authoritarianism, so are different models of democracy also evident among them. Some have adopted presidential forms of democracy while others have adopted parliamentary systems that we reviewed in Chapter 7.

A few developing countries earn the highest possible Polity IV score of +10, indicating that formal democratic rules exist and are basically followed by political leaders and citizens. Chile and Costa Rica are examples. But only a small number of developing countries meet these criteria. Consequently, this chapter will concern itself with developing countries that fall below this demanding standard. It will examine **weak democracies** that fall far short of the criteria, **electoral democracies** that meet many of them but not all, and electoral authoritarian regimes that combine elements of authoritarianism and democracy. The chapter will outline the characteristics of weak democracies, electoral democracies and electoral authoritarian regimes and offer case studies of countries that represent each of them. Nigeria exemplifies a weak democracy, Brazil an electoral democracy, and Iran a case study of the dilemmas electoral authoritarianism can create for ruling elites.

We have chosen these three countries for four reasons. First, they have large populations. Brazil has the largest population in Latin America, Nigeria the largest in Africa, and Iran has the second largest population in the Middle East after Egypt. Their governments' policy choices affect the capabilities of tens of millions of people. Second, they represent different levels of economic development. Brazil is an upper-middle-income country, Iran is a lower-middle-income country, and Nigeria is a low-income country. Third, they are from different regions of the world with Brazil in South America, Nigeria in sub-Saharan Africa, and Iran in the Middle East. Finally, they are important to the United States and other advanced democracies. Nigeria is an important oil supplier to the United States and attracted security concerns in 2009 when one of its citizens with connections to Al Qaeda attempted to blow up an American passenger plane. Brazil is important commercially for the United States and Europe and is likely to become an increasingly important supplier of oil supplies when recently discovered offshore oil fields come on line. Iran is set squarely between Iraq and Afghanistan in a volatile part of the world and is strongly suspected of working to gain nuclear weapons.

WEAK DEMOCRACIES

Weak democracies have regularly scheduled elections in which leaders of political parties compete to hold the most powerful political offices by seeking citizens' votes, but democracy is weakly institutionalized. Personal relationships and winning office often matter more than following formal rules.[4] Political rights to free and fair elections are often violated. Ballot boxes are stuffed, votes are bought, and candidates' supporters are intimidated at voting booths. Minorities' rights and civil liberties are violated. Democracy is relatively young in many weak democracies and political elites are not firmly committed to it.

Political parties in weak democracies tend be based on personality and patron–client relations rather than programs. Instead of designing policies that appeal to broad cross sections of the population, political parties design policies to benefit individuals and narrow groups of supporters. Political parties are usually electoral vehicles for individual politicians, not organizations representing broad constituencies.

Weak democracies also have weak states with little autonomy or capacity. They lack autonomy because many state officials have clientelist ties with individuals or small groups in society and work on their behalf rather than on behalf of broader publics. Many officials are not recruited on the basis of merit or insulated from direct political pressures. They do not work in accordance with clear guidelines or serve the public interest with a sense of professionalism. The temptations to behave in corrupt ways are strong because the rewards for doing so can be large, and the chances of getting caught and being punished are small.

This is not true of all officials. In some of these countries, officials in the central bank and financial ministries are highly capable. This has enabled presidents in some weak democracies to push through changes in economic policies that have improved economic growth rates. Such changes require the advice and cooperation of only a few officials. On the other hand, improving education for children requires the cooperation of tens of thousands of teachers and public school administrators spread across a country and it is difficult to achieve such cooperation. This makes improvements in education much tougher than cutting interest rates or strengthening requirements for banks. The lack of state capacity also makes improvement in health and safety difficult. States in weak democracies often lack the capacity to implement their decisions effectively throughout their territory. In many areas local political bosses, landlords, warlords, or criminal gangs are in control, not officials from the central government.

Finally, weak democracies have weak foundations in society. They lack essential raw materials for building strong opposition parties and civil society organizations. They are usually located in low-income countries in which a high percentage of people still live in rural areas and the middle class is small. The private business sector is weak and small and cannot offer much funding for opposition parties. Civil society organizations are small and limited mainly to the cities. Weak democracies are often the product of what the political scientists Steven Levitsky and Lucan Way call "rotten door transitions." They emerge after a weak authoritarian regime collapses, not because there is a strong demand for democracy from groups in society, strong support for the rule of law, a vibrant civil society, or a political culture supportive of democracy. Political elites and groups in society are only weakly committed to democracy as a means of winning and holding power. Examples of weak democracies include Kenya, Haiti, and Nigeria. Their Polity IV scores range from +4 to +7.

NIGERIA

Historical Background

Nigeria is Africa's most populous country and the eighth most populous country in the world. It is the world's seventh largest oil exporter and tenth largest gas exporter. It boasts valuable natural mineral resources and has large areas of fertile soil. When it gained independence from Britain in 1960, many people expected it to become one of the developing world's success stories. Instead, it remains one of the poorest countries in the world. In 2005, close to 70 percent of its people lived below the absolute poverty level of $1.25 per day.[5] More than 65 percent of adults are illiterate, and almost 10 percent of infants die before their first birthday.[6] Life expectancy at birth is only 47 years. These failures are in large part attributable to the complexity of ethnic and religious divisions in Nigeria, and the inadequacy of its political institutions for meeting the challenge these divisions present. Since 1999, when it became a democracy after years of military rule, it has improved its economic performance and made some headway in improving citizens' capabilities.

Nigeria is an artificial country created by British colonialism. The colonial borders enclosed more than 250 ethnic groups that had never been ruled by the same state. Thus, Nigeria lacked a history of common political institutions to which its people had some degree of loyalty. There was no agreement among its multiple ethnic groups over the rules of politics.[7] Nor did the British attempt to create such rules. They governed their Nigerian colony "on the cheap," relying on local leaders to maintain order and collect taxes. The northern part of the country was left in the hands of Muslim rulers, or emirs, under loose British supervision, while chiefs in the southern part of the country were under direct British control. The British made little effort to recruit and train a professional Nigerian civil service.[8]

Colonialism left four damaging legacies for Nigeria. One was a weak sense of nationhood. The Hausa-Fulani, Nigeria's largest ethnic group, dominate the north, while the Yoruba, the second largest, live mainly in the southwest, and the Igbo, in third place, live in the southeast. These ethnic divisions are overlaid by religious differences, because the Hausa-Fulani are predominantly Muslim while the Igbo and Yoruba are predominantly Christian. The center of the country is a mix of Muslims, Christians, and practitioners of traditional religions.

A second damaging colonial legacy was the "**divide and rule**" tactic that the British employed to pit ethnic groups against each other. The policy heightened ethnic awareness, and helped ensure that ethnicity would be the main line of political cleavage after Nigeria became an independent country. The third unfortunate legacy was a system of **personal rule** based on "**big men**" rather than the rule of law based on well-trained civil servants recruited through competitive examinations.[9] The chiefs who worked with the British colonial state did so "in the name of tradition" but without the checks on their power provided by traditional norms. They used personal relationships with British field administrators to accumulate wealth and power.[10] This form of rule, which relied on a hierarchy of local "big men" linked to superiors through personal connections and held together by a strong executive at the top, became the model for politics in independent Nigeria.[11]

The final damaging legacy was the creation of an increasingly active and interventionist state during World War II and the postwar years up until independence in 1960. The fragmented Nigerian elite who took over

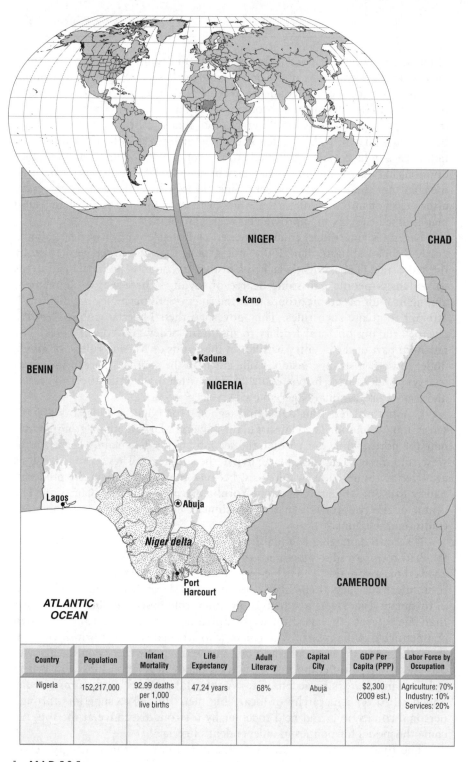

Country	Population	Infant Mortality	Life Expectancy	Adult Literacy	Capital City	GDP Per Capita (PPP)	Labor Force by Occupation
Nigeria	152,217,000	92.99 deaths per 1,000 live births	47.24 years	68%	Abuja	$2,300 (2009 est.)	Agriculture: 70% Industry: 10% Services: 20%

MAP 10.1
Nigeria

Nigeria at independence found this state well suited for their patronage needs. They used it as an employment agency for clients and a source of funding for projects in their regions to strengthen their political base, not to achieve some broader goal of economic and human development that would benefit all Nigerians.[12]

The State

Nigeria has a weak state that is unable to maintain law and order throughout the country, provide essential infrastructure, or meet the needs of its citizens for adequate education, safety, and health care. Nor does it provide them with secure civil and political rights. For several years large parts of the oil-producing Delta Region in southern Nigeria have been controlled by insurgents and criminal gangs. Cities in the central and northern parts of the country have experienced periodic clashes between Christians and Muslims, resulting in thousands of deaths. Electricity is supplied erratically by the state-managed Power Holding Company (PHC). The supplies are so unpredictable that Nigerians joke that PHC stands for Please Hold Candle.[13] Such jokes are a way of making the best of living under the rule of a weak state.

One major reason for the weakness of the state is that agencies are filled with patronage appointments rather than with civil servants selected on the basis of merit. Political leaders reward followers with state jobs and have dramatically expanded the number of civil service positions so as to increase the number of jobs they can dole out. Politics in Nigeria is in large part a competition between powerful "big men" and their clients. Clients help get big men elected and, in turn, are rewarded with government jobs, contracts for government construction projects, or simply a share in the theft of government funds. Corruption is rampant. In a setting where most of one's peers are corrupt, it makes little sense for officials to be the only honest person in their agency.

Some honest and dedicated officials, however, have made attempts to root out corrupt politicians and civil servants. One example is Nihu Ribadu, who was the head of the Economic and Financial Crimes Commission in 2007. Ribadu successfully prosecuted a number of corrupt politicians and became a hero among ordinary citizens. He ran into trouble, however, when he began prosecuting powerful politicians from the president's political party. One was the governor of a state who earned a salary of $25,000 a year but had bank accounts worth $35 million. The governor had been a major contributor to the president's winning campaign. Two weeks after the governor's arrest, the government announced that Ribadu would be resigning to attend a one-year course at the National Institute of Policy and Strategic Studies.[14]

The United States has had one constitution since 1789. Nigeria has had four since it gained independence from Britain in 1960. Its political history as an independent country has been marked by failed democracies and long periods of military rule. Military governments ruled Nigeria for 28 of its first

45 years. The first democratic period, lasting from 1960 until 1966, collapsed into a devastating civil war when the large Igbo ethnic group in the southeastern part of the country tried unsuccessfully to secede and form an independent country they called Biafra. The war caused an estimated 1 million deaths, many from starvation.

Military officers ruled Nigeria from the end of the civil war in 1970 until 1979 when Nigerians made a second attempt at democratic governance. This time, military officers waited only four years before seizing power. Coup leaders pointed to massive corruption and mismanagement as justification for returning to power, and although they promised a quick return to civilian rule, they remained in power for the next 20 years. Rather than reducing corruption and mismanagement, the military rulers became increasingly predatory. General Sani Abacha, who was president from 1993 until 1998, was the worst of them all. Nobel Prize-winning author Wole Soyinka predicted that Abacha would be Nigeria's "last despot," because he was such a bad leader that he discredited military rule.[15] When he died of a heart attack in 1998 there was widespread rejoicing.

Nigeria's present constitution came into effect in 1999. It is the most recent in a long line of attempts to craft an arrangement of state institutions that can hold such an ethnically and religiously diverse country together. It provides for a federal system of government, with power divided between the central government, with its capital in Abuja, and 36 states. But the balance of power is tilted heavily toward the federal government. It controls oil revenues that provide up to 80 percent of the government budget in some years, and decides how the revenues are to be allocated to the states.

The most powerful office in the central government is the presidency. The president is elected by voters every four years and can serve for no more than two terms. The president is both head of state and head of the executive branch of government. The president appoints a cabinet, which is named the Federal Executive Council. To satisfy the diversity of regions, ethnicities, and religions in Nigeria, the president must have at least one member of the cabinet from each of the 36 states.

The legislature, or National Assembly, has two chambers, a House of Representatives and a Senate. The 360 members of the House of Representatives are elected on the basis of states' population, while three people are elected to the Senate from each of the 36 states. Even though the president and legislative majorities in both houses have been from the same political party since 1999, there have been struggles over the budget and legislation between the two branches. A watershed moment in this power struggle occurred in 2006 when the Senate rejected a constitutional amendment proposed by President Olusegun Obasanjo that would have allowed him a third term in office.[16]

The court system has a Supreme Court, a Court of Appeal, and a system of state courts. In the first decades after Nigeria became independent, courts were highly regarded as independent institutions, which decided cases on the basis of the law. They lost a great deal of their independence during the years of military rule, but have begun to regain some of it since the return of civilian rule in 1999. In one striking instance of independence, the Supreme Court invalidated a 2001 election law that was supported by the president and a majority in the legislature, which would have benefited the president's political party in the upcoming elections in 2003.[17] In another example of judicial independence, courts overturned election victories in seven states for violations of electoral laws. These included some positions that had been won by politicians from the ruling political party.[18]

One of the unusual features of the Nigerian legal system is that 12 northern states with large Muslim populations can establish law courts based on Muslim law, or **shari'a** courts, in addition to secular courts. Their establishment alarmed many non-Muslims living in these states, as well as human rights activists inside and outside Nigeria. *Shari'a* law allows severe corporal punishment, including amputation of a hand for theft and stoning adulteresses to death. The punishments attracted international attention in 2002 when a *shari'a* court sentenced a young woman to be stoned to death for conceiving and having a child out of wedlock. Concerns about the courts have declined in recent years because the most draconian penalties are seldom applied. Amputations for theft have been rare, and in the case of the women sentenced to death by stoning, a *shari'a* appeals court overturned the ruling.[19]

Nigeria's military has intervened in politics often since independence and withdrew from governing most recently in 1998. While it offered itself as a responsible alternative to civilian rule, it often suffered from the same problems that afflicted civilian governments. The military was ethnically divided, patronage was often the basis for promotion as opposed to merit, and officers had relatively little professional training. In recent years, there have been efforts to create a more professional officer corps and strengthen civilian control over the military. One measure of progress occurred in 2008 when the president dismissed the heads of the army and navy and replaced them with his own choices.[20]

State and Society

Weak political parties do a poor job of linking citizens to the state and enabling them to choose among alternative sets of government policies. Political parties in Nigeria do not offer competing programs to address social and economic problems. Instead, they compete for votes by winning over local ethnic and religious leaders who can mobilize blocs of votes. It is more cost-effective for party leaders to use public money to build patron–client relationships than to provide effective public services. Oil revenues make this easier by permitting politicians to avoid raising taxes in order to pay off supporters.[21]

Political parties have strong regional bases rather than being national parties that appeal to voters across Nigeria. This pattern of party politics emerged in the first few years after achieving independence in 1960. Political parties were based almost exclusively in different regions because of their strong ties to particular ethnic groups. Recent changes in electoral laws have to some extent forced them to reach out to other ethnic groups and regions to win votes.

The most successful political party has been the People's Democratic Party (PDP), dominated by Hausa-Fulani "big men." Candidates from the PDP have won every presidential election since 1999. The transfer of power from President Obasanjo to President Yar'adua in 2007 was the first time in Nigeria's history that one elected president transferred power to another. This was a measure of progress for Nigeria, but the 2007 election was also marred by massive violations of election laws. In the six states of the oil-rich Niger Delta, thugs working for the PDP beat opposition politicians, stole ballot boxes, and filled them with ballots marked for PDP candidates. In Kano in the north, bagmen for opposing parties openly bought votes.[22] Independent observers in Nigeria, as well as international organizations such as Human Rights Watch, reported extensive cheating. The 2007 election is an example of how weakly formal rules are institutionalized in Nigeria. While elections have become the means of changing from one government to another, as opposed to doing so through military coups d'etat, presidential elections have also become "successively less fair, less efficient, and less credible."[23]

Civil society has become much more active in politics since the end of military rule. Business associations have begun to demand less government corruption, better roads, more reliable electricity, and fewer obstructions to starting new businesses. All too often, however, efforts to act collectively have been undercut when individual businesspeople go directly to influential politicians and civil servants to resolve problems. Efforts to coordinate businesses nationally are also hampered by ethnic and regional differences among them. Trust is in short supply between business and the government and among businesspeople themselves.

The end of military rule has also seen increased political activity by trade unions. They have demanded laws and regulations that would improve working conditions and have gone on strike to stop proposed cuts in government services. In 2000 and 2001 massive strikes forced the government to cancel plans to raise fuel prices. While they have had some success promoting working-class demands in large cities, ethnic and religious differences among workers have limited their achievements.

Ordinary people in the informal, unorganized sector and small farmers have even less influence in Nigerian politics. They have difficulty cooperating with each other, partly because of their large numbers, and also because like businesspeople and trade union members they are divided by ethnic and religious identities.[24]

Political Culture

Opinion surveys in 2000, just after Nigeria had returned to civilian rule, found overwhelming support for democratic politics.[25] But achieving an effective and stable democracy requires Nigeria to create a national political culture that takes precedence over local ones that reflect the culture of different ethnic and religious groups. Nigeria lacks social capital as much as it lacks economic capital. Its citizens lack the generalized trust and norms of reciprocity that are essential for collective action. Many lack confidence that other citizens will play by the rules and carry out their civic duties such as paying taxes, so they see no need to do so either. Such confidence requires "strong, effective institutions of governance to enforce and reproduce civic behavior."[26] Nigeria lacks such institutions. Corruption and cheating are taken for granted. This attitude is exemplified in a story told by the economist Paul Collier about his meeting with a former head of the Nigerian tax authority who had just resigned from his office. For two years, he had tried to get a minor piece of tax legislation passed. When he met with the chair of the legislative committee to discuss the legislation, the first question was, "How much?" The chair of the legislative committee on taxation "expected to be bribed by the tax authority. No bribe, no law. Why? Because that was normal; that was how it was done."[27]

Generalized social trust makes it possible to work with large numbers of people one does not know well to create civic associations and broadly based political parties. Such organizations bring together people as equals. In Nigeria, however, most relations are based on vertical ties between patrons and clients. "The masses of ordinary people at the bottom" of such a society find it difficult to "cooperate with one another because they are trapped in hierarchical networks, fragmented from one another, and generally distrustful. This social fragmentation is reinforced by ethnic, religious, and other identity cleavages that keep the oppressed from collaborating and enable the privileged to rally ready political support from their ethnic compatriots."[28]

The lack of trust can easily turn innocent events into violent confrontations. The Miss World Contest, scheduled to be held in the northern city of Kaduna in 2002, inspired rioting after a journalist raved about the contestants' beauty and suggested that the Prophet Muhammad might have married one of them if he were still alive. Outraged Muslims burned down the newspaper office, and, in the ensuing conflict more than 200 people were killed and 1,000 were injured.

Once violence begins, it can develop into a pattern of repeated retaliations. The city of Jos has been particularly hard hit by Christian-Muslim violence in recent years. It is in the central part of Nigeria along the fault line of the predominantly Muslim north and predominantly Christian south. There have been repeated clashes in Jos since 2001 over election results, efforts by the Christian majority to limit Muslim immigration into the state where Jos is located, and competition for jobs and land.[29]

With such a political culture it is not surprising that support for democracy has declined dramatically in Nigeria. In 2000, 84 percent of Nigerians said that they supported democracy, but "by 2005 that number had plummeted to 25 percent, lower than all the countries surveyed save Zimbabwe."[30]

Political Economy

Nigerians refer to the national budget as the "national cake." Politics is largely about getting the biggest slices. Nigerian politicians have extended the state's role into every major economic sector in order to create artificially high profits, or **rents** A major source of rents is the oil industry and much private business activity in Nigeria takes the form of **rent seeking,** or seeking to gain access to the rents provided by oil revenues. One of the easiest ways for a businessperson to make money in Nigeria is to get state contracts for constructing roads, bridges, or schools, or supplying the state with products ranging from office stationery to office equipment. In return politicians and civil servants granting the contracts get political support, monetary kickbacks, and shares in the company receiving the contract.

One reason for all this rent seeking is that Nigeria has not created institutions that provide incentives to invest in industry or manufacturing. Institutions do not provide secure property rights, effective regulation of markets to prevent cheating, or necessary infrastructure, such as reliable electrical power. Most astonishingly, Nigeria suffers from unstable fuel supplies. Its state-managed refineries have antiquated equipment and produce well below capacity. Most petroleum products are imported and the state-managed distribution system is riddled with corruption, inefficiency, and mismanagement.[31]

There has been economic progress in recent years. The transition to democracy has created greater political stability, which has in turn given businesspeople more confidence about investing in new businesses. In addition, President Olesegun Obasanjo, who served from 1999 to 2007, oversaw several reforms in the banking and financial sector of the economy. He chose a team of **technocrats,** or highly educated and skilled officials, to take over key institutions, including the ministry of finance and the central bank. These technocrats implemented reforms that have reduced inflation, strengthened banks, and increased transparency so that businesspeople have accurate economic information. Competitive bidding on state contracts was introduced and reduced the cost of these projects "by an average of 40 percent."[32] Finally, over 100 inefficient state enterprises were **privatized.** These reforms contributed to GDP growth rates of over 7 percent per year between 2003 and 2007. Economic consultants estimate that 24 percent of this growth was the result of world oil prices rising from $20 a barrel in 1999 to $145 a barrel in 2008, but most of the growth was in wholesale, retail, transportation, telecommunications, and manufacturing.[33] Nigeria has a long way to go, however, to create institutions that can sustain economic growth over the long term.

It is not clear whether Nigeria can sustain democratic politics or even survive as a country. The abysmal failures of previous military regimes helped democratic prospects by discrediting military rule. Larry Diamond, one of the world's foremost authorities in the study of democracy, writes that Nigeria still remains "one of the most predatory societies in the world."[34] Quite possibly, increasing ethnic and religious violence will outrun the capacity of Nigeria's institutions to constrain it.

ELECTORAL DEMOCRACIES

The second prevalent type of democracy in less developed countries is **electoral democracy.** At first glance, this concept can be confusing. All democracies have elections, so it might seem that all democracies are electoral democracies.

Political scientists use the concept to make the point that while all democracies have elections, the quality of democracy depends not just on having regularly scheduled elections, but on how free and fair they are and how strongly political and civil rights are enforced. Electoral democracies are an intermediate category of democracies between full and weak democracies. They have universal suffrage for all citizens, competitive political parties that can campaign mainly without intimidation, and that have access to important media. They also conduct regular elections using secret ballots without "massive voter fraud."[35] They have freer and fairer elections and better enforcement of political and civil rights than weak democracies such as Nigeria, but their elections are not as free and fair as those of full democracies such as Chile and Costa Rica. Nor is their enforcement of civil and political rights as effective. Citizens' civil and political rights are frequently violated by local strongmen in poor neighborhoods in cities and in rural areas.

The quality of democracies depends on the kinds of political parties countries have as well as on free and fair elections. Political parties in electoral democracies tend to rely heavily on patronage, or appeals to racial and ethnic identity, rather than presenting policy alternatives to voters. India's Congress Party, which has dominated the political scene since independence was achieved in 1948, started out with a socialist platform, but transformed itself into a party organized mainly on patronage networks. Brazil's Workers Party is an exception with its programmatic approach to politics.

Electoral democracies also have stronger states with higher autonomy and capacity than weak democracies. While many officials have clientelist ties with individuals or small groups in society, there are also substantial numbers of officials who are recruited on the basis of merit, and insulated from direct political pressures. These officials work in accordance with clear guidelines or serve the public interest with a sense of professionalism. The states also have greater capacity to implement their decisions throughout their territory than do those of weak democracies.

Finally electoral democracies have stronger societal foundations for democratic politics than weak democracies. They tend to be located in lower- and upper-middle-income countries that have a strong private business sector, organized labor unions, and numerous civil society organizations. Nevertheless, it can be difficult to make substantial improvements in capabilities for low-income citizens in electoral democracies. In many electoral democracies there are large inequalities in wealth and political power among citizens. Wealth tends to be concentrated in the hands of owners of large commercial and agricultural firms, urban professionals, and executives in domestic business firms or multinational corporations.

Economic inequality is reinforced by inequalities based on ethnicity and race. When countries have several major languages, religions, and ethnic groups, it can be very difficult for broad-based interest associations and political parties to form. Groups are challenged to organize beyond their specific region and ethnic or religious group. In the absence of broad-based movements that can successfully negotiate diverse identities in a large country, politicians tend to appeal to upper-income groups.[36]Even though lower-income citizens have more votes than upper-income groups, their influence is diluted by clientelism, ethnic and religious conflict, and the manipulation of democratic institutions.

Democracy specialist Larry Diamond lists Brazil, Mexico, India, and Indonesia as examples of electoral democracies.[37]

BRAZIL

Historical Background

"Brazil is the country of the future. And it always will be." For decades this cynical witticism reflected Brazil's failure to live up to its considerable potential. But there are signs it may finally be ready to deliver on its promise. For the past decade it has had very strong economic growth. In 2007, it discovered large new offshore oil fields that promise to make it a major oil exporter once they are on line. It has also received increasing international recognition. Rio de Janeiro was selected to host the 2016 Olympics. In several respects, however, Brazil remains the country of the future. It has one of the most unequal income distributions in the world. Its public education system is woeful, and violent crime linked to the drug trade is rampant. Two weeks after Rio de Janeiro was awarded the Olympics, drug traffickers shot down a police helicopter one mile from the stadium where the Olympic opening and closing ceremonies will take place.[38]

Brazil's path to its current set of politics, policies, and institutions began with its colonization by Portugal in the 1500s. The population was divided between a small European elite that owned large sugar plantations and a large number of slaves who had been brought from Africa to work on them. Independence from Portugal in 1822 brought little change to the social structure, as the same land-owning elite continued to dominate Brazil's politics for several decades. By 1900, however, the sugar barons were eclipsed politically by cattle ranchers and coffee growers. While this shift among landed elites moved the locus of power from the northeast, where the sugar plantations were based, to the southeast, where ranching and coffee growing predominated, it made little difference to most Brazilians, who remained poor, illiterate, and powerless.[39]

By 1930, with the presidency of Getulio Vargas, a new coalition with a different program took power. Instead of depending on landed elites, Vargas relied on industrialists, the middle class, industrial workers, and the military to promote rapid economic development through state-led industrialization. Vargas's imperious rule produced growing discontent and the military forced him out in 1945. But Vargas left a legacy that was to influence Brazilian politics for the next 40 years: state-led industrialization featuring cooperation between state officials and businesspeople; control of labor through corporatist practices; and the distribution of state benefits to key political constituencies.

The 1960s were marked by rapid industrialization, but also by growing economic and political polarization between social classes. Peasants began to seize land from large landowners and industrial workers initiated strikes

Country	Population	Infant Mortality	Life Expectancy	Adult Literacy	Capital City	GDP Per Capita (PPP)	Labor Force by Occupation
Brazil	201,103,000	21.86 deaths per 1,000 live births	72.26 years	88.6%	Brasilia	$10,100 (2009 est.)	Agriculture: 20% Industry: 14% Services: 66%

MAP 10.2
Brazil

against businesses. In 1964, the Brazilian President João Goulart sided with the peasants and workers and proposed major reforms that frightened elites. In 1964, the military overthrew the government and ruled until 1985.

Military leaders were intent on promoting rapid economic development through state-led industrialization. They offered businesses tariff protection, subsidies, and tax benefits, created hundreds of state-owned enterprises, repressed labor unions, and reduced social spending. Left-wing political parties were banned, and their leaders were driven out of the country, or arrested, imprisoned, and tortured.

Military leaders assumed that a rising standard of living would generate legitimacy for their rule. Between 1968 and 1974, the economy grew at more than 10 percent a year, and admirers began to refer to the "Brazilian miracle." But in the early 1980s Brazil plunged "into a prolonged period of economic stagnation" known as "the lost decade."[40] As economic difficulties mounted, criticism of the military regime grew, even among business elites and middle-class Brazilians who had formerly supported it. The army finally allowed a return to civilian rule in 1985. In 1988, a new constitution went into effect, and a year later, for the first time since the coup d'etat of 1964, there was direct, popular election of a president.

The State

The Brazilian state is relatively strong compared with those in other less developed countries and much stronger than the Nigerian state. It is able to maintain its authority across Brazil, collect taxes needed to fund government programs, and implement many policies effectively. Recent presidents have been successful in ending chronic inflation and indebtedness. Brazil has one of the most effective anti-HIV/AIDS strategies in the world. Although many state agencies are staffed with patronage appointees with little training, key economic agencies are run by skilled professionals. But in other respects the Brazilian state has not performed well. It has not been as successful as other countries at its income level in promoting literacy, improving health care, or controlling crime and violence.

Brazil has a presidential form of government. Presidents are directly elected by the voters for four years and are limited to serving two consecutive terms. Presidents initiate a considerable amount of the legislation, have the power to appoint many people to positions in the government, and can issue temporary emergency measures that have the effect of law.[41] But these formal constitutional powers are weakened by a fragmented party system that impairs presidents' ability to get legislation passed, and a fragmented bureaucracy that is responsive to pressure from powerful constituencies.

Members of Brazil's bicameral legislature are directly elected by voters. The upper house of the legislature is the 81-member Senate consisting of three senators from each state and the federal district. Senators, who have eight-year terms, are elected by plurality vote. The lower house is the Chamber of Deputies, whose 513 members are elected for four-year terms. In theory, states receive seats in the Chamber of Deputies in proportion to their population, but, in reality, smaller states, which are more rural, are disproportionately represented. This rural bias in the electoral system helps "explain why conservative landowners and agribusiness elites maintain positions of great influence in the Brazilian congress."[42]

The judicial system contains both federal and state courts. The Superior Court of Justice is the supreme court for most purposes. It has 33 justices, from which a smaller number are drawn to hear each case. The president nominates the members of the court from sitting Brazilian judges, and his choices must be confirmed by the Senate. After a two-year probationary period, they receive tenure for life. Brazil has a separate court to handle constitutional conflicts and questions of judicial review.[43]

Each of Brazil's 26 states elects its own governor and legislature. Because governors control a good deal of state spending and appoint large numbers of officials, they enjoy considerable power. Presidential and legislative candidates rely on the influence of governors in the states to get votes. Becoming governor of a large state is often an effective base for a presidential bid.

State and Society

Social class has been the most politically important cleavage in Brazilian politics, but in recent years race has emerged as another significant source of division. We begin with social class, and then turn to race.

Brazil is one of the world's most economically unequal societies. Social scientists measure income distribution in two different ways. One is to compare the percentage of a country's total income that goes to the top 10 percent of income earners, and the percentage that goes to the bottom 10 percent. The other is the **Gini Index**, which has a value from zero to 100. A Gini Index value of 0 equals perfect equality of income in which everyone receives the same share of a country's income, while a value of 100 equals perfect inequality. Table 10.1 shows how Brazil compares with other countries.

TABLE 10.1

Brazil's Income Distribution in Comparative Perspective

Country	Ratio of Income of Top 10% to Income of Bottom 10%	Gini Index
Haiti (2001)	45.43	68.0
Brazil (2001)	16.25	59.0
Costa Rica (2000)	9.65	46.0
United States (2000)	6.30	38.0
Germany (2000)	3.58	28.0
Sweden (2000)	3.18	25.0

Source: World Bank, *World Development Report 2006: Equity and Development* (New York: Oxford University Press, 2005), pp. 280–281.

Wealth, which includes ownership of homes, businesses, land, stocks, and bonds, is even more unevenly distributed in Brazil than income. Two percent of landowners own approximately 50 percent of the country's farmland.[44] This highly unequal distribution of income and wealth results in considerable inequalities in health care, safety, and access to education.

Yet Brazilian politics is not divided into a clear-cut struggle between the few at the top and the many at the bottom. Clientelism, in which wealthy patrons provide people with jobs or other benefits in return for their vote is a common practice in rural and urban areas alike. Such personal connections tie poor people to wealthier, more powerful people, rather than to organizations of other peasants or workers.

Political leaders have also used **state corporatism** to divide the members of the lower classes from each other organizationally. Under President Vargas, for example, workers were separated into different unions for different economic sectors, creating a highly fragmented labor movement. These unions were established and regulated by the state to limit their power. Aspects of state corporatism were continued under military rule. As a result, when Brazil finally made a transition to democracy in the late 1980s, it was left with a divided set of unions, and organized labor was separated from the much larger number of unorganized workers in the informal sector, including street vendors, day laborers, and maids.[45] The result is a working class whose political power is diluted.

Brazil's fragmented political organizations make it much easier for upper- and middle-class citizens to maintain their privileges than for poorer citizens to make changes that would improve their lives. To keep their privileges, members of the upper and middle classes need only to maintain existing institutions, while poor Brazilians need broad-based associations and political parties that enable them to capitalize on their larger numbers to change institutions and policies.[46]

Until recently Brazilian political parties were highly fragmented. Politicians readily switched from one party to another. Fragmentation has lessened in recent years, and the trend seems to be for parties to change "from loose patronage machines to programmatically coherent and distinctive groupings."[47]

Even with these recent changes the Brazilian party system makes it difficult for presidents to secure legislative backing for their proposals. Presidents are forced to rely upon coalitions of parties to accomplish their goals and sometimes purchase support by paying legislators for their votes.[48] Ministers appointed to government posts often have no real interest in supporting presidents' programs other than the specific benefits that programs bring them.[49] For presidents whose main base of support is from large landowners, business elites, and the middle classes, this is not much of a problem, because these groups can approach legislative committees or officials in the state bureaucracy for the favors they need. But formidable obstacles face presidents seeking to pass legislation that provides the poor with improved health care, better schools, and safer streets.

The major exception to these generalizations about political parties is the Workers' Party (Partido dos Trabalhadores), whose leader took office as President of Brazil in 2003. The Workers' Party grew out of the labor union movement during the years of military rule. It overcame the fragmentation induced by state corporatism and built a strong coalition of support at the municipal and state level among union members, poor farmers, landless workers, community activists, and radical academics. Its party members are much more program oriented than the leaders of other parties. Its leader, Luiz Inácio Lula da Silva, spoke openly of class struggle; he was highly critical of capitalism, and counted Fidel Castro as a friend. Lula ran for president in 1989, 1994, and 1998 before finally emerging victorious in 2002.

To win office Lula had to make concessions. Instead of campaigning while wearing the clothes of a worker, he appeared in business suits. More significantly, he toned down his anticapitalist rhetoric, reached out to middle-class voters, and reassured domestic and foreign business interests that he would pursue pro-market policies. Lula acknowledged that he needed the support of capitalists to sustain economic growth, which was essential to create jobs and provide revenue for his programs. Lula promised to maintain a budget surplus, restrain state spending, and keep interest rates high to attract investors and control inflation. These policies won the support of foreign investors, the International Monetary Fund, and large business managers in Brazil. But these pro-market policies strained his relations with core groups of supporters, including landless farmers and workers who expected him to do much more on their behalf. Intellectuals who had previously supported Lula criticized him, and peasants who had stopped engaging in unlawful land seizures resumed them.[50]

In addition to these concessions, Lula had to face up to the reality of Brazilian party politics. In the 2002 elections the Workers Party did not win a majority in either legislative house, requiring Lula to cobble together support from a coalition of small parties. Securing their support required him to use the same kind of tactics that presidents employed in the past. In 2005, leading officials of the Workers Party were discovered making monthly payments to legislators from other political parties in return for their support of Lula's legislative agenda.

Lula's administration and the Workers Party were tarnished by these charges of corruption. As a result, Lula was unable to win a majority of votes in the first round of the presidential election on October 1, 2006. In the second round of voting four weeks later, he won almost 61 percent of the vote, polling very well among low income voters. Despite the magnitude of his victory, the Workers Party won only a small percentage of seats in the legislature in the 2006 legislative elections. This meant Lula had to continue to rely heavily on patronage to win the support of other political parties for his legislative agenda.

Lula could not run for office again in the 2010 presidential elections because of term limits. He backed Dilma Rousseff, his chief of staff and former minister of energy and mines, as his successor, and campaigned energetically on her behalf. She had never held elective office, but on October 31, 2010, she won the presidency by a vote of 56 percent to 44 percent to become Brazil's first woman president. She received strong support among low-income voters, and was expected to continue social and economic policies broadly similar to those promoted by Lula.

The same political constraints that have made it difficult to improve the lives of poor Brazilians have also made it difficult to improve the lives of Brazilians of African descent. Brazil's racial politics differ in significant ways from those of the United States. Unlike the United States, where there are sharp distinctions between black and white citizens, racial categories in Brazil "are fluid and ambiguous."[51] There are many intermediate categories between black and white, and Brazilians use dozens of terms to describe one another's complexion. Brazil also differs from the United States in never having had state-imposed racial segregation. In fact, Brazilian constitutions since the 1930s have upheld racial equality, and the 1988 constitution defines racism as a crime.[52] Many Brazilians believe themselves to be citizens of a "racial democracy."

Despite constitutional guarantees of racial equality, Brazil is "profoundly stratified by color."[53] Citizens of African descent are more likely to live in poverty, have less schooling, and be illiterate than whites.[54] These inequalities did not become a significant political cleavage until the 1990s. Before then politicians saw no advantage in raising the issue of racial inequalities, and there were no large, well-organized, Afro-Brazilian groups that pressed the issue. Constitutional guarantees of equality, fluidity of racial identity, and the absence of legalized segregation made it more difficult for Brazilians of African descent to organize around racial issues than for blacks in the United States.[55]

It was not until the administration of President Fernando Henrique Cardoso in 1995 that a Brazilian government directly addressed racial inequalities and initiated several affirmative action programs to improve the lives of Afro-Brazilians.[56] But Brazil's pork barrel politics and fragmented political parties have made it difficult to pass affirmative action legislation, and get funding from the legislature to support it.[57]

Political Culture

The United States and Brazil are the two largest democracies in the Americas, but they have very different political cultures. The main themes of United States' political culture have been suspicion of a strong state, acceptance of free markets, individualism, and the promise of political equality in which all citizens are equal before the law. In many cases this promise of equality has been an ideal rather than a reality, but it has enabled African-Americans and women to use the ideal to advance their claims to equal treatment.

Brazil's political culture differs from that of the United States on each point. Most Brazilians support the need for a strong state that takes an active role in the economy. Through most of the twentieth century the state played a leading role in promoting industrialization in Brazil. Instead of embracing free markets, Brazilians have been highly skeptical of their benefits and focused more on their shortcomings.

Brazil's political and economic elites have not valued the political equality of all citizens. To the contrary, for most of Brazil's history elites believed in a hierarchical society in which some people are better than others and deserved to be the rulers. Well into the twentieth century the political elite in Brazil thought of themselves as a "political class" "with unique rights and privileges."[58] The rich considered themselves above the law and could punish poor peasants and workers with impunity. This political culture of inequality was reinforced by the teachings of a very conservative Catholic Church hierarchy in Brazil.

In such a society lower class people found it very difficult to make improvements in their lives through their own efforts. Many found it prudent to act individually and find a patron to protect them. But by the early 1960s, many became imbued with radical, Marxist ideas that promoted collective action on their behalf, which alarmed wealthy landowners, industrialists, and military leaders. The rise of Marxist ideas was complemented by the emergence of **liberation theology** in the Catholic Church. Many priests and nuns began to focus on those parts of the Gospels that emphasized helping the poor and powerless. Some even justified the use of revolution to improve the lives of the poor. The emergence of these radical political and religious ideas led to an increasing polarization of Brazilian politics and the military coup d'etat of 1964.

Brazilian political culture has changed in significant ways in recent decades. The military stepped down in 1985, and a new constitution went into effect in 1988. There is now more support for democracy and representative government, more emphasis on equal rights for all, greater acceptance of markets, and more criticism of bureaucratic inefficiency and waste. Economic growth, the development of a sizable middle class, and a decline in poverty rates have reduced the appeal of radical political ideas. Socialism and Marxism have lost much of their appeal. New associations and political movements have emerged to press for improvements in the lives of the poor, women, blacks, and indigenous peoples. The Catholic Church is now challenged by the rapid growth of Pentecostal Protestantism rather than by radical young priests and nuns. Yet the distinctive features that separate Brazilian political culture from the United States remain, albeit in a more muted form. Brazilians still accept a greater role for the state in the economy. A much higher percentage of Brazilians than citizens of the United States say that government should take more responsibility for ensuring that everyone is provided for and that governments should tax the rich and subsidize the poor.[59] They are more suspicious of free markets, and are more conscious of class conflict. The Workers Party that elected Lula as president in 2002 and again in 2006 is not simply a Brazilian version of the Democratic Party in the United States. It is further to the left politically and many of its supporters continue to believe in socialism.

Finally, while most Brazilians support the idea that democracy is a better system of governing than any alternative, they are extremely critical of politicians and political parties. They also have exceptionally low levels of trust in one another. In a 2005 survey only 9 percent said others could be trusted while 91 percent responded "one can't be too careful."[60] This does not mean that Brazil is in danger of a return to military rule or some other form of authoritarianism. It does mean that democracy is still a project under construction.

Political Economy

For most of the twentieth century, from the 1930s through the 1980s, Brazil pursued a strategy of state-led industrialization. Many state officials and economists believed local capitalists were not up to the task of catching up to the capitalists of the developed industrial countries through their own efforts. They needed the help of the state. Brazilian leaders proceeded to allocate credit to industry through state development banks and use tax incentives, subsidies, and wage and price controls to promote industrialization. Tariffs were manipulated to protect the domestic market from foreign competition.[61]

There are four reasons why state-led industrialization was so much more successful in Brazil than in Nigeria. First, Brazil began its drive for industrialization at a much more advanced level of economic development and technology than Nigeria did. Nigeria had a tiny industrial sector, while Brazil already had a significant one by the 1930s. Second, capitalists were politically stronger in Brazil than in Nigeria. While the Brazilian state provided investment and policies aimed at stimulating industrialization, most of the economic growth was driven by privately owned firms. While state elites had a great deal of power over which individual firms received investments, they were dependent on the private sector to provide sustained growth.[62] Nigerian political elites had no such constraints, especially because oil revenues flowed into the state treasury, and reduced their dependence on the private sector. Third, the Brazilian bureaucracy was more competent and professional than its Nigerian counterpart. Finally, Brazil had a longer period of independence than Nigeria, which contributed to a stronger sense of loyalty and identification with the state.

While state-led industrialization led to rapid industrialization in Brazil, it also had two major drawbacks. One was recurrent economic crises. Brazil's industrialization required high levels of foreign borrowing and oil imports to sustain it. When oil prices increased dramatically in 1973 and 1979, Brazil paid for imported oil by borrowing from abroad. Borrowing and high oil prices led to high levels of indebtedness and raging inflation that Brazil struggled to control between 1980 and 1995.

Another shortcoming of state-led industrialization was its disregard for the welfare of Brazil's large numbers of poor people. This abated somewhat with the return to democracy. Both President Fernando Henrique Cardoso (1994–2002) and Lula championed programs that reduced infant mortality rates, increased the percentage of children attending school, and initiated anti-HIV/AIDS strategies that became a model for other countries.[63] In these efforts they were supported by unions and social movements that became much more influential after the end of military rule. New unions emerged that were not tied to the state by corporatism and were more aggressive in demanding social services. This period also saw the growth of a reform movement lobbying for universal health care.[64] A final factor that contributed to the expansion of educational opportunities and health care was the dropping of literacy requirements for voting in 1985. When that happened, political parties had incentives to seek the votes of poor people by promising to expand social services.[65]

Both Cardoso and Lula pursued policies that diverged from the previous policy of state-led industrialization. When Cardoso became president in 1995, he promoted privatization. His administration sold a number of state-owned enterprises to private investors in a bid to make them more efficient and productive. These sales provoked massive protests by workers, students, and radical intellectuals, who regarded them as a sellout to global capital. But Cardoso persisted with the policy, and, as president, Lula followed suit.

The past decade has been an exhilarating one for many Brazilians. After suffering through prolonged periods of economic volatility in which the economy was ravaged by inflation and unemployment, Brazil seems to have entered a phase of sustained, stable growth. It has achieved international recognition for its economic and political successes instead of being known for debt crises, hyperinflation, and coups d'etat. Democratic politics has become more institutionalized, and the lives of many poor Brazilians have improved. Despite all these achievements problems remain. The discovery of oil promises a great increase in national income, but oil has often had very undesirable effects on countries' economics and politics. It remains to be seen how well Brazil's institutions cope with oil wealth. Brazil also faces considerable challenges in improving the welfare of its poorest citizens, controlling crime and violence, and in relieving the intense racial and economic inequalities that exist. Whether Brazil will finally redeem its considerable potential or see its current good fortune fizzle out as other opportunities have in the past is at issue.

ELECTORAL AUTHORITARIANISM

The distinguishing feature of electoral authoritarian regimes is their use of competitive multiparty elections to "mask the reality of authoritarian domination."[66] Chief executives and legislators are chosen by voters in multiparty elections, but the electoral rules are tilted so strongly in favor of the ruling party or faction that opposition parties or movements have little chance of taking power. Full political and civil rights are frequently denied to the leaders of opposition political parties and their supporters, even when such rights are guaranteed in the constitution.

The most stable electoral authoritarian regimes have a strong ruling party. Such parties provide an institutional setting for sorting out disputes among leaders of different factions. In addition, leaders have strong incentives to keep their policy disagreements inside the party rather than trying to find support for them outside the party. To go outside the party is to lose all access to power and the chance to shape policies in ways that benefit one's constituents. Egypt and Malaysia are examples of countries with ruling political parties and very durable electoral authoritarian regimes.

Electoral authoritarian regimes that mix authoritarianism and multiparty elections without benefit of a ruling political party tend to be more unstable. Leaders of factions who disagree with regime policies take their case directly to the voters during elections for legislators and presidents. This creates serious problems for the regime with divisions between factions that want to increase the importance of democratic institutions and those that want to decrease them. This has been a continuing issue in Iran.[67]

All electoral authoritarian regimes combine elements of democracy and autocracy, but some countries tolerate the democratic elements more than others. Russia's rulers, for example, see the benefits of allowing a small degree of democracy because of its advantages to the regime. A democratic facade helps provide legitimacy for the regime and elections provide rulers with information about what citizens are thinking and how they are reacting to the regime's policies.[68] In contrast, many of the conservative clerics who rule Iran have contempt for democracy and see few benefits from the democratic elements in Iran's version of electoral authoritarianism.

IRAN

Historical Background

The Islamic Republic of Iran is a **theocracy**, a country in which religious leaders rule. These religious leaders have differed, however, on the specific set of rules and procedures for choosing leaders and policies. In the late 1990s and early 2000s, leaders who believed the elected branches of government should have more power won the presidency and control of parliament, but their success did not result in political liberalization. Conservative religious leaders and their allies blocked the initiatives of these leaders and turned Iran in an increasingly authoritarian direction.[69]

The 2009 presidential election seemed to offer another chance for political opening. The candidate favored by Iran's Supreme Leader was the incumbent president Mahmoud Ahmadinejad. Ahmadinejad is best known in the United States for his harsh criticisms of United States' policies in the Middle East and his denial of the Holocaust. In Iran he is known as a supporter of conservative cultural and social policies. He portrays himself as a populist with a responsibility to defend the poor from corrupt elites. His main opponent was Mir Hossein Mousavi, a former prime minister who promised to follow more liberal cultural and social policies and to strengthen democratic institutions. In a striking change from past practice his wife, a very well known sculptor, intellectual, and Islamic feminist, campaigned alongside him. Mousavi seemed to have no chance of winning. As the campaign progressed, however, the crowds turning out to support Mousavi became larger and larger. His supporters identified themselves by wearing green armbands or other items of clothing. By the final week of the campaign public opinion polls suggested he had a very good chance of winning. Immediately following the vote, however, the Interior Ministry announced that Ahmadinejad had won with 63 percent of the vote to

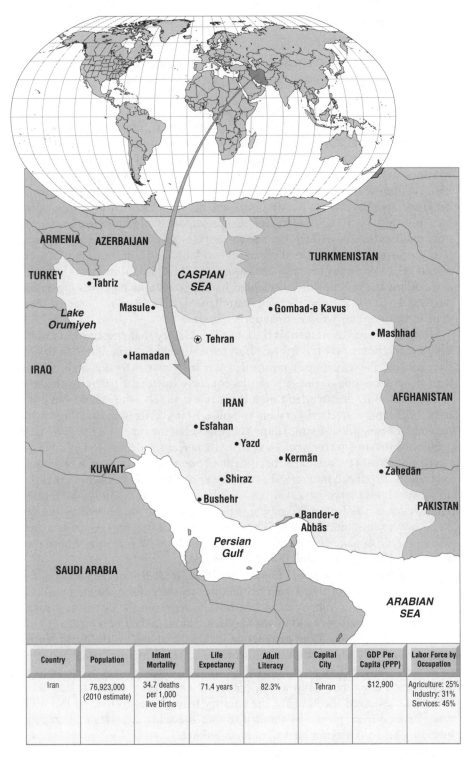

Country	Population	Infant Mortality	Life Expectancy	Adult Literacy	Capital City	GDP Per Capita (PPP)	Labor Force by Occupation
Iran	76,923,000 (2010 estimate)	34.7 deaths per 1,000 live births	71.4 years	82.3%	Tehran	$12,900	Agriculture: 25% Industry: 31% Services: 45%

MAP 10.3
Iran

Mousavi's 34 percent. Mousavi's supporters immediately charged the regime with massive fraud. Demonstrations erupted to protest the vote and grew into some of the largest ever seen, with one estimate claiming that 3 million Iranians took to the streets to object to the stolen election.

The regime used security forces to attack, arrest, imprison, torture, and kill demonstrators. One of those killed was 26-year-old Neda Agha-Soltani who was shot as she walked along a street in Tehran close to where demonstrations were taking place. A bystander filmed her last moments of life with his cell phone as she bled to death on the sidewalk. He posted them on YouTube and Facebook. Within hours she became known worldwide as the face of resistance to the Iranian regime. It is impossible to know with accuracy how many others have died. On the anniversary of the protests the following year the government blanketed the capital with hundreds of thousands of security forces to prevent memorial demonstrations honoring those who lost their lives. While the regime has intimidated its opponents, its base of support has narrowed and the Supreme Leader, **Ayatollah** Ali Khamenei, has become more dependent on security forces to suppress dissent.[70]

Iran's present government is the latest in a history that stretches back some 2,500 years. For most of its history, Iran was known as Persia. In the sixth century B.C. the Persian Empire controlled territory that extended well beyond Iran's current borders. But it was subsequently invaded first by Arabs who brought Islam to the area, and then by Turkic invaders who ruled from 1501 until 1722 and converted Persians to **Shiite Islam**. This is the smaller of the two major branches of Islam, Sunni Muslims being the other. Of the more than 1 billion Muslims in the world less than 10 percent are Shiites. The split between the two branches dates back to the seventh century over who should succeed the Prophet Muhammad as the leader of Islam. Shiites believe that this authority should have passed to his hereditary successors known as *Imams*. The twelfth of the *Imams* is known as the *Mahdi* who Shiites believe did not die, but went into hiding in 941. They believe he will reappear again as a messiah to establish just rule on earth. The clerics who now rule Iran believe they are the legitimate rulers until the *Mahdi* returns.

When European imperial powers, such as Great Britain and Russia, extended their influence into Persia in the nineteenth century, the ruling Turkic dynasty remained nominally in power. In fact, however, the British controlled large parts of its economy and financial system, and had their eyes on Persia's oil. In 1921, Colonel Reza Khan carried out a coup d'etat against the Turkic rulers with the aim of building an independent and strong state that could stand up to Western powers. He established the Pahlavi Dynasty in 1925. He tried to westernize Persia and build a modern army and bureaucracy. It was Reza Khan who changed the name of the country from Persia to Iran in 1935. He was removed from power by the British and Russians in 1941, and was followed by his son, Mohammed Reza Shah Pahlavi.

After World War II, Iran experienced a brief period of democratic politics. In 1951 Mohammad Mossadegh was elected prime minister. He tried to take control of Iran's oil industry from the British and use its revenues for national development. But his efforts were thwarted by the British government and the United States Central Intelligence Agency. They backed a coup d'etat that overthrew Mossadegh in 1953 and returned the Shah to power.

The Shah became a strong ally of the United States and pursued some progressive policies. He introduced Western law rather than Islamic *shari'a* law, dramatically increased the number of schools, strengthened the rights of women, and implemented land reforms transferring land from large landowners to farmers with small holdings. But his rule was brutal and authoritarian, sustained by a ruthlessly effective security service, and backed by one of the largest armies in the world.

The Shah's goal was to make Iran an economically developed modern country, but his policies angered many Iranians. They included shopkeepers and merchants in Iran's traditional bazaars who opposed his corruption and favoritism toward selected businesspeople, workers who derived few benefits from his policies, intellectuals and college educated middle-class Iranians who resented his oppressive authoritarianism, and conservative Islamic clerics who were opposed to westernization. The Shah's close ties to the United States guaranteed that anger aimed at the Shah would also be targeted at the United States.

In 1979, the Shah was overthrown by a revolution led by the Islamic cleric Ruhollah Khomeini. After the Shah was forced into exile, there was a ferocious struggle among the elements of Khomeini's coalition for control of the state. One group believed that the clerics most trained in Islamic jurisprudence should rule. This is the concept of ***velayat-e-faqih,*** or "guardianship of the jurisprudent," which holds that a cleric should be the leader of the country. Others wanted a secular democratic state in which elected legislators would make laws, not religious clerics claiming to speak for God.[71]

Khomeini and the clerics prevailed in the struggle over who would inherit the Iranian revolution. He supported students who took over the American Embassy in the capital city of Tehran and held U.S. diplomats hostage for 444 days. Khomeini praised the students for demonstrating to the world that Iran could stand up to "the Great Satan," as he called the United States. The clerics were also abetted by Iraq's attack on Iran in 1980. Khomeini used the war to rally Iranians to defend their country and spread their Shiite faith to neighboring countries. Khomeini died in 1989 after the war ended, but by then his regime was firmly in place. To make sure his vision survived his death, Khomeini and his close advisers devised state institutions to ensure the rule of the clerics. In designing the constitution they gave highest authority to nonelected offices held by clerics, but they also provided for an elected president and elected legislators. This mix of authoritarian and elective offices has created increasing political tensions since the late 1990s.

The State

The single most powerful office is that of the **Supreme Leader,** who is responsible for safeguarding the legacy of the Islamic Revolution of 1979. He ensures that government agencies "function in line with Islamic tenets and principles of the revolution."[72] He appoints the head of the judiciary and has direct control over the armed forces, which include the regular army and the Iranian Revolutionary Guards Corps (IRGC), or **Revolutionary Guards**. The Revolutionary Guards were created following the revolution because Ayatollah Khomeini did not trust the regular army. Their main responsibility is defending the revolution. They suppress protests, command Iran's missile force, and collect domestic and foreign intelligence.[73] The Guards also command the Basij Resistance Force, or **Basij,** composed of volunteers who help the Guards intimidate political opponents and enforce Islamic codes of conduct, including proper dress for women in public. The current Supreme Leader is Ayatollah Khamenei, whose name should not be confused with that of his predecessor, Ayatollah Khomeini. See Figure 10.1.

The Supreme Leader appoints the 6 religious members of the 12-member **Guardian Council**. The Council has the power to block parliamentary bills it believes are incompatible with Islamic law or in conflict with the constitution. It also decides who gets to run in parliamentary elections. A measure of its power is that in 2004 it disqualified around 2,000 candidates as part of a strategy to ensure that moderate opponents of the regime could not get on the ballot. Another powerful nonelected institution is the **Expediency Council**. Its members are also appointed by the Supreme Leader. It has the authority to arbitrate conflicts between the Guardian Council and the parliament. This authority has made it a very important decision-making institution.

Alongside these institutions that are not responsive to voters and reflect the power of the clerics are institutions whose officials are directly elected by voters. The **Assembly of Experts** is a popularly elected body that has the authority to elect the Supreme Leader and supervises his activities. This gives the impression that the voting population indirectly chooses the Supreme Leader, but this is not the case. Candidates for seats in the Assembly of Experts are carefully screened and approved by the Guardian Council, which is appointed by the Supreme Leader. Candidates who do not meet the approval of the Guardian Council are not allowed to run.

The **President** is the head of the executive branch of the government and is elected by popular vote for a four-year term. Presidents control the budget, and they appoint the cabinet and governors of provinces, both of which must be approved by parliament. Candidates can run for president only after being screened by the Supreme Leader and the Guardian Council and the Supreme Leader must ratify the voters' choice for president.

Iran has a single-house, or unicameral, parliament called the **Majles**. It has 290 members elected for four-year terms by popular vote. Unlike the office of president, women can be elected as members of the Majles. The Majles has the authority to approve the president's nominees for his cabinet, to question cabinet members about their ministries' policies, and pass legislation. But like presidential power, legislative power is hedged in on all sides by more powerful indirectly elected or appointed religious leaders.

The Iranian civil service is inefficient and weak. It does not fare well in comparison with other lower-middle-income Middle Eastern and North African countries. Only war-torn Iraq ranks lower in government effectiveness.

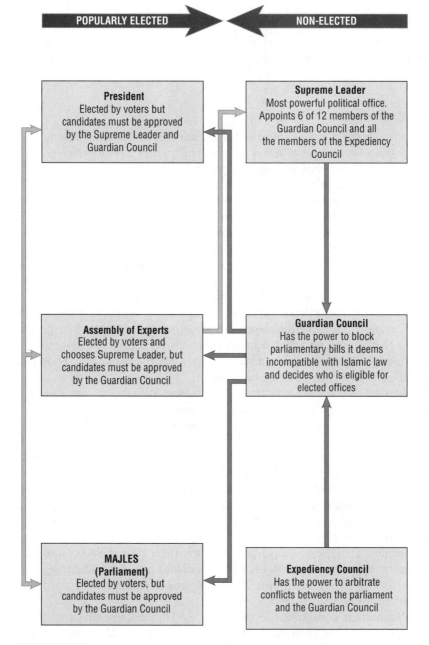

FIGURE 10.1
Iranian Political Institutions

One indicator of the bureaucracy's weakness is extremely high levels of corruption. In 2009, Transparency International rankings, Iran ranked among the top 10 most corrupt countries in the world. A popular Iranian saying is, "In the United States, people become rich and then go into politics; in Iran, people go into politics to become rich."[74]

State and Society

The struggle for political power in Iran centers on competition among factions rather than on competition among political parties for citizens' votes. Four loose political factions struggle for power in Iran. The boundaries between these factions are not clearly defined, and there are tensions between political leaders within the factions, but they form recognizable groupings in Iranian politics. The leaders of the first three factions are all influential clerics who were followers of Khomeini during the revolution. They have held a variety of powerful political positions since the revolution, and are now elderly. The leaders of the fourth faction come from a younger generation; this faction has more lay leaders than the other factions. The leaders of all four factions are committed to the principle of *velayat-e-faqih*. They are all "insiders," who want to maintain the present regime, but they differ on the best ways of doing so. The main points of difference are the appropriate balance of power between elected and nonelected institutions, cultural policy, economic policy, how much priority should be given to improving the lives of the poor, and relations with the United States and Europe.

At one end of the spectrum are **conservatives** who are opposed to democracy and insist that religious leaders retain power. They view "the essential purpose of the state as the realization of God's will on earth" and believe they best understand what God's will is.[75] They do not believe in individual rights or in a pluralism of ideas. They insist on strict dress codes for women, control of media and film to screen out decadent Western cultural influences, and a ban on alcohol sales. While they have been supportive of merchants in Iran's traditional bazaars, they have not supported the development of a modern industrial economy. They claim to be strongly committed to economic justice and improving the lives of the poor. In foreign policy, they pursue confrontation with the United States and Europe and are very strong supporters of Iran's nuclear program. Their best known leader is the current Supreme Leader Khamenei, and they have been the dominant faction since 1989.

Pragmatists comprise a second faction. They believe that the economic policies of the conservatives and their dismissal of elected institutions endanger the long-run stability and legitimacy of the regime. The pragmatists are concerned with promoting economic growth and draw their support from professionals, some members of the business community, and highly educated technocrats in the bureaucracy. They want to develop a competitive industrial economy and believe opening up Iran to foreign investment will further this goal. Better relations with the West are a necessary step in this direction. They believe economic growth will improve the lives of citizens more than providing government subsidies and other forms of government aid. Politically, they would like to see more power given to democratic institutions and less repression of dissent. Culturally, they are less restrictive than the conservatives and believe conservatives' rigid codes of conduct are antagonizing the support of Iran's younger population. The pragmatists' best known leader is Hashemi Rafsanjani. They had their greatest influence from 1989 to 1997 when Rafsanjani was President of Iran.

Reformists have gone the furthest of any of the factions in inching toward democracy. This faction believes that Islam and democracy can coexist. No one group of religious leaders can claim special insight into God's will that allows them to monopolize power. While they support the concept of *velayat-e-faqih*, they argue that the Supreme Leader "must defer to the elected branches of the government."[76] Reformists want to go even further than the pragmatists in loosening cultural controls, and improving relations with the West. Their best known leader is a mid-level cleric, Mohammed Khatami. This faction had its greatest influence when Khatami was president from 1997 to 2004, but has increasingly lost influence since then.

Finally, the most recent faction to emerge is the **principlists** faction. It is composed of a younger generation of leaders, many of whom served in the Revolutionary Guards and fought in the war with Iraq. They believe many of the leaders in the older generation who came to power after 1979 have become corrupt through power and wealth. They have targeted Hashemi Rafsanjani of the pragmatist faction and his followers in particular. The principlists argue for a return to the original principles of the revolution, "meaning strict moral enforcement, social justice, and anti-imperialism."[77] They are strongly critical of the United States and Israel and are strong backers of Iran's nuclear program. This faction was energized by the surprising popularity of the reformist Khatami during his first term as president, and alarmed by the growth of United States military force in neighboring Afghanistan after 2001 and in Iraq after 2003. This faction's best known leader is President Mahmoud Ahmadinejad. He was elected president in 2005 and again in 2009 with the backing of Supreme Leader Khamenei and the Revolutionary Guards and the Basij. By openly backing Ahmadinejad, Khamenei has undermined his role as an effective arbiter among the factions and even alienated some of the clerical elite within the regime.[78]

Leaders of the factions use elections to gain control of the presidency and parliament. Regularly scheduled elections for parliament and president allow candidates supporting differing policy positions to run for office but they campaign without benefit or help from well-organized, programmatic political parties. Ayatollah Khomeini banned all political parties in 1981 except for the Islamic Republic Party, which was then the ruling party of the clerics. Khomeini disbanded this party in 1987 because of growing divisions within the party and his fear that party politics might "polarize the society."[79] Political parties reemerged in Iran, although none of them have strong organizations, a large membership, or roots in society. Most are formed to promote a particular candidate and have no enduring organization. Their reemergence was tolerated because parties must now be approved by the Ministry of the Interior, which can deny them permits if the Ministry deems them anti-Islamic. This requirement guarantees that no party proposes significant change and even leaders of those with moderate views can be suppressed. During the fall of 2009 and spring of 2010, leaders of the three largest reformist parties were arrested and put in prison.[80]

Political leaders are linked to groups in society mainly through patron–client relations. Each of the factions has built up large patronage networks that penetrate deep into state agencies and extend out into society. They try to capture state agencies in order to reward their followers with jobs, gain access to state funds, and provide business opportunities for supporters. An example of how this system operates can be seen in the case of organizations that were formed to make connections between merchants in Iran's bazaars and clerics who supported Ayatollah Khomeini. When Khomeini came to power in 1979, the members of these organizations benefited by being given positions in the government and gaining access to assets seized from the Shah and his business supporters. They developed a vested interest in keeping the regime in power to further their own goals, rather than benefiting merchants as a group. Instead of using their power to represent the merchants of the bazaar as a social class or group of businesses with common interests, they used it to promote their own interests.[81]

There are a large number of business and professional associations in Iran, but they do not play an important a role in representing their members' interests to the state. Businesspeople tend to work through clientelist connections to seek particular benefits for themselves rather than working through business associations to represent their business sector collectively. Labor unions are in an even more difficult situation than businesspeople. Unions are tightly controlled by labor laws, and independent labor unions are not permitted in Iran. Workers can establish Islamic Labor Councils, but the leaders of these councils must be approved by a state agency. Union leaders who lead strikes can be imprisoned. In recent years conservative governments have cracked down on labor unions with increasing harshness.

Social movements have emerged as an alternative way of making demands on the state. The best example is the **Green Movement,** which was formed during the 2009 presidential election. Its primary goal was preventing the reelection of President Mahmoud Ahmadinejad, and its longer-term goal was slowing the accumulation of political power by the conservative and principlist factions. The groups making up the movement organized large rallies to support Mir Hossein Mousavi during the election campaign, and then organized huge protests when the election was stolen. From a movement in support of Mousavi, prior to the election, it was transformed into a civil rights movement after the election. It originally drew support mainly from university students, professionals, parts of the urban middle class, and women's groups, but after the election its support broadened to include both the middle and working class, as well as some clerics. Like many social movements, it is decentralized and diverse, with supporters who want to overthrow the current regime, and others who prefer a more gradual approach to reform. The regime responded violently to the challenge **the Green Movement** posed, using beatings, arrests, torture, and murder. It is unclear whether it can survive such repression.

Political Culture

Akbar Ganji, a leading Iranian political dissident, draws on congruence theory to argue that a democratic political culture "based on mutual trust, tolerance of diversity and difference, and readiness to compromise is a precondition for a stable democracy."[82] All are lacking in Iran.

Iranian political culture is distinguished by a combination of great pride in the country's long history and accomplishments, and extreme resentment toward the foreign countries that have humiliated Iran. It is a potent mix that Iran's current leaders use to proclaim Iran's regional and international importance and to fiercely defend its independence from efforts by outside powers to influence its policies. They have exploited these feelings to gain support for their nuclear program in the face of criticisms by the United States and other countries by drawing on Iranians' resentment of past humiliations inflicted on them by Britain, Russia, and the United States.

Iran's version of Islam has also shaped its political culture. Shiites are a tiny minority of all the Muslims in the world. Their minority status has led to exaggerated pride in their uniqueness and defensiveness because of their vulnerability as a minority. Conservative clerics draw upon Shiite puritanism to argue for the restoration of values and the way of life preached by the Prophet. But Shiite Islam has no equivalent of the Pope who can speak for all Shiite Muslims. Shiite religious scholars take different views on important political and religious issues. Even though Ayatollah Khomeini was the leader of the Islamic Revolution, his views were openly challenged by other clerics, who supported giving a bigger role to democratic institutions and greater rights for women,[83] Ayatollah Khamaeini, the current Supreme Leader, has also been criticized on the same grounds by other clerics.

A clear majority of Iranians desire a democratic political system. A 2005 World Values Survey found that over 92 percent agreed that having a democratic political system was a "very good" or "fairly good idea." But self-expression values important for creating and sustaining democracy are in short supply. One of these values is trust in other people. Only 11 percent agreed most people could be trusted while 89 percent believed one "can't be too careful" in dealing with others. Another self-expression value is tolerance toward people with different lifestyles. In comparison with citizens in Latin democracies, such as Brazil and Chile, Iranians are much less tolerant of people with different religious and sexual preferences. Iranians do not believe that most other citizens will obey laws and carry out their civic obligations. Finally, many Iranians long for a strong leader, with 74 percent agreeing that having a strong leader is "good" or "very good."[84] This political culture persists because political elites have not "developed a state of law that made life predictable and governed by rules rather than personal connections."[85]

Political elites' promises have also led many Iranians to believe it is the government's responsibility to provide jobs, decent wages, and low prices for food and other necessities. Ayatollah Khomeini repeatedly promised to help poor Iranians by keeping prices low and subsidizing their incomes. The current Supreme Leader, Khamenei, President Ahmedinejad, and other leaders have echoed these promises. In a 2005, World Values Survey Iranians were asked to locate themselves on a ten-point scale with 1 being "people should take more responsibility to provide for themselves" and 10 being "the government should take more responsibility." The answers tilted strongly toward government taking more responsibility. The same survey found there was very strong support for having the government tax the rich and subsidize the poor.

Coupled with these views is considerable distrust of private ownership of business, especially of large industrial corporations. The survey found a higher percentage of respondents believed that government ownership of business should be increased than those who thought private ownership should be increased. These values stem from decades of experience with the Shah's version of crony capitalism as well as the attacks of Khomeini and subsequent clerical leaders on the exploitative nature of capitalism. President Ahmadinejad has made improving the rights of poor Iranians the major issue of his presidency. He has drawn on his own background as the son of a blacksmith, as well as teachings in Shiite Islam to condemn the rich for exploiting the poor. Although he received a degree from a leading Iranian university, he lives in the same house in a lower-middle-class neighborhood that he lived in before he became president. He has a bad haircut and wears cheap suits, shoes, and windbreaker when he appears in public. The message to the working class is, "I am one of you."[86]

Political Economy

Ayatollah Khomeini and his successors have made progress in achieving their goal of improving the lives of poor Iranians. Poverty rates have dropped considerably and access to education and health care have improved for poor families. Girls born in poor families in rural areas have been some of the main beneficiaries of expanded educational opportunities, but access to educational opportunities have expanded for girls in general. A higher percentage of women graduate from college than men. The Islamic Republic has also reduced infant mortality rates by focusing on providing clean water and health care services to villages, even in remote areas of the country.[87]

Governments have achieved these goals by using an "interventionist-redistributive social contract"[88] in which the state intervenes extensively in the economy to subsidize the costs of key food items such as bread and sugar in return for support. Middle-class Iranians who own cars also benefit from these food subsidies, and benefit more than the poor from subsidies that keep the price of gas artificially low.

Some of the major beneficiaries of Iran's interventionist state have been organizations with links to the conservative faction, such as the semipublic charitable organizations known as *bonyads*. One of the largest and best known is the Foundation of the Oppressed and Disabled. This *bonyad* and others have moved far beyond charitable activities. The Islamic Republic funded the *bonyads* with assets seized from wealthy Iranians and the Shah, and the *bonyads* used these assets to invest in all sectors of the Iranian economy including real estate, construction, transportation, and automobile companies. They now control assets worth billions of dollars and some of their directors are multimillionaires. The *bonyads* are not taxed and have no government oversight, even though they are funded directly from government budgets. They are accountable only to the Supreme Leader.[89]

Another organization that has benefited is the Revolutionary Guards. Like the *bonyads* they have extended their activities well beyond their original mission of defending the revolution into a wide range of commercial activities including construction, mining, and defense industries. Their commercial activities have flourished since Ahmadinejad became president in 2005. He has approved hundreds of construction and petrochemical contracts for companies owned by the Guards. These contracts are worth billions of dollars.[90] Like the *bonyads*, they are accountable only to the Supreme Leader.

This interventionist-redistributive political economy is funded largely with oil and gas revenues that provide 70 percent of the government budget and is dominated by the state, which controls some 65 to 70 percent of the economy. This political economy allows political elites to make many of the key decisions about how state revenues are allocated without having to be responsible to citizens. State-owned banks are used to make loans to politically favored firms at very low interest rates. The government funds large infrastructure projects that can be doled out to businesses in return for kickbacks. Finally, the government controls licensing for imports. Politically favored firms get monopolies over the import of key consumer goods.

These features have led to a highly inefficient and troubled economy. Iran's heavy dependence on oil makes it vulnerable to shifting prices of oil in international markets. It has had slow economic growth rates, high inflation, and high unemployment. Real GDP growth rates have declined every year since 2005 when Ahmadinejad won the presidency. Inflation is officially said to be 12 percent per year, but is in all probability more than 20 percent. Unemployment is officially 12 percent, but nonofficial estimates put it in the 24 percent range.[91] These economic problems are compounded by the disproportionate number of young people in the population and a labor force that grows by 800,000 new job seekers each year. Iran needs a growth rate of approximately 6.5 percent per year to employ them, but its growth rate has been well below this.[92] Large numbers of young people have left Iran for the United States, Canada, and Europe, and thousands more seek to leave each year in search of better job prospects.

Making changes to improve productivity are very difficult politically. Ending subsidies is difficult because of ideological commitments and fear of antagonizing key parts of the regime's political base.[93] There are also powerful individual leaders and organizations such as *bonyads* and the Revolutionary Guard who benefit from the present political economy. In early 2010, President Ahmadinejad proposed phasing out price subsidies and using half of the revenue saved by ending the subsidies for targeted cash transfers to citizens. Most of the transfers would go to poorer citizens. The proposal met strong resistance from groups who would lose from the change. It also became apparent that the Iranian state lacked information needed to decide who would qualify for cash transfers as well as the administrative capacity to enact such a plan efficiently.[94]

The Iranian regime has had success in improving citizens' capabilities in education and health. Poorer Iranians have benefited in particular. But the means the regime has used have created extensive economic and political problems. Unemployment and inflation rates are high, and the economy is overwhelmingly dependent on oil revenues and vulnerable to rises and falls in the price of oil. Politically, Iran has become increasingly authoritarian since 2004. Its experience demonstrates the difficulty authoritarian regimes can encounter when they try to use competitive multiparty elections as a means of winning legitimacy. Even when rulers tilt the playing field in the regime's favor, elections can get out of hand as they did in Iran in 2009. The leaders of the regime then have to either let the results stand or rig them and risk mass demonstrations. Iran's leaders chose the latter course. They have used security forces to suppress open dissent, but their base of support is possibly the narrowest it has been since 1979. The clerics are becoming increasingly dependent on the Revolutionary Guards and Basij to hold on to power as they become increasingly authoritarian.[95]

COMPARING CAPABILITIES AMONG NIGERIA, BRAZIL, AND IRAN

We profiled Nigeria, Brazil, and Iran because they typify different political models found among less developed countries. Nigeria typifies weakly institutionalized democracies, Brazil has many of the features of other electoral democracies, and Iran is a variant of electoral authoritarianism that has moved in an increasingly authoritarian direction. A comparison of how these countries perform in terms of our criteria for the Good Society provides clues as to which types of political regimes better meet the standards of the Good Society.

Physical Well-Being

In Chapter 1, we argued that infant mortality rates are the best indicator of well-being. Current infant mortality rates in Brazil, Iran, and Nigeria are correlated with the level of economic development: the higher the per capita

TABLE 10.2

Infant Mortality Rates per 1,000 Live Births in 1980, 1990, and 2008

	1965	1980	1990	2008
Brazil	107	72	46	18
Iran	156	89	55	27
Nigeria	157	117	120	96

Source: World Bank, World Development Indicators. www.google.com/publicdata. Accessed June 18, 2010.

income the lower the poverty rate. See Table 10.2. But a long-term perspective reveals important differences among the countries. Iran and Nigeria had almost identical infant mortality rates in 1965 but Iran brought its rate down much more quickly than Nigeria. A second difference among the countries is that in both Brazil and Iran infant mortality rates followed a steady downward path. They did not in Nigeria. The infant mortality rate in Nigeria dropped from 1965 until 1975, but then leveled off during the years of military rule. It did not begin dropping again until the late 1990s. Third, authoritarian governments have had very different levels of success in lowering infant mortality. Brazil and Iran both reduced infant mortality under authoritarian governments, but Nigeria had a terrible record under military rule.

Informed Decision Making

The pattern for literacy is similar to that for infant mortality rates with the higher the income per capita, the better the results. As in the case of infant mortality, however, the current level of literacy hides patterns within countries. One of Brazil's biggest successes has been increasing school attendance and literacy among children from poor families. One of Iran's biggest successes has been increasing educational access for girls. Nigeria followed the same pattern in literacy that it did with infant mortality. There was no progress in improving adult literacy in Nigeria during the last decade of military rule, but there has been improvement under democratic governments. See Table 10.3.

TABLE 10.3

Adult Literacy Rates, 15 Years and Older, Selected Years (Percentage)

	1980	1991	2000	2007
Brazil	75%	—	86%	90%
Iran	—	65%	77% (2002)	82% (2006)
Nigeria	—	55%	55% (2003)	60% (2008)

Source: World Bank, World Development Indicators. http://data.worldbank.org/country. Accessed June 18, 2010.

> ◤ **TABLE 10.4**
>
> **Homicide Rates in Brazil, Iran and Nigeria per 100,000 Population**
>
> | | |
> |---|---|
> | Brazil | 30.8 |
> | Nigeria | 17.7 |
> | Iran | 2.9 |
>
> Source: Data set for *The Good Society*

Safety

Safety, as operationally defined by homicide rates, does not fit the previous patterns in which the wealthier country had the best record. There are big differences among the countries and Brazil, the wealthiest, has the highest homicide rate. See Table 10.4.

These data must be treated with some skepticism, but they give a general indication of overall differences in homicide rates among the countries. What they do not give is a sense of the overall level of safety in these countries, which differs by region and social class. Nigerians living in parts of the oil-producing Niger Delta or in the city of Jos, on the borderline between predominantly Muslim and Christian populations, are not likely to feel as safe as those in other parts of the country. Poor Brazilians living in huge urban slums known as *favelas* are not as likely to feel safe as wealthy Brazilians living in exclusive neighborhoods. Nor can Iranians who have had the courage to openly challenge the regime likely feel as safe as regime supporters.

Democracy

Individuals' ability to participate effectively in political choices that govern their lives is essential for sustaining conditions that improve their health, education, and safety. Authoritarian governments can make decisions to improve these capabilities, as they have in Iran, but without the right to political participation, free speech, and associations, citizens cannot be assured that governments will continue to work to improve capabilities. There are considerable differences in the ability to participate effectively among Nigeria, Brazil, and

> ◤ **TABLE 10.5**
>
> **Voice and Accountability in Brazil, Nigeria, and Iran 2008**
>
> | | Voice and Accountability Score | Percentile Rank |
> |---|---|---|
> | Brazil | +0.51 | 61.1% |
> | Nigeria | −0.60 | 31.3% |
> | Iran | −1.48 | 8.2% |

TABLE 10.6	
Polity IV Scores for Brazil, Nigeria, and Iran, 2008	
Brazil	+8
Nigeria	+4
Iran	−6

Iran. One way to measure this is to use the World Bank Governance Indicators Dataset for "voice and accountability." Countries were scored on a −2.50 to 2.50 scale on this index. The higher a country's score, the more its citizens were deemed to have "voice and accountability." The percentile rank shows the percentage of countries ranked below the country in Table 10.5.

Measured this way approximately 60 percent of countries had lower voice and accountability than Brazil. Only 8 percent scored lower than Iran.

An alternative is to use Polity IV ratings for 2008 measuring levels of democracy with +10 being the most democratic and −10 being the most authoritarian. See Table 10.6.

In summary, with the exception of homicide, Brazil does a better job than Nigeria or Iran in creating conditions that enhance the capabilities of its citizens. Overall, electoral democracies perform better at enhancing capabilities than weak democracies because of a combination of higher economic development and more institutionalized democracy. All electoral democracies do not perform better than all electoral authoritarian regimes in each category of capabilities. Some electoral authoritarian regimes such as Malaysia's have done very well in creating conditions that enhance the capabilities of their citizens.

CONCLUSION

In this chapter we have examined three common types of regimes in less developed countries, with a representative country from each of them. Our conclusions about the performance of different kinds of regimes have to be tentative because they are based on case studies rather than large samples of countries from each type of regime. One conclusion is that electoral democracies tend to do a better job of enhancing citizens' capabilities than electoral authoritarian regimes.

The second conclusion is that authoritarian regimes do not have an advantage over democracies in promoting economic development. Contrary to claims that authoritarian regimes can make decisions quickly and effectively because they do not have to be concerned about offending vested interests, we saw that neither the military in Nigeria nor the clerics in Iran could make decisions quickly and effectively. The military in Nigeria was hampered by patron–client politics and massive rent seeking. The clerics in Iran are hampered by factional struggles and rent seeking. Many leading clerics have personal interests in maintaining Iran's present economic policies and so do the constituencies with which they have close ties, such as the *bonyads* and Revolutionary Guards. In contrast, democratically elected governments in Nigeria have made economic decisions that have brought strong economic growth in the past decade. Brazil's democratically elected governments have made tough economic decisions that seem to have ended Brazil's perpetual economic crises and contributed to a decade of rapid growth.

Finally, while Brazil and Iran have both brought down infant mortality rates and increased educational opportunities for children of poor families, poor Brazilians have more opportunity to participate effectively in political choices that affect their lives than poor Iranians. The poor in Brazil form an important voting constituency of the Workers Party. Leaders of the Workers Party strive to improve their capabilities not just because of ideological commitment, but because they need their votes to win office. Competitive elections are decisive in determining who holds the most powerful offices in Brazil, and they give the poor political leverage. In Iran, competitive elections are not decisive in determining who holds the most powerful political offices or in shaping regime policies. The Supreme Leader and other nonelected clerics, not elected leaders, make the ultimate policy decisions. While President Ahmadinejad appealed to the poor for votes in the 2005 and 2009 presidential elections, and promised to bring them benefits from oil revenues, it was nonelected leaders who held the power to determine whether these promises were implemented or not. As long as the Supreme Leader and other powerful conservative clerics support Iran's interventionist-redistributive political economy, the regime will make efforts to improve the incomes and capabilities of poor citizens, but poor citizens in Iran do not have as much political leverage in Iran as they have in Brazil.

mypoliscikit EXERCISES

Apply what you learned in this chapter on MyPoliSciKit (www.mypoliscikit.com).

 CHAPTER MENU ICON
Review this chapter using learning objectives, chapter summaries, practice tests, and more.

 VIDEO CASE STUDIES
Analyze recent world affairs by watching streaming video from major news providers

 FLASHCARD ICON
Learn the key terms in this chapter; you can test yourself by term or definition.

 COMPARATIVE EXERCISES
Compare political ideas, behaviors, institutions, and policies worldwide.

CRITICAL THINKING QUESTIONS

1. Why has Nigeria had so little success in achieving economic and human development despite huge revenues from oil?
2. Brazil is set to become a major oil exporter in the next few decades. What are the likely effects of dramatic increases in oil revenues on Brazil's politics?

3. Why are broad-based associations and political parties more important for the improvement of capabilities for poor Brazilians than for wealthier Brazilians?
4. If the goal is to improve capabilities, does it really make any difference whether poor families in Iran get better health care through authoritarian means or democratic ones?
5. Why have reformers in Iran not been more successful in their struggles with conservatives and principlists to liberalize politics and cultural policy?

KEY TERMS

SUGGESTED READINGS

Atul Kohli, *State-Directed Development: Political Power and Industrialization in the Global Periphery* (New York: Cambridge University Press, 2004). A very good comparative study of why Nigera, Brazil, and other less developed countries have had such different development outcomes.

Kurt Weyland, *Democracy without Equity: Failures of Reform in Brazil* (Pittsburgh, PA: University of Pittsburgh Press, 1996). Explains why democracy has not led to greater improvements in the lives of poor Brazilians.

David D, Ferranti, Guillermo E. Perry, and Francisco Ferreira. *Inequality in Latin America and the Caribbean: Breaking with History?* (Washington, D.C: World Bank, 2003). Explores origins and persistence of economic and social inequality in Latin America and the prospects for alleviating inequality.

Afshin Molavi, *The Soul of Iran* (New York: W. W. Norton and Company, 2002). A very readable introduction to Iranian history and culture that combines interviews with Iranians from different backgrounds and social classes.

Ray Takeyh, *Hidden Iran: Paradox and Power in the Islamic Republic* (New York: Henry Holt and Company, 2006). A very good discussion of Ayatollah Khomeini's continuing influence on Iran and descriptions of the main political factions.

NOTES

1. Simon Long, "Two Concepts of Liberty," in "Survey: India and China," *The Economist* (March 3, 2005); Larry Diamond, "Thinking About Hybrid Regimes, *Journal of Democracy* 13:2 (April 2002), p. 28; and Pranab Bardhan, "Democacy and Distributive Politics in India," unpublished manuscript. www.globetrotter. berkeley.edu/macarthur/inequality/papers/#Bardhan. Accessed July 2, 2010.

2. Somini Sangupta, "Education Push Yields Little for India's Poor," *The New York Times* (January 17, 2008).

3. Data are from World Bank, *World Development Report 2009* (New York: Oxford University Press, 2009) and CIA *World Fact Book*.

4. Daniel N. Posner and Daniel J. Young, "The Institutionalization of Political Power in Africa," *Journal of Democracy* 18:3 (July 2007), p. 127.

5. World Bank, "2008 World Development Indicators. Poverty Data. A Supplement to World Development Indicators 2008 (World Bank: Washington, D.C., 2008) p. 20. www.worldbank.org.

6. CIA World Fact Book. https://www.cia.gov/library/publications/the-world-factbook/index.html, accessed June 21, 2010.

7. Pierre Englebert, "Pre-Colonial Institutions, Post-Colonial States, and Economic Development in Tropical Africa," *Political Research Quarterly* 53:1 (March 2000).

8. Atul Kohli, *State-Directed Development: Political Power and Industrialization in the Global Periphery* (New York: Cambridge University Press, 2004), pp. 301–306.

9. Ibid., p. 306.

10. Catherine Boone, "States and Ruling Classes in Postcolonial Africa: The Enduring Contradictions of Power," in Joel S. Migdal, Atul Kohli, and Vivienne Shue, editors, *State Power and Social Forces: Domination and Transformation in the Third World* (New York: Cambridge University Press, 1994), pp. 117–118.

11. William Reno, *Warlord Politics and African States* (Boulder, CO: Lynne Rienner Publishers, 1998), p. 21.

12. Kohli, pp. 314–315.

13. Lydia Polgreen, "Africa's Crisis of Democracy," *The New York Times* April 23, 2007.

14. "The Good, the Bad, and the President," *The Economist* (January 5, 2008), p. 38. See also Richard Joseph, "Challenges of a 'Frontier' Region," pp. 103–104.

15. Wole Soyinka, *The Open Sore of a Continent* (New York: Oxford University Press, 1997), p. 15.

16. Daniel N. Posner and Daniel J. Young, "The Institutionalization of Political Power in Africa," p. 126.

17. Darren Kew and Peter Lewis, "Nigeria," in *Introduction to Comparative Politics*, 3rd edition, ed. Mark Kesselman, Joel Krieger, and William A. Joseph (New York, Houghton Mifflin Company, 2004) p. 547.

18. Richard Joseph, "Nigeria's Season of Uncertainty," *Current History* (May 2010), p. 181.

19. Lydia Polgreen, "Nigeria Turns from Harsher Side of Islamic Law," *New York Times*, December 1, 2007.

20. "Master of His Commanders," *The Economist* (November 7, 2008).

21. Paul Collier, *The Bottom Billion: Why the Poorest Countries Are Falling Apart and What Can Be Done About It* (New York: Oxford University Press, 2007), p. 46.

22. "Big Men, Big Fraud, and Big Trouble," *The Economist* (April 28, 2007), pp. 55–56, 58.

23. Richard Joseph, "Challenges of a 'Frontier' Region," *Journal of Democracy* 19:2 (April 2008), p. 96.

24. Larry Diamond, "Nigeria's Federal Democracy: Will It Survive?" Presentation for the United States Institute of Peace, May 20, 2002. /papers, accessed June 12, 2010.

25. World Values Survey, 2000 http://www.wvsevsdb.com/wvs/WVSAnalizeQuestion.jsp, accessed June 12, 2010.

26. Larry Diamond, "Nigeria's Federal Democracy: Will It Survive?" p. 5. Accessed June 12, 2010.

27. Paul Collier, *The Bottom Billion: Why the Poorest Countries Are Falling Behind and What Can Be Done about It?* (New York: Oxford University Press, 2007), p. 46.

28. Larry Diamond, "Nigeria's Federal Democracy: Will It Survive?" p. 6.

29. Chris Kwaja and Darren Kew, "Analysis: Nigeria's Smoldering Crisis in Jos." http://web1.globalpost.com, accessed June 13, 2010.

30. Lydia Polgreen "Africa's Crisis of Democracy," *The New York Times,* April 23, 2007

31. Richard Joseph, Richard Joseph, "Challenges of a 'Frontier' Region," p. 182.

32. Paul Collier, *The Bottom Billion*, p. 49.

33. Charles Roxburgh, Nobert Dorr, Acha Leke, Amine Tazi-Riffi, Arend van Wamelen, Susan Ward, Mutsa, Chirongsa, Tarik Alatovik, Charles Atkins, Nadia Terfous, and Till Zeino-Mahmalat, "Lions on the Loose: The Progress and Potential of African Economies." The McKinsey Global Institute, June 2010, pp. 10, 30–31.

34. Larry Diamond, "Nigeria's Federal Democracy: Will It Survive?" p. 8.

35. Freedom House, *Freedom in the World*, 2009. www.freedomhouse.org, accessed June 30, 2010.

36. David De Ferranti, Guillermo E. Perry, and Francisco Ferreira, *Inequality in Latin America: Breaking with History?* p. 137.

37. Larry Diamond, "Thinking Abour Hybrid Regimes," *The Journal of Democracy* 13:2 (April 2002), Table 2.

38. Alexei Barrionuevo, "Violence in the Newest Olympic City Rattles Brazil," *The New York Times* October 20, 2009.

39. David De Ferranti et al., *Inequality in Latin America*, pp. 112–122, 186.

40. Kohli, p. 171.

41. Ben Ross Schneider, "The *Dessarollista* State in Brazil and Mexico," in Meredith Woo-Cumings, *The Developmental State* (Ithaca, NY: Cornell University Press, 1999), pp. 291–293.

42. Alfred P. Montero, "Brazil," in William A. Joseph, Mark Kesselman, and Joel Krieger, *Introduction to Politics of the Developing World* , 3rd ed. (New York: Houghton Mifflin Company, 2004), p. 219.

43. Information on the judiciary is from Charles H. Blake, *Politics in Latin America: The Quests for Development, Liberty, and Justice* (Boston: Houghton Mifflin Company, 2005), p. 179.

44. Ibid., p. 180.

45. Kurt Weyland, *Democracy Without Equity*, pp. 55–56.

46. Ibid., p. 4.

47. Frances Hagopian, Carlos Gervasoni, and Juan Andres Moraes, "From Patronage to Program: The Emergence of Party-Oriented Legislators in Brazil," *Comparative Political Studies* 42:3 (March 2009), p. 361.

48. Ibid., pp. 160–161.

49. Ibid., pp. 273–274.

50. "Political forces: Country Briefings, Brazil," *The Economist* (April 6, 2004), Web edition.

51. Mala Htun, "From 'Racial Democracy' to Affirmative Action: Changing State Policy on Race in Brazil," *Latin American Research Review* 39:1 (February 2004), p. 61.

52. Mala Htun, "Racial Quotas for a 'Racial Democracy,'" *NACLA Report on the Americas* (January/February 2005), p. 21.

53. Ibid., p. 20.

54. Mala Htun, "From 'Racial Democracy' to Affirmative Action," p. 63.

55. Ibid., p. 64.

56. Ibid., pp. 75–76.
57. Mala Htun, "Racial Quotas for a 'Racial Democracy,'" p. 24.
58. Schneider, p. 289.
59. http://www.wvsevsdb.com/wvs/WVSAnalizeQuestion.jsp, accessed June 21, 2010.
60. http://www.wvsevsdb.com/wvs/WVSAnalizeQuestion.jsp, accessed June 21, 2010.
61. Ben Ross Schneider, "The *Desarrollista* State in Brazil and Mexico," pp. 280–288.
62. Ibid., p. 282.
63. World Bank, "Brazil: Country Brief," www.worldbank.org.
64. James McGuire, "Democracy, Social Policy, and Mortality Decline in Brazil," Paper prepared for delivery at the 23rd Congress of the Latin American Studies Association, Washington, D.C., September 6–8, 2001, p. 21.
65. Ibid., p. 23.
66. Larry Diamond," Thinking About Hybrid Regimes," *The Journal of Democracy*, 13:2 (April 2002), p. 24.
67. Jason Brownlee, *Authoritarianism in an Age of Democratization* (New York: Cambridge University Press, 2007), pp. 64–72, 157–181.
68. Nikolai Petrov, Masha Lipman, and Henry E. Hale, "Overmanaged Democracy: Governance Implications of Hybrid Regimes," Carnegie Endowment for International Peace, Russia and Eurasia Program, Number 106, February, 2010.
69. Iran combines authoritarianism with competitive elections, but its type of regime has been difficult to classify. It can be classified as a theocracy because religious leaders are the rulers. The political scientists Marc Morje Howard and Philip G. Roessler classifed it as a competitive authoritarian regime in the late 1990s. Francis Fukuyama categorized it as an electoral authoritarian regime in 2010, but Steven Levitsky and Lucan Way prefer to call it a tutelary regime because the un-elected clerics have such strong veto power. See Marc Morje Howard and Philip G. Roessler, "Liberalizing Electoral Outcomes in Competitive Authoritarian Regimes," *American Journal of Political Science* 52:2 (April 2006), p. 370; Francis Fukuyama, "Iran, Islam and the Rule of Law," *Wall Street Journal* (June 27, 2009); and Steven Levitsky and Lucan A. Way, "Autocracy by Democratic Rules: The Dynamics of Competitive Authoritarianism in the Post-Cold War Era," Paper Prepared for the Conference, "Mapping the Great Zone: Clientelism and the Boundary between Democratic and Democratizing," Columbia University, April 4–5, 2003. [This is a revised version of a paper prepared for the Annual Meeting of the American Political Science Association, Boston, MA, August 28–31, 2002, p. 4.
70. Karim Sadjadpour, "Iran—One Year after the Disputed Election and Violent Crackdown," June 11, 2010. www.carnegieendowment.org, accessed June 15, 2010.
71. Reuel Marc Gerecht, "The Koran and the Ballot Box," *The New York Times* (June 21, 2009).
72. Khamenei speech entitled "Reforms, Strategies, and Challenges" quoted in Karim Sadjadpour, "Reading Khamenei: The World View of Iran's Most Powerful Leader," (Washington, DC: Carnegie Endowment for International Peace, 2008), p. 8.
73. Greg Bruno, "Iran's Revolutionary Guards," Council on Foreign Relations Backgrounder (June 22, 2009). www.cfr.org.
74. Cited in David E. Thaler, Alireza Nader, Shahram Chubin, Jerrold D. Green, Charlotte Lynch, and Frederi Wehrey l, *Mullahs, Guards, and Bonyads: An Exploration of Iranian Leadership* Dynamics (Santa Monica, CA: RAND National Defense Research Institute, 2010), p. 37.
75. This discussion of the first three factions draws on Ray Takeyh, *Hidden Iran* pp. 31–57.

76. Ray Takeyh, *Hidden Iran*, p. 48.
77. Kjetil Bjorvatin and Kjetil Selvik, "Destructive Competition: Factionalism and Rent-Seeking in Iran," *World Development* 36:11 (2008), p. 2316
78. Kevan Harris, "Arjomand: The Critical Turn of Ulema-State Relations," PBS *Frontline: Tehran Bureau*, April 11, 2010.
79. Razavi, "The Road to Party Politics in Iran," *Middle Eastern Studies* 46:1 (2010), pp. 32–35, 38.
80. Arash Aramesh, "Iran Paralyzes Political Parties by Arresting Leaders, March 23, 2010. www.insideiran.org, accessed June 1, 2010.
81. Arang Keshavarzian, "Regime Loyalty and *Bazaari* Representation under the Islamic Republic: Dilemmas of the Society of Islamic Coalition," *International Journal of Middle East Studies* 41 (2009), pp. 232–236.
82. Akbar Ganji, "The Struggle against Sultanism," *Journal of Democracy* 16:4 (October 2005), pp. 40–41.
83. Hooman Majd, *The Ayatollah Begs to Differ: The Paradox of Modern Iran* (New York: Anchor Books, 2009), pp. 214–215.
84. World Values Survey. www.worldvaluessurvey.org.
85. H.E. Chelabi and Arang Keshavarzian, "Politics in Iran," in *Comparative Politics Today: A World View*, 9th edition, ed. Gabriel A. Almond, G. Bingham Powell, Jr., Russell Dalton, and Kaare Strom (New York: Pearson Longman Publishers, 2008), p. 581.
86. Hooman Majd, *The Ayatollah Begs to Differ*, pp. 29–30.
87. World Bank, World Development Indicators. www.google.com/publicdata. Accessed June 25, 2010.
88. The phrase is from T. Yousef, "Employment, Development and the Social Contract in the Middle East and North Africa." Technical report, Washington, D.C. 2004, cited in Dvjavad Salhehi-Isfahani, "Revolution and Redistribution in Iran: Poverty and Inequality 25 Years Later," Department of Economics, Virginia Tech University, August 2006, p. 4.
89. David E. Thaler et. al., *Mullahs, Guards, and Bonyads*, pp. 56–58; and Bjorvatin and Selvik, "Destructive Competition: Factionalism and Rent-Seeking in Iran," World Development 36:11 (2008)," p. 2317.
90. Jerry Guo, "Letter from Tehran: Iran's New Hard-Liners," *Foreign Affairs* (September 30, 2009). www.foreignaffairs.org.
91. Jahangir Amuzegar, "Iran's Economy in Turmoil," International Economic Bulletin (March 2010). http://www.carnegieendowment.org/publications/index.cfm?fa=view&id=40354
92. Kjetil Bjorvatn and Kjetil Selvik, "Destructive Competition: Factionalism and Rent-Seeking in Iran," p. 2315.
93. Ray Takeyh, *Hidden Iran*, p. 38.
94. Kevan Harris, "The Politics of Subsidy Reform in Iran," *Middle East Report* (Spring 2010). http://merip.org/mer/mer254/harris.html
95. Elliot Hen-Tov, "Understanding Iran's New Authoritarianism," *The Washington Quarterly* 30:1 (Winter 2006-2007), pp. 176-177 and Kevan Harris, "Arjomand: The Critical Turn of Ulema-State Relations." PBS Front Line, Tehran Bureau, April 11, 2010.

Communism, Postcommunism, and the Good Society

INTRODUCTION

On April 20, 1975, a long line of North Vietnamese tanks rolled into Saigon, the capital of South Vietnam, accompanied by large numbers of troops. The Communist Party of Vietnam had succeeded in its decades-long struggle to unify Vietnam under its leadership. The event was cause for great celebration in North Vietnam. It was a cause for alarm in the United States. Many American policy makers feared that other countries in Southeast Asia, including Malaysia, Thailand, and Indonesia would be the next to fall to communist control like dominoes lined up in a row.

A domino effect did not occur in Southeast Asia. A domino effect did occur in Eastern Europe 15 years later when communist party rule collapsed in one country after another in rapid succession during 1989. Two years later, the communist regime lost power in the Soviet Union, where the communists had first come to power. The republics that had formed the Soviet Union broke up into individual countries with Russia as the largest. By 1992, there were only five communist regimes left in the world: China, Cuba, Laos, North Korea, and Vietnam. All of the countries that had been ruled by a communist party faced the task of remaking their political and economic institutions. The remaining communist regimes faced the task of trying to understand what had gone wrong in Eastern Europe and the Soviet Union and making changes to ensure they did not follow those communist regimes into oblivion.

This chapter is divided into three parts. The first examines the institutional features that defined communist regimes for much of the twentieth century. The second examines the collapse of most of these regimes and the kinds of regimes that emerged from the wreckage. The final section focuses on case studies of two regimes: electoral authoritarianism in Russia and one-party rule in China.

THE INSTITUTIONAL BASIS OF COMMUNIST REGIMES

For most of the twentieth century **communist regimes** shared two features that distinguished them from other types of authoritarian regimes. These were communist party control of the state and state-owned and centrally planned economies.

Communist Party Rule

Communist parties are vanguard parties led by a small elite who believe they understand the long-term interests of workers better than the workers themselves. Party leaders believe workers are prone to get bogged down in concerns about short-term issues such as working conditions, pay, and hours of work. Workers cannot see that the only way they can permanently improve their lives is through overthrowing capitalism and building a communist society. The role of a communist party is to lead workers in achieving these goals. To do so it must have a small, carefully selected membership rather than a mass membership. In most countries, party membership is less than 10 percent of the population.

Communist parties are organized hierarchically. Power is concentrated in the hands of a very small number of leaders at the top of the party hierarchy. The main principle of organization is "**democratic centralism.**" The key word is centralism. Party leaders make decisions and these decisions are binding on lower levels of the party. In theory, party leaders are elected by lower-ranking party members. In practice, however, these elections are controlled by party leaders. Party leaders present lower-level party organizations with a list of names and these people are "elected" as the leaders. Democratic centralism also is supposed to allow open discussions of policy proposals in which all party members can offer their views and opinions. Once agreement is reached all members of the party are obliged to work to implement the decisions. In practice, offering one's own views and opinions can be dangerous, and lower-level party members follow the decisions reached by the party leadership.

The party and state have separate organizational hierarchies in communist countries, with the party controlling the state. All major policy decisions are made by the top leaders of the communist party and these decisions are implemented by government agencies. One of the key problems for any communist party is how to ensure that the state does what the party wants it to do. There are three main ways of ensuring this. First, while the party and government have separate organizational structures, there is considerable overlap in personnel between the two. Some of the top leaders of the communist party also have top positions in the state. A second means of maintaining control is the use of **nomenklatura.** Communist parties maintain lists of official positions that can be filled only with the approval of party committees. These committees control initial appointments to positions, promotions, and dismissals. This puts government officials' careers in the hands of party officials. The third way communist parties control the state is to make sure that a high percentage of government officials at all levels of government are communist party members whose first loyalty is to the party, not to the government ministry or bureau in which they work.

The final feature of twentieth- century communist party rule was tight party control over all organizations in society. No other political parties were allowed to compete with the communist party, and no interest groups or organizations independent of communist party control were allowed. Communist parties controlled trade unions, women's associations, youth organizations, sports associations, universities, newspapers, and television stations. Communist parties used repressive state security forces to maintain control through surveillance, arrests, and terror. The best known of these agencies was the Soviet Union's Committee for State Security known by its Russian language initials as the KGB.

State-Owned, Centrally Planned Economies

The second main institutional feature of twentieth-century communist regimes was state-owned enterprises whose activities were coordinated by

central planning. Economic planners decided what would be produced, the quantity to be produced, and the price at which goods would be sold. Farms were either owned by the state or collectively owned by the farmers who worked on them. The owners of collective farms were merely owners on paper, because the state told them what to plant and set prices for their crops. Most economic activity took place within countries, although there was trade with other communist party-led countries. Communist economies were largely isolated from world markets.

State-owned, centrally planned economies had several flaws, which led to a lack of efficiency, productivity, and innovation. These economies were good at achieving **extensive growth,** which entailed mobilizing large amounts of labor and material to build or produce things. But they were not adept at promoting **intensive growth,** which entailed using labor and material efficiently. The difference between extensive and intensive growth can be illustrated through ditch digging. Two men working with shovels can dig a ditch faster than one man, and ten men can do so faster than two. Similar logic applies to factory production. Adding workers and raw materials can increase a factory's output. But this kind of growth has limits. While 10 men might be more productive at digging a ditch than 2, 10,000 would simply get in each other's way. Similarly, 100 workers in a factory might produce twice as much as 50, but 1,000 won't necessarily produce 10 times more than 100 workers. To achieve sustained economic growth it is necessary to shift from extensive to intensive growth. Intensive growth entails being smarter about how to use resources, not simply using more of them.

Centrally planned economies created few incentives for being smarter about how to use resources. Workers had little incentive to work hard because they knew they would never lose their jobs. Managers had little incentive to raise productivity because their firms had no competition from other firms and they knew their firms would never go bankrupt. Managers also had little incentive to try to increase efficiency because they were paid for meeting their factory's quota and the best way to achieve the quota was to use time-tested production methods.

THE COLLAPSE OF COMMUNIST REGIMES IN EASTERN EUROPE AND THE SOVIET UNION

The political and economic institutions of communist regimes were first put into place in the Soviet Union. Vladimir Lenin, the leader of the 1917 revolution that established communist party rule in the Soviet Union, conceived and implemented the idea of a vanguard party that would lead workers in revolution and in building communism. In the 1930s, Joseph Stalin oversaw the creation of a state-owned, centrally planned economy with collectivized agriculture. These institutions spread to other countries through conquest and revolution. At the end of World War II, the Soviet Union imposed communist regimes in the countries it controlled. These included Czechoslovakia,

Hungary, Poland, and the eastern part of Germany. In China and Vietnam, communist parties came to power through social revolutions and adopted Soviet political and economic institutions.

By 1980, all of these countries were facing economic problems, as "extensive" economic growth reached its limits and the problems of central planning multiplied. The problems were particularly severe in the Soviet Union, but many Communist Party members, government officials, and factory managers continued to live well and had no incentive to make changes. But a new generation of leaders that emerged in the 1980s acknowledged that the Soviet Union was falling farther and farther behind the West, and that it was essential to reform the system in order to save it.

In 1985, Mikhail Gorbachev became head of the Communist Party and began reforms aimed at renewing economic growth. They led instead to the collapse of communist regimes in Eastern Europe and the collapse of the Soviet Union. Gorbachev pursued three strategies to reform the Soviet Union: *glasnost*, *perestroika*, and *demokratizatsiia*. **Glasnost,** or openness, encouraged freer expression of opinion. Gorbachev hoped reducing censorship and letting information flow more freely would publicize policy failures and thereby promote the need for change. Glasnost would create momentum for reform by placing the obstructionist wing of the Communist Party on the defensive, and lead citizens to support Gorbachev's broader reform program. **Perestroika,** usually translated as restructuring, was aimed primarily at loosening state control of the economy and creating more freedom for firms to respond to demands from consumers. The term was also applied more broadly to the restructuring of social relations and political institutions. Finally, *demokratizatsiia* introduced a very limited version of democracy. It shifted some power from the Communist Party to the government by creating new legislative institutions and allowing competitive elections for the legislature. Gorbachev believed candidates supporting his program could form a coalition for reform that could defeat corrupt and obstructionist elements within the Communist Party.

Gorbachev also introduced "new thinking" in Soviet foreign policy. The Soviet Union could not afford to continue its military competition with the United States. Gorbachev wanted to ease this competition, and the economic drain it created on the Soviet economy, by achieving better relations with the United States and Western Europe. He also began to relax the Soviet Union's hold over Eastern Europe. These countries were no longer as valuable as security buffers between the Soviet Union and Western Europe as they had been in earlier decades. They had also become an economic burden on the Soviet Union. Gorbachev did not want to continue subsidizing them. He pressed their leaders to enact their own versions of *perestroika*, *glasnost*, and *demokratizatsiia* to improve economic performance and strengthen their legitimacy. The decision to relax Soviet control over Eastern Europe and press leaders of communist regimes to reform led to the collapse of one regime after another. These regimes had been imposed by the Soviet Union and had never achieved legitimacy for many citizens. In some countries, large-scale uprisings against communist party rule in previous decades had been suppressed by Soviet troops sent into those countries. Gorbachev's reforms gave citizens an opportunity to challenge communist party rule. They knew the Soviet Union would not intervene to save the regimes, and began pushing for democratic reforms. Without Soviet backing, the regimes collapsed. Poland's was the first to fall, and it was followed by the fall of every communist regime in Eastern Europe. The most dramatic event occurred in November, 1989 when the border dividing East and West Germany was opened and huge crowds of East Germans crossed the border into West Germany.

Even after the collapse of Eastern European communist regimes, few people expected that the Soviet Union would collapse. The Communist Party seemed to be firmly in control there, but Gorbachev's ambitious reforms divided the party. The reforms went too far, too fast for conservative elements in the party, and not far or fast enough for progressives. Conservatives struck first. Hard-line communists in the party, military, and secret police led a coup against Gorbachev in August 1991. The effort collapsed after only a few days, discrediting opponents of reform. But it also weakened Gorbachev, when it became apparent that some of the coup leaders had been members of his own government.

The winner in this struggle was **Boris Yeltsin**. Yeltsin had been a protégé of Gorbachev, but when the reforms went too slowly, he became increasingly critical. Although Gorbachev eventually dismissed him from the inner ranks of Communist Party leaders, demokratizatsiia had created institutions that gave Yeltsin an alternative route to power. In 1991, he was elected President of the Russian Republic and won popular acclaim for his leadership in thwarting the conservatives' coup effort. Yeltsin realized that the way to defeat Gorbachev was to encourage the collapse of the U.S.S.R. With no Soviet Union, Gorbachev would have no country to govern. Thus, Yeltsin schemed with presidents of the other republics to withdraw from the Soviet Union and become independent countries. The strategy worked. In December 1991, the Soviet Union came to an end. Its 15 republics formed independent countries with Russia being the largest of these countries. The fifteen new countries retained some weak ties with each other by creating the Commonwealth of Independent States (CIS).

These former communist-led countries have taken very different political directions. Most of the former Eastern European communist countries have made relatively smooth transitions to democracy and market economies. Russia and many of the other former 14 republics of the Soviet Union have not made smooth transitions. Some have unstable weak democracies, while others have various forms of personal rule or electoral authoritarianism.

Communist regimes did not collapse everywhere. Communist regimes remain in power in China, Cuba, Laos, North Korea and Vietnam. The specific reasons for their survival differ from regime to regime, but they had four things in common that help explain why they did not collapse. First, they had greater legitimacy than the Eastern European regimes. Communist party rule had not been imposed on them from outside. Second, they were more independent of Soviet control and influence than the Eastern European countries and were not as deeply affected by Gorbachev's reforms. Third was a willingness to use overwhelming force against threats to their rule. Lastly, these regimes managed to avoid prolonged, debilitating divisions that would have weakened their rule and enabled critics to mobilize supporters and topple them. Although they stayed in power, the collapse of so many other communist regimes alarmed them, and forced them to think about what they needed to do to remain in power in the future.

RUSSIA AND CHINA AS POSTCOMMUNIST REGIMES

In this section, we examine Russia and China as case studies of postcommunist regimes. Both have had to deal with the legacies of communist institutions. Russia is no longer ruled by a communist party, but its contemporary politics and economics have been profoundly shaped by past communist party rule and economic policies. China is still ruled by a communist party, but it is no longer a communist country in the way communist countries were defined for most of the twentieth century. Its Communist Party allows more individual freedom and seeks less control over groups in society than in the past. Much of its economy is in private hands and is coordinated by market supply and demand rather than central planning. Collective farming has been dismantled and replaced by family farming. Finally, the economy depends heavily on international trade and it is a member of the World Trade Organization.

RUSSIA

Russia, formally known as the **Russian Federation,** has the largest land area of any country in the world. Its population of approximately 140 million is a little less than half that of the United States. It is the world's second largest producer of oil after Saudi Arabia, and the largest producer of natural gas. Its other natural resources include gold, various minerals, and vast expanses of timber. Approximately 80 percent of the population is ethnically Russian, but close to 100 ethnic groups make up the rest of the population.

When the Soviet Union collapsed, many people in the West assumed that the end of Communist Party political control and central planning would free Russians to pursue democracy and markets. But that optimism was misplaced because it underestimated the difficulty of reform. Russia has become an electoral authoritarian regime and its economy is a mix of private and large state-owned firms. Adult literacy rates are extremely high and infant mortality rates have gone down since 1995, but male life expectancy is only 62 years, lower than that in many less developed countries.

Historical Background

The autocratic czarist regime that had ruled Russia since the sixteenth century collapsed in 1917. World War I revealed the regime's weaknesses, including poor civilian and military leadership. Russian troops were poorly equipped and led. As defeats accumulated and central authority weakened, soldiers deserted the army, peasants seized land owned by nobles, and workers took over factories. The czar was forced to step down and a provisional government was formed to lead the country.

By late 1917, Vladimir Lenin, the leader of the Bolsheviks, a wing of the Russian Social Democratic Labor Party, believed that the provisional government also lacked support of the people. Its weakness provided an opportunity to seize power in the name of workers, even though Russia did not meet the standard criteria for a socialist revolution. Approximately 80 percent of the population consisted of peasants, and capitalism was not well developed in Russia.

No one was more surprised at the success of the 1917 October Revolution in Russia than many of the Bolsheviks themselves. They came to power without a blueprint for how to build socialism and communism, and much of what they did was in reaction to the rush of events. With the new government beset by domestic and foreign enemies intent on its defeat, the Bolsheviks responded forcefully. Lenin suppressed other political parties, giving the Communist Party a monopoly of power, and created an internal security force to collect intelligence and arrest opponents. At the same time, the Bolsheviks initiated economic changes. For their first six years in power they followed the New Economic Policy (NEP), which nationalized banks and major businesses, while leaving small firms in the hands of their owners and allowing peasants to keep the lands they had seized from the nobility. The NEP recognized private property, included a place for market exchange, and implied that the transition to a command economy in which the state socialized production would be gradual.

It was only in the late 1920s and early 1930s that the defining economic institutions of Soviet communism were implemented. The leader who initiated these changes was Joseph Stalin, who replaced Lenin as party leader following Lenin's death in 1924. Stalin's economic revolution had three parts. First, Stalin pursued a policy of agricultural collectivization in which privately owned farms were abolished and replaced by collectivized farms owned by the state. Collectivization gave control over farms and grain supplies to the state, which used them to feed urban workers and earn foreign exchange that could be used to develop Soviet industry. When farmers resisted collectivization, their defiance was broken by force and a famine that was deliberately created by authorities.[1] The second part of Stalin's "revolution from above" was the creation of a state-owned, centrally planned economy. Finally, Stalin chose to invest in capital goods such as power plants, steel, railroads, infrastructure, and military equipment, at the expense of consumer goods.

In addition to transforming the economy, Stalin increased the use of terror to annihilate opponents in the party, government, and military. Party leaders who had worked with Stalin in making the Bolshevik revolution of 1917 were falsely accused of collaborating with foreign spies, prosecuted in elaborate "show trials" in which they were forced to confess their guilt, and then executed.

Country	Population	Infant Mortality	Life Expectancy	Adult Literacy	Capital City	GDP Per Capita (PPP)	Labor Force by Occupation
Russia	139,390,000 (2010 estimate)	10.32 deaths/ 1,000 live births	66.2	99.4%	Moscow	$15,100 (2008 estimate)	Agriculture: 10.0% Industry: 31.9% Services: 58.1% (2008)

MAP 11.1
Russia & CIS

Source: CIA World Fact Book

Ordinary people also experienced the terror, as hundreds of thousands of them were either executed or arrested and sent to labor camps in Siberia.[2] Scholars debate the number of people Stalin condemned to death, with estimates that begin at one million and go up from there.[3]

After Stalin died in 1953, the leaders of the Soviet Union moved to create a more collegial, less personalized form of governance, designed to limit the power of any one individual. Soviet politics became more stable and the economy continued to grow. In the 1960s and 1970s most people in the United States viewed the U.S.S.R. as a superpower and a formidable threat. Beneath this impressive appearance, however, the Soviet Union was in serious trouble. Mikhail Gorbachev's efforts to reform the Soviet Union led instead to its collapse and the creation of new countries from its former republics. The largest of these was Russia.

The State

When Russia became an independent country, it operated initially with the same political institutions it had as a republic in the Soviet Union. Boris Yeltsin, who had been elected President of Russia in 1991 before the Soviet Union collapsed, remained in office, and Russia's parliament, which was dominated by members of the Communist Party, also continued to function. But by 1993 an acute conflict between Yeltsin and the legislature deadlocked the policy-making process. Yeltsin's solution was to dissolve parliament, assign a commission to write a new constitution, and ask voters to approve it by referendum. The document remains in force today.

The constitution provides for a strong **president**.[4] The president's powers include the authority to appoint and dismiss the prime minister and members of the cabinet, and to issue decrees that have the force of law so long as they do not violate the constitution. The president determines Russia's overall domestic and foreign policy, but focuses primarily on foreign affairs, defense, and domestic security policy. The president is commander-in-chief of the armed forces, and controls the **Russian Security Council**, which coordinates all of Russia's security agencies as well as government ministries with responsibility for foreign affairs, defense, and domestic security. Elected directly by the voters, the president is limited to two terms in office. The first presidential election held under the rules of the new constitution was won by Yeltsin in 1996. His designated successor, Vladimir Putin, was victorious in 2000 and 2004, but could not run for a third term in 2008. The 2008 presidential election was won by Putin's handpicked successor, Dmitry Medvedev, and Putin became the prime minster. In 2008 the president's term of office was extended from four to six years beginning with the 2012 presidential election. See Figure 11.1

The **prime minister**, though appointed by the president, must be approved by the lower house of parliament, the State Duma. While the State Duma must approve the president's selection of prime minister, once in office prime ministers have been responsible to the president, not to parliament. Unlike prime ministers in parliamentary systems, such as Canada's and Sweden's, the

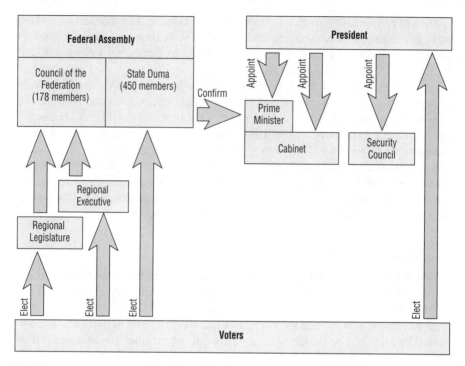

FIGURE 11.1
Russian Political Institutions

Russian prime minister required the president's support, not the parliament's, to stay in office. Prime ministers are responsible for managing the day-to-day business of the government and focus mainly on economic and social policy. Prime Minister Putin has much more authority than an ordinary prime minister, and remains "the ultimate decision maker in Russia."[5]

The bicameral legislature, or **Federal Assembly**, is relatively weak. The upper house of the Federal Assembly is the **Federation Council**, which plays a role somewhat similar to the United States Senate. The Federation Council represents Russia's administrative divisions, and has 178 members, which includes two members from each of Russia's regional governments, no matter what their population. Beyond this similarity, however, the analogy breaks down. The members of the Federation Council are chosen differently from Senators, and the chamber has far less power. By the terms of the 1993, constitution they were to be directly elected by voters, but since 2002 they have been indirectly elected: A region's governor chooses one of the representatives and the region's legislature chooses the other.

The lower house, the **State Duma**, has 450 deputies directly elected by voters to four-year terms. The December 2007 Duma election was the first to use an electoral system in which all 450 members are chosen from party lists using proportional representation. In previous Duma elections only half the members were elected using proportional representation, while the other half were elected from single member districts by plurality vote. The Duma is where most legislative activity takes place, and while its decisions can be vetoed by the Federation Council, the Duma can override the veto with a two-thirds vote. The State Duma is the more powerful of the two institutions, but its influence over legislation and its ability to act as a check on the executive branch has been greatly weakened since 2000. **United Russia,** a political party supporting Russia's presidents has controlled a large majority of seats in the Duma since the 2003 Duma election. Presidents have used United Russia's control of the Duma to process their priorities.[6]

Russia has a Constitutional Court to decide controversies between political institutions and to rule on the constitutionality of laws. Thus far the Court has been very cautious about challenging the president. In addition to the Constitutional Court, a system of courts handles civil and criminal cases, with the Supreme Court at the top of the hierarchy. These courts have a reputation for corruption and being susceptible to political influence. A young lawyer explained how he earns money as follows: "I go to a judge and say, 'I really need to win this case.' He says, let's say, 100,000 rubles. I go to my client and tell him 130,000."[7] Steven Kotkin, the director of the program in Russian and Eurasian Studies at Princeton, bluntly asserts that Russia lacks an independent judiciary.[8]

The Russian state is highly centralized. One of Putin's central goals during his presidency was to reassert central government control over regional governments. During the Soviet years, regional units of government had been tightly controlled from Moscow by the Communist Party. The collapse of the Soviet regime gave regional leaders opportunities to build power and accumulate wealth. Yeltsin's strategy was to share power with them, hoping to hold the country together and construct a federal system of government. Putin reversed this approach and restricted regional leaders' influence by creating seven federal "super districts," each of which oversees several regional governments. The super districts are headed by presidential appointees who make sure that regional leaders comply with federal laws. Putin further restricted the governors' power by gaining the authority to remove them if they violate federal laws and by changing the way regional governors are selected. Previously, governors were elected. Now the president has the power to appoint governors, who must be confirmed by regional legislatures.

While Putin successfully centralized state power in the hands of the president, the state remains relatively weak. The World Bank ranks the effectiveness of Russia's government well below that of China and Brazil. For the most part, the state lacks professional, capable civil servants recruited on the basis of merit and promoted on the basis of performance. There are some highly capable, dedicated civil servants in Russia. Those in charge of fiscal and monetary policy did a good job of managing economic policy after 2000, but elsewhere corruption is endemic. Police are notorious for asking for bribes. A correspondent for the *Economist* magazine tells the story of a businessperson stopped by a traffic police officer in Moscow in 2008 and handed a note with "30.000 rubles" written on it. When asked why the fine was so high, the officer replied he had bought an apartment for his mother and needed money to fix it up."[9] In 2009, Transparency International ranked Russia the 146th most corrupt country in the world out of 180 rankings. Russia's ranking tied it with low income sub-Saharan African countries such as Cameroon, Kenya, and Sierra Leone.[10]

State and Society

The main theme of state–society relations in Russia since 2000 has been a decline in political competition and political accountability and a corresponding increase in the control of political parties, interest groups, and major media by central state authorities. The authorities do not want to eliminate democratic competition entirely. Political leaders find controlled competition helpful for providing useful information about the public's preferences and grievances. But these leaders want "always to win and to be confident that this will continue."[11] They have taken several steps to make sure this happens. One has been to eliminate a number of political parties by making it difficult for them to find financing and attract voters. Tight state supervision over party financing guarantees that no businesspeople will give money to political parties not approved by the central authorities. To do so invites retaliation by the government. A second step is to use the legal process to write election laws that are so complicated that it is difficult for parties to comply with them. Candidates can be disqualified for even minor violations. A third step has been to increase the number of signatures parties need to get on the ballot and the percentage of seats a party must win to get seats in the Duma. Finally, voting procedures have been changed to make it easier to manipulate voters' choices and to stuff ballot boxes if necessary.[12] These tactics reduced the number of officially recognized political parties from 44 in 2003 to 10 in 2009.[13]

The United Russia Party is Russia's dominant party.[14] It is what Russians call a **"party of power,"** or a party designed to get politically powerful leaders elected.[15] While party competition exists, the playing field is tipped in favor of United Russia. Major media outlets give its candidates extensive coverage while denying it to those from other parties. Newspaper journalists critical of its candidates are harassed by tax authorities, sued in courts, and even arrested.[16] United Russia proclaims a vague "social conservatism," which is "a blend of market economics, promotion of the middle class, nationalism, and support for order and stability."[17] Although these broad themes help attract supporters, they are not translated into coherent policies. The party leaders' real interests are in pork and patronage for themselves and their followers in the regions.[18]

The central authorities do not want United Russia to be the sole political party, as the Communist Party was in the Soviet Union. This would destroy the pretense that Russia is a democracy with competitive elections and weaken the regime's legitimacy. Smaller political parties are allowed to exist, and even to elect some members to the Duma. Some of these small parties have been created by the authorities to give the appearance of alternatives to United Russia but they in fact support United Russia. The consequence is that "party competition is more nominal than real, and voters cannot have "meaningful choices over policy alternatives."[19]

In addition to gaining control over the electoral process, the Putin administration also increased state control over interest groups. After the collapse of the Soviet Union, large numbers of interest groups emerged in Russia to represent the interests of businesspeople, professionals, workers, and human rights activists. The most influential of these are business associations, especially the Russian Union of Industrialists and Entrepreneurs (RUIE), which represents the interests of big business. Despite some success in influencing tax and regulatory policy, the RUIE has been unwilling to challenge the state when officials act illegally to seize business firms. The organization's influence has also been undermined by wealthy businesspeople's preference for going directly to officials with their problems rather than working through the association. Small business owners are much more vulnerable to corrupt police officers, organized crime, and government inspectors, as they are not represented effectively by associations.[20]

In addition to seeking control over organized business associations, Putin sought to break the political power of extremely wealthy, powerful **oligarchs** who used political connections in the 1990s to establish banks, gain control of television stations, and purchase oil companies. They enjoyed considerable influence in government when Boris Yeltsin was president. When Putin took office in 2000, two of the oligarchs, Vladimir Gusinsky and Boris Berezovsky, used their media outlets to criticize his policies. In July, Putin called a meeting with 20 of the oligarchs, telling them they could keep their wealth but warned them to stay out of politics. Soon afterwards government investigators launched legal charges against Berezovsky and Gusinsky. They were stripped of their main assets, including their television stations, and both went into exile.[21] In 2003, Mikhail Khodorkovsky, another oligarch who was funding opposition parties, was arrested, sentenced to a nine-year prison term and his assets were seized.[22] In 2010, he was found guilty on dubious charges of embezzlement and sentenced to six more years in prison. Other oligarchs have gotten the message and become more cooperative fearing that they will suffer a similar fate.

The largest labor organization in Russia is the Federation of Independent Trade Unions of Russia. It succeeded the official trade union federation of the Soviet era, which was used by the Communist Party to control labor rather than give it a voice. Even though 95 percent of all workers who are organized into unions are members of the Federation, it has little political influence. Its member unions are fragmented and unable to cooperate for collective action. They struggle with each other to gain members instead of coordinating their activities to unite workers against business. One main reason for this is that leaders of the Federation of Independent Trade Unions prefer to establish relationships with individual state officials as a means of gaining influence rather than organizing workers for collective action.[23]

Finally, the authorities have gained control of the three major television stations through which an estimated 90 percent of Russians get their news about politics. Much of these stations' political coverage focuses on the government's accomplishments. To make sure they get their stories straight, the heads of the networks coordinate coverage with the Kremlin's press service. There is also a nastier side to control of the news. Crusading journalists who offer a more critical perspective have been intimidated and even murdered.

Still, independent sources of information and news exist. For example, citizens can use the Internet to get access to news sources that are not controlled by the authorities. One television station offers relatively independent reporting to urban areas of Russia. But few people take advantages of these alternative sources of news, and the authorities allow them to exist because they offer the fig leaf of freedom of expression in Russia and provide leaders with alternative sources of information about developments in society.[24]

Political Culture

Russian political culture has been shaped by Russia's history of authoritarian rule. Czars ruled for hundreds of years and Communist Party officials for most of the twentieth century. Democratic institutions were not introduced until the 1990s and lacked strong support. The majority of Russians were not committed to democratic values or to democracy as the most desirable arrangement for resolving conflicts and making public policy. They valued it only so far as it was useful in improving their standard of living. When many Russians' standard of living fell in the 1990s, they associated democracy with this failure. Many of them welcomed President Putin's strong leadership that produced improvements in their standard of living, social stability, and restoration of Russian power and influence in the world. These Russians' political ideal is of a paternalistic state that projects power abroad and looks out for the interests of its citizens at home.[25]

Many Russians have strong nationalist feelings and want a restoration of Russia's lost influence in world affairs. One of the most popular songs in 2005 was "I Was Made in the USSR." The title refers to a time when the Soviet Union was a world superpower. The lyrics closely copied Bruce Springsteen's "Born in the USA," and used the same tune.[26] Russians have strong patriotic feelings. One measure of patriotism is one's willingness to fight for one's country. In a 2006, survey 83 percent of Russians said they were willing to fight for their country. In the United States only 63 percent said they were.[27]

In domestic affairs many Russians say they want a strong, paternalistic state that looks out for their interests. When asked in 2006 if "the government should take more responsibility for ensuring that everyone is provided for," 43 percent responded that it should. In the United States, only 9 percent responded in similar fashion and in China the figure was 15 percent. It is not surprising that Russians are more inclined to want a larger role for the government in taking care of citizens than Americans. What is surprising is that a much higher percentage of Russians want the government to provide for everybody than Chinese do.[28]

There is considerable support in Russia for a strong leader who is decisive and effective and does not have to bother with parliament or elections. Fifty-seven percent of Russians agreed this was a "very good" or "fairly good" idea. This desire for a strong leader who overrides parliament to achieve desirable aims is coupled with a lack of support for fundamental democratic values such as freedom of speech. One of the most important self-expressive values is the willingness to tolerate free speech even from those with whom one strongly disagrees. Most Russians have little tolerance for views they find offensive. They want rights for themselves that they are not willing to give to others.[29] One of the reasons President Putin was so popular with many Russians was that he fit their expectations of how a leader should behave. While many in the West grew increasingly critical of his authoritarian policies, only a small percentage of Russians felt similarly.[30]

It is important to emphasize that not all Russians have the public political ideal of a paternalistic state with a strong leader who overrides parliament. In the early 1990s right after the collapse of the Soviet Union, there was initially strong support for democracy. But this support eroded as standards of living declined and social instability increased. Support for the Russian state increased sharply after 2000 when President Putin was elected, but began to decline again in 2005 as citizens became increasingly critical of government corruption and lack of responsiveness.[31] Russians do not view their current form of government as ideal, but they appreciate it because it has brought improvements to their lives.

The Russian political scientist Alexander Lukin suggests the current regime is "quite stable" because it is "based on the dominant Russia political culture."[32] He concedes that lower oil prices that lowered citizens' standard of living, or government policy that diverged markedly from what he calls the "popular political ideal," could destabilize the regime, Other political scientists believe the regime might be stable in the short term, but not for the long term. They argue that Russia's version of electoral authoritarianism cuts leaders off from free flows of information about the effects of their policies on society. This makes it increasingly likely that the leaders will make decisions that go against the wishes of large numbers of citizens. If this happens there are no ways for citizens to express their discontent except to take to the streets in demonstrations. This happened in 2005 when the government proposed a change in how benefits would be allocated to pensioners and others. The regime's inability to anticipate and respond flexibly to emerging problems is likely to eventually set off leadership struggles that will destabilize it.[33]

Political Economy

Much of the current regime's support is due to its handling of economic problems that bedeviled President Yeltsin in the 1990s. Yeltsin's government inherited a sinking economy after the Soviet Union collapsed in 1991. His economic advisers convinced him the only economic option for reviving the economy quickly was "**shock therapy**": making a transition to a market economy as rapidly as possible. Shock therapy included letting the market set prices instead of government planners; selling state-owned firms to private investors; slashing state spending in order to reduce budget deficits; and encouraging foreign investment.[34]

For most of the 1990s, none of the four components of shock therapy worked as planned. Inflation skyrocketed once prices were allowed to float and be determined by market forces, with devastating consequences for millions of Russians living on fixed salaries and pensions. The benefits of selling state enterprises were no more apparent than letting the market set prices. Instead of winding up in the hands of businesspeople intent on making them more efficient and productive, many of those enterprises were acquired by the people who had managed them when they were state-owned firms, or were bought by people with political connections. New owners sometimes sold off their firms' assets in order to make a quick profit instead of investing to make them more competitive. Nor was the state able to reduce deficits, as recession reduced revenues and the government continued to subsidize ailing businesses. Finally, increased dependence on international investment and trade contributed to an economic crisis in 1998. World oil prices dropped, reducing revenues, and making it impossible for Russia to pay its debts.

Shock therapy's failures led to an intense debate over the appropriate roles of states and markets in Russia. Members of Russia's Communist Party and other supporters of socialist economics were willing to give markets some role in the economy but wanted a much larger role to the state. They wanted to return some firms to state ownership, subsidize firms to help them survive economic difficulties, put greater restrictions on foreign investment, and increase welfare spending to assist the victims of market reforms. On the other side were a number of small parties that supported continued market reforms and reduced state intervention. In the middle were parties and groups that generally favored markets but believed the state should maintain control over key economic sectors. This last position was the one taken by President Putin.

His economic policies differed considerably from those pursued by President Yeltsin in the early 1990s. While Yeltsin was willing to go along with his economic advisers' recommendations for a rapid transition to a market economy, Putin pursued a combination of support for markets with a large role for the state in strategically important industries. Putin believes that state control of strategic economic sectors—oil and gas in particular—is essential to restoring Russia's power in the world. Accordingly, huge companies such as Gazprom, the fifth-largest corporation in the world in 2006 as measured by stock value, and other huge companies were tightly controlled by men in Putin's inner circle.[35]

By one estimate, the state's share of industrial output and employment grew from about 30 percent in 2003 to about 40 percent in 2006. The model that has emerged is of "an economic system increasingly built around huge state-owned or state-directed companies," rather than relying on competition among private firms. These state-owned and state-directed companies have become powerful political instruments. Domestically, their profits have allowed the government to purchase independent televisions stations, and to subsidize favored industries with cheap energy. Internationally, they have permitted the government to threaten other countries by cutting off their access to oil. For example, in 2006 Gazprom's executive "warned Europe not to block its expansion into European markets, lest it decide to sell its natural gas elsewhere."[36] Russia has also intimidated major multinational corporations. In December 2006 the government pressured Royal Dutch Shell into selling controlling stakes in a huge gas and oil field in Russia's Far East to Gazprom. The government accused Royal Dutch Shell of violating environmental laws and threatened it with delays, obstructions, and legal action.[37]

President Medvedev came into office in May 2008 promising to improve the performance of a Russian economy that is, in his words, "a primitive economy based on raw materials and endemic corruption."[38] He argued Russia needs improved infrastructure, and to diversify away from its current heavy dependence on the oil, gas, and metals that make up 80 per cent of its exports. Instead of being able to pursue this agenda, Mevedev had to focus on responding to the world recession that began in 2008. Stock prices collapsed, the price of oil dropped, and foreign investment dried up. The government responded with a large stimulus package to offset the effects of the economic downturn, but much of the spending went into older industries rather than the development of new ones. Economic growth revived in 2010, but with relatively little job creation, and there has also been little progress in developing the high-technology industries promised by Medvedev.

Progress has been limited because President Medvedev and his advisers believe that it is essential to maintain current political arrangements that inhibit the development of new sectors of the economy. The interests of the Russian elite are in conflict with the requirements of economic modernization. The elite depend on "rent from natural resources or administrative interference in the market. Competition and the rule of law undermine this arrangement. Corruption holds it together, and ensures the loyalty of the bureaucracy."[39] One of Medvedev's major advisers asserts that "consolidated state power is the only instrument of modernisation in Russia. And, let me assure you, it is the only one possible."[40] Yet consolidated state power in Russia is more likely to perpetuate present economic arrangements than spark rapid economic diversification and modernization.

Russia has had mixed success in promoting capabilities. Infant mortality rates have been cut almost in half since 1990 from 23 per 1,000 to only 12 per 1,000, with most of this reduction coming since 2000. It has also sustained a very high literacy rate that it inherited from the Soviet Union. The biggest failure has come in life expectancy. Since the late 1990s Russia's average life expectancy has been below the world average. Male life expectancy was 62 years in 2008, lower than that of many less developed countries. Women's life expectancy was 74 years. The difference is explained largely by alcohol and tobacco use by men. Murder rates have also risen, along with deaths from suicide and AIDS. High death rates that are double the average of developed countries and low birth rates caused population to shrink by 700,000 people a year. In 2006 the Putin government increased child support payments and offered parents a bonus for having a second child. This has helped increase birth rates somewhat but not sufficiently to reverse the overall decline in population size.

CHINA

China has the largest population of any country with approximately 1.3 billion people, and is the fourth largest in area. Since 1980, it has had one of the fastest economic growth rates in history, averaging almost 10 percent per year. It now has the second largest economy in the world measured by purchasing power parity. Rapid economic growth has raised millions of people out of poverty and raised others into the middle class, and even created a rich elite. But these successes have not come cheap. Inequality has increased dramatically among individuals and between regions, with wealthier Chinese and coastal regions enjoying the fruits of growth, while poorer Chinese and interior regions have been left behind. Rapid industrialization and urbanization have caused extensive environmental damage, with severe health costs for many Chinese.

Historical Background

In 1976, citizens of the United States proudly celebrated 200 years of independence. For Chinese citizens 200 years is not much to brag about. The first Chinese empire emerged in 221 BCE. In subsequent centuries Chinese emperors developed a centralized state that ruled over a country larger than the continental United States. When Europeans first came to China, they were impressed with the size of its cities, the dynamism of its economy, and the sophistication of its art. European access was limited to a few ports because there was little China needed from Europeans. By the middle of the nineteenth century, however, several European countries had pulled ahead of China economically and militarily, and began to press its leaders to open their country to trade. This pressure increased at a time when the ruling dynasty was in decline. The British easily defeated the Chinese during the Opium War (1839–1843) and demanded reparations for the costs of the war as well as the opening of China to British products. Other European countries soon followed suit, and divided China into "spheres of influence," which were a humiliating sign of the country's weakness.

In 1911, a rebellion led to the collapse of the dynasty, and a year later Sun Yat-sen, a Western educated nationalist, was named president of the new Republic of China. But he was unable to establish a stable regime, and five years later the country disintegrated into regions controlled by competing warlords. Two political parties emerged to lead the struggle to reunify China: the **Nationalist (or *Guomindang*) Party** and the Chinese Communist Party (CCP). The newly created Soviet Union threw its support behind the Nationalist Party and advised the smaller CCP to ally with it against the warlords. The Nationalists drew support mainly from landlords, wealthy farmers, and big business interests, while the Communists received their support from poor peasants and urban workers.

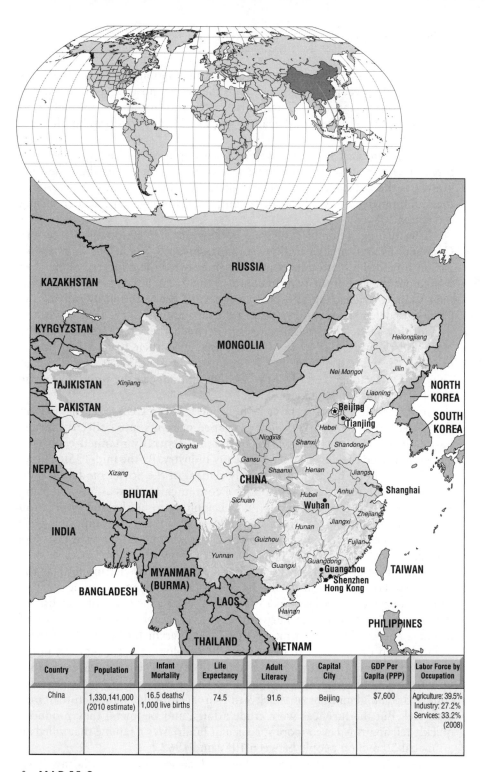

Country	Population	Infant Mortality	Life Expectancy	Adult Literacy	Capital City	GDP Per Capita (PPP)	Labor Force by Occupation
China	1,330,141,000 (2010 estimate)	16.5 deaths/ 1,000 live births	74.5	91.6	Beijing	$7,600	Agriculture: 39.5% Industry: 27.2% Services: 33.2% (2008)

MAP 11.2
China

Source: CIA World Fact Book

Chiang Kai-shek, who became leader of the Nationalist Party after Sun's death in 1925, decided the alliance with the Communist Party was unworkable. His troops massacred Communist Party members, and proceeded to re-unify the country, either by defeating warlords' armies or forming alliances with them.

The Communist Party attempted to regroup in southern China but was forced to flee to a remote area in northwestern China. This flight became known as the Long March, a journey of 6,000 miles that only 10 percent of the Communists survived. Mao Zedong became the party's leader during the march.

The turning point in the struggle between the Nationalist Party and Communist Party came in 1937, when Japan invaded China. The Japanese invasion forced the Nationalists into the interior of the country, where they waited out the end of the war. In contrast, the Communists greatly expanded their support by enacting reforms that benefited peasants and by rallying the Chinese to defend their country against the Japanese. After the Japanese defeat in World War II, civil war broke out between the Communists and the Nationalists, and by 1949 the Communists, with their formidable, battle-hardened army, had driven the Nationalists out of China to the island of Taiwan. On October 1, 1949 Mao Zedong announced the founding of the People's Republic of China.

In its first few years in power, the leaders of the CCP relied heavily on the Soviet model of socialism. They grouped peasants into collective farms, nationalized business enterprises, initiated a centrally planned economy, and emphasized the development of heavy industry. By the mid-1950s, however, Mao Zedong became increasingly critical of the Soviet model on both economic and ideological grounds. Economically, it was not creating enough jobs, and food production was beginning to fall behind population growth. Ideologically, Mao regarded the Soviet model as incompatible with socialist principles because it empowered bureaucrats rather than peasants and workers.

Mao's first effort to create an alternative to the Soviet model was the **Great Leap Forward** (1958–1960). Its goal was to catch up economically with West European countries within 15 years and create a new kind of socialism in the process. The Great Leap Forward was based on the mass mobilization of peasants and workers, substituting "ideological fervor for material rewards" to motivate people.[41] Instead of focusing on developing heavy industry in the cities, Mao sought to balance rural and urban development. The Great Leap is now remembered for its spectacular failures. For example, peasants were encouraged to build millions of "backyard" furnaces for the manufacture of iron and steel. But the furnaces were crude affairs, and the metal they produced quickly fell apart. An even more spectacular failure was a famine that killed an estimated 30 million people between 1959 and 1962.[42]

The failures of the Great Leap Forward caused Mao to withdraw from day-to-day decision making. Two senior party leaders, Liu Shaoqi and Deng Xiaoping, took the lead in restoring economic growth. They relied on careful economic planning and even used market incentives to get peasants to grow more crops. Deng's justification for trying different approaches to jump-start growth is reflected in his famous remark, "It doesn't matter if a cat is white or black as long as it catches the mouse."[43] Mao did not find the comment amusing and regarded Deng Xiaoping as a counter-revolutionary whose policies encouraged people to focus on making money and exploiting others to do so rather than building socialism. Mao believed that what China needed instead was a "**Great Proletarian Cultural Revolution** (1966–1976) that would reshape people's thinking in line with his version of socialism. A major goal of the Cultural Revolution was to purge the party of "capitalist roaders" and "class enemies" such as Liu Shaoqi and Deng Xiaoping, and to rid the country of old culture, habits, ideas, and customs. Mao charged the Red Guards, young students, with the task of rooting out capitalist influences by burning Western books and novels; purging universities, high schools, factories, newspaper offices, and local governments of "class enemies"; and brutalizing, even murdering, many former capitalists, landlords, and their children.

The Cultural Revolution "imposed great suffering on tens of millions."[44] It only came to an end when conflicts between Red Guard factions threatened public order. In 1969 a new party leadership restored a measure of political and social stability, but it was not until after Mao died in 1976 that a stable Party leadership finally came in to power and set China on a new course.

Deng Xiaoping returned from his humiliation during the Cultural Revolution to become China's leader in 1978. With the aid of numerous officials who had been purged during the Cultural Revolution, he began to build a very different socialism from that envisaged by Mao. Deng's policies aimed at strengthening the Communist Party and gaining legitimacy for it by promoting rapid economic growth that would improve citizens' lives. He reassured the Chinese there would be no more turmoil-inducing mass movements such as the Great Leap Forward and the Cultural Revolution. He initiated legal reforms that gave citizens some protection from arbitrary state policies. He also allowed more cultural diversity than had been permitted in the recent past.

The most far-reaching of Deng's reforms, however, were those that gave a greater role to markets and market incentives. They were summarized in the phrase "**reform and opening**," meaning reform of the domestic economy and opening to the world economy. Three economic reforms were particularly important. First was to end collective farming. Communes were broken up and households were allowed to decide what to grow. The households were not given ownership of land—agricultural land is still not privately owned in China—but farmers could now make their own decisions and benefit from their efforts, rather than having to plant what officials told them and share the benefits with other farm families. As a result of this reform, agricultural output grew and farmers' income rose.

The second economic reform was to open China to world markets. Initially, the opening was limited to special zones in coastal provinces and a few cities that gave foreign companies permission to invest, build factories, and export their goods. These areas experienced an economic boom that powered China's rapid export trade in the 1980s and 1990s.[45] The final reform was to allow privately owned businesses, as well as businesses jointly owned by local governments and private investors called township and village enterprises (TVEs). In 1978, when the reforms began, state-owned enterprises accounted for 78 percent of industrial output, but by 2002, that figure had fallen to 41 percent. In the same period, the share of privately owned firms rose astronomically from 0.2 percent to 41 percent.[46]

While Deng Xiaoping approved of reducing state control of the economy, he had no intention of letting it proceed so far that it threatened Party control. Indeed, Deng supported market-oriented reforms because he believed they would increase Party legitimacy and support. While economic growth did indeed produce benefits to many, it also affected groups of people differently. For many urban Chinese, the reforms were too slow and brought charges of corruption by students who accused Party elites of using the reforms to enrich their families. In 1989, student protests filled **Tiananmen Square** in Beijing, and spread to other major cities. As the protests spread they attracted wider support from middle-class and working-class citizens. For weeks the party dithered about how to respond, until the hard-liners who opposed any concessions prevailed. Very early on the morning of June 4, 1989, soldiers cleared Tiananmen Square of protestors, and shot and killed large numbers of students.

Since the **Tiananmen Square protests**, the leaders of the Communist Party have followed the same basic strategy instituted by Deng Xiaoping: relying on markets and integration into the global economy to drive economic growth, while strengthening the power of the Communist Party so that it stays in power. The central issue of Chinese politics is how long this strategy can work. Rapid, market-led economic growth is producing a much more complex society with new social classes, organizations, and political cleavages that may potentially challenge Party rule.

The State

The CCP dominates Chinese politics, and within the party power is largely in the hands of the party's leader and 25 to 35 party officials around him.[47] As the party's first paramount leader, Mao held power by arbitrating disputes among party factions and using mass mobilization, and ideological campaigns to control them.[48] Politics became a "game to win all" in which opponents were reduced to impotence.[49] Since then, party leaders have tried to create rules that make their power more predictable and less threatening than it was in Mao's time. For example, the succession process for who becomes the next leader of the party has been institutionalized. When Mao was chair, there was no way to remove him short of a coup and he served as party leader until he died. Party leaders are now expected to step down after two terms in office, as Jiang Zemin did in 2002 when he transferred leadership to Hu Jintao. The next major change in leadership is scheduled for 2012 and the likely successor to Hu Jintao was selected in 2010.[50]

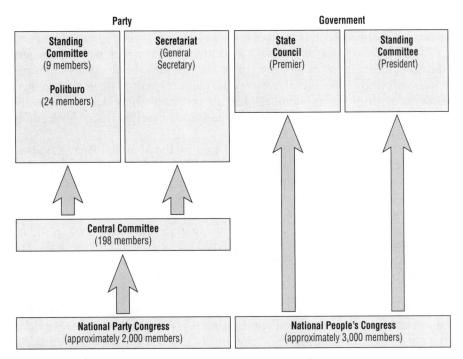

FIGURE 11.2
Party and Government in China

Another change has been to institutionalize decision making so that major decisions are made at regular meetings of party institutions, rather than outside of them.[51] Also, Hu Jintao initiated recruitment to the top ranks of the party based on merit rather than connections.

The most powerful institutions in the CCP are the **Politburo** (short for Political Bureau) and its Standing Committee, which make all major policy decisions. The Politburo usually has two dozen members, nine of whom were members of the Standing Committee.

The party leader is always the **General Secretary** of the party's **Secretariat**. This organization's power derives from its responsibilities for overseeing implementation of Politburo decisions and managing the party's personnel. The General Secretary has considerable influence over promotions and transfers of personnel to important positions in the party and government.

According to the party's constitution, members of the Politburo and the Secretariat are elected by the **Central Committee**, an organization of around 200 full members. In reality, the selection process is the reverse of what the party constitution says. Who gets into the Central Committee is determined by members of the Politburo, and the Central Committee simply approves the names presented to it for Politburo membership. An exception can occur when there is an irresolvable power struggle among top leaders in the party. In these cases, Central Committee members do play a role in selecting the leader and other members of the Politburo. The last time this happened was after Mao Zedong's death when Deng Xiaoping was chosen as party leader. The party constitution also gives the Central Committee a major policy-making role, but this, too, exists more in theory than in fact because the Central Committee meets only once a year for about a week. While it is not powerful as a policy-making institution, its members are all powerful individuals within the Communist Party. They hold top party positions at the provincial level and in the central government.

Central Committee members are elected by the **National Party Congress** according to the party constitution, but with over 2000 delegates who meet for one to two weeks every five years, it is largely a rubber stamp designed to approve the choices of the party leaders. Below these national party institutions are provincial, city, and county institutions.

All major policies are made by the party's Politburo and Standing Committee, and the decisions are implemented by government agencies. For example, while the Politburo determines the main goals of educational policy, the ministry of education implements that policy throughout the school system, and teachers are employees of the ministry of education, not the Communist Party. While the party and government have separate organizational structures, there is considerable overlap in personnel between the two at the top levels. For example, the Communist Party leader, is also the president of china and head of state. The premier of the government is always a member of the party Politburo and its Standing Committee. Party and government policy is coordinated by the fact that a high percentage of government officials are also Communist Party members.

China's premier is the head of the government with responsibility for leading and coordinating its tasks. The premier heads China's cabinet, the **State Council**, which includes many of the same kinds of ministries one finds in European countries such as finance, foreign affairs, and national defense. It also includes a ministry of public security that is responsible for maintaining order in China.

In addition to a **premier** who oversees and coordinates government ministries and agencies, China has a head of state, the **president**, whose position is mainly ceremonial. It is the president, however, who represents China at meetings with other world leaders and negotiates with them. When a Chinese leader meets with U.S. presidents, the leader comes as the President of China, not as Secretary General of the CCP.

The Communist Party's leaders choose the premier, cabinet ministers, and president, even though the constitution assigns that function to the legislature, the **National People's Congress** (NPC). The National People's Congress is a government institution, which should not be confused with the Communist Party's National Party Congress. The unicameral National People's Congress can have as many as 3,000 members who are indirectly elected by people's congresses at the provincial level of government for five-year terms. It meets only two to three weeks each year and has very little power. When it is not in session it is represented by a Standing Committee of approximately 150 members.

For decades the NPC was a rubber stamp for party policies, but its members have become more outspoken in their criticisms of party policies in recent years. In 2006, legislators opposed government proposals to strengthen property rights, claiming they were too sympathetic to the interests of capitalists and the government should do more to promote equity and social justice.[52] The government withdrew its proposals in the face of such criticism. While the NPC has become more of a forum for debate over policies than in the past, it still lacks the ability to determine its own agenda independent of the Communist Party.[53]

One of the most widely discussed governmental reforms was the decision in the late 1980s to allow villages to elect village leaders among competing contestants. Some scholars believe these elections provide the basis for an extension of democratic practices to higher levels of government. Others believe the elections have little significance because party leaders rather than elected government officials still have real power in many villages. The party has also tried limited experiments with elections in townships, counties, and urban areas.[54] The impact of these elections on democratization is similarly unclear.[55]

China's judicial system is headed by a Supreme People's Court. There is no system of judicial review, and the court system is subordinate to the Communist Party. During the Cultural Revolution, judges were attacked by the Red Guards as elitists, and courts were shut down. Many legal reforms have been implemented since the Cultural Revolution, and the number of lawyers and lawsuits against businesses and government agencies has increased dramatically. Despite these reforms, the Communist Party still exercises a great deal of influence over lawyers, judges, and decisions. It controls appointments of key personnel and "is fundamentally unwilling to allow real judicial constraints on the exercise of its power."[56] Another problem is widespread corruption. "In public perception, the Chinese judiciary is one of the most corrupt government institutions."[57]

Criminal cases in China are handled by the "people's procuratorate." When officials bring a case to trial, the accused is almost invariably convicted. Prison terms are long, and the death penalty is applied for a wide range of offenses, including certain economic crimes. Amnesty International estimated in 2009 that China executed more people than all of the other countries in the world combined.[58]

State and Society

The CCP does not allow any organized opposition to its rule, but its leaders have learned they cannot survive by relying only on control and coercion. This lesson was brought home to them by the Tiananmen Square demonstrations in1989, the collapse of communist regimes in Eastern Europe in 1989, and the fall of the Soviet Union in 1991, which left them "profoundly shaken."[59] They concluded from these examples of instability that it was imprudent for the party to permit an organized opposition to form that could potentially challenge it. Another lesson was not to allow experiments with democracy at the national level, as Gorbachev did in the Soviet Union. In addition to drawing lessons about what to avoid, the Chinese communists also drew lessons about what they could do to ensure their continued rule. One was to become more ideologically flexible, and the other was to co-opt social elites instead of repressing and antagonizing them. Consequently, the party scrapped its ideology of class struggle and since 2000 has presented itself as a party that represents "the advanced productive forces in society" and governs in the "interests of the vast majority of people."[60] It also actively seeks the support of social elites. It has tried to coopt private entrepreneurs by supporting market-oriented economic development and even recruiting them as members of the Communist Party. At the same time it has tried to attract professionals and intellectuals by subsidizing their research and appointing them to desirable positions.[61] Increasingly the party is becoming "the party of elites, including commercial elites," and less a party representing the interests of workers and peasants.[62]

Another of the lessons Chinese scholars drew from their comparative studies of communist collapse elsewhere was the importance of managing ethnic issues and avoiding ethnic chauvinism. But Communist Party leaders have not made the kinds of adjustments in dealing with ethnic minorities that they have in dealing with Chinese social elites."[63] Ethnic Chinese make up 92 percent of China's population, but in some border areas, such as Tibet, ethnic Chinese are a minority. Tibetans have resented Chinese control of their territory as have the Uighurs, a Muslim minority in China's northwest Xinjiang province. In order to strengthen their rule in these outlying areas, the Party has promoted the migration of ethnic Chinese to the areas, threatening the majority status of Tibetans and Uighurs in their home regions. Tibetans and Uighurs resent China's political and economic policies, and Uighur resentment boiled over into riots in 2009, but Chinese authorities show little inclination to change the policies. [64]

One of the biggest tests of the state's ability to control social behavior has been its controversial **one-child policy.** At China's rate of population growth in 1980, its population of 800 million would have doubled by 2005 to 1.6 billion. Chinese authorities initially limited parents to having just one child but relaxed the strict one-child policy because of intense resistance from families in rural China and foreign criticism of its excesses.[65] Local officials have population control targets they are expected to meet and there is strong government pressure on them to meet the targets. The one-child policy helped hold the population to approximately 1.3 billion, but it had three unintended consequences. One was an increase in the number of aborted female fetuses: parents who were limited to one child wanted to make sure it was a boy. One farmer told *New York Times* reporter Nicholas Kristof in 1993, "You go to the doctor and pay him 200 or 300 yuan. He tells you if your wife is pregnant with a boy or a girl. Then if it's a girl, you get an abortion."[66] As a result, hundreds of thousands of girls are "missing" who would otherwise have been born. Another unintended consequence has been to contribute to the labor shortage now facing some coastal cities.[67] Finally, the policy has led to a dearth of young people compared to old.

The CCP has also tried to exert social control through controlling the flow of information that reaches citizens. This has been made more difficult by China's openness to the world and by the internet. The authorities do not want to lose the advantages of such openness, but the Propaganda Department censors close newspapers and block access to Internet sites "when and where it sees fit." Journalists and bloggers who cross the fuzzy line of what is permitted are threatened or arrested. The party has negotiated censorship regulations with Google and Yahoo as the price for these companies to get licenses to operate in China.[68]

Political Culture

For most of China's history, it was the dominant country in Asia. Most Chinese assume this is China's natural place in the region, and they want China to be a world power as well. They take great pride in its economic development and cultural accomplishments. Along with pride is considerable resentment over the way Western powers humiliated China in the nineteenth and early twentieth centuries. This mix of pride and bitterness has produced what China specialist David Shambaugh calls "competing nationalisms." On the one hand, pride has contributed to a "confident nationalism" based on China's economic success and renewed role as a major power in international politics. This is the nationalism China showcased at the summer Olympic Games in 2008. On the other hand, there is a resentful nationalism based on past treatment by Western powers and current slights. It showed itself in 2008 in angry Chinese reactions to pro-Tibet and anti-Chinese demonstrations in the United States and Europe.[69]

The current regime has benefited from these strong nationalist feelings. But nationalism is not the only reason for high levels of satisfaction with the regime. A 2002 study of political culture and regime support in several Asian countries by China scholar Andrew Nathan found that China had the highest level of regime support among the countries in the survey. An extraordinarily high 94.4 percent of Chinese respondents agreed with the statement "our form of government is the best for us." Most surprising of all, 81.9 percent of respondents said they were "satisfied with how democracy works in our country." Chinese were more satisfied about the way democracy works in their country than Japanese, even though China is by any measure an authoritarian regime, while Japan is a democracy. These findings demonstrate how democracy can be defined in very different ways. They also suggest the regime has been successful in promoting "democracy with Chinese characteristics" as a form of democracy that works in the best interests of the Chinese people.[70]

One explanation for why the regime is awarded such high marks is the credit it receives for the increase in the Chinese people's overall standard of living in recent decades. Another reason is the greater personal freedom citizens

TABLE 11.1

Differing Chinese and Russian Political Values in 2006–2007

Value	Russia (2006)	China (2007)
Governments should take more responsibility for ensuring that everyone is provided for.	43%	15.3%
Need a strong leader who does not have to bother with parliament or elections.	20%	5.4%

Source: World Values Survey 2005–2008. www.worldvaluessurvey.org

now enjoy in comparison to the past. Finally, Andrew Nathan suggests that the traditional norms and values Chinese learn early in their lives have led to positive evaluations of the regime's performance. Many older Chinese have strong traditional values that are nondemocratic. Nathan and his colleagues found the "stronger the traditional social values a person has, the lower the support for democratic values."[71] Urban and educated Chinese are more likely to support democratic values, and as their numbers grow, it is reasonable to expect "regime legitimacy to come under greater challenge."[72]

Finally, it is worth noting that Chinese have very different expectations of what governments should do in comparison with Russians. Lengthy communist party rule in both countries might be expected to have shaped similar expectations of government, but it has not, as can be seen in Table 11.1. In general, fewer Chinese look forward to a nanny state or desire a strong leader than the Russians.

Political Economy

The final lesson Chinese leaders drew from their study of communist regime failure in Eastern Europe and the Soviet Union was that to stay in power the party needed to "sustain economic growth in order to provide jobs and raise standards of living."[73] If they failed to do so, nationalism and past economic success would not keep them in power. The challenge the Communist Party leaders face in this respect is especially daunting: With the world's largest population they have to create 12 million new jobs a year just to keep up with new workers entering the work force.[74]

Chinese leaders describe the country's political economy as "**socialism with Chinese characteristics.**" It has four components. First, markets will set prices in most sectors of the economy and there will be a large role for privately owned firms. Second, small- and medium-sized state-owned enterprises that perform badly and persistently require bailouts from government banks will be shut down or sold. Third, China will compete in world markets. Joining the World Trade Organization (WTO), which manages rules of trade among countries, in 2001 was a sign that China was willing to open its formerly closed markets in order to gain access to foreign markets. Finally, despite all of these changes, the leadership insists that China is, and will remain, socialist. It will do so by keeping a large state-owned enterprise sector and by retaining collective ownership of farm land.

The Party leadership is acutely aware that the turn toward markets has drawbacks as well as advantages. In the 1990s, leaders believed the benefits of growth would "trickle down" from the rich to the poor, and from the urban areas to the rural areas, but "rising inequality and social unrest have called this view into question."[75] While China has prospered, raising tens of millions of people out of abject poverty, some people have done much better than others. At the top there is now a small capitalist class made up of highly successful businesspeople. Below them is a middle class composed of "smaller entrepreneurs, managers and other white-collar employees of foreign or large companies and professionals." These two groups account "for less than 13 percent of the urban population, making them about 5 percent of the country as a whole."[76] At the other extreme is a new class of about 40 to 50 million urban poor, comprising workers who have lost their jobs and their family members.[77] Their numbers have been swollen by millions of peasant migrants to the cities looking for jobs as part of the informal labor force. The urban poor now make up a "large portion of the average city's citizenry." [78]

The appearance of rich entrepreneurs who live in gated communities and drive luxury cars alongside the urban poor is reflected in data on increasing income inequality. The Gini Index, where 0 equals perfect equality and 100 perfect inequality, has risen from 33 at the beginning of the reforms in the late 1970s to around 49 in 2005, "meaning that China has shifted from being one of the most egalitarian countries in Asia to becoming one of the least." China's National Statistics Bureau found that 45 percent of China's wealth was in the hands of the top 10 percent of the population, while "the poorest 10% shared only 1.4%."[79]

The second major cleavage in China today is between urban and rural dwellers. Deng Xiaoping's reforms began in the rural areas and led to rapid increases in most farmers' incomes in the 1980s. By the 1990s, however, the impact of these reforms on income growth had for the most part ended. Farmers received a onetime boost in income from the breakup of communes and a switch to the household responsibility system. But the latter left most farmers with plots of land that are too small to yield increasing incomes. Consequently, rural income growth stagnated in the 1990s. In contrast, in many cities, especially those along the east coast, per capita income has grown rapidly. The gap between average incomes of urban and rural residents was about 3:1 by 2005, according to United Nations Development Program.[80]

These inequalities also extend to inequalities in access to capabilities in education and health care. Many rural schools are not as good as urban schools, and in urban areas the children of rich parents go to better schools than children of poor workers. The children of migrant workers in the cities are particularly disadvantaged. They are penalized by China's household registration system that divides Chinese into urban and rural residents. Migrant workers' registration papers identify them as rural dwellers and and their children are expected to attend schools in their parents' rural village. As a result "tens of millions of children of migrant workers are, in effect, forced to stay in the countryside for schooling looked after by other relatives."[81] They are also disadvantaged in the competition to get into universities.

Access to health care has also become much more unequal. In the mid-1970s and early 1980s, an estimated 90 percent of Chinese citizens had some form of health care coverage. Urban workers were covered by state owned enterprises and rural citizens by rural cooperatives. When many state-owned enterprises closed and rural cooperatives collapsed after the introduction of household farming, many Chinese lost their access to health care. The central government did not replace the lost health care with an alternative comprehensive system of health care.[82] Wealthier Chinese can pay for private care, but such care is beyond the reach of many citizens. Migrant workers are among the most vulnerable. Many have no health coverage at all and those that do get coverage at their place of work lose it when they lose their job. In the last four months of 2008 as the effects of the world recession hit China and plants began to lay off workers, an estimated 10 million migrant workers lost access to health care, when they lost their jobs. In 2002, approximately a third of rural residents did not receive any kind of health care and in 2006 less than half of urban residents had any coverage.[83]

China's leaders are now making efforts to moderate the dark side of markets and increase security for vulnerable parts of the population.[84] They emphasize creating a "harmonious society" less divided by "huge disparities in wealth and access to services such as schools and hospitals, and one less troubled by protests."[85] In response to these problems the party has promised a number of new policies, some of which are targeted especially at rural areas and the rural poor. Recent evidence suggests increases in spending for unemployment benefits, living subsidies, and food subsidies have helped improve people's lives.[86] It remains to be seen how well and how rapidly these reforms will be implemented.

Looming over these policy challenges are major environmental problems. China's economic growth has been fueled by coal, which provides about 70 percent of China's energy and is a major reason that 16 of the world's 20 most polluted cities are in China. The rapid increase in automobile and truck use contributes further to air pollution in China, which has surpassed the United States to become the biggest producer of carbon dioxide. China's water supplies are becoming depleted because of increasing use of water for irrigation and rapidly growing cities. Much of the water supply is polluted and contaminated water is a major cause of death among children under five in the rural population. Air pollution causes as many as 750,000 premature deaths a year. Chinese authorities had to take drastic measures to improve air quality in

Beijing for the 2008 Olympics, but have not taken such measures for other equally polluted cities.[87]

Authorities have taken a number of steps to address pollution problems. In January 2010, Prime Minister Wen Jiabao created a National Energy Commission. China is now the world's largest maker of wind turbines and solar electric panels. China is also building more efficient coal power plants and nuclear reactors to cut its dependence on coal and oil. This will still leave China heavily dependent on coal for many years. Despite the race to build new wind turbines and solar panels, wind, solar, and biomass will provide only 8 percent of China's energy by 2020.[88] Furthermore, many government officials as well as businesspeople and industrialists put a higher priority on economic growth than on the environment.[89]

Analysts differ over China's future prospects. Some see a bright future for China, with its economy continuing to grow rapidly and China becoming the dominant power in the world.[90] Ted C. Fishman, for example, argues the twenty-first century will be "The Chinese Century" as the twentieth century was "the American century." He argues China's combination of disciplined low-wage workers, growing numbers of engineers and scientists, innovative entrepreneurs, and increased spending on research and development give it advantages no other country has. Chinese firms can produce a wide range of labor-intensive exports such as shoes and toys more cheaply than any other country. They are also exporting increasingly sophisticated products.[91]

China specialists are less impressed with China's prospects. They point out that it has many problems including concerns about the Communist Party's ability to sustain its legitimacy, extensive corruption, and large numbers of protests in cities and rural areas. Some China specialists believe China is likely to succeed in handling these problems over the next decade or so, while others believe China will not be able to cope with them successfully. They do not, however, believe this will necessarily lead to the regime's sudden collapse as happened in the Soviet Union, but that China faces long-term political and economic stagnation.[92] Nathan compares the leaders of the regime to "a team of acrobats on a high wire, staving off all crises, while keeping" their act together. They are currently managing to stave off crises, but they "cannot afford to slip."[93]

COMPARING CAPABILITIES BETWEEN RUSSIA AND CHINA

Despite its spectacular economic growth rates since 1980, China is a poorer country than Russia. In 2009, its per capita income was $6,600 in purchasing power parity terms. The corresponding figure for Russia was $15,100.[94] Russia has a considerable advantage in per capita income over China, and leads China in some indicators of capability, but China is catching up quickly in the areas where it lags behind.

TABLE 11.2

Infant Mortality Rates in Russia and China per 1,000 Live Births

	1970	1980	1990	2000	2008
Russia	33	28	23	20	12
China	83	46	37	30	18

Source: World Bank, World Development Indicators at www.google.com/publicdata, accessed July 30, 2010.

Physical Well-Being

We have suggested that the best way of measuring whether governments meet the physical needs of their citizens is to look at infant mortality rates. If governments fail here, there is no chance for infants to develop other capabilities. Russia started off with a large lead over China in 1970, but China has reduced infant mortality rates much more rapidly than Russia since then and is approaching Russia's infant mortality rate with less than half Russia's per capita income. See Table 11.2

In a little less than 40 years, China cut its infant mortality gap with Russia from 50 infant deaths per 1,000 to 6 per 1,000. It is notable that the Chinese infant mortality rate continued to fall, despite reductions in health care for many citizens in China in the past two decades.

Informed Decision Making

Both countries have done an excellent job of teaching literacy as can be seen in Table 11.3.

The countries are almost identical in youth literacy rates, while Russia has a slight edge in adult literacy. This difference reflects lower literacy rates among older adults in China, many of whom live in rural areas. China has achieved these rates with a much lower income than Russia.

Safety

China is a much safer country than Russia as measured by homicide rates. See Table 11.4. China's homicide rate is lower than that of Scotland, Finland,

TABLE 11.3

Youth and Adult Literacy Rates in Russia and China, 2008

	Youth Literacy % people 15–24	Adult Literacy % people over 15
Russia	99.9%	99.5%
China	99.3%	93.7%

Source: World Bank, World Development Indicators. www.worldbank.org/indicator

TABLE 11.4

Homicide Rates in Russia and China per 100,000

Russia	29.7
China	2.2

Source: Data set for *The Good Society*, 2nd Edition

Switzerland, and the United States. Russia's, on the other hand, places it among the most homicide prone countries in the world.

The World Bank's World Governance Indicators provide an alternative method of comparing violence among countries. Its "rule of law" indicator measures "the quality of police and courts as well as the likelihood of crime and violence."[95] The scores range from 2.5 to –2.5, with more positive scores indicating higher quality of policing and courts and less likelihood of crime and violence, and negative scores indicating lower quality policing and courts and greater likelihood of crime and violence. The percentage indicates a country's ranking relative to other countries. The results for Russia and China can be seen in Table 11.5.

On the basis of this indicator , which includes the quality of justice as well as likelihood of crime and violence, neither country scores well. There is still a large difference between Russia and China. Russia's rule of law ranking was better than that of only 20 percent of the other countries ranked by the World Bank, while China's ranking was better than 45 percent of the countries.

Democracy

Individuals' ability to participate effectively in political choices that govern their lives is essential for sustaining conditions that improve their health, education, and safety. For example, while the Chinese authorities have had considerable success in raising citizens out of poverty and improving their health, they also threaten citizens' health by pursuing industrialization policies detrimental to health. Citizens have very little ability to change these

TABLE 11.5

Rule of Law in Russia and China, 2008

	Score	Percentile Rank
Russia	–0.91	20%
China	–0.33	45%

Source: World Bank, Governance Matters, 2009. www.worldbank.org/governance, accessed June 16, 2010.

> ### TABLE 11.6
>
> **Voice and Accountability in Russia and China, 2008**
>
> | | Voice and Accountability Score | Percentile Rank |
> | --- | --- | --- |
> | Russia | −0.97 | 21.6 |
> | China | −1.72 | 5.8 |
>
> *Source:* World Bank, Governance Matters, 2009. www.worldbank.org/governance, accessed June 16, 2010.

---

policies. One way to measure citizens' ability to express their views to governments and government accountability to citizens is to use the World Bank's Governance Indicators Dataset for "voice and accountability." Countries were scored on a −2.50 to 2.50 scale on this index. The higher a country's score, the more its citizens were deemed to have "voice and accountability." The percentile rank shows the percentage of countries ranked below the country. See Table 11.6.

Measured this way both countries perform poorly in providing voice and accountability for citizens, although Russia does better than China. Less than 6 percent of the countries in the world had lower voice and accountability scores than China.

Polity IV scores draw an even sharper distinction between Russia and China. In a ranking system in which a 10 is the most democratic and −10 is the most authoritarian, Russia received a Polity score of 4 in 2008, while China received a −7. In summary, while neither country does well in providing individuals with the ability to participate effectively in political choices that govern their lives, Russia does a better job than China.

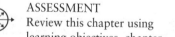EXERCISES

Apply what you learned in this chapter on MyPoliSciKit (www.mypoliscikit.com).

 ASSESSMENT
Review this chapter using learning objectives, chapter summaries, practice tests, and more

 VIDEO CASE STUDIES
Analyze recent world affairs by watching streaming video from major news providers.

 FLASHCARDS
Learn the key terms in this chapter; you can test yourself by term or definition.

 COMPARATIVE EXERCISES
Compare political ideas, behaviors, institutions, and policies worldwide.

CRITICAL THINKING QUESTIONS

1. Vladimir Putin received job approval ratings of over 70 percent for most of his term in office as president of Rusia and was chosen as president by overwhelming margins by voters. If the great majority of Russians approved of him and his policies, what does it matter that Russia has an electoral authoritarian regime rather than a democratic one?
2. Evidence from surveys in Russia and China finds that their authoritarian regimes fit their countries' political culture. If this is the case, isn't it inappropriate for citizens from a very different political culture such as that of the United States to criticize these regimes?
3. Why has China's communist party-state been able to survive the kind of political upheavals that toppled communist party-states in Eastern Europe and the Soviet Union?
4. The collapse of communist regimes in Eastern Europe and the Soviet Union caused leaders of the CCP to undertake one of the biggest comparative studies in recent history. What was their dependent variable? What were their main independent variables?
5. Why have leaders of China's Communist Party supported market-oriented economic policies, even though they have led to growing income inequality and favor businesspeople over workers?

KEY TERMS

Communist regime   311
Democratic
   centralism   312
Nomenklatura   312
Central planning   313
Extensive growth   313
Intensive growth   313
Glasnost   314
Perestroika   314
President (Russia)   319
Russian Security
   Council   319
Prime Minister
   (Russia)   319
Federal Assembly   320
Federation Council   320

State Duma   320
United Russia   321
Party of power   322
Oligarchs   323
Shock therapy   325
Nationalist
   (or *Guomindang*)
   Party   328
Great Leap Forward
   (1958–1960)   330
Great Proletarian
   Cultural Revolution
   (1966–1976)   331
Reform and opening   331
Tiananmen Square
   Protests   332

Politburo   333
Secretariat   333
General Secretary of the
   Communist Party   333
Central Committee   333
National Party
   Congress   334
State Council   334
Premier   334
President   334
National People's
   Congress (NPC)   334
One-child policy   336
Socialism with Chinese
   characteristics   338

SUGGESTED READINGS

Nikolai Petrov, Masha Lipman, and Henry Hale, "Overmanaged Democracy in Russia: Governance Implications of Hybrid Regimes," Carnegie Endowment for International Peace, Russia and Eurasia Program, No. 106, February 2010. An excellent brief analysis of Russia as a version of electoral authoritarianism they call "overmanaged democracy." Particularly useful for explaining why Russian leaders want some degree of democracy.

Thomas F. Remington, *Politics in Russia* (New York: Longman, 2010). An excellent study of the Russian state, political parties, interest groups, political culture, and state and market in Russia.

Bruce K. Dickson, *Wealth into Power: the Communist Party's Embrace of China's Private Sector* (New York: Cambridge University Press, 2008). An excellent analysis of how and why the interests of China's Communist Party leaders and business elites have become intertwined and why China's capitalists have become one of the most important bases of support for the party.

Minxin Pei, *China's Trapped Transition: The Limits of Developmental Autocracy* (Cambridge, MA: Harvard University Press, 2006). The book argues that China is caught in a "trapped transition" from a command economy to a market economy. Necessary political reform has lagged far behind economic reform and this will cause problems in the future. Ruling elites are likely to protect their careers and privileges rather than make the needed reforms.

David Shambaugh, *China's Communist Party: Atrophy and Adaptation* (Washington, DC: Woodrow Wilson Center Press, 2009). An excellent explanation of how China's Communist Party used comparative analysis of the collapse of communist regimes in Eastern Europe and the Soviet Union to make changes in China to avoid a similar collapse.

NOTES

1. Stephen F. Cohen, *Bukharin and the Bolshevik Revolution* (New York: Oxford University Press, 1980), p. 339.
2. Aleksandr I. Solzhenitsyn, *The Gulag Archipelago* (New York: Harper and Row, 1974–1978).
3. Stephen White, "Russia," in *Politics in Europe*, 4th ed., M. Donald Hancock, eds. (Washington, D.C.: Congressional Quarterly Press, 2007), p. 464.
4. Arthur S. Banks, Thomas C. Muller, and William R. Overstreet, eds. *Political Handbook of the World 2005–2006* (Washington, D.C.: Congressional Quarterly Press, 2006), p. 964.
5. James F. Collins, Maria Lipman, Nikolay Petrov, and Henry Hale. "Medvedev's Presidency: What's New, What's Not." Carnegie Endowment for International Peace, March 9, 2010. www.carnegieendowment.org.
6. White, p. 481.
7. Gideon Lichfield, "Survey of Russia: Watch Your Back," *The Economist* (May 20, 2004), www.economist.com, accessed June 30, 2010.
8. Steven Kotkin, "Gasputin," *New Republic* (May 29, 2006), p. 30.
9. "Grease my palm," *The Economist* , November 27, 2008. www.economist.com, accessed November 30, 2008.
10. Transparency International, "Corruptions Perception Index 2009," www.transparency.org, accessed July 15, 2010.
11. Nikolai Petrov, Masha Lipman, and Henry Hale, "Overmanaged Democracy in Russia: Governance Implications of Hybrid Regimes," Carnegie Endowment for International Peace, Russia and Eurasia Program, No. 106, February 2010, p. 4.
12. Ibid., pp. 6–9.
13. Ibid., p. 7.
14. Vladimir Gel'man, "Russia's Party Politics," June 6. 2008, p. 2. wwwchathamhouse.org, accessed July 4, 2010.

15. White, pp. 489–490. Arthur S. Banks, Thomas C. Muller, and William R. Overstreet, editors, *Political Handbook of the World 2005–2006* (Washington, D.C.: Congressional Quarterly Press, 2006), p. 964.
16. Michael McFaul and Nikolai Petrov, "What the Elections Tell Us," *Journal of Democracy* 15(3) (July 2004), p. 24.
17. Banks, Muller, and Overstreet, p. 966.
18. Thomas F. Remington, "Prospects for a Democratic Left in Russia," *The Journal of Policy History* 15(1) (2003), p. 133.
19. Thomas F. Remington, "Politics in Russia," in *Comparative Politics Today*, 9th edition, ed. Gabriel A. Almond, G. Bingham Powell, Jr., Russell J. Dalton, and Kaare Strom (New York: Pearson Longman. 2008), pp. 392–393.
20. Gideon Lichfield, "Survey of Russia: Watch Your Back," *Economist* (May 20, 2004), www.economist.com, accessed July 2, 2010.
21. Ibid.
22. Anders Aslund, "Putin's Decline and America's Responsibility," Carnegie Foundation for International Peace, Policy Brief 41 (August 2005), p. 2, www.carnegieendowment.org, accessed July 2, 2010.
23. Thomas F. Remington, "Politics in Russia," pp. 385–386.
24. Petrov, Lipman, and Hale, "Overmanaged Democracy in Russia," pp. 17–18.
25. Alexander Lukin, "Russia's New Authoritarianism and the Post-Soviet Political Ideal," *Post-Soviet Affairs*, 25:1 (2009), pp. 66–92.
26. Arkady Ostrovsky, "Enigma Variations," *The Economist*, November 27, 2008. It is worth noting that the song is titled "Born in the USSR," not "born in Russia." Many Russians look back to the USSR with nostalgia.
27. World Values Survey. http://www.wvsevsdb.com/wvs/WVSAnalizeQuestion.jsp, accessed June 15, 2010.
28. World Values Survey. www.worldvaluessurvey.org. Accessed June 15, 2010.
29. Lukin, p. 71.
30. Ibid., pp. 77–78.
31. William Mishler and Richard Rose, "Generation, Age, and Time: The Dynamics of Political Learning during Russia's Transformation," *American Journal of Political Science* 51:4 (October 2007), p. 826.
32. Lukin, p. 87.
33. Petrov, Lipman, and Hale, "Overmanaged Democracy in Russia," pp. 25–28.
34. Joseph E. Stiglitz, *Globalization and Its Discontents* (New York: W. W. Norton 2002), p. 53.
35. Andrew E. Kramer and Steven Lee Myers, "Workers' Paradise Is Rebranded as Kremlin, Inc.," *The New York Times* (April 24, 2006), www.nytimes.com, accessed July 12, 2010. See also Marshal I. Goldman, "Political Graft: The Russian Way," p. 316.
36. Kramer and Myers, "Workers' Paradise is Rebranded as Kremlin, Inc."
37. "After Sakhalin," *The Economist* (December 13, 2006). www.economist.com, accessed July 5, 2010.
38. "Another Great Leap Forward," *The Economist* (March 11, 2010). www.economist.com, accessed March 15, 2010.
39. Ibid.
40. Ibid.
41. Andrew Nathan, *China's Transition* (New York: Columbia University Press, 1997), p. 29.
42. Ibid., p. 6.

43. Frederick C. Teiwes, "Politics at the 'Core': The Political Circumstances of Mao Zedong, Deng Xiaoping and Jiang Zemin," China information: *A Journal of Contemporary China Studies*, Vol. XV, No. 1, p. 27.

44. Nathan, *China's Transition*, p. 6.

45. "A Great Leap Forward," *The Economist* (October 5, 1991), pp. 19–21.

46. Minxin Pei, *China's Trapped Transition: The Limits of Developmental Autocracy* (Cambridge, MA: Harvard University Press, 2006), pp. 2–3.

47. Michel Oksenberg, "China's Political System: Challenges of the Twenty-First Century," *China Journal* 45 (January 2001), p. 22.

48. Lowell Dittmer, "The Changing Shape of Elite Power Politics," *The China Journal* 45 (January 2001), p. 53.

49. Tang Tsou, "Chinese Politics at the Top: Factionalism or Informal Politics? Balance-of-Power Politics or a Game to Win All?" *The China Journal* 34 (July 1995), cited in Frederick C. Teiwes, "Normal Politics with Chinese Characteristics," *The China Journal*, 45 (2001), p. 71.

50. Chen Li, "China's Team of Rivals," *Foreign Policy* (March/April 2009).

51. Andrew Nathan, "Authoritarian Resilience," *Journal of Democracy* 14(1) (January 2003), p. 9.

52. Joseph Khan, "A Sharp Debate Erupts in China over Ideologies," *New York Times*, March 12, 2006, www.nytimes.com, accessed July 7, 2010.

53. Minxin Pei, *China's Trapped Transition*, p. 64.

54. John L. Thornton, "Long Time Coming: The Prospects for Democracy in China," *Foreign Affairs* (January/February 2008), pp. 6–8.

55. Ibid., pp. 72–73.

56. Minxin Pei, *China's Trapped Transition*, p. 65.

57. Ibid., pp. 70–71.

58. "The Death Penalty in 2009," http://www.amnesty.org/en/death-penalty/death-sentences-and-executions-in-2009, accessed December 27, 2010.

59. David Shambaugh, *China's Communist Party: Atrophy and Adaptation* (Washington, D.C.: Woodrow Wilson Center Press, 2009), p. 53.

60. Ibid., p. 111.

61. Minxin Pei, *China's Trapped Transition*, pp. 89–92.

62. Shambaugh, *China's Communist Party*, p. 112.

63. Ibid., p. 75.

64. Minxin Pei, "Uighur Riots Show Need for Rethink by Beijing," *Financial Times* (July 9, 2009).

65. William A. Joseph, "China," p. 638; Nicholas D. Kristof and Sheryl Wudunn, *China Wakes*, pp. 228–229.

66. Nicholas D. Kristof and Sheryl Wudunn, *China Wakes: The Struggle for the Soul of a Rising Power* (New York: Vintage Books, 1994), p. 230.

67. Howard W. French, "As China Ages, a Shortage of Cheap Labor Looms," *The New York Times* (June 30, 2006), www.nytimes.com, accessed June 15, 2009.

68. David Shambaugh, *China's Communist Party*, p. 107.

69. David Shambaugh, "China's Competing Nationalisms." *International Herald Tribune*, May 5, 2008. www.brookings.edu. Accessed July 9, 2010.

70. Andrew J. Nathan, "Political Culture and Diffuse Regime Support in Asia," Working Papers Series No. 43, Asia Barometer, A Comparative Survey of Democracy Governance and Development, Tapei, 2007, pp. 4–6.

71. Ibid., pp. 12–15.

72. Ibid., pp. 17–18.

73. Minxin Pei, "How China Is Ruled," *The American Interest*, 3:4 (March/April 2008). pp. 46–47.

74. Guoguang Wu, "China in 2009," *Asian Survey* 50:1 (2010), p. 27.

75. Tony Saich, "China in 2005," *Asian Survey* (January/February 2006), p. 45.

76. An Chen, "The New Inequality," *Journal of Democracy* 14:1 (January 2003), p. 54.

77. Dorothy Solinger, "Path Dependence Re-examined: Chinese Welfare Policy in the Transition to Unemployment," *Comparative Politics* 38:1 (October 2005), p. 93.

78. Ibid., p. 96.

79. Saich, "China in 2005," p. 42.

80. Joseph Khan, "A Sharp Debate Erupts in China over Ideologies."

81. "Invisible and Heavy Shackles," *The Economist* (May 6, 2010).www.economist. com, accessed May 10, 2010.

82. Meredith Wen,"Averting Crisis: A Path Forward for China's Health Care System," Carnegie Endowment for International Peace Issue Briefing, March, 2009, p. 1.

83. Ibid., p. 6.

84. Ibid., p. 48.

85. James Miles, "Survey of China," p. 4.

86. Qin Gao, "Redistributive Nature of the Chinese Social Benefit System: Progressive or Regressive?" *The China Quarterly* 201 (March 2010), pp. 1–19.

87. Elizabeth C. Economy, "The Great Leap Backward: The Costs of China's Environmental Crisis," *Foreign Affairs* (September/October 2007), pp. 38–49.

88. Keith Bradsher, "China Leading Global Race to Make Clean Energy, " *New York Times* (January 31, 2010). Crisis," *Foreign Affairs* (September/October 2007), pp. 38–49.

89. Economy, pp. 50–56.

90. Ted C. Fishman, *China Inc.: How the Rise of the Next Superpower Challenges America and the World* (New York: Scribner, 2005).

91. Ted C. Fishman, "The Chinese Century," *New York Times Magazine* (July 4, 2004); and *China Inc.: How the Rise of the Next Superpower Challenges America and the World*.

92. Shambaugh, *China's Communist Party*, pp. 24–32.

93. Andrew J. Nathan, "Authoritarian Impermanence," *Journal of Democracy* 20:3 (July 2009), p. 40.

94. CIA World Fact Book 2007. www.cia.gov, accessed July 30, 2010.

95. Daniel Kaufmann, Aart Kraay, and Massimo Mastruzzi, *Governance Matters IV: Governance Indicators for 1996–2004* (Washington, D.C.: The World Bank, 2005), http://info.worldbank.org/etools/docs/library/206973/GovMatters_IV_main.pdf, accessed June 16, 2010.

APPENDIX

TABLE 1.1

Infant Mortality Rates

Country	Rank	Rate	Country	Rank	Rate
Singapore	1	2.31	Canada	36	5.04
Bermuda	2	2.46	Ireland	37	5.05
Sweden	3	2.75	Greece	38	5.16
Japan	4	2.79	San Marino	39	5.34
Hong Kong	5	2.92	Taiwan	40	5.35
Macau	6	3.22	Isle of Man	41	5.37
Iceland	7	3.23	Italy	42	5.51
France	8	3.33	European Union	43	5.72
Finland	9	3.47	Cuba	44	5.82
Anguilla	10	3.52	United States	45	6.26
Norway	11	3.58	Faroe Islands	46	6.32
Malta	12	3.75	Croatia	47	6.37
Andorra	13	3.76	Belarus	48	6.43
Czech Republic	14	3.79	Lithuania	49	6.47
Germany	15	3.99	Northern Mariana		
Switzerland	16	4.18	Islands	50	6.59
Spain	17	4.21	Cyprus	51	6.6
Israel	18	4.22	Serbia	52	6.75
Slovenia	19	4.25	Poland	53	6.8
Liechtenstein	20	4.25	Slovakia	54	6.84
Korea, South	21	4.26	Saint Pierre and		
Denmark	22	4.34	Miquelon	55	6.87
Austria	23	4.42	Cayman Islands	56	6.94
Belgium	24	4.44	New Caledonia	57	7.05
Guernsey	25	4.47	Estonia	58	7.32
Luxembourg	26	4.56	French Polynesia	59	7.55
Netherlands	27	4.73	Virgin Islands	60	7.56
Jersey	28	4.73	Chile	61	7.71
Australia	29	4.75	Hungary	62	7.86
Portugal	30	4.78	Puerto Rico	63	8.42
Gibraltar	31	4.83	Latvia	64	8.77
United Kingdom	32	4.85	Costa Rica	65	8.77
New Zealand	33	4.92	Kuwait	66	8.96
Monaco	34	5	Ukraine	67	8.98
Wallis and Futuna	35	5.02	Macedonia	68	9.01

TABLE 1.1 (*CONTINUED*)

Country	Rank	Rate	Country	Rank	Rate
Netherlands			Malaysia	101	15.87
Antilles	69	9.09	West Bank	102	15.96
Bosnia and			Montserrat	103	16.08
Herzegovina	70	9.1	Georgia	104	16.22
Nauru	71	9.25	Antigua and		
American Samoa	72	10.18	Barbuda	105	16.25
Russia	73	10.56	Oman	106	16.88
Greenland	74	10.72	Cook Islands	107	16.9
Uruguay	75	11.32	Thailand	108	17.63
Argentina	76	11.44	Saint Helena	109	17.63
Saudi Arabia	77	11.57	Bulgaria	110	17.87
Tonga	78	11.58	Gaza Strip	111	18.35
Fiji	79	11.58	Mexico	112	18.42
Mauritius	80	12.2	Tuvalu	113	18.43
Brunei	81	12.27	Sri Lanka	114	18.57
Barbados	82	12.29	Albania	115	18.62
Seychelles	83	12.3	Suriname	116	18.81
Botswana	84	12.59	Colombia	117	18.9
Qatar	85	12.66	Solomon Islands	118	19.03
Panama	86	12.67	Armenia	119	20.21
United Arab			China	120	20.25
Emirates	87	12.7	Philippines	121	20.56
Moldova	88	13.13	Ecuador	122	20.9
Palau	89	13.14	Libya	123	21.05
Grenada	90	13.23	El Salvador	124	21.52
Saint Lucia	91	13.43	Venezuela	125	21.54
Dominica	92	13.65	Lebanon	126	21.82
Aruba	93	13.79	Tunisia	127	22.57
Turks and Caicos			Brazil	128	22.58
Islands	94	13.89	Vietnam	129	22.88
Saint Kitts and			Romania	130	22.9
Nevis	95	13.94	Belize	131	23.07
British Virgin			Bahamas, The	132	23.17
Islands	96	14.65	Uzbekistan	133	23.43
Jordan	97	14.97	Honduras	134	24.03
Saint Vincent			Samoa	135	24.22
and the			Paraguay	136	24.68
Grenadines	98	15.14	Nicaragua	137	25.02
Jamaica	99	15.22	Marshall Islands	138	25.45
Bahrain	100	15.25	Kazakhstan	139	25.73

(*continued*)

TABLE 1.1 (*CONTINUED*)

Country	Rank	Rate	Country	Rank	Rate
Turkey	140	25.78	Korea, North	176	51.34
Syria	141	25.87	Gabon	177	51.78
Dominican			Madagascar	178	54.2
Republic	142	25.96	Azerbaijan	179	54.6
Micronesia,			Yemen	180	54.7
Federated			Kenya	181	54.7
States of	143	26.1	Cambodia	182	54.79
Egypt	144	27.26	Togo	183	56.24
Algeria	145	27.73	Mayotte	184	56.29
Guatemala	146	27.84	Senegal	185	58.94
Peru	147	28.62	Bangladesh	186	59.02
Maldives	148	29.53	Burundi	187	59.64
Guyana	149	29.65	Haiti	188	59.69
Trinidad and			Cameroon	189	63.34
Tobago	150	29.93	Mauritania	190	63.42
Indonesia	151	29.97	Benin	191	64.64
India	152	30.15	Uganda	192	64.82
Kyrgyzstan	153	31.26	Pakistan	193	65.14
Zimbabwe	154	32.31	Guinea	194	65.22
Iran	155	35.78	Comoros	195	66.57
Morocco	156	36.88	Gambia, The	196	67.33
Sao Tome and			Cote d'Ivoire	197	68.06
Principe	157	37.12	Swaziland	198	68.63
Mongolia	158	39.88	Tanzania	199	69.28
Timor-Leste	159	40.65	Western Sahara	200	69.66
World	160	40.85	Lesotho	201	77.4
Tajikistan	161	41.03	Laos	202	77.82
Cape Verde	162	41.35	Congo, Republic		
Eritrea	163	43.33	of the	203	79.78
Kiribati	164	43.48	Central African		
Iraq	165	43.82	Republic	204	80.62
South Africa	166	44.42	Ethiopia	205	80.8
Bolivia	167	44.66	Congo,		
Papua New			Democratic		
Guinea	168	45.23	Republic of the	206	81.21
Turkmenistan	169	45.36	Equatorial Guinea	207	81.58
Namibia	170	45.51	Rwanda	208	81.61
Nepal	171	47.46	Sudan	209	82.43
Burma	172	47.61	Burkina Faso	210	84.49
Bhutan	173	49.36	Malawi	211	89.05
Vanuatu	174	49.45	Nigeria	212	94.35
Ghana	175	51.09	Djibouti	213	97.51

TABLE 1.1 (*CONTINUED*)

Country	Rank	Rate	Country	Rank	Rate
Chad	214	98.69	Niger	220	116.66
Guinea-Bissau	215	99.82	Liberia	221	138.24
Zambia	216	101.2	Afghanistan	222	151.95
Mali	217	102.05	Sierra Leone	223	154.43
Mozambique	218	105.8	Angola	224	180.21
Somalia	219	109.19	Montenegro[3]		23.6

Source: CIA World Factbook, Country Comparison 2009 estimates.

[3] UN World Population Prospects, 2006 Revision.

TABLE 1.2

Adult Literacy Rates

Country	Rank	Rate	Country	Rank	Rate
Cuba	1	99.8	Sweden	19	99
Estonia	1	99.8	Switzerland	19	99
Latvia	1	99.8	United Kingdom	19	99
Barbados	4	99.7	United States	19	99
Slovenia	4	99.7	Hungary	43	98.9
Belarus	4	99.7	Italy	43	98.9
Lithuania	4	99.7	Samoa	45	98.7
Ukraine	4	99.7	Trinidad and		
Kazakhstan	9	99.6	Tobago	45	98.7
Tajikistan	9	99.6	Croatia	45	98.7
Armenia	11	99.5	Bulgaria	48	98.3
Azerbaijan	11	99.5	Spain	49	97.9
Turkmenistan	11	99.5	Uruguay	49	97.9
Russia	11	99.5	Saint Kitts		
Kyrgyzstan	15	99.3	and Nevis	51	97.8
Poland	15	99.3	Cyprus	52	97.7
Moldova	17	99.2	Romania	53	97.6
Tonga	17	99.2	Argentina	53	97.6
Albania	19	99	Mongolia	55	97.3
Antigua and			Israel	56	97.1
Barbuda	19	99	Greece	56	97.1
Australia	19	99	Maldives	58	97
Austria	19	99	Macedonia	58	97
Belgium	19	99	Uzbekistan	60	96.9
Canada	19	99	Bosnia and		
Czech Republic	19	99	Herzegovina	61	96.7
Denmark	19	99	Chile	62	96.5
Finland	19	99	Serbia	63	96.4
France	19	99	Grenada	64	96
Germany	19	99	Costa Rica	65	95.9
Guyana	19	99	Bahamas	66	95.8
Iceland	19	99	Venezuela	67	95.2
Ireland	19	99	Brunei		
Japan	19	99	Darussalam	68	94.9
Republic of			Portugal	68	94.9
Korea	19	99	Saint Lucia	70	94.8
Luxembourg	19	99	Hong Kong	71	94.6
Netherlands	19	99	Paraguay	71	94.6
New Zealand	19	99	Kuwait	73	94.5
Norway	19	99	Singapore	74	94.4
Slovakia	19	99	Fiji	74	94.4

TABLE 1.2 (*CONTINUED*)

Country	Rank	Rate	Country	Rank	Rate
Thailand	76	94.1	Libya	110	84.2
Palestinian			Gabon	111	84
Territories	77	93.8	Saudi Arabia	112	82.9
Panama	78	93.4	Iran	113	82.4
Philippines	78	93.3	South Africa	113	82.4
China	80	93.1	Lesotho	115	82.2
Qatar	81	93.1	Oman	116	81.4
Mexico	82	92.8	Botswana	117	81.2
Colombia	83	92.7	Cape Verde	117	81.2
Malta	84	92.4	Syria	119	80.8
Indonesia	85	92	El Salvador	120	80.6
Malaysia	86	91.9	Honduras	121	80
Seychelles	87	91.8	Jamaica	122	79.9
Zimbabwe	88	91.2	Swaziland	123	79.6
Jordan	89	91.1	Nicaragua	124	76.7
Ecuador	90	91	Solomon Islands	126	76.6
Sri Lanka	91	90.8	Belize	127	75.1
Bolivia	92	90.7	Tunisia	128	74.3
Suriname	93	90.4	Vanuatu	129	74
Vietnam	94	90.3	Cambodia	130	73.6
United Arab			Kenya	131	73.6
Emirates	95	90	Egypt	132	71.4
Brazil	95	90	Madagascar	133	70.7
Myanmar	97	89.9	Djibouti	134	70.3
Peru	98	89.6	Algeria	135	69.9
Lebanon	98	89.6	Tanzania	136	69.4
Dominican			Guatemala	137	69.1
Republic	100	89.1	Nigeria	138	69.1
Turkey	101	88.7	Laos	139	68.7
Saint Vincent			Zambia	140	68
and the			Cameroon	141	67.9
Grenadines	102	88.1	Angola	142	67.4
Dominica	103	88	Democratic		
Equatorial			Republic of		
Guinea	104	87	the Congo	143	67.2
Namibia	106	85	Uganda	144	73.6
Sao Tome and			Rwanda	145	64.9
Principe	107	84.9	Malawi	146	71.8
Republic of the			India	147	61
Congo	108	84.7	Sudan	148	60.9
Mauritius	109	84.3	Eritrea	149	60.5

(*continued*)

TABLE 1.2 (*CONTINUED*)

Country	Rank	Rate	Country	Rank	Rate
Burundi	150	59.3	Senegal	168	39.3
Ghana	151	57.9	Mozambique	169	38.7
Papua New			Ethiopia	170	35.9
Guinea	152	57.3	Sierra Leone	171	34.8
Comoros	153	56.8	Benin	172	34.7
Haiti	154	54.8	Guinea	173	29.5
Yemen	155	54.1	Niger	174	28.7
Togo	156	53.2	Chad	175	25.7
Morocco	157	52.3	Mali	176	24
Mauritania	158	51.2	Burkina Faso	177	23.6
Timor-Leste	159	50.1	Liberia[1]		57.5
Pakistan	160	49.9	Georgia[1]		100
Cote d'Ivoire	161	48.7	North Korea[1]		99
Central African			Pakistan[1]		49.9
Republic	162	48.6	Afghanistan[1]		28.1
Nepal	162	48.6	Iraq[1]		74.1
Bangladesh	164	47.5	Somalia[1]		37.8
Bhutan	165	47	Tiawan[1]		96.1
Guinea-Bissau	166	44.8	Montenegro[2]		96.4
Gambia	167	42.5			15189

Source: United Nations Development Programme, Human Development Report 2009 , page 171.
http://hdr.undp.org/en/reports/global/hdr2009/.
[1]CIA World Factbook.

TABLE 1.3

Homicide Rates Around the World per 100,000

Country	Rank	Rate	Country	Rank	Rate
Luxembourg	1	0.4	New Zealand	12	1.5
Japan	2	0.5	Slovenia	12	1.5
Morocco	2	0.5	Solomon Islands	12	1.5
Singapore	2	0.5	England & Wales	13	1.6
Hong Kong			France	13	1.6
(Spec Admin			Malta	14	1.7
Reg China)	3	0.6	Poland	14	1.7
Austria	4	0.7	Tunisia	14	1.7
Egypt	4	0.7	Bosnia and		
Fiji	4	0.7	Herzegovina	15	1.8
United Arab			Cyprus	15	1.8
Emirates	4	0.7	Marshall Islands	15	1.8
Norway	5	0.8	Croatia	16	2
Qatar	5	0.8	Malaysia	16	2
Micronesia	6	0.9	Belgium	17	2.1
Palau	6	0.9	Hungary	17	2.1
Bahrain	7	1	Maldives	17	2.1
Germany	7	1	Nepal	17	2.1
Greece	7	1	Oman	17	2.1
Iceland	7	1	China	18	2.2
Tonga	7	1	Czech Rep	18	2.2
Vanuatu	7	1	Korea, south	18	2.2
Bermuda	8	1.1	Bangladesh	19	2.3
Denmark	8	1.1	Slovakia	19	2.3
Ireland	8	1.1	Azerbaijan	20	2.4
Samoa	8	1.1	Lebanon	20	2.4
Italy	9	1.2	Macedonia	20	2.4
Jordan	9	1.2	Northern Ireland	20	2.4
Spain	9	1.2	Romania	20	2.4
Sweden	9	1.2	Tajikistan	20	2.4
Syria	9	1.2	Armenia	21	2.5
Australia	10	1.3	Mauritius	21	2.5
Algeria	11	1.4	Yemen	21	2.5
Andorra	11	1.4	Israel	22	2.6
Brunei			Scotland	22	2.6
Darussalam	11	1.4	Finland	23	2.8
Kuwait	11	1.4	Iran	24	2.9
Netherlands	11	1.4	Libya	25	2.9
Portugal	11	1.4	Liechtenstein	26	2.9
Serbia	11	1.4	Switzerland	26	2.9
Canada	12	1.5	Peru	27	3

(continued)

TABLE 1.3 (*CONTINUED*)

Country	Rank	Rate	Country	Rank	Rate
Bulgaria	28	3.1	Kyrgyzstan	54	8.1
Monaco	28	3.1	Thailand	55	8.2
Saudi Arabia	29	3.2	Anguilla	56	8.3
Somalia	30	3.3	Belarus	56	8.3
Afghanistan	31	3.4	Zimbabwe	57	8.4
Djibouti	32	3.5	Latvia	58	8.6
Seychelles	32	3.5	Indonesia	59	8.9
Uzbekistan	32	3.5	Lithuania	60	9.1
Montenegro	33	3.6	Comoros	61	9.3
Pakistan	33	3.6	Nauru	62	9.9
Viet Nam	34	3.8	Dominica	63	10.3
Palestinian			Cape Verde	64	10.7
Territories	35	4	Mexico	65	10.9
Bhutan	36	4.3	Ghana	66	11.6
Uruguay	37	4.7	Timor-Leste	67	11.7
Grenada	38	4.9	Madagascar	67	11.7
Argentina	39	5.3	Suriname	68	11.8
Bolivia	39	5.3	Kazakhstan	69	11.9
Haiti	39	5.3	Benin	70	12.7
Lao People's			Swaziland	70	12.7
Democratic Rep	40	5.4	Namibia	71	12.8
Sao Tome and			Mongolia	72	13.1
Principe	40	5.4	Panama	73	13.4
Chile	41	5.5	Gambia	74	13.5
India	41	5.5	Togo	75	13.7
USA	42	5.9	Trinidad and		
Cuba	43	6	Tobago	75	13.7
Georgia	44	6.2	Honduras	76	13.8
Kiribati	45	6.5	Senegal	77	14.2
Albania	46	6.6	Barbados	78	15.1
Estonia	47	6.7	Mauritania	79	15.2
Iraq	47	6.7	Papua New		
Kenya	47	6.7	Guinea	79	15.2
Turkey	48	6.9	Burma	80	15.7
Moldova	49	7.2	Eritrea	81	15.9
Sri Lanka	49	7.2	Saint Vincent and		
Costa Rica	50	7.3	the Grenadines	82	16
Uganda	50	7.3	Cameroon	83	16.1
Antigua and			Guinea-Bissau	84	16.3
Barbuda	51	7.7	Dominican Rep	85	16.8
Turkmenistan	52	7.8	Ecuador	85	16.8
Ukraine	53	8	Liberia	85	16.8

TABLE 1.3 (CONTINUED)

Country	Rank	Rate	Country	Rank	Rate
Gabon	86	17.1	Equatorial Guinea	106	24
Guinea	87	17.3	Tanzania	107	26.1
Nicaragua	88	17.4	Guatemala	108	26.3
Nigeria	89	17.7	Rwanda	109	26.6
Paraguay	90	17.8	Sudan	110	28.6
Malawi	91	18	Central		
Mali	92	18	African Rep	111	29.1
Burkina Faso	93	18.1	Russian		
Cambodia	94	18.5	Federation	112	29.7
Congo	95	18.8	Belize	113	30.1
Korea, north	96	18.9	Brazil	114	30.8
Puerto Rico	96	18.9	Venezuela	115	32.5
Chad	97	19	Jamaica	116	33.7
Guyana	98	19.2	Sierra Leone	117	34
Ethiopia	99	19.3	Congo, the Dem		
Mozambique	100	20.2	Rep of the	118	35.2
Niger	100	20.2	Burundi	119	35.4
Philippines	101	21	Angola	120	36
Saint Lucia	102	21.3	Lesotho	121	37.3
Botswana	103	21.5	South Africa	122	39.5
Bahamas	103	22.5	Cote d'Ivoire	123	45.7
Saint Kitts			El Salvador	124	56.4
and Nevis	104	22.7	Colombia	125	61.1
Zambia	105	22.9			1961.6

Source: "Global Homicide: Murder Rates around the World," The Guardian Datablog. http://www.guardian.co.uk/news/datablog/2009/oct/13/homicide-rates-country-murder-data.

Data from 2004 for most countries. Colombia data from 2003–2005 average.

The Guardian datablog using statistics from Eurostat, WHO, UN.

TABLE 1.4

Polity IV Index

Democracies		Semi-Democracies		Semi-Authoritarian		Authoritarian	
Canada	10	Dom Rep	8	Central African Republic		Cuba	−7
Costa Rica	10	Belgium	8	Guinea	−1	Belarus	−7
Austria	10	Guatemala	8	Uganda	−1	China	−7
Denmark	10	Czech Republic	8	Singapore	−2	Laos	−7
Finland	10	Mexico	8	Chad	−2	Vietnam	−7
Germany	10	Argentina	8	Yemen	−2	Azerbaijan	−7
United States	10	Bolivia	8	Angola	−2	Bahrain	−7
Greece	10	Brazil	8	Tajikistan	−3	Kuwait	−7
Hungary	10	Latvia	8	Egypt	−3	Libya	−7
Ireland	10	Moldova	8	Jordon	−3	Syria	−7
Chile	10	Paraguay	8	Rwanda	−3	Eritrea	−7
Italy	10	Montenegro	8	Fiji	−4	Myanmar	−8
Lithuania	10	Serbia	8	Sudan	−4	Oman	−8
Netherlands	10	Indonesia	8	Tunisia	−4	UAE	−8
Trinidad & Tobago	10	South Korea	8	Cameroon	−4	North Korea	−9
Norway	10	Philippines	8	Congo	−4	Turkmenistan	−9
Uruguay	10	Ghana	8	Gabon	−4	Uzbekistan	−9
Poland	10	Lesotho	8	Togo	−4	Qatar	−10
Portugal	10	Senegal	8	Zimbabwe	−4	Saudi Arabia	−10
Slovak Rep.	10	El Salvador	7	Equatorial Guinea	−5		
Slovenia	10	Honduras	7	Gambia	−5		
Spain	10	Columbia	7	Bangladesh	−6		
Sweden	10	Ukraine	7	Bhutan	−6		
Switzerland	10	East Timor	7	Kazakhstan	−6		
U.K.	10	Lebanon	7	Iran	−6		
Australia	10	Turkey	7	Morocco	−6		
Japan	10	Benin	7				
Mongolia	10	Kenya	7				
New Zealand	10	Madagascar	7				
Papua New Guinea	10	Sierra Leone	7				
Taiwan	10	Estonia	6				
Cyprus	10	Guyana	6				
Israel	10	Nepal	6				
Mauritius	10	Sri Lanka	6				
Albania	9	Georgia	6				

TABLE 1.4 (*CONTINUED*)

Democracies		Semi-Democracies		Semi-Authoritarian	Authoritarian
Bulgaria	9	Mali	6		
Croatia	9	Niger	6		
Jamaica	9	Burundi	6		
Nicaragua	9	Guinea-Bissau	6		
France	9	Liberia	6		
Panama	9	Malawi	6		
Macedonia	9	Mozambique	6		
Peru	9	Namibia	6		
Jamaica	9	Haiti	5		
Romania	9	Ecuador	5		
India	9	Venezuela	5		
Botswana	9	Russia	5		
South Africa	9	Armenia	5		
Swaziland	9	Demo Republic of Congo	5		
		Zambia	5		
		Mauritania	4		
		Nigeria	4		
		Kyrgyzstan	3		
		Malaysia	3		
		Cambodia	2		
		Pakistan	2		
		Algeria	2		
		Djibouti	2		
		Thailand	1		
		Ethiopia	1		
		Tanzania	1		
		Burkina Faso	0		

TABLE 3.1

Failed States Index

Sustainable

Country	Rank	Rate	Country	Rank	Rate
Norway	1	18.3	Australia	8	25.9
Finland	2	19.2	Netherlands	9	27
Sweden	3	20.6	Luxembourg	10	27.6
Switzerland	4	21.2	Austria	11	27.6
Ireland	5	21.6	Canada	12	27.7
Denmark	6	23.2	Iceland	13	29
New Zealand	7	23.3			

Moderate

Country	Rank	Rate	Country	Rank	Rate
Japan	14	31.2	Greece	31	46.1
Portugal	15	32.7	Oman	32	47.2
Belgium	16	33.5	Lithuania	33	48
United Kingdom	17	33.6	Slovakia	34	48.6
Singapore	18	33.8	Malta	35	48.8
United States	19	34	Poland	36	49.6
France	20	35.3	Hungary	37	50.7
Germany	21	36.2	Estonia	38	51.2
Slovenia	22	36.3	United Arab		
Chile	23	37.5	Emirates	39	51.8
Uruguay	24	41.2	Qatar	40	51.9
South Korea	25	41.6	Costa Rica	41	52.5
Czech Republic	26	42.6	Latvia	42	54.6
Spain	27	43.3	Barbados	43	57.2
Italy	28	43.9	Montenegro	44	58
Mauritius	29	44.7	Bahrain	45	59
Argentina	30	44.7	Panama	46	59.7

Warning

Country	Rank	Rate	Country	Rank	Rate
Croatia	47	60.1	Ghana	54	66.2
Bahamas	48	60.9	Trinidad	55	66.7
Romania	49	61.3	South Africa	56	67.4
Bulgaria	50	61.5	Tunisia	57	67.6
Mongolia	51	61.9	Seychelles	58	67.7
Antigua and			Grenada	59	67.9
Barbuda	52	62.8	Brunei		
Kuwait	53	63.4	Darussalam	60	68.1

TABLE 3.1 (*CONTINUED*)

Country	Rank	Rate	Country	Rank	Rate
Jamaica	61	68.6	Venezuela	101	79.5
Botswana	62	68.8	Guatemala	102	80.6
Malaysia	63	68.9	Djibouti	103	80.6
Cyprus	64	68.9	Cuba	104	80.6
Brazil	65	69.1	Algeria	105	80.6
Libya	66	69.4	Mozambique	106	80.7
Belize	67	69.5	Russia	107	80.8
Ukraine	68	69.7	Tanzania	108	81.1
Albania	69	70	Ecuador	109	81.2
Samoa	70	71.4	Madagascar	110	81.6
Micronesia	71	71.9	Lesotho	111	81.8
Paraguay	72	72	Belarus	112	82.3
Kazakhstan	73	72.5	Swaziland	113	82.4
Guyana	74	73	Nicaragua	114	82.6
Suriname	75	73.2	Bosnia	115	83.3
Senegal	76	74.2	Papua New		
Armenia	77	74.3	Guinea	116	84.1
Macedonia	78	74.4	Indonesia	117	84.1
Gabon	79	74.4	Zambia	118	84.2
Mexico	80	75.4	Turkmenistan	119	84.3
Benin	81	75.5	Israel/West Bank	120	84.6
Namibia	82	75.6	China	121	84.6
Sao Tome	83	76.7	Azerbaijan	122	84.6
Vietnam	84	76.9	Angola	123	85
Peru	85	77.1	Moldova	124	85.1
Morocco	86	77.1	Philippines	125	85.8
Honduras	87	77.2	Comoros	126	86.3
El Salvador	88	77.2	Bolivia	127	86.3
Saudi Arabia	89	77.5	Togo	128	87.2
Dominican			Cambodia	129	87.3
Republic	90	77.7	Bhutan	130	87.3
India	91	77.8	Equatorial		
Jordan	92	77.9	Guinea	131	88.3
Turkey	93	78.2	Mauritania	132	88.7
Cape Verde	94	78.5	Rwanda	133	89
Mali	95	78.7	Laos	134	89
Maldives	96	78.8	Egypt	135	89
Fiji	97	78.8	Kirgizstan	136	89.1
Gambia	98	79	Colombia	137	89.2
Thailand	99	79.2	Solomon Islands	138	89.6
Serbia	100	79.2	Syria	139	89.8

(*continued*)

TABLE 3.1 (*CONTINUED*)

Alert

Country	Rank	Rate	Country	Rank	Rate
Iran	140	90	Bangladesh	160	98.1
Tajikistan	141	90.3	North Korea	161	98.3
Eritrea	142	90.3	Ethiopia	162	98.9
Burkina Faso	143	91.3	Nigeria	163	99.8
Liberia	144	91.8	Kenya	164	101.4
Georgia	145	91.8	Burma	165	101.5
Sierra Leone	146	92.1	Haiti	166	101.8
Uzbekistan	147	92.8	Ivory Coast	167	102.5
Republic of Congo	148	93.1	Pakistan	168	104.1
Lebanon	149	93.5	Guinea	169	104.6
Malawi	150	93.8	Central African		
Guinea-Bissau	151	94.8	Republic	170	105.4
Cameroon	152	95.3	Afghanistan	171	108.2
Nepal	153	95.4	Iraq	172	108.6
Burundi	154	95.7	Dem. Rep. of		
Niger	155	96.5	the Congo	173	108.7
Sri Lanka	156	96.7	Chad	174	112.2
Uganda	157	96.9	Sudan	175	112.4
East Timor	158	97.2	Zimbabwe	176	114
Yemen	159	98.1	Somalia	177	114.7

Source: The Fund for Peace at: http://www.fundforpeace.org/web/index.php?, accessed June 1, 2010

TABLE 5.1

Economic Freedom Index

Country	Rank	Rate	Country	Rank	Rate
Hong Kong	1	8.97	Sweden	40	7.28
Singapore	2	8.66	Peru	41	7.26
New Zealand	3	8.3	Georgia	42	7.25
Switzerland	4	8.19	Guatemala	42	7.25
Chile	5	8.14	Latvia	44	7.22
United States	6	8.06	Jamaica	45	7.19
Ireland	7	7.98	Portugal	45	7.19
Canada	8	7.91	Belgium	47	7.18
Australia	9	7.89	Armenia	48	7.17
United Kingdom	9	7.89	Zambia	49	7.13
Estonia	11	7.81	Botswana	50	7.12
Denmark	12	7.74	Kazakstan	50	7.12
Austria	13	7.67	Greece	52	7.11
Luxembourg	14	7.65	Bahamas	53	7.1
Panama	14	7.65	Czech Republic	54	7.09
Finland	16	7.62	Kenya	54	7.09
Mauritius	16	7.62	Trinidad and		
Taiwan	16	7.62	Tobago	56	7.07
United Arab			Albania	57	7.06
Emeriates	19	7.58	South Africa	57	7.06
Bahrain	20	7.56	Thailand	59	7.04
Costa Rica	20	7.56	Nicaragua	60	6.96
Netherlands	20	7.56	Italy	61	6.95
Malta	23	7.54	Uruguay	61	6.95
Iceland	24	7.53	Mongolia	63	6.91
Norway	24	7.53	Slovenia	64	6.9
Slovakia	26	7.52	Uganda	64	6.9
Germany	27	7.5	Malaysia	66	6.88
El Salvador	28	7.48	Belize	67	6.87
Honduras	28	7.48	Mexico	68	6.85
Japan	28	7.46	Namibia	69	6.83
Kuwait	30	7.46	Philippines	69	6.83
South Korea	32	7.45	Ghana	71	6.8
France	33	7.43	Kyrgyz Republic	71	6.8
Jordan	34	7.4	Romania	73	6.79
Lithuania	35	7.38	Poland	74	6.78
Cyprus	36	7.36	Barbados	75	6.75
Oman	36	7.36	Bulgaria	76	6.74
Hungary	38	7.33	Papua New		
Spain	39	7.32	Guinea	77	6.71

(continued)

◣ TABLE 5.1 (*CONTINUED*)

Country	Rank	Rate	Country	Rank	Rate
Israel	78	6.69	Brazil	111	6
Egypt	79	6.68	Iran	112	5.99
Fiji	80	6.64	Guyana	113	5.98
Montenegro	81	6.58	Sierre Leone	114	5.97
China	82	6.54	Bangladesh	115	5.93
Russia	83	6.5	Malawi	116	5.93
Serbia	84	6.47	Togo	117	5.9
Azerbaijan	85	6.46	Benin	118	5.89
India	86	6.45	Burkina Faso	119	5.87
Haiti	87	6.44	Ecuador	120	5.83
Turkey	88	6.42	Colombia	121	5.81
Macedonia	89	6.4	Gabon	122	5.8
Tunisia	90	6.39	Cameroon	123	5.79
Paraguay	91	6.38	Syria	124	5.76
Lesotho	92	6.36	Mozambique	125	5.74
Indonesia	93	6.35	Senegal	126	5.72
Moldova	94	6.34	Ethiopia	127	5.71
Croatia	95	6.33	Ukraine	128	5.68
Tanzania	96	6.32	Nepal	129	5.58
Nigeria	97	6.31	Burundi	130	5.54
Madagascar	98	6.29	Algeria	131	5.34
Mali	99	6.28	Niger	132	5.11
Dominican			Chad	133	5.09
Republic	100	6.27	Dem. Republic		
Vietnam	101	6.22	of the Congo	134	5
Rwanda	102	6.2	Guinea-Bissau	135	4.84
Bolivia	103	6.18	Central African		
Morocco	104	6.16	Republic	136	4.79
Argentina	105	6.1	Republic of		
Bosnia and			the Congo	137	4.44
Herzegovina	105	6.1	Venezuela	138	4.33
Sri Lanka	105	6.1	Angola	139	4.04
Cote d'Ivoire	108	6.09	Myanmar	140	3.69
Mauritania	109	6.05	Zimbabwe	141	2.89
Pakistan	110	6.01			

Source: Economic Freedom of the World.

GLOSSARY

Absolute Poverty: Poverty so severe that it is life threatening.

Active Labor Market Policies: Government programs designed to move the unemployed back into the labor market by giving them additional training, creating jobs, subsidizing employment, or helping them with their job search.

Assembly of Experts (Iran): The Assembly of Experts is elected by voters and has the authority to select Supreme Leaders, supervise their activities, and remove them from power.

Authoritarianism: A form of politics in which a single ruler or small elite make decisions without constitutional checks on their use of power.

Authority: When power is exercised in a way that people recognize as legitimate or appropriate.

Ayatollah: Ayatollah means "sign of God." An ayatollah is a high-ranking cleric, outranked only by grand ayatollahs and imams.

Basij: A volunteer militia in Iran under the command of the Revolutionary Guards who enforce Islamic codes of conduct and are used to break up political demonstrations and protests.

Bicameral: A legislature that is composed of two chambers, consisting of an upper and lower house.

"Big men": Politically powerful leaders in Nigeria.

Bonding Behavior: People identify with their in-group based on ethnicity, race, language, or religion.

Bonyads: Bonyads are semi-public charitable foundations in Iran that receive state and private funding. They own numerous firms in various sectors of the Iranian economy.

Bridging Behavior: People reach across differences in ethnicity, race, language, and religion to ally for common purposes.

Bureaucracy: A part of the executive branch that is supposed to administer and implement policy in a neutral and professional way.

Cabinet: A group of officials in the executive branch that advise the head of the government and are in charge of various ministries within it.

The Capabilities Approach: This approach argues that societies should be evaluated according to the freedoms their members enjoy to develop their human potential and to choose the ways of living they have reason to value.

Causation: A change to one thing that occurs at one point in time that produces or is responsible for a change to something else that occurs at a later point in time.

Central Bank: Central banks control the money supply in each country and manage its value in foreign exchange.

Central Committee: Communist Party institution that approves appointments to the politburo and party policies in annual sessions.

Central Planned Economy: Economy in which decisions about what is produced, how much is produced, and at what price is made by a state planning agency.

Centralized Wage Bargaining: When there is a high degree of inter-union and inter-employer cooperation in wage setting; when wage agreements by the peak organizations of unions and employers set the framework for lower level bargaining.

Charismatic Leader: A leader who is believed to have extraordinary ability well beyond that of ordinary people and who is capable of achieving extraordinary goals on behalf of the leader's followers.

Civil Rights: Those rights guaranteed by the state to all individuals as citizens. These are equal rights that the state guarantees to all its citizens, such as the right to marry or the right to use public accommodations.

Class Identification: A subjective judgment people make as to which class they belong to.

Classical Definition of Democracy: A form of participatory democracy in which the people are directly involved in making the laws that govern them.

Clientelism: A method states and political parties use to win support by dispensing favors to individuals or small groups.

Colonialism: The establishment of formal political control by one country over another.

Communist Party: A political party based on Marxist beliefs and organized as a vanguard party to lead workers and peasants in revolution to overthrow capitalism and build socialism and communism.

Communist Regime: Where a Communist Party controls the state and suppresses independent organizations in society. The means of production are state owned and economic production is centrally planned.

Comparative Political Analysis: Forming and testing hypothesis in the study of comparative politics.

Comparative Politics: A subfield of political science that studies similarities and differences among countries' politics, why they exist, and their consequences.

Congruence Approach: An approach to political culture that assumes countries need congruence, or a match, between their political culture and political institutions to be stable.

Conservatives (Iran): Strongly supports theocracy and minimizing the power of voters to choose leaders or policies.

Constitution: Describes the powers and functions of the different parts of the state. It lays out how power is distributed within the state and between the state and its citizens.

Constructivism: This approach to political culture assumes that identities are not simply found ready-made, but are socially constructed; they are continually refined and redefined.

Control Variables: When researchers hold other factors constant so they can determine if their independent variable, as opposed to some extraneous factor, was responsible for a change to their dependent variable.

Core Executive: Consists of the head of the government, often the president or prime minister, their closest advisors, and members of their cabinet.

Corporatist Interest Groups: When a few interest groups include a large proportion of potential members and are often given some official recognition by the state and included in the policy-making process.

Correlation: An observed change in one variable is associated with an observed change in another variable without necessarily establishing whether the former caused the latter.

Corruption: The use of public office for private gain.

Council of Guardian: A twelve member body that has the power to block legislative bills it believes are incompatible with Islam and can prevent individuals from running for parliamentary seats.

Crisis of Governability: When states have trouble making their laws effective. The authority of the state is not respected and public order and services provided by the state deteriorate.

Cultural Relativism: The premise that countries should be evaluated according to their own cultural values, as opposed to being judged according to values outsiders impose on them.

Culture: A society's widely shared values, beliefs, norms, and orientations toward the world.

Dealignment: When voters' identification with political parties weakens and their preferences become more fleeting and volatile.

Democracy: Rule by the people, in which the government reflects the will of the people and is accountable to it.

Democratic Centralism: Organizational principle of communist parties in which lower level party organizations instruct higher levels. Once issues are decided, the result is binding on all members of the party.

Dependent Variable: What the analyst is trying to explain; what the independent variable acts upon.

Despotic Power: Power to make decisions without having to follow organizational procedures.

Diffusion Effects: Describes how what happens in one country spreads or is adopted by neighboring countries.

Divide and Rule: A strategy that pits groups against each other so they are unable to act collectively.

Divided Government: When different parties have a majority in different parts of the state's elected institutions, such as its executive and legislative branches.

Double Ballot Elections: If no candidate receives a majority in the first election, a second, run-off election is then held between the two candidates who received the most votes.

Economic Development: The process increasing a country's wealth by diversifying and producing goods and services more efficiently.

Electoral Authoritarian Regime: Holds regularly scheduled elections and allows multiple political parties to participate in them but the elections are not free and fair, and election rules are tilted strongly in favor of the ruling political party.

Electoral Democracies: Democracies where elections occur, but they are not always free and fair, voter fraud is a problem, political parties tend to be patronage based rather than programmatic, and corruption is significant.

Electoral Systems: Describes the system by which votes are counted to yield a winner, such as majority, or plurality rule. The rules by which winners in elections are chosen.

Empirical Analysis: A factual, objective presentation of material.

Ethnic Group: A group of persons who recognize each other as sharing common cultural or religious beliefs, language, and history.

Ethnic Identity: A sense of collective belonging that can be based on common cultural or religious beliefs, language, and history.

European Central Bank: The central bank for those countries that are members of the European Union and use the Euro as their currency.

European Union: An economic and political union of 27 European countries committed to regional integration.

Executive Branch: That part of the government charged with executing the laws passed by the legislature. It is charged with implementing or carrying out policy.

Expediency Council (Iran): The Expediency Council's members are appointed by the Supreme Leader in Iran, and has the authority to arbitrate conflicts between the Council of Guardians and the parliament.

Extensive Growth of Markets: Refers to the broader geographic reach of market systems to include more people and places.

Extensive Growth: Economic growth achieved by mobilizing large amounts of labor and material to build or produce products.

Fascism: A political movement that emphasizes nationalism and the primacy of the state, embodied by a single leader, over the individual and social groups.

Federal Assembly: Russia's bicameral legislature composed of the Federation Council and the State Duma.

Federal Systems: Political systems where power is shared between national and regional governments that have their own independent authority to tax and make policy.

Federation Council: Russia's upper house which represents Russia's regional administrative divisions.

Fiscal Policy: Governments make fiscal policy which uses the budget—government revenues and expenditures—to manage overall demand in the economy.

Free Rider Problem: When services or goods are available that people can use without paying for them.

GDP: A country's economic output that includes the total amount of goods and services consumed, invested within the country, disbursed by the government, and spent on exports minus the value of imports.

General Secretary of the Communist Party: Head of the secretariat and the most powerful position in the Communist Party.

Generalized Reciprocity: The norm that if you do something for someone they will return the favor in the future.

Generalized Trust: The belief that most people in a society can be trusted,

not just one's family members and friends.

Genocide: A state-conducted policy of deliberately and systematically killing all members of a particular ethnic group, nationality, or religion.

Gini Index: The Gini Index is used to measure the extent of income inequality in a country. A Gini Index value of 0 equals perfect equality of income in which everyone receives the same share of a country's income while a value of 100 equals perfect inequality.

Glasnost: Used to describe Soviet leader Mikhail Gorbachev's policy in the late 1980s of "openness," in which freer expression of opinion was encouraged within the Soviet Union.

Global Production Chains: Where different parts of an interconnected production process are outsourced to different firms that are located in different countries.

Globalization: Refers to the greater integration and worldwide exchange of ideas, goods, currencies, investments, and culture.

The Government: The government refers to those who run, or are in control of, the executive branch of the state. It alludes to those who occupy executive leadership positions within the state.

Great Leap Forward (1958–1960): Mass campaign initiated by Mao Zedong to catch up economically with the West within 15 years and create a new kind of socialism in the process.

Great Proletarian Cultural Revolution (1966–1976): Mass campaign initiated by Mao Zedong to reshape citizens' thinking in line with Mao's version of socialism. Major goals of the Cultural Revolution were to purge the party of "capitalist roaders" and "class enemies" and rid the country of old culture, habits, ideas, and customs.

The Green Movement (Iran): The Green Movement emerged to support the presidential campaign of Mir Hossein Mousavi in Iran in 2009 and since then has called for strengthening human rights and civil liberties.

Harmful Spillover Effects: These are costs that the public, or third parties, suffer as a result of other's transactions or activities.

Head of Government: The leader of the executive branch, often either the president or prime minister.

Head of State: The official who represents the country and is considered its formal, symbolic leader.

Human Development Index (HDI): This index has three components: health, as measured by life expectancy at birth; knowledge, as measured by literacy rates and school enrollments; and standard of living, as measured by income's purchasing power.

Human Development: The process of expanding the choices people have to lead lives they value. These include being well-fed and healthy; being safe from violence; being literate and numerate; and enjoying political participation.

Hypothesis: Proposed relationship among variables. An educated guess about how one thing affects something else.

Imams: Hereditary successors to the Prophet Mohammed that Shiite Muslims believe are infallible.

Imperialism: The economic or political domination of one region or country by another. It is a relationship of inequality in which powerful countries subjugate weaker ones.

Independent Variable: The agent of change in a hypothesis. What the analyst believes explains the change to the dependent variable.

Infrastructural Power: Power to implement decisions effectively.

Institutions: Institutions refer not only to rules but to the organizations that

make them. Institutions create patterns of behavior that give order to society.

Instrumentalism: This approach to identity assumes that self-seeking political elites manipulate political identity for personal advantage.

Intensive Growth of Markets: Refers to the broader range of activities that are satisfied through the market.

Intensive Growth: Economic growth achieved by using labor and material more efficiently.

Interest Groups: An organized group that seeks to influence public policy.

International Monetary Fund (IMF): Created in 1945, the IMF's purpose is to provide a safety net for countries when they experience financial crisis, which occur when they cannot pay their debts.

Judicial Review: When courts have the power to overturn or invalidate laws that violate a country's Constitution or basic law.

Judicialization of Politics: The increasing use of courts to settle policy issues.

Judiciary: A system of courts that interpret and apply the law.

Kleptocracy: Rule based on theft of state assets and income.

Legislature: An assembly that is a law-making body.

Legitimacy: The willingness of citizens to believe that rulers rightfully hold and exercise power and should be obeyed.

Liberation Theology: Catholic doctrine that believes the church should focus on improving the lives of the poor.

Mahdi: The Mahdi is the twelfth Shiite Imam. Shiites believe he did not die, but went into hiding in 941 and will reappear again as the messiah to establish just rule on earth.

Majles: The Majles is Iran's unicameral legislature.

Market Systems: Market systems exist where productive assets are privately owned and employed to earn profits for their owners. Production is geared to produce goods for sale, and prices are set by market forces through supply and demand.

Martial Law: Law applied by military forces which gives them the right to set curfews, and ban public gatherings and demonstrations in the name of maintaining public order and safety.

Marxism: Based on the work of Karl Marx (1818–1883) who believed that capitalism would develop in such a manner as to create a revolutionary working class that would overthrow it.

Medicare: Government provided medical insurance in the U.S. for people 65 or older.

Military Regime: A group of military officers chooses the ruler and participates in policy making. Key leadership positions in the state are staffed by military officers.

Modernization Theory: A theory that held modernizing, "traditional" societies would follow the same developmental sequence as Western, more developed countries, which included industrialization, urbanization, specialization, and democratization.

Monarchy: A regime in which the ruler is selected on the basis of royal lineage.

Monetary Policy: Policy through which governments manage the money supply in order to influence interest rates so as to promote economic stability and growth.

Multimember Districts: A district from which more than one representative is elected.

Nation: A group of people sharing a collective identity that desire to govern themselves through their own state.

National Party Congress: In theory it has supreme authority in the Communist Party, electing members of the central committee and approving party policy.

In practice, it has little influence and approves what the party leadership presents to it.

National People's Congress (NPC): China's unicameral legislature which is in session for only two or three weeks a year and has little power.

Nationalism: A sense of pride in one's nationality and a desire to control a state representing that nationality.

Nationalist (or *Guomindang*) Party: The political party that governed China from 1928 until its defeat by the Communist Party in 1949.

Neopatrimonial Regimes: These regimes combine the outward appearance of a modern bureaucracy but bureaucrats are appointed on the basis of clientelist ties with rulers, serve at their will, and use their positions to extort money for private gain.

New Social Movements: New social movements are distinguished from their predecessors by their focus on issues of identity (feminism) and quality of life (environmentalism) as opposed to economic demands (redistribution).

Newly Industrialized Countries (NICs): Countries with economies that have become advanced enough to make a wide range of industrial products that are competitive in global markets.

Nomenklatura: Means by which Communist parties control state agencies and social organizations by appointing leaders to them.

Normative Analysis: A judgmental and evaluative presentation of material.

Norms of Reciprocity: Favors that are given with the expectation that they will be repaid. Similar to "Generalized Reciprocity" defined above.

Oligarchs: Extremely wealthy businesspeople in Russia who used political connections in the 1990s to establish banks, gain control of television stations, and become owners of valuable natural resources.

Ombudsman: Investigates complaints by citizens against a government agency or official.

One-child Policy: China's effort to slow population growth by limiting most parents to one child.

One-party Regime: Access to political office is controlled by a single ruling party, and the leaders of that party control policy making.

Operationalize Variables: When we substitute specific, real-life, measurable alternatives in place of concepts that are too abstract and general for use in testing hypotheses.

Opportunity Structures: The relative openness of a political system to political participation and influence.

Outliers: Countries that do not fit an expected pattern in a scattergram.

Parliamentary Systems: Sovereignty resides in the legislature which selects the executive. The executive is responsible to the legislature which, in turn, is responsible to the voters.

Parochials: Citizens who focus on their own lives, ignore what political leaders are doing, and do not participate in politics in any way.

Participants: Citizens who take an interest in politics, are aware of how government policies affect their lives, and participate in politics.

Party Discipline: When legislators from the same party display unity and vote together as a bloc in response to government proposals.

Party of Power: Russian term for a political party created to elect powerful leaders to office.

Party Systems: Party systems occur when party conflict takes a regular, stable form in terms of the number of parties competing, the relative vote share each party receives, and the types of interests they represent.

Patronage: Rewards offered to individuals in return for their electoral support.

Patron-Client Relations: An unequal exchange in which poor clients give their political support in return for some reward, such as money, farm land, credit, protection, or access to services, from rich patrons.

Perestroika: Policy followed by Soviet leader Mikhail Gorbachev in the 1980s to describe his policy of restructuring, or loosening state control of the economy and creating more freedom for firms to respond to consumer demand.

Personal Rule: A system of rule in which a leader controls policy making and selection of state personnel without effective constraints from an organization or the public.

Pluralist Interest Group Systems: Where large numbers of interest groups compete with each other for members and exert influence by lobbying the government.

Politburo: Main policy-making institution of a communist party.

Political Culture: A society's widely shared beliefs, values, and orientations toward politics.

Political Economy: The manner in which states influence the economy and, reciprocally, how the economy affects states; the mutual influence of politics and economics.

Political Participation: The means by which citizens influence the laws that govern them. Efforts people make to influence the state.

Political Parties: Political parties are distinguished from other forms of political participation by putting forward candidates to run the government.

Political Rights: Those rights that pertain to participating in the establishment or administration of the government, such as the right to vote.

Postindustrial Society: A society in which more than fifty percent of the labor force is engaged in service occupations, as opposed to industry and agriculture.

Power: The ability to influence people's ideas and behavior; to influence others to comply with your wishes.

Pragmatists (Iran): The pragmatist faction puts primary emphasis on improving economic growth by relying more on market forces.

Premier: Head of government who oversees and coordinates the work of government ministries and agencies

President (Russia): The most powerful political office in Russia. The president is elected by voters for four year terms, but beginning in 2012, will be six years.

President (China): Serves as head of state and represents China in meetings with other world leaders. The Chinese Communist Party's Secretary General is also the president.

Presidential Systems: Where both the legislature and president share power and are elected independently by the people.

Prime Minister (Russia): Head of the cabinet appointed by the president and in charge of day to day government operations.

Primordialism: This approach assumes that group identities emerge naturally from human differences in ethnicity, race, and religion, can be traced far back into the past, and tend to persist with little change once formed.

Principlists (Iran): The principlist faction is composed of a younger generation of leaders who believe many of the older leaders have become corrupt and abandoned the principles of the Islamic Revolution. They are hard-line conservatives on cultural policy and confrontational toward the United States, Europe, and Israel.

Privatize: When state-owned firms are sold on the market to private business people.

Programmatic Parties: Parties that mobilize supporters on the basis of the party's platform that its representatives are committed to enact when in office.

Proportional Representation: Seats in the legislature are awarded to parties based upon the percentage of the vote they receive.

Reform and Opening (China): Policies initiated by Deng Xiaoping to introduce market forces and open the economy to foreign investment and trade.

Reformists (Iran): The reformist faction that wants to give more authority to elected institutions and permit more cultural freedom.

Regime: A set of rules and procedures for choosing leaders and policies and the government that embodies those rules.

Regulatory Policy: Policies that compel economic actors to act in certain ways, setting explicit rules they must follow.

Relative Poverty: Being poor, relative to other people's income and wealth.

Religious Identity: Identity based on religious beliefs.

Rent Seeking: Companies seeking profits by lobbying government officials for protection from competitors instead of making better products for customers and improving productivity.

Rentier States: States which depend upon natural resources such as oil for most of their revenues.

Rents: Artificially high profits created by state actions to limit competition for goods and services.

Revolution: A rapid, fundamental, and violent change in a society's values, politics, society, leadership, and policies.

Revolutionary Guards (Iran): An all volunteer elite military force who are responsible to the Supreme Leader and are supposed to defend the Islamic Revolution.

Secretariat: Communist Party institution with responsibility for overseeing the implementation of politburo decisions.

Security Council (Russia): Coordinates all of Russia's security agencies and government ministries with responsibility for foreign affairs, defense, and domestic security.

Self-expression Values: Valuing freedom of speech, tolerance toward people with different lifestyles, and willingness to challenge authorities.

Shari'a Law: Muslim law based on the Qur'an and the teachings of the Prophet Mohammed.

Shiite Islam: The smaller of the two major branches of Islam. Sunni Muslims are the other. The split between the two branches dates back to the seventh century over who should succeed the Prophet Mohammed as the leader of Islam.

Shock Therapy: A term applied to Russia's attempt to make the transition from a centrally planned economy to a market economy as rapidly as possible.

Social Capital Approach: This approach seeks to explain how people manage to collaborate to achieve goals, and why people often find it difficult to cooperate even when it would benefit them.

Social Capital: The ability of members of a group to collaborate for shared interests. It is based on trust among people and their ability to work together for common purposes.

Social Character Approach: An approach to political culture which assumes societies have prevailing cultural beliefs and values that give them a distinctive character.

Social Dilemma: A situation in which everyone realizes they would benefit from cooperation but they still find it difficult to do so.

Social Market Economy: An economic model that combined capitalism with a good deal of government regulation and welfare state spending.

Social Movements: Social movements are less formally organized than interest groups and engage in unconventional forms of political activism that require a higher level of commitment and sacrifice from their supporters.

Socialism with Chinese Characteristics: Chinese concept for describing their current economy which will continue to be socialist despite a large role for private firms, markets, and integration into the global economy

The State: A state has four qualities: (1) It is an organization that, has a specific administrative form; (2) is sovereign, meaning it has ultimate power over people under its control; (3) exerts this power through its control over the means of violence; and (4) extends this power over a bounded territory that defines the limits of its rule.

State Corporatism: Refers to state recognized and favored business and labor organizations that cooperate with the state to make public policy.

State Council (Russia): It comprises the premier and cabinet, which is composed of vice premiers and ministers who head government ministries.

State Duma: Russia's lower house whose members are elected by proportional representation in a single nationwide district.

Strong States: Strong states are not captured by any social group and are able to govern and implement their policies. They are able to make their rules stick.

Subjects: Citizens who do not participate or take an active interest in politics, but have a sense of how government policies affect their lives and passively obey laws.

Supreme Leader: The most powerful political leader in Iran charged with safekeeping the legacy of the Islamic Revolution of 1979.

Technocrat: A highly educated and trained civil servant who makes decisions based on technical rather than political grounds.

Theocracy: A regime in which religious leaders rule.

Tiananmen Square Protests: Student-led protests in China in 1989 against corruption and government unresponsiveness. The protests lasted for weeks until they were suppressed brutally by the military.

Totalitarianism: An extreme form of authoritarianism that seeks total control of citizens' behavior and thoughts and tries to transform society in accord with ideological goals.

Transfer Payments: When the government distributes money to individuals as specified by law, such as issuing checks to those who qualify for unemployment insurance.

Unicameral: A legislature that is composed of one chamber that debates and votes on bills.

Union Density Rate: The proportion of workers who belong to labor unions.

Unitary Systems: Political systems where power is centralized at the national level in the federal government.

United Russia: Russia's dominant ruling political party.

Velayat-e-faqih: The guiding principle of the Islamic Republic of Iran. It is translated into English as "guardianship of the jurisprudent," and holds that the clerics most trained in Islamic jurisprudence should rule and that a cleric should be the leader of the country.

Veto Points: Places in a decision-making or policymaking process at which proposals can be defeated or blocked.

Wage Solidarity: The principle that workers doing similar work should be paid similarly and that wage differentials between the top and the bottom should be reduced as much as possible.

"Washington Consensus" or Neoliberalism: A diagnosis promoted by many Western governments and international agencies that attributed poor economic performance to too much state regulation and prescribed free trade, balanced budgets, and competition as the cure.

Weak States: States that have trouble making their laws effective or acting independently of social groups.

Welfare Effort: A measure that divides welfare spending by GDP to compare different countries' relative commitments to the welfare state.

The World Bank: The World Bank provides loans, credits, and grants to low and middle-income countries in order to promote development.

INDEX